Dear Harry,

For a number of years Dr. Clark was in business, operating his own establishment. He "walked the walk," so to say, and is now writing from his experience with many stories.

Last fall, we enjoyed him as a speaker and are now delighting in his book. We hope you also are blessed.

Love from your friends,
John & Coralie
Dec. 2014

Life Is
NOT
A
Snapshot
(It's A Mosaic)

R.E. Clark

GnG Publishers

122 Skinner St.

Centerton, AR 72719

First Edition Published by GnG Publishers 10/01/13

ISBN: 0615889352

ISBN-13: 978-0615889351

Printed in the United States of America

The mosaic photo on the cover of this book was created using AndreaMosaic 3.33 - Copyright © 1997-2010 by Andrea Denzler

Because of the dynamic nature of the Internet, any web addresses or links contained in this book may have changed since publication and may no longer be valid.

DEDICATION

My life is truly a mosaic.
Therefore,
this book is dedicated to the thousands
who have been snapshots in time
and
because of those moments
have become tiny bits and pieces
of me.
Without each of you,
from scattered places all over this globe,
I would be much less than I am
and
would never have been able to write
this book.

Thank you!

Table of Contents

• ACKNOWLEDGMENTS

No book writes itself and no author can claim the privilege of having written alone. I am grateful on several levels, as I consider all of the people I should acknowledge, in bringing this project to a close.

First, I must thank the hundreds who purchased my first devotional, *Glasses In the Grass: Devotions For My Friends*. Your confidence in me concerning that first devotional writing has encouraged me greatly in the writing of this book. I honestly could have never imagined the response that I received in my first effort.

Second, I must acknowledge my wife who has without fail encouraged me to write. She has watched the Lord's hand as He has redirected my life and allowed me the wonderful opportunity to minister far and wide through the written word. Thank you, Trudy for your loving reassurance in those times when I thought I should just stop. This second devotional is finished because of you.

Third, I could never complete a project like this without the help of my daughter and ministry assistant, Kayre. Not only has she served again as my editor and proofreader, she has picked up the slack in my normal duties as an associational missionary and helped me to remain faithful in my ministry to the churches of Northwest Baptist Association.

Finally, a note to all of the people hidden away in the mosaic that you see on the bottom of the cover I created for *Life Is Not A Snapshot: It's A Mosaic*. The photo that was lifted out of the mosaic is one of over 10,000 pictures from mission trips that were used to create the composite that became the mosaic. The actual photo was taken just outside of Monte Christi in the Dominican Republic. All of you have been instrumental in providing life stories that helped me apply scripture in such a way that this book is a collection of devotions from life—for life.

• JANUARY

For Frodo!

Happy Resolution Day!

You have completed another year. All of the *x's* have been placed over all of the days that passed so quickly in the former year. It's time to look ahead. Your journey has brought you along a path to this day of developing a personal set of resolutions for the New Year.

If you are like most, your list is usually too long. Your intentions are well-founded and expectations are high. The problem is that the mountain you have constructed is just too steep to climb. After a few days of the new year have evaporated, we take a gaze towards the peak and simply give up.

Another element that rises up to confront our list of resolutions is memory. We, umm, now what was I going to say... Oh yes, we forget.

In Psalm 119, David listed the first three "I wills" of his resolution:

"I will meditate on Your precepts." ~ Psalm 119:15a
"I will contemplate Your ways." ~ Psalms 119:15b
"I will delight in Your statutes." ~ Psalms 119:16a

Then he added a fourth and final statement of resolution:

"I will not forget Your word." ~ Psalms 119:16b

The word "forget" means to mislay. It is not so much intentionality, but carelessness that brings our resolutions to naught. I prefer to make this fourth statement of resolution positive instead negative:

"I will remember Your word."

As in David's words found in Psalms 143:5, "I remember the days of old; I meditate on all Your works; I muse on the work of Your hands," so we must purposefully be mindful of God's words and works. The idea of remembering is to make mention of regularly.

This last "I will" of David is like the final paragraph of a formal resolution that begins with the phrase, BE IT FINALLY RESOLVED. No matter what has been said before, if there is no intent to perform, then the resolves become meaningless.

And this is where most of our resolutions fail. It is not that our intents were too grandiose. It was not that we lacked the ability to perform. It was not that we were challenged by forces seen or unseen and fell on the field of battle. We just forget!

In "The Lord of the Rings: The Return of the King", Aragon stands with the men of Middle Earth before the black gate of Sauron. With a "BE IT FINALLY RESOLVED" challenge to these warriors, he declares, "For Frodo!" Then he turns and rides toward the enemy.

He chose to remember what the whole battle was about even though he knew not the outcome. Whatever this year will bring to your path, be it good or bad, always remember God's word and His ways.

BE IT FINALLY RESOLVED…

01/02

The Final Frontier

I was a Trekkie, before it was in vogue to be a Trekkie. And for those who have no idea what a Trekkie is, I love following all things Star Trek.

Now before you begin seeing me in costume or wearing pointed ears or attempting to speak Vulcan, please know that I am a nominal Trekkie. I just like to watch the programs and the movies.

Space…the final frontier. These are the voyages of the starship Enterprise…NOT!

Space isn't really the final frontier. There is a frontier that we all face each day, but perhaps we more especially think about it as we launch into a new year. That frontier is the future.

Like space, the future always stretches itself out before us. To live is to have a future. I suppose that all of us would like to peel back the covering of tomorrow and take a peek. Truthfully, though, when we really grasp that next page of our lives and start to turn it we refrain. We are happy to just let tomorrow take care of itself.

We serve a God that never faces tomorrow. He is eternal and omnipresent. Time does not occur to God. He is the same yesterday, today, and forever.

Especially in the Old Testament, God would reveal the future through one of His prophets. This was the case during the time of Isaiah. God unveiled the future both short term and long term through the prophet Isaiah. He showed the coming judgment of Israel and the coming of Jesus as the Messiah and Deliverer.

God's message about the future was not always rosy. In Isaiah 8, God spoke through the the prophet and warned of the coming Assyrian invasion. He foretold of the enemy's advance being like a flood that would rise to the neckline. But then He reminded the people that their name was Immanuel (Isaiah 8:8).

Here is the good news about the future if you are a believer and follower of Christ. We do not walk into the unknown alone! Immanuel is walking with you. Immanuel— God with us! He is the Captain of our vessel as we traverse the great unknown.

And as Isaiah wrote in the midst of a despairing prophecy, "I will wait on the Lord, who hides His face from the house of Jacob; and I will hope in Him." ~ Isaiah 8:17

The Future…the final frontier and God will be there for the entire ride!

	01/03

Masterpiece

Artists have the ability to take a flat piece of canvas and turn it into a three dimensional masterpiece. Using dark and light colors along with the effects of shadows and light, the person viewing the work is drawn deep into the painting. All the while in reality the eye is viewing a two dimensional object.

As far as I know, we do not have a single piece of artwork that was ever completed by the shepherd boy David. This same David became the king of Israel following the reign of Saul.

Though we have no portraits or drawings done by David, we do have large portions of scripture that serve the purpose of drawing a picture for us. David was a wordsmith. His love for words was recorded both as text to be read and text to be sung.

In 2 Samuel, David's words are recorded as a psalm. He is detailing his struggles during the time that he was chased and hounded daily by Saul. He also describes the glorious protective presence of God throughout his ordeal.

Like an artist, he used the contrast of light and dark to describe an otherwise indescribable God. Speaking of God in meteorological terms, he said, "He bowed the heavens also, and came down with darkness under His feet. / He made darkness canopies around Him, dark waters and thick clouds of the skies." ~ 2 Samuel 22:10, 12

In these two verses and those surrounding them David speaks of God's presence and intercession as a billowing thunderhead. Its huge top ascending to the heights, the lightning flashing from cloud to cloud and cloud to ground, the constant roll of thunder like a marching army, and the wind as the very breath of God blasting away His enemies.

Then when all seems dark and hopeless, he dips his pen in the black ink and splashes light upon the canvas of our minds. "For You are my lamp, O Lord; the Lord shall enlighten my darkness." ~ 2 Samuel 22:29

Here in full glorious display the God that seems distant and removed, the God who seems untouchable and reclusive, the God who seems abstract and one dimensional, bursts forth in brilliant light!

If this is a dark day for you, then look up my friend! Let the light of heaven revealed in the face of God fill the dark canvas of your mind with His marvelous light.

Then stand before Him, like one who is absorbed by a masterpiece and take Him into your darkness. You will be amazed at the contrast.

01/04

Pleasing Others

One of the first manners that we are taught is to follow a request with the little word please. In this use it serves as a key which we quickly learn to use in acquiring something that will ultimately serve us.

The intent of our parents teaching us to use this little adverb was to bring about a certain level of refinement in our character and that is all well and good. But too often, children quickly learn that its use brings pleasure to them personally.

The Apostle Paul uses the word please in the closing remarks of his letter to the Romans. He used the verb form of the word please as he spoke of our relationship to other believers in the body of Christ.

"We then who are strong ought to bear with the scruples of the weak, and not to please ourselves. Let each of us please his neighbor for his good, leading to edification. For even Christ did not please Himself; but as it is written, 'The reproaches of those who reproached You fell on Me.'" ~ Romans 15:1-3

It becomes very clear that Paul's intent was not to teach good manners, but instead to edify others. The word means to encourage to the point of emotional excitement.

His intent was not that we do everything to make people happy. That path is walked by many and it can be a discouraging experience to live as a people-pleaser. First, because we can never really determine what pleases another. Secondly, as fallen men and women we can never be pleased. The result is frustration on the parts of both parties.

Paul instructs that our focus in pleasing is to build up each other. It begins by being keenly aware of the other person's weaknesses. Not only to be aware, but to serve as an aid to their lack. The giving of support will always cost you something. A portion of your strength will need to be lent to the weaker person.

We then see that our goal is the edification of our neighbor. The word edification is sometimes simplified to the concept of building up, but it actually means to place a roof over a family. Having a roof over your head goes a long way towards strengthening a family.

Do we have a good example to follow in this pleasing exercise? Yes, we do. It is Christ Himself. Paul clearly states that Christ in His ministry did not seek to please Himself, but instead took the weaknesses of those who had reviled Him and bore them Himself.

I hope you will say please as a follow up to your requests, but more so I hope you will seek to please God by lifting up a weaker believer today. In doing so, you become more like Christ and the roof is broadened over the family of God.

01/05

With Fear and Trembling

It seems that we have become very casual in our approach to salvation. It has been a long time since I have personally seen anyone rushing down an aisle with tears flowing and a sense of terror in the presence of a holy and righteous God.

Do not take this in a wrong way. I believe that God wants us to be in a friendly relationship with Him. Did He not call Abraham His friend? Jesus called the disciples His friends as well. We have, however, taken this idea of friendship so far that we might think of God as our buddy whom we can just slap on the back, give Him a wink, and think that He will understand our shortcomings. Not so fast!

Paul wrote about our salvation in his letter to the Philippians. "Therefore, my beloved, as you have always obeyed, not as in my presence only, but now much more in my absence, work out your own salvation with fear and trembling; for it is God who works in you both to will and to do for His good pleasure." ~ Philippians 2:12-13

How long has it been since you have used the words salvation, fear, and trembling in the same sentence?

These are strong words. We get our English words phobia and tremor from them. Paul instructs us that we are to be working out our salvation. This is not working "for" or "through", but working "out." The idea is that of setting our salvation in order, making sense of what we now have. As we deeply consider this great gift, it should cause us to shake when we think of being without it.

But how are we to even get a grasp of this great fact? It comes by God working in us. God provides the energy to accomplish His purpose in us. We simply receive the gift of salvation, but as God works in us to perform His will, we should day by day come under the overwhelming influence of salvation's work in our lives. The result will be no less than fear and trembling.

Spend some time today considering this great work that is being accomplished in your life as God energizes His plan for you.

01/06

Moments

Life has its moments. They may be defined with words like: happy, sad, disastrous, exciting, memorable, or with one of a thousand other such descriptives. Each of these high points or low points is so dramatic that a marker is placed in our minds and hearts forever.

During the earthly ministry of Jesus, several such occasions arose. One of them was the dividing of the loaves and fish. This one miracle is spoken of in all four of the gospels.

John's account of this miracle is recorded for us in the sixth chapter of his gospel. John also records for us what transpired the next day following this moment of miracle.

Many followed Jesus looking for another miracle; a free lunch if you please. It was in this setting that Jesus laid forth the truth about Himself being the very bread from heaven. He challenged the hearers to eat of Him and never hunger again.

This caused great consternation among those following Him and John tells us, "From that time many of His disciples went back and walked with Him no more. Then Jesus said to the twelve, 'Do you also want to go away?' But Simon Peter answered Him, 'Lord, to whom shall we go? You have the words of eternal life. Also we have come to believe and know that You are the Christ, the Son of the living God.'" ~ John 6:66-69

Here was a life moment. A place of decision that could not be avoided nor ever returned upon again for reconsideration. It was a point of no return.

Divide Creek runs its course through the Canadian Rockies. At a point in its flow the creek divides around a large boulder. Waters which flow to one side of the boulder rush on into Kicking Horse River and finally into the Pacific Ocean.

Waters which travel to the other side of this dividing rock course their way into the Bow River. They later connect to the Saskatchewan River, on into Lake Winnipeg, the Nelson River, Hudson Bay, and to the Atlantic Ocean. Once the waters divide at this rock there is no turning back.

Jesus is the Rock in the midst of your life's stream. Every decision will be forced to one side or the other by His presence. Will you turn back and follow Him no more or will you decide with the disciples that you have no other place to go? It's one of those moments…

01/07

This Is The Day

I became a Christian at the dawn of the worship wars. These were the first days of the transition that carried us from the hymnal to the chorus.

For those who were caught up in those first skirmishes, (I dare not call them battles, though it seemed at times that blood might be spilled) the assumption was that this was the first such transition that had ever occurred.

You and I both know better. Styles of music have changed time and again over the centuries. Wait long enough and hymns will be in vogue again.

Better than the hymns are those verses of scripture that seem to just flow like a melody. One of these is Psalm 118:24: "This is the day the Lord has made; we will rejoice and be glad in it."

This particular verse which is part of a song since it is found in the Psalms, became a chorus that we all sang a few years back. I still hear it from time to time, but not as much as I did in the first days of my journey as a believer.

Its words seem perfect to enjoin believers in a time of praise as they gather for corporate worship and thank God for the very day of which they are partaking.

It is interesting to take a broader look at this one verse in context. The psalmist reaches this pinnacle of praise after giving us a list of everyday life occurrences. Some of these happenings are very harsh. Yet in the end he concludes that this is a day to rejoice and be glad.

He spoke of his distress as he was surrounded by those who hated him. He told of his distrust of men in whom he could place no confidence. He declared that his destruction was continually a possibility as his enemies surrounded him like a swarm of bees.

It was on a day like that in which he broke forth in praise and adoration. He summarized all of his woes as he lifted his eyes toward heaven and sang, "The Lord has chastened me severely, but He has not given me over to death." ~ Psalms 118:18

However this day turns out for you, will you join with the psalmist in singing a little chorus? Can you sing it in the face of the most difficult day? This really is the day that the Lord has made!

01/08

Valley of Trouble

Have you ever jokingly remarked about someone as they entered a room, "Here comes trouble!" In most cases the person is a child who likes to have their own way too much. Sometimes though the child grows up and is still a trouble maker of sorts. At least it seems when there is trouble, they are in the proximity.

Now before you get into your judgmental mood and start naming names, I would suggest that you hear the rest of the story. Then you can be free to name the first trouble maker you can think of in that moment.

The children of Israel had been wandering the wilderness for 40 years when they crossed the Jordan River and defeated the walled city of Jericho. It was a grand victory.

God had set parameters upon the spoils of this one city. Very simple instructions were given: "And you, by all means abstain from the accursed things, lest you become accursed when you take of the accursed things, and make the camp of Israel a curse, and trouble it. But all the silver and gold, and vessels of bronze and iron, are consecrated to the Lord; they shall come into the treasury of the Lord." ~ Joshua 6:18-19

There was the clear warning. The spoils of this city were the Lord's alone. If anyone took of this city's treasures, then trouble would come to Israel.

Here comes trouble! One man decided that he would take just a little of that which belonged to the Lord. In comparison to the whole of the city it was minuscule. But it was the cause of great trouble.

The man's name was Achan. Interestingly, his very name meant troublesome in Hebrew. Who knows, but that his parents gave him this name because of his troublesome character.

Because of his actions, Israel was defeated in their attempt to conquer the city of Ai. Joshua vehemently accused God of bringing them to this place to destroy them. God, however, quickly pointed the finger at the trouble that was in the camp of Israel.

The judgment upon Achan and his family was harsh. They were stoned to death and then burned along with all of their possessions. "Then they raised over him a great heap of stones, still there to this day. So the Lord turned from the fierceness of His anger. Therefore the name of that place has been called the Valley of Achor to this day." ~ Joshua 7:26 The Valley of Achor can be translated the Valley of Trouble.

Well, now, here comes trouble as you take a long look into the mirror of your own life! What have you buried away that belongs to the Lord? Dig it up immediately and lay it before Him. Watch your troubles melt away in the light of your obedience.

01/09

Privacy Notice

Several times each year I receive in the mail a notice from each of the companies with which I conduct business. The heading on the pamphlet usually has some form of this statement: PRIVACY NOTICE.

The legal department of that company then proceeds to inform me of how they are going out of their way to protect my privacy. If you are like me, you immediately sit down and read all of the legalese and feel so much more protected in your cocoon of safety…NOT!

Honestly, we have all pretty much come to the place of accepting the fact that we have no privacy left unto us. We simply put up with the intrusions.

Yet there is a part of us that needs to be disturbed more often. It is that deep inner part of us that we too often forsake to examine. Maybe we have unconsciously decided that it is the only place left that is safe from prying eyes.

But it is a place that needs to be invaded. Until its walls are torn down and we take a long serious look at who we really are, I'm not sure we can ever fully know the depth of unbroken communion with the Lord.

David's words in Psalm 19 speak of this examination of our deep inner world. "Who can understand his errors? Cleanse me from secret faults. Keep back Your servant also from presumptuous sins; let them not have dominion over me. Then I shall be blameless, and I shall be innocent of great transgression. Let the words of my mouth and the meditation of my heart be acceptable in Your sight, O Lord, my strength and my Redeemer." ~ Psalms 19:12-14

Oswald Chambers spoke of this deep introspective walk through ourselves. He said, "The only way we can be of use to God is to let Him take us through the crooks and crannies of our own characters. It is astounding how ignorant we are about ourselves! We do not know envy when we see it, or laziness, or pride… How many of us have learned to look in with courage? We have to get rid of the idea that we understand ourselves; it is the last conceit to go. The only One who understands us is God."

You are on notice. The God who knows you from the inside out wants you to know you from the outside in. You have been delivered a privacy notice from heaven today. Not an agreement to protect your privacy, but to declare that you have none.

As David said, "Let the words of my mouth and the meditation of my heart be acceptable in Your sight, O Lord, my strength and my Redeemer."

01/10

Loyal Children

We live in the day of perfect children. They aren't really perfect, we just think they are. Everything is handed to them on silver platters and few kids have ever had to want for anything.

I can hear the cries of child abuse going up even now. I am not speaking here of causing a child to be without basic necessities. But seeing the way so many kids are spoiled rotten today really worries me. I was on an airplane a few days ago. A boy was sitting a few rows ahead of me. He looked to be about nine or ten years old. He had in his hands an iPad, an iPhone, an iPod, and some other game device. His dilemma as I watched him was trying to figure out what he would turn on next. This kid had well over $1000 worth of electronics at his ready disposal!

Certainly these possessions do not portend destruction for this young man, but I wonder if his father has ever prayed as David did for his son, Solomon. "And give my son Solomon a loyal heart to keep Your commandments and Your testimonies and Your statutes, to do all these things, and to build the temple for which I have made provision." ~ 1 Chronicles 29:19

As David was about to step down from the throne and Solomon was to become king David spoke in terms of reality. This day of celebration had begun by David proclaiming before the people, "My son Solomon, whom alone God has chosen, is young and inexperienced; and the work is great, because the temple is not for man but for the Lord God."~1 Chronicles 29:1 David had a desire to build the temple, but God had forbidden him to do so. Because of this restriction, David prepared all of the materials for the building and left it to his son to perform the actual task. Surely, it was a proud day for him as a Father, but he was honest enough to admit the inexperience of his son.

Riches were not a problem for Solomon. If he had lived today, he would have had a huge flat screen television, and all of the electronic goodies that his credit cards could buy. His father had left a huge kingdom for him to rule and made every provision for his success. But he still needed a loyal heart. The word "loyal" means a mature heart that is at peace.

Stop now and pray for your children. Pray not for them to be prosperous, but at peace with all men and with God Himself. Admit that they are still young and inexperienced. Never pray for a task equal to their ability, but pray that God will make them loyal to the task He has planned for their lives. Prepare for your departure and trust them with the completion of the task.

01/11

Obituary

Another funeral today—I checked the obituary column. It's not my funeral.

Now that may seem a bit morbid to you as you consider this devotional reading, but you would have to understand my background a little to better comprehend my opening sentence.

I have been attending funerals for a very long time. One of my earliest memories as a child is that of attending my grandfather's funeral. I was seven or eight years old. I served as a pall bearer. At least my hand was on the coffin as I walked with the men who were actually carrying his casket.

That picture has never left my mind.

Since then I have attended the funerals of nearly all of my close family. When my obituary is written it will be very long. Not because of a great list of accomplishments, but instead the list of those who have preceded me in death will be so extensive.

Days like this sure leave a person reflecting on how brief our existence really is.

Since I have been a pastor for over three decades, it has been my responsibility and may I say my privilege to minister at the side of many grieving families. Truthfully, I have lost count, but each funeral was in some way remarkable.

It may have been the power of a life lived or the brevity of a person's days or even the struggle that someone fought before succumbing to the call that none of us can escape. Each person leaves a deep and indelible mark upon a life lived.

One day it will be my obituary that is being read—not by me, of course! My life will have run its course. All opportunities will be lost for both the living and the dead as they relate to my circle of influence. Memories will replace reality and eternity will be engaged by the one whose name you have read in the obituary column.

So what conclusion can possibly be reached that allows the living to face the inevitability of death? As I have said many times from the pulpit, "I'm so glad you asked!"

And here is my concluding summation on this thing we call death, as I join the Apostle Paul in his confidence: "For I am persuaded that neither death nor life, nor angels nor principalities nor powers, nor things present nor things to come, nor height nor depth, nor any other created thing, shall be able to separate us from the love of God which is in Christ Jesus our Lord." ~ Romans 8:38-39

01/12

Like Precious Faith

Do you remember ever being picked last? As the choices dwindled and the choosers worked through their decision making, you stood there praying that you would not be the last one still in the choosing line. There is no way around this process. Someone must be last. Someone will get the short stick. It's just a part of this life we live, but there is some good news when it comes to the matter of faith.

Every believer is given the exact same faith at the point of belief. Peter stated it this way as he began his second epistle: "Simon Peter, a bondservant and apostle of Jesus Christ, to those who have obtained like precious faith with us by the righteousness of our God and Savior Jesus Christ." ~ 2 Peter 1:1

He used one word in the original that has been translated as two words in English. The Greek word *eesoteemos* is translated "like precious" as it describes the faith that has been given to all believers. It literally means of equal value. No one gets picked last! No one gets the short end of the stick!

Jesus described this equality of the gift of faith in the parable of the workers. A man hired some men to work at daylight and they agreed that he would pay them what was right. He hired others at noon and they agreed to work as well for what was right. Finally, he hired others just minutes before sunset and made a similar agreement. As the men lined up to be paid, he started with those hired last and gave them their wages. The men hired at noon received an equal amount, and so did those hired early. Of course, complaining arose among those who had worked longer, but the employer reminded them that each had agreed to work for what he would determine was right. After all, it was his to offer in the first place. He had been fair with each group independent of the labor provided. (Matthew 20:1-16)

Perhaps today you are feeling a little under appreciated. Maybe it seems like you've received the short end of the stick. Take heart! The end of the day has not come yet. Each believer has obtained "like precious" faith. All stand on level ground at the foot of the cross.

	01/13

Can You Hear?

Hearing can be relative at times. The ability to understand can be affected by conditions under which the sound arrives at our ear. But there are times that we simply are unhearing. The sound is clear. The message is distinct. We just refuse to hear.

I have heard of many a person who wears hearing aids using the volume control of the device to tune out what they do not wish to hear. All of us I suppose become selectively hard of hearing at times. At least that makes me feel better about being unhearing now and again.

As the disciples heard Jesus speaking the message of God, they learned that He often spoke in parables. The words were clearly discernible, but the message was entirely missed. Jesus would then take them aside and explain the meaning of the parable to them.

In essence, he corrected their hearing. He turned their unhearing into hearing.

On one such occasion the disciples came to Him and asked, "Why do You speak to them in parables?" ~ Matthew 13:10

Jesus responded by quoting from the prophet Isaiah about a time when Israel would no longer see nor hear even though they were seeing and hearing. Jesus said, "Therefore I speak to them in parables, because seeing they do not see, and hearing they do not hear, nor do they understand." ~ Matthew 13:13

It is amazing to me that this same Jesus who had given many deaf people their ability to hear physically would not override the choice made by many in that day to be unhearing.

Herein lies a great truth and a great sadness. Many will physically hear God's word. It may come by sermon, song, or some other manner, but it will fall on spiritually deaf ears. The message unheard by choice.

Jesus used parables not to keep people from hearing, but because they were unhearing. They had made a choice not to hear. They had turned the little volume control of their souls down until they could no longer discern the voice of God.

The good news for the hearer is this: "Blessed are your eyes for they see, and your ears for they hear; for assuredly, I say to you that many prophets and righteous men desired to see what you see, and did not see it, and to hear what you hear, and did not hear it." ~ Matthew 13:16-17

God is still speaking. Listen and hear!

01/14

Overcoming the World

Have you ever noticed that people like stories about overcomers? It really doesn't matter the issue or obstacle that they have surmounted. We love to hear about personal victory in the face of overwhelming odds.

One such overcomer was Booker T. Washington. He was born into slavery in 1856. He wrote that he could remember the day that a man stood before him, his mother, and siblings and heard that man read what he later understood to be the Emancipation Proclamation.

Washington was a master of overcoming difficulties. He established the Tuskegee Institute under the premise that with self-help, people could go from poverty to success. The school was literally built from the ground up by those who attended there while being educated. He was quoted as saying, "A measure of a man's success is not what he achieves, but what he overcomes."

As Christians, we too are overcomers. We were under the influence of sin and like slaves we were mastered by it until the day that Christ issued our spiritual emancipation proclamation from the cross.

Our relationship with God changes our very nature. John put it this way in his first epistle: "For whatever is born of God overcomes the world. And this is the victory that has overcome the world—our faith. Who is he who overcomes the world, but he who believes that Jesus is the Son of God?" ~ 1 John 5:4-5

Unlike Booker T. Washington's focus on self-help as the leverage to overcoming, as Christians, we are born again and changed into overcomers by the element of faith.

John asks the question and answers it in the same breath. "Who is he who overcomes the world, but he who believes that Jesus is the Son of God?" Jesus is the author, object, and finisher of our faith.

This little poem by an unknown author sums up what faith accomplishes in our overcoming the world:

> A little brown cork fell in the path of a whale
> Who lashed it down with his angry tail.
> But in spite of its blows it quickly arose,
> And floated serenely before his nose.
> Said the cork to the whale:
> "You may flap and sputter and frown,
> But you never, never, can keep me down;
> For I'm made of the stuff
> That is buoyant enough
> To float instead of drown."

Keep on floating by faith till Jesus comes!

01/15

What A Waste!

My many mission trips have caused one marked difference in how I live all of the other weeks that I am here in a land of plenty. I have a strong aversion to waste.

I have seen enough REALLY hungry people in my travels that it bothers me to see how much we simply throw away here in the United States. Maybe it bothers me most when a church has dinner on the grounds. That's potluck for those of you who live anywhere north of Interstate 10.

Food is piled up, picked over, and plopped into the garbage can. That "garbage" would make a fine meal in a lot of places in this world.

Now lest you think of me as a hoarder, I would take you to a biblical account that shows the correct time to throw away that which is perfectly good. The occasion transpires in the early days of David's reign as king of Israel.

David had set up rule in Jerusalem. The Philistines still occupied Bethlehem. Surrounding David were the mighty men who had gathered in his support and defense.

"And David said with longing, 'Oh, that someone would give me a drink of water from the well of Bethlehem, which is by the gate!' So the three broke through the camp of the Philistines, drew water from the well of Bethlehem that was by the gate, and took it and brought it to David. Nevertheless David would not drink it, but poured it out to the Lord." ~ 1 Chronicles 11:17-18

I know what you are thinking, "What a waste!" But David could not bring himself to drink that which had come at such risk. These three men had accomplished the feat of bringing him water at great expense. In essence, the water became their shed blood to him and all he could do was pour it out unto the Lord as a sacrifice.

How amazingly different this response is to the extravagance that most expect in our world today. We spend our days attempting to satisfy a thirst from the well of Bethlehem. We care not nor do we take the time to measure the cost of acquiring such dainties.

Our waste alone could make a tremendous difference in the world in which we interact. Would you dare pour out that which you have greatly desired and have now obtained?

Yes, some will declare it to be a waste, but that which is surrendered to the Lord never becomes rubbish. Ask God now what needs to be released unto Him and be amazed at His response.

01/16

All By Myself

Have you ever concluded that if you were going to get something done you had best do it yourself? Of course you have and so have I.

Our reasons may have varied greatly in why we chose that route, but in the end it just came down to a matter of not knowing what the outcome might be. So, we endeavor by doing it ourselves to assure the end result. You know, as well as I, that even doing it yourself does not always guarantee a good end to a project. Chances are however, sooner or later, we will seize control and do it ourselves…just in case.

Something similar happened in the life of Abraham. God gave him instructions as recorded in Genesis 15. He was to take a selection of animals, kill them, divide them into two pieces, and lay them on each side of a path.

Now this may seem weird to you and I, but Abraham would have been very comfortable in doing this since it was a common custom in his day.

Two individuals would perform a similar act in preparation of making a covenant between the two. These two people would then walk arm in arm along the path between the severed animals.

Looking back down the path they would declare their faithfulness to one another. Their oath would pronounce that unfaithfulness bring them to the same end as the animals scattered along the pathway.

After Abraham had laid out the path of animal carcasses, God caused a deep sleep to fall upon him. At that point God came and walked the path alone. "And it came to pass, when the sun went down and it was dark, that behold, there appeared a smoking oven and a burning torch that passed between those pieces. On the same day the Lord made a covenant with Abram…" ~ Genesis 15:17-18

In essence, God decided to do it Himself to assure the outcome. Even though Abraham is noted for his faith, he was still human and in the frailty of the flesh he was sure to fail. God knew this about Abraham just as He knows our own weaknesses.

This same God who appeared in a cloud of smoke and fire showed Himself again to Israel as they journeyed from Egypt to the Promised Land. Daily they were guided and protected under a cloud by day and a pillar of fire by night. (Exodus 14:20)

You and I can thank God that when it comes to our salvation, He has guaranteed the outcome. He sent His only Son to walk alone among the pieces of humanity. All who trust Him can be assured that He alone is faithful to complete that which He has begun in those who have believed.

Praise God! He did it all by Himself!

01/17

Set My Soul Afire

The writing of devotions has become a serious focus for me over the past few years. The more of them that I compose the more I see of the greatness of God and the unending source of revelation about Him.

Certainly there is space in our devotional time for our words and thoughts to be lifted before the gate of heaven. Even as David said in Psalm 5, "Give ear to my words, O Lord, consider my meditation. Give heed to the voice of my cry, my King and my God, for to You I will pray. My voice You shall hear in the morning, O Lord; in the morning I will direct it to You, and I will look up." ~ Psalms 5:1-3

I think that we are very good at getting our voice heard before the Lord. Especially in this world of tragedy and hurt, we have lots to cry about during our devotional times.

How much time do we take though to just be silent before the Lord? How often do we simply lay open the Bible, focus upon a verse or two, and wait for God to speak?

I fear that our devotional time may be a bit hurried. Sometimes things happen. I understand that, but devotional time must become an intentional time.

As a boy, it was an exciting time when I could get my hands on a magnifying glass. Out I would go into the yard with a single mission: to use that glass to focus the power of the sun upon a leaf or a piece of paper. Talk about fun! Remember, these were the days when imaginations still were used.

Just like my use of a magnifying glass to focus the sun, our devotional time becomes a focal point that takes the rays of God's glory and burns one single spot upon our hearts.

That's my desire in writing these words each day. My words are not the power or energy that sets a heart ablaze. My words are only the magnifying glass. As you hold them at just right angle, the amassed energy of God's word is focused upon your life and POOF!…a flame is set into motion.

General Charles "Chinese" Gordon was a British soldier. While in the Sudan, he had a certain sign before his tent each morning which meant that he must be left alone. His Bible is in the Queen's apartments at Windsor. If you look closely at it you will see that this companion in his daily devotional time is so worn that you can scarcely read the print.

Let the word of God become your companion today. Hold it at just the right angle so that it can set your life on fire. Better for the your Bible to be worn out instead of you. Better for the fire of God to burn in you than for you to burn out.

01/18

Defective Love

A man visited his pastor with a problem to discuss. He told the pastor that he was having a difficult time loving his wife. The pastor told him that scripture clearly taught that husbands are to love their wives. The man said he could not.

The pastor then told the man that he was commanded by scripture to love his neighbor and that he should love her as a neighbor. The man said again that he could not. The pastor finally told the man that scripture was very clear. If he could not love her as a wife or a neighbor then he must love her anyway because the command of God is plain: We are to love our enemies!

Sometimes loving is hard to do, but we are indeed required to follow the supreme command of God which is to love. Love is not an option!

Jesus was asked once what was the greatest commandment. Amazingly, He did not name any of the "big 10." He answered, "You shall love the Lord your God with all your heart, with all your soul, and with all your mind. This is the first and great commandment. And the second is like it: You shall love your neighbor as yourself. On these two commandments hang all the Law and the Prophets." ~ Matthew 22:37-40

In these verses Jesus summarized all of the Law and compacted it into two statements that deal with love. Here we learn that love functions in two dimensions. One is vertical and the other is horizontal. When we love God completely then loving others can be done simply.

Kenneth Boa in his book, "Handbook to Prayer," said, "Another way of summarizing our calling and purpose as followers of Christ is to love God completely, to love self correctly, and to love others compassionately."

The man in my opening story did not have a problem loving his wife. He had a problem loving God completely. His defective love for God led to a deficient love of self. Because the vertical dimension of love was interrupted he could not love horizontally.

If you are having a problem loving yourself or someone else as you should today, the problem in not in you or around you. It's above you! Look up and love God again with all your heart, soul, and, mind.

01/19

Life On the Wire

When it comes to balancing acts there is no greater name than Wallenda. This family of acrobats known as the Flying Wallendas have set several world records in their high wire feats of daring.

In this hurry-up, moment by moment intensity that we live in day by day we can all find ourselves suspended high above the crowds on a thin wire of support.

Is this what God expects for us or have we created a false level of expectancy when it comes to our everyday lives? Busyness and risk seem to be the norm. Not only the norm, but these conditions and lifestyles are admired and we are prompted to climb higher and walk farther on the high wire of life. All of this is expected to be done of course without a net!

Interestingly, the Bible uses a word from which we directly get our English word acrobat. The Greek word is translated as circumspectly and can be found in Ephesians 5:15. Here's the word in context:

"See then that you walk circumspectly, not as fools but as wise, redeeming the time, because the days are evil. Therefore do not be unwise, but understand what the will of the Lord is." ~ Ephesians 5:15-17

We are to go about our everyday lives in a circumspect way, that is, like acrobats. Now before you get squeamish and faint you need to understand fully what God is saying to us.

First, I think we need to understand that life really is lived on the high wire. Karl Wallenda the patriarch of the Flying Wallendas is quoted as saying, "Life is on the wire, the rest is just waiting."

Second, you need to be wise. Here is the truth: You and I are not Wallendas!

We need to be fully aware that there will always be forces that are attempting to knock us off of our high wire. Karl Wallenda fell to his death at the age of 73 as he attempted to walk between two buildings in Puerto Rico.

Two things attributed to his fall: high winds and loose cables that supported the wire upon which he walked. Just as Paul said in these verses, the days are evil. We need to guard against the things that are attempting to destroy us.

Finally, never walk beyond the will of God. Never take more of a risk than God is requiring, but never shirk the level of risk that always exists when we do the will of God.

Here is the good news. God's will is the safest place to be. His will is literally the safety net beneath our high wire.

Now go out there and walk like an acrobat!

01/20

A New Thing

It is my understanding that a person cannot dream anything that they have not experienced. Our dreams are just a compilation of occurrences that get reassembled in our subconscious and sometimes come out in very strange forms.

Whether this is a fact or not I will not set out to prove. I know that I have had some really weird dreams and perhaps I am comforted in believing that what I remember could not possibly be apart from what I have already experienced.

God, on the other hand, has shown throughout time to have used the dreams of men to convey His message. Because of His intervention, we are able to see new things that have never existed before either in time or space.

In Isaiah 43 God is introduced as Jacob's Creator. That is, I think, the key to understanding God's revelation. As Creator, He can do things in a brand new way.

We, as mere humans, are limited to a box as it was described by Solomon in Ecclesiastes. "That which has been is what will be, that which is done is what will be done, and there is nothing new under the sun." ~ Ecclesiastes 1:9

Isaiah, however, records God's words as they relate to the gathering of Israel from the four corners of the earth and His promises to go with them through every trial whether it be flood or fire.

The Lord said, "Do not remember the former things, nor consider the things of old. Behold, I will do a new thing, now it shall spring forth; shall you not know it? I will even make a road in the wilderness and rivers in the desert." ~ Isaiah 43:18-19

Now lest you think that all of this was written just for Israel's benefit, you should know that these things were written for our benefit as well. God never changes. What He did for Israel, He can do for you today.

God can do a new thing in your life right now! It starts by forgetting your past and looking to the Creator. He who needs nothing to begin, can make things that do not even exist come into being in the here and now.

Once again listen to the word of the Lord. "Behold, I will do a new thing, now it shall spring forth; shall you not know it?"

God wants to make a way through your wilderness and bring water to your wasteland. It will be a new thing. It will spring up out of nowhere and you will know it has occurred.

Come out of your dream world! Wake up to the reality of God's great work in your life as the Creator! It's going to be a new day!

	01/21

Qualified

Qualification is used in a lot of ways today. I still remember being qualified to buy my first home.

I also remember walking on a car lot as a young man. I was married and we had our first child with us as we looked at new vehicles. A salesman came out and asked me what I was doing on the lot. I told him I was there to buy a car. He told me to go home! Evidently his evaluation of a young married couple with a child was that we did not qualify. I went to another dealer and bought a car that day. Now that I think back on that day, he was probably right…I should have went home!

The Apostle Paul began to offer thanks to God when he thought of how God had qualified him for salvation. "…giving thanks to the Father who has qualified us to be partakers of the inheritance of the saints in the light. He has delivered us from the power of darkness and conveyed us into the kingdom of the Son of His love…" ~ Colossians 1:12-13

We can give thanks that our qualification for salvation is not based on our own abilities. We were not judged like a player of some sport who must acquire a certain score or time in an event to qualify. We were not assessed to determine if we could pay for our salvation. God did not look us over like the salesman did me many years ago and determine that we should just go home. He qualified us! Someone said that God does not call the qualified; He qualifies the called.

This is good news for us! This qualifying makes us eligible to receive a portion of the inheritance that He purchased for us by the blood of His own Son. He has taken us out of the kingdom of darkness and placed us securely into the light of Christ's Kingdom.

Stop today and give thanks for that moment in your life when you were made to stand in the light. If as you read this you are yet in the darkness, stop now, and ask God to deliver you. You are pre-qualified for salvation for Christ has come as the Light to convey you into His love. Oh, happy day!

01/22

Trail Blazers

The early explorers of our expansive country would use a process called trail blazing to mark out paths across forests and mountains. Symbols left by hatchet marks upon trees or by stacking rocks in certain formations would allow others to follow safely through otherwise unmapped territory.

Today we travel highways and interstate systems that carry us quickly across the countryside. These too are blazed with road signs which give us directions in strange places.

Few people have no access to some sort of GPS equipment. From units mounted in automobiles, to cell phone apps, or even wrist watches, we have access to satellites that can give us directions with the familiar voice that implores us to turn right or left just ahead.

I doubt that there is a single route that could be taken where a turn would not be required. So it is in a spiritual sense also. Turning, or as it is better known, repenting is necessary to finding the road to heaven.

It is the word of God through the work of the Holy Spirit that implores us to make a turn. Some of these turns are dramatic, while some are gentle redirection that heads us toward God and away from a path of total lostness.

For the people of Thessalonica it was a radical turn that put them on the pathway of salvation. "For from you the word of the Lord has sounded forth, not only in Macedonia and Achaia, but also in every place. Your faith toward God has gone out, so that we do not need to say anything. For they themselves declare concerning us what manner of entry we had to you, and how you turned to God from idols to serve the living and true God…" ~ 1 Thessalonians 1:8-9

The Thessalonians made an immediate and decisive change consequent upon a deliberate choice. Theirs was a voluntary act in response to the presentation of truth.

The result was a change of direction; a full U-turn if you please. So radical was their change of direction that they became blazes upon the trail of life. Their very lives declared the gospel without even speaking a word.

God wants you and I to be markers along the trail of life. We can be like the voice of the GPS lady sounding forth the directions that lead to home:

"Make a U-turn and arrive at your destination."

01/23

Strengthened With Power

Power is an interesting concept. For the most part it is completely relative since everyone and all things have some form and quantity of power. One's power is only of real use if it surmounts the power of another person or thing.

As boys, we would never let a freshly dumped load of dirt go to waste. Like bees to honey the neighborhood boys would gather to play King of the Mountain.

The rules are very easy for this game. Everyone battles everyone else for supremacy on the peak of the dirt mountain. Allies were not considered. Shared effort was not utilized. It was every "man" for himself. Challengers were flung in every direction until either all were defeated or the king was dethroned.

It sure was better than a video game where the only power needed is in your thumbs!

Power is spoken of often in the scriptures. At least 117 times it is the translation of the Greek word *dunamis*. This is the same word from which we derive the word dynamite.

It speaks primarily of strength and ability including miraculous feats. Unlike our English word dynamite which only has destructive power, *dunamis* can also speak of creative power.

In the Apostle Paul's last letter he wrote to his young protégé' Timothy. In the first few lines of this letter he reminded Timothy of his salvation experience and the subsequent power that had been given him because of his relationship with Christ.

"For God has not given us a spirit of fear, but of power and of love and of a sound mind. Therefore do not be ashamed of the testimony of our Lord, nor of me His prisoner, but share with me in the sufferings for the gospel according to the power of God…" ~ 2 Timothy 1:7-8

The power that we have as believers is not inherent. It comes as a gift from God. Unlike boys trying to fling each other from the top of a dirt mound in their own strength, God has given us an inner dynamo by the Holy Spirit to carry out His commission.

"…that He would grant you, according to the riches of His glory, to be strengthened with might {power} through His Spirit in the inner man…" ~ Ephesians 3:16

Are you staring up the face of a mountain today? Concern not yourself with the height of the peak, the steepness of the grade, or the occupier of the mountain.

Go in the strength of God! Seize the mountain in the name of Jesus!

01/24

Mysterious Visitors

Some things that happen to us are so mysterious that we just do not talk about them very much. Other happenings are disturbing because of pain or disappointment and we avoid them as well. The story I am about to tell you falls into the mysterious category.

Many years ago I owned a country grocery store. Most of the time I operated my business by myself. When you own a small grocery business like mine you get to know everyone very well. You serve the community in many roles.

When a customer needed some meat you were the butcher. When a lady needed assistance in completing her supper plans you became a chef. A noisy auto called for your abilities as a mechanic. Financial troubles turned you into a loan officer. A cough or a sniffle required one's pharmaceutical skills. It was indeed an interesting occupation to own a small country grocery business.

My mysterious story happened one afternoon during what is normally a slow time. It is the time when folks have had their lunch and the kids aren't home yet from school. It was just me and the sound of equipment running when he appeared.

To this day I cannot remember the door opening. He was just there in front of me. He had long unkempt hair and clothes that seemed to have been worn for many days and nights. He was a man and there he stood. A stranger that would be easily recognized in the setting of a small country grocery store.

He did not say anything and before he might have, I asked a question. I do not really know why I asked it, but I did.

"Are you hungry?"

As much as I can remember that day, he simply nodded yes.

I prepared a couple of sandwiches from my deli selection, gave him a pint of milk, and five dollars from the cash register drawer. Each of these he received graciously, but I do not remember any vocal response.

He turned and walked out of my store. I went immediately to the window to see which way he would be walking, but I saw no one. I walked outside—no one. I walked around the building—again no one.

My story is still a mystery and I do not tell it very often. It was a sacred moment for me. I can only resolve a part of it by remembering this verse of scripture: "Do not forget to entertain strangers, for by so doing some have unwittingly entertained angels." ~ Hebrews 13:2

01/25

Unrolling the Scroll

Perhaps it was a fair morning in Goshen when the Egyptian emissary rode into the camp. The children of Israel had grown accustomed to the toils of their taskmasters. What had begun as a small troop of people 400 years before was now a multitude and Pharaoh worried about them assuming too much power.

With the unrolling of a scroll the Egyptian would read the proposal of Pharaoh to control the population of the Israelites. All male children would be unmercifully slaughtered. No excuses. No exceptions.

We never know what a day will hold. We can't imagine an Egyptian riding into our lives and bringing the worst news imaginable. But it happens. It may have already occurred in your life today and as you read this you are wondering how you will survive the unrolling of the scroll.

That is where faith comes into the equation. Faith does not always change the circumstances, but it provides the way through whatever is occurring in your life.

This is where the actions of Moses' parents by faith are recorded for our edification. "And a man of the house of Levi went and took as wife a daughter of Levi. So the woman conceived and bore a son. And when she saw that he was a beautiful child, she hid him three months. But when she could no longer hide him, she took an ark of bulrushes for him, daubed it with asphalt and pitch, put the child in it, and laid it in the reeds by the river's bank. And his sister stood afar off, to know what would be done to him." ~ Exodus 2:1-4

Hebrews 11:23 tells us this was an act of faith. "By faith Moses, when he was born, was hidden three months by his parents, because they saw he was a beautiful child; and they were not afraid of the king's command."

Great instruction is given to the believer as it relates to faith in these few verses. First, we should always do what we can. Moses' mother hid him for three months and then placed him in a basket upon the Nile River.

She did what she could while she could do it. Faith does not preclude our own efforts, but we should know when we have done all we can.

Second, faith trusts that what we have done is enough and the results are fully in the hand of the Lord. His sister simply stood by and watched what would become of the baby.

Third, faith leaves no room for fear. Moses' parents would not allow Pharaoh's command to diminish their faith.

Tomorrow I'll tell you the rest of the story. Until then, are you doing what you can while you can? Even if it means placing your most precious possession afloat, will you by faith trust everything to God today?

Be sure to read tomorrow's devotion for the rest of the story…

01/26

Doing What You Can

Yesterday's devotional dealt with the functioning of faith in the lives of Moses' parents. Again, hear the words of Hebrews 11 as his parents are listed in the hall of faith.

"By faith Moses, when he was born, was hidden three months by his parents, because they saw he was a beautiful child; and they were not afraid of the king's command." ~ Hebrews 11:23

The three things learned about faith in this story are:

1. Faith requires that we do what we can do.
2. Faith requires that we know when we have done all we could do.
3. Faith never gives place to fear.

Can you imagine those first three months of Moses' life? He must have been held continually and soothed by his mother as she did her best to keep him quietly hidden. But his mother was also preparing for his departure and ultimate salvation.

Each day she would have gathered a few reeds and lovingly wove them tightly into a little basket. A basket that would become an ark upon the crocodile infested Nile River.

She surely must have remembered the story of Noah faithfully building the ark for 120 years never knowing exactly which day the rains would come. She must have known about Noah coating that ark with pitch within and without as she did all she could to prepare an ark of safety for her boy child.

And as always happens, the day came. The day when she knew she had done all she could to save her son. She placed him in the tiny ship and by faith set it afloat amongst the bulrushes of the river. With the same faith that kept fear from her heart concerning the command of Pharaoh, she walked away from the river bank leaving both boy and boat in the sure Hand of Providence.

What are you facing today that requires you to turn it all over to the Hand of the Lord? Is it time to lay down your most precious possession and walk away trusting God for the outcome?

Can God really be trusted? Find out tomorrow as we conclude the story of Moses' Nile River Cruise.

01/27

Providential Care

As we continue the story of Moses, it becomes apparent that God's hand of providence was clearly at work. Because God is omniscient, He sees all at all times. It amazes me that a God who exists outside of time is always in sync with our time.

The current on the river that day was at just the right speed. A little push of a cool breeze across the bow of Moses' ark of bulrushes guided it gently past a sleeping crocodile. If you listen closely you can hear the bottom of the pitch covered basket as it scrapes the river bottom and comes to rest in the shallows.

Not any shallow spot on the longest river in the world, but the exact spot that Pharaoh's daughter would be bathing! Now that's providence!

Shall I go on? This Egyptian maiden draws Moses up out of the river. Hence, his name, Moses, which means to be drawn out. Curiosity prompts her to open the basket "and when she opened it, she saw the child, and behold, the baby wept. So she had compassion on him, and said, 'This is one of the Hebrews' children.'" ~ Exodus 2:6

It may not be so, but I believe that God sent an angel to pinch Moses right then and there. What person could not have compassion on a crying baby? In God's providence we even cry at the right time!

Is this enough for you or shall I describe the providence of God even more? Miriam, Moses' sister, having followed the floating basket down the river, just "happened" to be right there to hear the remarks of Pharaoh's daughter.

"Then his sister said to Pharaoh's daughter, 'Shall I go and call a nurse for you from the Hebrew women, that she may nurse the child for you?' And Pharaoh's daughter said to her, 'Go…'" ~ Exodus 2:7-8

And it gets even better! "So the maiden went and called the child's mother. Then Pharaoh's daughter said to her, 'Take this child away and nurse him for me, and I will give you your wages.' So the woman took the child and nursed him." ~ Exodus 2:8-9

In God's providence, He required the same king, who had ordered all Hebrew boys to die, to pay Moses' mother to feed her own child. Thus saving the life of Moses and healing the shattered heart of a mother!

Could you tell me again about your situation? And when you do, I will graciously remind you of God's providential care. What a mighty God we serve!

Tomorrow I shall tell you of what Moses' mother might have whispered into his ear as she nursed him through those first few years.

01/28

Who'll Take Billy's Place?

Over the past three days we have journeyed through the first few months of Moses' life. Over and again the Hand of Providence has been clearly seen. Now consider the truth that all of these things have been written for the benefit of us as believers in the 21st century!

Truly, that is providential!

The mother of Moses is now on Pharaoh's payroll. She is nursing Moses every few hours of each and every day. He is no longer in hiding. She can cuddle him openly and sing lullabies of the Promised Land to him as he drifts off to sleep seeing the face of his own dear mother.

Over and again, she would whisper the stories of his forefathers: Abraham, Isaac, and Jacob. She would have told him of God's providence in placing Joseph in Egypt as the deliverer of his own people. And yes, she would have told him of God's promise to ultimately deliver them from the oppression of the Egyptians. Little could she have known that she held the deliverer in her arms.

Imagine the eyes of Moses growing wide as his mother described her preparation of the ark of reeds, the careful placing of it in the river, and the discovery of Pharaoh's daughter.

Was she able to call the baby she held her son? Did he know that his mother caressed him against her breasts?

We will never know those answers on this side of glory, but we do know that the influence she had upon him was lasting. The book of Hebrews tells us, "By faith Moses, when he became of age, refused to be called the son of Pharaoh's daughter, choosing rather to suffer affliction with the people of God than to enjoy the passing pleasures of sin, esteeming the reproach of Christ greater riches than the treasures in Egypt; for he looked to the reward. By faith he forsook Egypt, not fearing the wrath of the king; for he endured as seeing Him who is invisible." ~ Hebrews 11:24-27

You may be wondering if you are making a difference or not today? Know that you are! The seeds that you are planting in the hearts and minds of your children and acquaintances will surely burst forth one day.

God in His providence has placed you in your particular circle of influence. While you are there, never waste one precious moment. Take every opportunity to plant the hope of the gospel. Remember, somebody has to take Billy Graham's place!

Tomorrow: Out of Egypt!

01/29

Out of Egypt

The day would have finally come when Moses' mother would need to surrender her son to Pharaoh's daughter. It must have been a bittersweet occasion. Memories would have been attached to each tear that fell into the thirsty sands of Egypt.

Certainly she would be remembering the day she counted toes and fingers as Moses took his first few breaths. She would have remembered the anxiety at delivering a male child and the horrible edict declared by Pharaoh that all the Hebrew boys were to be slain.

Of course, she would remember each threading of the reeds that created an ark of safety for this fine boy to sail down the Nile into the arms of Pharaoh's daughter. And today she would remember her promise to Moses that she would pray every day for him as he began his life in the palace.

We are not told much of the next four decades of Moses' life, but we can only imagine the splendor he must have enjoyed. Every desire was met with the snap of a finger. His mother would have been praying each day of her life that the deliverer would be delivered. And her prayers were answered. For that day came...

Again, the book of Hebrews describes faith at work in Moses' life: "Esteeming the reproach of Christ greater riches than the treasures in Egypt; for he looked to the reward. By faith he forsook Egypt, not fearing the wrath of the king; for he endured as seeing Him who is invisible. By faith he kept the Passover and the sprinkling of blood, lest he who destroyed the firstborn should touch them. By faith they passed through the Red Sea as by dry land, whereas the Egyptians, attempting to do so, were drowned." ~ Hebrews 11:26-29

Yes, the day came when prayers were answered. The day when the memories of Moses were revived and he forsook Egypt. He did not just depart from the geographical place called Egypt. He FORSOOK it! To forsake means to leave behind with full intent of never returning. Only faith can bring about such a change of direction. So, we read three times in these verses, it was by faith that he walked out of Egypt.

His mother's words as she nursed him were now bringing forth fruit. By faith, he forsook, by faith he feared not, by faith he followed the instructions for the Passover, and by faith he found a pathway through the Red Sea.

Who of you today is praying for your little Moses? Has time passed and it seems that there is no answer? By faith, keep believing and never forget. Soon your Moses will get out of Egypt!

01/30

Fixing Your Fence

Fences can be found everywhere. I have seen them built out of all sorts of materials as I have traveled on mission trips. Some are as simple as sticks stuck into the ground. Others are elaborate and filled with intricate design. I have seen others that are somewhat natural such as cactus planted in long rows. Extra security can be added with almost anything from broken glass bottles on the top of the fence to razor-sharp wire.

One must wonder at times if fences are meant to keep people out or to keep people in as if in a self-made prison of sorts. Take for example fences around graveyards...it does make you wonder!

Paul used the analogy of being a prisoner of the Lord in Ephesians. "I, therefore, the prisoner of the Lord, beseech you to walk worthy of the calling with which you were called, with all lowliness and gentleness, with longsuffering, bearing with one another in love,…" ~ Ephesians 4:1-2 The word "prisoner" is a very strong word with the meaning of captive by way of shackles. Fences are not necessary for a shackled man; or are they?

No sooner than he uses the word prisoner, he speaks of walking. He then describes the pattern of that walk or lifestyle. He tells us that we are called out to a calling. This is a public bidding to serve the Lord. It is not set aside only for those in a church ministry, but for all believers in everyday life.

Paul then uses several words to give dimension to our walk. These are lowliness, gentleness, longsuffering, and love. Humility, patience, and benevolent charity constitute the last three, but I want to focus on the first word, lowliness.

This word means humility of mind. It comes from a compound word in the original language. It means more than being humble. It is active humility that is maintained by keeping one's mind fenced in. Now here's a fence that makes sense!

Humility is not an easy function of the human existence. It is easy to become proud of one's humbleness! Paul used language that gives us important instruction in how to walk worthy of our calling. It begins with building a fence around our minds; not to keep others out, but to keep us in check.

Maybe it's time today to ride around the perimeter of your mind and make sure there are no gaps in the fence.

01/31

The Written Word

How many times have you been reintroduced to someone you have not seen in a long time and you have as a first response a shock that they have gotten so old? Then you look in the mirror and find out that the same thing has happened to you as well!

Changes happen to us both internally and externally and for the most part they occur in an almost imperceptible fashion. There is little that we can do about the effects of aging, but we can do some things about that which occurs to us from the outside.

For example, our circumstances can change quickly and we must respond in an appropriate way. We assess the situation and then we must decide whether we are facing the inevitable or if we can make a difference.

The Old Testament patriarch Job must have come to the conclusion that what had happened to him by the hand of God could not be changed. It was what it was, but his response to it was still his own.

Hear his voice as he groans under the weight of the change of his circumstances: "Oh, that my words were written! Oh, that they were inscribed in a book! That they were engraved on a rock with an iron pen and lead, forever! For I know that my Redeemer lives, and He shall stand at last on the earth; and after my skin is destroyed, this I know, that in my flesh I shall see God, whom I shall see for myself, and my eyes shall behold, and not another. How my heart yearns within me!" ~ Job 19:23-27

Wow! I am not sure that I have ever attained that level of faith, but I do desire to reach the point that I could react to change like Job did.

As I considered the words of Job today, I was touched by his desire to leave a permanent record of his life's struggles. After describing his suffering and loss in life, he said, "Oh, that my words were written!"

I am traveling today to my first writer's conference. Change has occurred in my life. In the beginning of my ministry I used words as a preacher from the pulpit. As I come nearer the end of my days, I have joined Job in saying, "Oh, that my words were written!"

I am looking forward to the learning experience. My desire is to use the written word more effectively to communicate the gospel and the hope that lies in Jesus Christ.

FEBRUARY

Grits and Eggs

I can still remember lots of little occasions that transpired when I was a boy. Some of these remembrances have left an indelible mark in my life. These have gone into the mosaic that is me.

Other experiences , however, were those in which I participated directly and played an even more important role. As I considered the following verse of scripture this morning, one such memory rushed back to the front of my mind.

Paul said to the Colossians, "Let your speech always be with grace, seasoned with salt, that you may know how you ought to answer each one." ~ Colossians 4:6 After reading this verse, I began to think about what it meant to have your speech seasoned with salt. That's when I thought about grits.

Now unless you have some connection to the South, then you may not know much about grits. Grits are primarily a breakfast food. It is coarsely ground corn that is cooked in hot water and serve like a hot cereal.

One thing about grits for me: They must be seasoned! Without salt they are pretty much tasteless. Another thing about grits, at least for me, they must be served with eggs.

And that's where my boyhood memory picks up again…

I was about six or seven years old the morning that my daddy took me fishing. On our way to the lake, we stopped at a place called the Toddle House to eat breakfast. I placed my order and was almost stumped when the waitress asked how I wanted my eggs.

Of course, she meant scrambled, fried hard, over easy, etc., but I only knew one way to serve eggs. So I responded, "On top of my grits!" That's where my mama always put them and I thought it was the only way to eat grits and eggs.

You see, the waitress and I were speaking the same language, but we could not understand each other. Our knowledge of grits and eggs was on two different planes. We were using the same words, but with different meanings.

There is a world around us that speaks our language socially, but our speech as a Christian can be completely misconstrued. Therefore, what we have to say is tasteless and as weird as eggs on top of grits.

Make sure that your speech is stimulating so that people will desire even more of what you have to say about Christ. Well-seasoned speech will provide the answer—don't worry about the question. The best answer is always Jesus!

02/02

Fear This

Fear is a powerful emotion. Fear is also a God-given emotion. Fear will provoke one of several different responses in us. Two are primary: fight or flight. For these two reasons we tend to avoid fear at all costs. I'm sure that I'm not alone in having made some poor decisions in times of fear. But let me remind you that fear is a God-given emotion. Therefore, it cannot be bad in and of itself. It is our response that is defective.

Truthfully, there is a lack of fear that is evident in the church today. I'm not sure there would be a very big crowd if the marquee read, "SUNDAY OF FEAR: ALL WELCOME!"

We have even tried to soften the meaning of fear as it relates to God. We want to focus on the idea of reverence and respect, but that's not what we see in the book of Acts. "So great fear came upon all the church and upon all who heard these things." ~ Acts 5:11 The context of this verse is the death of two people in the church and I do mean IN the church! Ananias and Sapphira sold a parcel of land and brought the money as a gift to the church. This sounds like a nice thing for them to do, right?

Again, let's see the context. Prior to their gift a man named Joseph had sold land and given all of the proceeds to the church. The very next thing we read is that this couple did the same thing except for one small detail. They acted as if they had given all, but contrived a plan to keep a portion for themselves. Because of this untruth, they both died IN the church moments after laying their gift on the altar. That's the full context of verse 11. When this news spread great FEAR came upon the church!

I can hear some of you thinking now, "I knew giving was a bad idea!" You know better than that! Peter clearly told them that the land was theirs to keep or sell. The proceeds were theirs to give, share, or keep. The sin that took their life was two-fold. First, they lied. Second, they did not fear God. I believe the lie precipitated from a lack of fear.

Do you fear God? Don't wait for an incident like the one recorded in Acts 5 to prompt you to fear. Fear God today and you will never have to live through an Ananias and Sapphira experience.

Throw It Away

I bought my new laptop a few weeks ago and I'm going to throw it away. It's not broken. It runs just fine. It's just out of date.

That's how fast things are changing. And, no, you can't have my computer since I'm not really throwing it out like an old relic. It really was out of date though the day I took it out of its protective packaging.

We are all forced to deal with more change than we care to, but change we must or be left to eat dust. Is there anywhere we can look to where stability and changelessness exist?

You won't find such a place here on earth, but if you look up like the Psalmist did you will discover the wonders of an unchanging God. "Of old You laid the foundation of the earth, And the heavens are the work of Your hands. They will perish, but You will endure; yes, they will all grow old like a garment; like a cloak You will change them, and they will be changed. But You are the same, and Your years will have no end." ~ Psalms 102:25-27

Here was a person overwhelmed by life. He had concluded that his days were nothing more than smoke. He was being carried away on the wind and would never be seen again. Whatever he had been was no more. It had been consumed with the deterioration of life or cut down by enemies.

He described himself as a pelican in the wilderness. Far removed from its natural habitat, this bird was alone and dying from the elements. The ocean was just too far to fly away to and loneliness was consuming him.

Aware that his world was ever changing—growing old and quickly passing away, he must have looked up momentarily from his predicament and caught a fresh vision of the only thing around him that was not changing.

With his vision fixed above the fray of life he saw his unchanging Maker. He remembered that the God of today was the God of yesterday and would be the God of tomorrow. His God was always the same—an unchanging assurance in the midst of a quickly changing world.

So before you throw away your life like an outdated laptop, look up, look over, and look beyond your present situation. When you do, you will find an unchanging God of hope.

Well-Remembered

A. Battista said, "A well-trained memory is one that permits you to forget everything that isn't worth remembering." It seems that more often than not I find myself remembering the bad stuff. This is the problem of a depraved heart and a mind scarred by sin. Is there a way to do as Mr. Battista said and "forget everything that isn't worth remembering"?

Paul often began his letters with comments about those to whom he was writing. One such occasion was in his letter to the church at Thessalonica. In First Thessalonians 1:2-3 he wrote, "We give thanks to God always for you all, making mention of you in our prayers, remembering without ceasing your work of faith, labor of love, and patience of hope in our Lord Jesus Christ in the sight of our God and Father…".

Paul begins with thanksgiving as he prays for them. Out of this he begins to list that for which he is now remembering the Thessalonians.

He tells them that his remembrance of them is without ceasing which could be translated as uninterrupted. The characteristics of this church were always fresh on Paul's mind. I wonder if Battista's remarks about forgetting what isn't worth remembering could be turned around to include the value of a memory that will always remember things that are worth remembering? This was the case with Paul and the Thessalonians.

He remembered their faith, love, and hope. But there was a quality in these items that caused Paul to remember them continually. What burned these descriptives into Paul's mind? He gives us the answer as he describes each quality. It was their WORK of faith that he remembered. They toiled diligently in their faith as if it was their occupation and Paul noted that. They LABORED in their love. Their love was so deep that it was as if it was ingrained in them. They loved to the point of weariness and Paul could not forget it. Finally, he remembered the PATIENCE of their hope. They had the fortitude to stay with it and not give up or give in because of Jesus. Their continual hope prompted Paul to never forget them.

What will you be remembered for in this life? Hopefully, you are not living in a way that others will only want to forget. If you need a good pattern to follow, I highly recommend the church at Thessalonica.

In My Opinion

Most of us never fail to have an opinion. At least that's my opinion about opinions and it always seems to me that my opinion is correct!

Now you know that I speak in jest, but opinions can be very strong at times. More dangerous than a strong opinion is to have a fickle opinion. It always amazes me in every opinion poll there are those who have no opinion. I think that the same few folks run from poll to poll announcing that they have no opinion and that is their opinion on the matter!

As Elijah confronted the false prophets on Mount Carmel, he also challenged the people to formulate an opinion concerning who was the real god. "And Elijah came to all the people, and said, 'How long will you falter between two opinions? If the Lord is God, follow Him; but if Baal, follow him.' But the people answered him not a word."~1 Kings 18:21

There were those same people all of those thousands of years ago who had no opinion. At least they did not or could not voice one at this moment. They spoke not a word.

Elijah's challenge was for them to have an opinion. Truthfully, they had two opinions about one subject. Who is the real God? Elijah said that they were faltering between two opinions. This word "falter" means to hop, skip, or jump. In modern language they were "flip-floppers."

They were constantly running back and forth between the God of heaven and Baal. I get a picture in my mind or should I say, in my opinion, that they were like children playing a game. But Elijah challenged them to settle on one opinion about the real God. He wanted them to stop flip-flopping. His words left no room for two opinions or no opinion. Whoever they chose, he told them to follow that one.

Are you following after God today? Are you still trying to make up your mind? Listen, God has proven Himself over and again. He can be trusted because He never changes. The same God who revealed Himself by fire on Mount Carmel is the God you can follow today. Quit being a flip-flopper! Choose today and follow your God. This is no time to be in the no opinion column.

A Penny At A Time

At some point I will be a millionaire. I have been working on it my whole life, but given enough time and enough dropped coins, I'm going to make it one day.

You see, I pick up pennies. I'll pick up any change that I find laying around on floors, parking lots, or the ground, but most of the time I just come across pennies. Actually, I come across a lot of them and I will always pick them up and place them securely in my pocket.

Like I said, given enough time I'm going to be rich beyond my wildest dreams!

Each of those reclaimed coins serve as a minuscule piece of my million dollar plan. Bit by bit, I am getting closer to my goal. I don't know what being a millionaire feels or looks like, but I'll let you know as soon as I arrive.

As I have walked through life picking up coins, I have become a little wiser along the way. I have come to realize that just as pennies one at a time can add up to a million dollars, so our lives are being assembled one day at a time into the completed picture of God's fully revealed intent for us.

David concluded in Psalm 139 that his very design as a human being was beyond comprehension. "I will praise You, for I am fearfully and wonderfully made; marvelous are Your works, and that my soul knows very well." ~ Psalms 139:14

In the latter half of the last century Edwin Land invented the film that was used by Polaroid in what became known as the Polaroid Land camera. This film was developed on site by the camera. A picture was taken and about one minute later the photographer was holding a photograph. It was an amazing feat of technology.

Since those days it seems that we have become more and more impatient for the instantaneous. Now we expect everything to happen in the moment with no elapsed time. Maybe that's why people won't pick up a dropped penny. They just don't see its value as a small part of a million.

God is giving us our whole fearfully-and-wonderfully-made lives one snapshot at a time. Each of those snapshots fit together into a marvelous mosaic like bits and pieces of broken glass. Don't let what seems like a penny's worth of your life fall to the ground in disregard. Remember, the mosaic of a finished life will look awkward with those tiny bits and pieces missing.

The Answer Man

Many years ago I was a veterinarian and a pediatrician. I was also a commodities trader and a financial counselor. Actually, I owned a grocery business out in the country. The operator of a grocery/feed store/restaurant/gas station is required to wear many hats. Lots of people seek out answers on a myriad of questions.

It was not really a big step for me to leave that business over 30 years ago and become a pastor. This is not to diminish the value or importance of my call to the ministry, but being a pastor is very much like being a small grocery store owner in a country setting.

Folks were always needing an answer for their pertinent questions. These varied from what they could prepare for supper to what they could feed their chickens. Sometimes I had to be the family doctor and "prescribe" some over-the-counter remedy. And there were times that I had to diagnose that clicking sound coming from under the hood of their auto.

I was an answer man.

No one likes to only be an answer man though. You get weary of people only calling on you when they need an answer. Imagine if your children or friends only came to see you when they needed an answer. You begin to realize that you are loved for the answers...not for who you are.

We see hundreds of occasions in scripture where people called on God for an answer. Moses, Aaron, and Samuel are named as ones that had sought out God's answer. "Moses and Aaron were among His priests, and Samuel was among those who called upon His name; they called upon the Lord, and He answered them." ~ Psalms 99:6

Now there is nothing inherently wrong with seeking out the Lord for an answer. Where we go wrong is when we only go to God for the answer. Oswald Chambers said, "The meaning of prayer is that we get hold of God, not of the answer."

Get hold of God today. Approach Him not as your answer man. Simply crawl up into His lap because His lap is yours to crawl into for comfort. Lean your head against His breast and relax. The amazing thing that you will find is most of your questions don't matter anymore when you recline upon Him. And those questions that just *must* be answered—they will be when we seek Him instead of an answer.

How Much Will It Cost Me?

FREE!

Have I got your attention? There is nothing that will turn heads like the little word free. Everybody is looking for something for nothing. I am no different. I am constantly on the lookout for a deal. It might be a discount or buy one get one, but free is the best.

Unless you are offering something to the Lord.

Consider what had transpired in the life of King David. Out of pride, David took a census of the people. He counted the people to measure the size of his kingdom and his power as a ruler.

God's displeasure in David's choice was immediately felt. The prophet Gad brought a word of impending judgment to David and a new choice to make. He could experience seven years of famine, be chased by his enemies for three months, or suffer three days of a plague under the hand of the Lord.

David chose to accept the direct hand of the Lord as punishment and 70,000 people died. God stayed the plague as it approached Jerusalem near the property of Araunah. The prophet then instructed David to build an altar upon that site and offer sacrifices there.

This is where so many people make a mistake. Often the first question that comes to mind when an offering unto God is considered is, "How much will it cost?" But not so with David.

Araunah offered to give everything that David needed for free, but David would have no part of this. "Then the king said to Araunah, "No, but I will surely buy it from you for a price; nor will I offer burnt offerings to the Lord my God with that which costs me nothing." So David bought the threshing floor and the oxen for fifty shekels of silver." ~ 2 Samuel 24:24

The next time that you get ready to offer something to the Lord what will be your first thought? Will it be how cheaply can I get by with my obedience? Let us join with David in his commitment: "Nor will I offer burnt offerings to the Lord my God with that which costs me nothing."

Antiques

Who am I? Here's a hint:

"I love those who love me, And those who seek me diligently will find me. Riches and honor are with me, Enduring riches and righteousness. My fruit is better than gold, yes, than fine gold, And my revenue than choice silver."

Do you know who this is?

If you open your Bible to Proverbs 8 you will find out even more. The description above comes from verses 17-19. The answer is wisdom. Wisdom is personified in this chapter of Proverbs, that is, an inanimate object is given human characteristics.

I chose these few verses as a sampling of wisdom's character in light of the over-abundance of commercials, signs, storefronts, etc. that are trying to buy your gold and silver. Their premise is that precious metals are all that can save us from financial disaster. I could not say if this is true or not. I suppose having a pot of gold is nice, but it is a little tough to eat!

So, is there real value in having wisdom in your possession? I think there is! First, wisdom costs you nothing. You need only seek after her and she will be found. Among the dozens of attributes listed in Proverbs 8 the verses listed here speak of riches that are provided by wisdom, but there is one key word that describes these riches. They are enduring.

The word could be translated durable and comes from the same word that we get our English word antique. The idea here is not that wisdom is old or old-fashioned. It is instead the fact that if an item is to be noted as an antique is has to have the quality of durability or it would not be around to be an antique. Like silver and gold which can be melted, beaten, and shaped, wisdom comes through the process still holding its original composition. That is what makes it durable!

Wisdom stands at the crossroad of life and cries out to all who pass by, "To you, O men, I call, And my voice is to the sons of men. O you simple ones, understand prudence, and you fools, be of an understanding heart." ~ Proverbs 8:4-5 It's time to stop and invest in that which will last. You won't need a safe to store it and you won't have to fear anyone stealing it from you. Love wisdom and she will love you.

Back To The Sea

Never turn your back to the sea. That's what I was told when I visited Hawaii a few years ago. Not many days after I had returned home the news reported that a man was swept out to sea by a rogue wave as he and his wife strolled along the shoreline.

A search of Google for "man swept to sea" produces over nine million hits. Story after story unfolds of people who are on the beach one moment and gone in the next. Never turn your back to the sea!

The National Oceanic and Atmospheric Agency reports that the narrow fringe comprising 17 percent of the contiguous U.S. land area is home to more than 53 percent of the nation's population. That's a lot of people living very close to the dangers that come from the sea.

There are a lot of people who live just as dangerously when it comes to their spiritual walk. Jesus spoke a parable of the two foundations. In this parable he compared the man whose home rested upon the bedrock to the one whose home was built upon the sand.

"But why do you call Me 'Lord, Lord,' and not do the things which I say? Whoever comes to Me, and hears My sayings and does them, I will show you whom he is like: He is like a man building a house, who dug deep and laid the foundation on the rock. And when the flood arose, the stream beat vehemently against that house, and could not shake it, for it was founded on the rock. But he who heard and did nothing is like a man who built a house on the earth without a foundation, against which the stream beat vehemently; and immediately it fell. And the ruin of that house was great."~Luke 6:46-49

Much less than half of the population will attend a church during any given week. Of those who do attend, I wonder how many will really go with the intent of obeying what they will hear from the Lord?

Those who do not attend are like the vast population who live constantly with their backs to the sea. It is only a matter of time before a rogue wave or a storm catches them unaware and sweeps them to destruction.

Worst though are those who will hear and not obey. They will be like those who hear the warning of impending danger and remain behind to experience the same fate. The wave of truth will sweep them away in a moment.

We all in one sense live on the same narrow beach of existence. Heed the word of God and never, never turn your back to the Lord.

Power of a Shadow

Six degrees north of the equator on the edge of the Sahara Desert is a place where you come to appreciate a spot of shade. My mission trip took me to Nigeria and deposited me in the village of Okuku. The sweltering heat never abated. Shadows were a favorite place.

In an almost obscure way, Luke, the writer of the book of Acts, was moved by the Spirit to include a bit of information that could almost be overlooked. The setting is the first days of the church. The work of the Apostles had just begun in Jerusalem.

"And believers were increasingly added to the Lord, multitudes of both men and women, so that they brought the sick out into the streets and laid them on beds and couches, that at least the shadow of Peter passing by might fall on some of them." ~ Acts 5:14-15

These were the days of miracles. God in His sovereignty used the Apostles through signs and wonders to draw the multitudes to the early church. The ministry of Peter was aflame with the power of God.

Many had witnessed the healing of the lame man at the gate of the Temple and now the sick were gathered at Solomon's Porch with the hopes of a miracle in their lives. The word had spread and the story on the street was that even the shadow of Peter could heal.

Luke does not say that this was a fact. We do not know if indeed Peter's shadow falling on a sick person brought about healing. What then is the reason for this obscure tidbit of information?

Those who had gathered at the Temple were under the throes of their individual illnesses. The sweltering heat of life beat upon them relentlessly. Just as I sought a shady spot in Nigeria, so these sought relief from their misery.

Amazingly, this shadow was cast by a man who a few days before had denied his knowledge of Jesus and had gone so far as to curse His name. Now people sought out his shadow. Only the Spirit of God could make this difference.

You and I cast a shadow in this life. The shadow is not really us nor is the shadow possible without the "Son" shining brightly upon us. Our responsibility is to keep facing the "Son" and the shadow will take care of itself.

Just as Peter was probably unaware of where his shadow had fallen, you and I will have influence that we will never know about in this life. Keep your face toward the "Son" and let your shadow bring hope to those upon which it falls.

Outside of Time

"Will you be using Medicare?"

That was the question I was asked by the receptionist that was making my appointment at the optometrist office. I looked around to see if she was speaking to someone else. Certainly she was mistaken. I looked down to see if I had forgotten my walker or at least my cane. I looked up and God reminded me: "To everything there is a season, a time for every purpose under heaven…"~Ecclesiastes 3:1

I am still a few years away from joining the Medicare parade. I am just going to assume that she was the one that needed glasses—not me! But the truth is, time has marched on and left in its tracks many who could not keep up the pace.

But I looked up. That's always where the answer for time lies. Not in a world that is crumbling away around our feet, but in the everlasting eternality of the God of this universe. This same God moved upon the heart of the wisest and richest man who has ever lived to write a very simple statement about time. He declared, "To everything there is a season, a time for every purpose under heaven."

Great comfort can be gained from this simple yet profound conclusion about a subject that confounds all who have lived through its meticulous passing. Without fanfare the ticks fall away from the clock and time evaporates like a wispy cloud that wandered before the face of the sun.

Two truths leap from this single verse about time. First, everything has its season. There is time for all things to bloom and have a brief moment to live. That season will be filled with sun and cloud, with gentle dew and stormy hail, and with gentle breeze and mighty gale. And as seasons come and go, so will everything pass away.

Second, there is time for every purpose to be fulfilled. When the receptionist asked me if I would be filing my doctor's visit under Medicare, God's purpose for that question in time and about time was fulfilled. It caused me to look up and be reassured by the Everlasting Father who exists outside of time.

You have been given a portion of time. It is a fixed quantity, but it is of undetermined quality. That part is up to you! You can take the time given to you today and wrap it in the protective covering of God's purpose and secure it tightly by His word which will never pass away.

Now get back into the parade of time while it's still your season. March on and keep looking up. Medicare will take care of itself.

A Charmed Sucker

A fourth grader couldn't have a greater possession to share with his secret love than a nickel-sized Charm Sucker. This marvel on a stick was designed to last all day, but did not fare well when dropped on a hard floor.

This is how my day turned to disaster.

I was in love with a seventh grade girl. She, of course, did not know that I existed. My entire fortune was spent daily and renewed each morning by my mother as I left for school. Each day I received a nickel to buy a piece of candy from one of the machines at school.

On this day I would give my all for the one I loved so deeply.

I had watched as her class passed through the lunch line each day and as she came into the lunch room seating area. My plan was to take the entirety of my vast riches, which was a Charms Sucker purchased with all the money I had in this world, and slip it into her coat pocket. She would discover this gift from her secret lover later in the day. I would be satisfied in my sacrifice for love.

I watched her enter the line. I timed my exit. Carrying my lunch tray and my treasure, I made my way to the sharp turn she would make at the corner of the teachers' table. And that's when my plan all fell apart.

I do mean fell apart. As I passed her in the congested aisle, I reached for her pocket. In slow motion, the cellophane wrapped jewel of my passion came within millimeters of finding safety in the deep recesses of her pocket. And then it happened…

The expression of my admiration fell to the tiled floor in front of her, the teachers, all of humanity, and heaven itself. It seemed to take forever to strike the floor, but inevitably it did. I could not believe that a sucker could shatter into that many pieces!

So ended my first attempt at love.

I am so grateful that Christ did not fail in his effort to find me as His love. Listen to His call from this verse in the Song of Solomon: "O my dove, in the clefts of the rock, in the secret places of the cliff, let me see your face, let me hear your voice; for your voice is sweet, and your face is lovely." ~ Song of Solomon 2:14

Jesus is calling for you today to come forth from your hiding place. He desires a relationship with you. Answer His call today. He can take your shattered attempts at life and love and make you His Beloved. You are His dove.

How Do I Love Thee?

How do I love thee? Let me count the ways. So begins the famous poem by Elizabeth Barrett Browning. God, however did not leave the standard of our love up to the emotional whims of an exercise in romance. He declares, "You shall love the Lord your God with all your heart, with all your soul, and with all your strength."~Deuteronomy 6:5

As this day for declaring true love unfolds, will you take time to proclaim your true and undying love for the One who loved you before you were lovable? The Apostle Paul wrote that God commends His love toward us while we are yet sinners. (Romans 5:8) Clearly the demonstration of God's love is active as seen in the word commend. It lends the idea of companionship or association. God loves us by standing with us in an open declaration of His love. And He does all of this while we are yet in a sinful state!

This is so contrary to the flaunting of love in our world today. Love is thrown about in a careless and selfish manner that demands all sorts of pre-conditions. In other words, I will love you if you are beautiful or successful or prosperous. I will love you if you will love me first and offer me substantial proof of your endearment

Only when we fully grasp the depths of His love for us can we begin to fulfill the command of loving God with all of our heart, soul, and strength. It will no longer be considered a command, but a response to His love for us in our unlovable condition.

How Do I Love Thee? may have been written in an attempt to describe love for a mortal, but its words describe well our fulfillment of loving God with all our being:

> How do I love thee? Let me count the ways.
> I love thee to the depth and breadth and height
> My soul can reach, when feeling out of sight
> For the ends of being and ideal grace.
>
> I love thee to the level of every day's
> Most quiet need, by sun and candle-light.
> I love thee freely, as men strive for right.
> I love thee purely, as they turn from praise.
>
> I love thee with the passion put to use
> In my old griefs, and with my childhood's faith.
> I love thee with a love I seemed to lose
> With my lost saints. I love thee with the breath,
> Smiles, tears, of all my life; and, if God choose,
> I shall but love thee better after death. ~ Elizabeth Barrett Browning

Break Time

Mr. Earl was my savior and he didn't even know it. It was always a happy time for me when Mr. Earl would lean on the fence that separated his property from ours and call my daddy over for a talk.

Taking a break wasn't in my daddy's vocabulary. He worked hard and so did I as a boy. There seemed to always be another project, whether it was raking leaves, digging ditches, or removing the remains of a stump left over from the last hurricane's revenge.

I was glad for that fence. It provided a place for two men to gather for a few minutes and discuss whatever men discuss. For me, it was a moment of rest from whatever that day's project was.

Now that I think about it, I'm not sure why the fence was there. We were the best of neighbors. We needed no separation point, but for some reason the fence had been erected. It's sort of like a fence around a graveyard. You wonder if it's there to keep people in or to keep people out!

There is a separating point in our spiritual lives also. Scripture calls it a wall. "For He Himself is our peace, who has made both one, and has broken down the middle wall of separation…"~Ephesians 2:14

Unlike the fence between neighbors, this wall is not one of peace, but of enmity. The wall is there because of previous failures. It was erected the moment man sinned and fell from God's perfect grace. It is never a place of rest, but instead a place of struggle.

Just like the fence between us and Mr. Earl, you may be wondering why the wall between you and God is there. As far as you know, it always has been, and you would be correct in your assumption, for we are conceived in sin and failure.

But there is good news! God has sent a Savior to tear down the wall of separation. His desire is that there be nothing between Him and you. He wants to deliver you from your labor and give you rest.

Hear His voice today as He calls to you. "Come to Me, all you who labor and are heavy laden, and I will give you rest." ~ Matthew 11:28

He is not asking you to lean on the fence and then return to the work. He is calling for you to lay down your burden and lean upon Him for eternal rest.

02/16

Oh, Chicken Feathers

A lady approached her pastor with tears in her eyes. "I have spread tales about you, pastor. I am so sorry," she cried. The pastor offered his full and free forgiveness, but then made a strange request of the woman. "Do you own any chickens," he asked. The lady answered in the affirmative and then heard the pastor's instructions.

He told her to go home and kill one of her chickens and begin to travel around town with the dead chicken. She was to pluck a feather from the bird and and lay it on the doorstep of each home where she had told the tale about the pastor. She was to then return to the pastor. Sorrow prompted her immediate obedience.

After returning, the pastor told her, "Now go back to each door and collect the feathers!" The woman replied with amazement, "Pastor, by this time those feathers have blown all over town!" Then she fell silent as the reality of her actions settled upon her.

The wisest man who ever lived wrote the book of Ecclesiastes. In the fifth chapter he said, "Walk prudently when you go to the house of God; and draw near to hear rather than to give the sacrifice of fools, for they do not know that they do evil. Do not be rash with your mouth, and let not your heart utter anything hastily before God. For God is in heaven, and you on earth; Therefore let your words be few." ~ Ecclesiastes 5:1-2

The two words translated "walk prudently" carry the meaning of guarding your steps. But they also hold a deeper connotation of not being a tale bearer. Interesting is the fact that Solomon warned about tale bearing in the house of God. He further gave instruction on how to make sure that we were not tale bearers. Draw near to hear rather than speak. Do not speak too quickly. In other words the best way to prevent gossip is to keep your mouth closed!

The incentive for this lies in the truth that God is in heaven and from His perspective of omniscience He knows all that transpires here on the earth. Not only what we say, but our intent in saying it. As Solomon said, "Let your words be few." And as I say, "It will keep your chickens alive and feathered!"

02/17

God Speak—I Obey

The dew still lay heavy upon the grass as all in the camp were asleep. All, that is, but one man. This man not only was awake; he had not slept during the long night. The man was Abraham.

He is joined by his servants and a sleepy-eyed young lad. The boy is his son, Isaac. The donkey is burdened with several days provision and wood that will be used for a sacrifice. Abraham does not know where he will lead this group for as it has been for many decades in his life he is a sojourner. God leads; he follows; and that's just the way it is. But this journey is different, for he goes under orders that any other man of lesser faith would never engage. God has told him to go to a mountain that He would show him and offer his son as a sacrifice. (Genesis 22:2)

The next three days are a blur to Abraham as he contemplates God's command, but there on the horizon stands Moriah. The mountain of God's choosing and the place of ultimate obedience. Up the rocky trail Abraham and Isaac climb with wood and fire for the sacrifice. Abraham's heart shudders as his son asks his father where is the sacrifice. His mind races as he responds that God will provide the sacrifice.

The exact spot is reached and in submission Isaac helps his father build an altar, stack the wood, and prepare for the dreaded moment. Isaac yields as his father binds him and lays him upon the altar. Abraham's dagger is drawn from its sheath. His arm is raised high and begins to make the fatal plunge into his son's chest, but Abraham hears the voice of God, "Do not lay your hand on the lad, or do anything to him; for now I know that you fear God, since you have not withheld your son, your only son, from Me." ~ Genesis 22:12

George Bowen was a missionary to India in the mid-1800's. He wrote in his book, "Love Revealed", "God sometimes bestows gifts just that love may have something to renounce. The things that He puts into our hands are possibly put there that we may have the opportunity of showing what is in our heart. Oh, that there were in us a fervor of love that would lead us to examine everything that belongs to us, to ascertain how it might be made a means of showing our affection to Christ!"

Have a blessed day as you seek to obey God's every command and lay at His feet every gift that He has bestowed into your life.

02/18

Spiritual Spelunking

I have been spelunking since I was a boy. I enjoy it immensely and will still take the opportunity to engage a little spelunking expedition if I get the chance.

Unless you are a spelunker you should be asking by now if spelunking is normal or at a minimum legal. I'm not sure how normal it is, but it is legal. At least in places like Carlsbad, Merimac, and Ruby Falls, it is. You see, spelunking is nothing more than exploring caves.

Almost every cave has a limestone formation that looks like a magnificent hanging of draperies. If it is large enough, an entire area will be called the Drapery Room. Each time I see one of these formations, I think of the huge set of curtains that separated the holy place in the tabernacle from the holy of holies.

Sometimes you can see cracks that run from top to bottom in these formations. These always remind me of the moment when the great curtain in the Temple was torn from top to bottom.

The writer of Hebrews relates this event to our access of God's holiness by the death of Christ. As the body of Christ was rent and His blood shed for us, we pass through Him into God's holy presence. As Christ declared His work of salvation to be finished, we then can "…hold fast the confession of our hope without wavering, for He who promised is faithful." ~ Hebrews 10:23

I cannot help but imagine that the priests that were serving in the Temple that day must have stood in amazement at the unseen hand that tore the massive curtain from top to bottom. But I also imagine that they soon got out their needle and thread and started sewing the curtain back together.

That's always the way of religion. It never removes the barrier between man and God; it preserves it.

Why not do a little spiritual spelunking today? Take a step behind the curtain of your religious activity and see that God never commanded that the curtain be re-sewn.

God is not interested in repairing the old. He is engaged in removing the barrier between you and Himself. Go ahead. Step into the deep recesses of His holiness and you will find a crack from top to bottom in the drapery of love He has for you.

02/19

Controlling the Future

Bill Jenny could guess the correct time within half-a-minute at any hour of the day or night. The British Medical Association put Jenny through a battery of test to determine his almost supernatural ability, but could not determine exactly what had given him this ability.

The key to his time-telling prowess was his occupation. Jenny was employed for over thirty years as the clock tender in the Savoy Hotel in London. This hotel houses 1505 timepieces. It takes four days of every week to wind these clocks. Mr. Jenny has immersed himself in time. The result was a remarkable ability to keep time very accurately.

Time is God's idea. From the very first few verses of the Bible we learn that God set into motion the days, seasons, and years for our benefit. He, of course, being eternal is above and beyond time. God exist in the eternal here and now.

While the disciples stood with Jesus, as He was about to ascend to heaven, they began to question Jesus about the time that He would establish His kingdom here on the earth. His response was very simple and to the point. "And He said to them, 'It is not for you to know times or seasons which the Father has put in His own authority.'" ~ Acts 1:7

We all have a tendency to desire some control over the future. First, we want to know what's going to happen and secondly when it is going to happen. We know that there is really nothing that we can do to change the inevitable, but we desire the knowledge anyway.

The disciples prove that this is nothing new. They wanted the mystery resolved about the Kingdom of God, but Jesus declared that information to be in His Father's control.

He told them that God held both the times and seasons in His hands. God has both the exact time of occurrence and the time that would elapse until then in His sovereign control.

This is good news for us who obsess over time. We do not have to be like Mr. Jenny who could tell you the time of day at any given moment. It is not our business to keep God's clock wound, because His clock never runs down.

Relax in the moment knowing that He holds the next.

	02/20

Rubber Boots

I woke up to find my bed suspended on concrete blocks and the floor immersed in several inches of water. No, it was not a bad dream. I was six years old and these were exciting times!

Growing up in south Louisiana means for the most part that you will live near some body of water. Along with the close proximity to water comes the almost sure guarantee that at some point in your life you will experience a flood. That's how I found myself as a boy, high and dry, above the flood waters that had invaded our home during the night.

I still remember the afternoon before as I stood with my dad on the bank of the canal that ran next to our home. I watched him place a marker on the bank to serve as a gauge in determining how much the water was rising. And like most children who trust their parents implicitly, I went to sleep that night unaware that our home would flood.

At some point my parents lifted my bed above the rising waters while I slept through it all. For me, as a little boy, it meant that I got to wear my rubber boots the next morning as I traipsed through the water now washing through the interior of our house.

All of us at some point in our lives will experience a flood. It may not be a literal flood of rising water, but a flood nevertheless. It might be a flood of sorrow and worry. It could be an overwhelming wave of grief. It may come as an ever rising tide of debt. Sometimes we are surrounded by enemies that force us to seek higher ground.

The psalmist found himself in just such a predicament as he wrote, "The floods have lifted up, O Lord, the floods have lifted up their voice; the floods lift up their waves." ~ Psalms 93:3

Our faith needs to be like that of a confident six year old boy who simply trusts his parents enough that he can sleep through a flood, find himself perched above the water high and dry, and enjoy it to the point that he can wear rubber boots in the house.

The psalmist answered his concerns about the flood in declaring, "The Lord on high is mightier than the noise of many waters, than the mighty waves of the sea." ~ Psalms 93:4

Sleep now without your boots next to the bed.. The Lord is high above your flood!

02/21

Abandonment

The captain of a ship is responsible for everyone on board. All of his actions must be consistent with protecting this most precious cargo. It is his decision alone to decide the critical point where the order to abandon ship should be given. I would not want to be in the shoes of a captain that had to make that fateful decision.

Just as in the case of abandoning ship, the word abandon is nearly always used in a negative sense. Something or someone is left behind in every situation.

All of us have experienced abandonment at some level. It may have been in a disconnected way. You might have driven past an abandoned vehicle along a busy highway and wondered the reason why someone walked away from it. You may have seen the shuttered windows of an abandoned house and briefly considered the tragedy that brought a family to the place of leaving a residence empty of hopes and dreams.

You may have cringed at the news of a human life cast aside and no longer regarded as valuable. In that moment, you realize that there could be nothing any worse that being abandoned. But there is a positive side to abandonment also.

The word abandon means to release control, to no longer own, or have a right to maintain. This is the negative side of abandonment. The positive side is to give oneself over with total surrender and without restraint.

God will bring each of us to the place where we must abandon all to Him. When many turned from following Jesus because His demands were too great he asked His disciples if they too would abandon Him.

It was Peter who answered, "Lord, to whom shall we go? You have the words of eternal life." ~ John 6:68

All of us must come to this point in our lives. Like the captain of a ship, we are the captain of our own souls. We are responsible for the decision that leads us to point of abandonment. Will we come to the same conclusion that Peter did? There must be that moment in our lives when we surrender all and release all rights of keeping our ship afloat.

It is time to cry out, "Abandon ship!" Then leaving all behind, climb over the rail of life, and fall safely into the hands of the One who has the words of eternal life.

02/22

Light In the Darkness

Oft times as a boy, my job was to hold the flashlight for my father. It's funny now to think about how many times he had to guide my hand back to the place where the light would shine on whatever it was he was repairing or installing at the time. As hard as I would try, my hand would drift until the light lined up with my eye instead of his. All I wanted was to see, but that was not the point of me holding the light; the light was for my daddy, not me.

Light is referenced hundreds of times throughout the scriptures. God begins His creative work by declaring that there should be light...and it was. Instantly, like the turning on of a flashlight multiplied millions of times over, God pierced the darkness and the world was filled with light.

God sent light as a pillar of fire before the children of Israel as they journeyed the wilderness. He required the light upon the golden lamp stand in the Tabernacle to burn continually as a source of light inside the heavily curtained interior. (Exodus 27:20)

Gideon's army broke the pitchers hiding their torches as they rushed upon the sleeping Midianites and a strong enemy was routed as God once again dispersed the darkness of doubt with a display of His glory. (Judges 7:19)

In Psalm 119 the word of God is declared as a lamp to our feet and a light unto our path. Solomon tells us in Ecclesiastes that the light of a God is sweet. Micah reminds us that when we sit in darkness, God will be our light.

On and on go the descriptions of God as a light for us to see by in a darkened world. But there is no greater declaration than that of Christ as He stood and proclaimed, "I am the light of the world!"

That light now shines through you and I as we walk in this darkened world. He still is the light of the world and the darkness cannot comprehend the light. The smallest light in the darkest room becomes a beacon of hope.

So Jesus spoke of us as a city set upon a hill whose light shines out across the way and beckons the weary traveler to come and find rest. He instructed us to place our lights out in the open and never under a basket to be hidden.

His light is there for you, but He is guiding that light today like a flashlight in your hand so that someone else can see also. Don't resist. Let your light shine, so all the world can see Him—the true Light of the world.

02/23

Outside of Our Knowledge

Take a sheet of paper. You may choose any size that you wish. Consider the borders of that sheet to be the extent of all knowledge available to mankind. Now draw a circle on that paper that would represent all of the knowledge that you possess. Again, you may draw the circle any size, but one would assume it to be less than the entire size of the sheet of paper.

Now place a dot on the sheet outside of your circle of knowledge. That dot represents God.

The demonstration above will disprove every denier of God's existence. No atheist can justify a belief that there is no God, because God simply exists outside of the realm of his knowledge. To deny God is to proclaim oneself all knowing. Since no one knows all, then no one can claim to know that there is no God.

Ah, but you would then say, the one who claims that there is a God cannot do so with surety either. In this you would be correct, except for the matter of faith. Since God exists outside of our ability to know, then it truly is a matter of faith. And faith is the gift of God to us for God wants to be known by us.

The wisest man who ever lived was Solomon. Gifted by God with supreme intellect, he ruled as king of Israel. He authored what we know as the book of Proverbs. In one of the maxims he wrote, "He who trusts in his own heart is a fool, but whoever walks wisely will be delivered." ~ Proverbs 28:26

Remember the circle you drew on your piece of paper? That circle is your heart. It's easy to understand how Solomon could conclude the folly of trusting in something so small in relation to all that exists. And more than this is the fact that God exists outside of these incorrigible hearts which Jeremiah declared desperately wicked.

We are not without hope, however. Solomon tells us that a man can walk wisely and be delivered. The wisest decision you can make is to redraw your circle of knowledge. Place your pen on the paper once more and draw a new circle around the dot that represents God. Now He is inside your heart and you will know as He is known.

Stop trusting your little heart-circle of knowledge. Give your life to God today and be rescued from yourself. It's time to have your life redrawn.

	02/24

Remnants

Michigan cherries were always my selection from the bulk candy counter at F.W. Woolworth's. These scrumptious jellybean-like candies were scooped up by the lady behind the counter and put into a bag and weighed by the pound. Of course, you could get a bag full for just a little change back then.

Mr. Woolworth got the idea for his business from his former employer. While working as a clerk, the owner of the store told Frank to gather up the remnants of left over goods and offer them at reduced prices in a clearance sale.

Frank placed all of the items in a bin, marked them a nickel, and watched customers buy them all rapidly. Thus began his vision to open a five and dime store. Though his first business failed, he continued in his attempt to operate a discount style operation. By 1911, there were over 1000 F.W. Woolworth stores across the United States and it all began with a sale of remnants.

God has always used the principle of the remnant in preserving His people and His purpose. Time and again, in the biblical narrative it seems that sure defeat and ultimate extinction of God's people is at hand.

In those darkest moments, the doctrine of the remnant shines through in full array. One of those times was during the reign of Ahab and Jezebel. The people had turned from God and the nation seemed about to succumb under the wickedness of their king and queen.

God had set Elijah aside as His prophet. Elijah confronted the false prophets of Baal on Mt. Carmel, where God demonstrated His power, as fire fell to consume the sacrifice offered there.

The result: A death warrant was issued upon Elijah and he ran for his life into the wilderness. There he cried out to the Lord declaring that he alone was left as a defender of the faith.

God's response: The remnant principle is once again revealed as He said, "Yet I have reserved seven thousand in Israel, all whose knees have not bowed to Baal, and every mouth that has not kissed him." ~ 1 Kings 19:18

Never take measure of the darkness nor make a tally of those who you think are serving God today. God always has a remnant whom He has set aside and protected.

Take heart. Though it seems that you alone are left, it is far from the truth. God ALWAYS has a remnant and at His appointed time they will be gathered and positioned front and center.

02/25

Heartsick

Hope is a word that is used very casually. Many times we hope with little expectation. For example, we hope that it will not rain, but ultimately we are fully aware that the outcome is not in our control. This flippant hope usually ends in disappointment.

In Proverbs 13:12 we read, "Hope deferred makes the heart sick, but when the desire comes, it is a tree of life." The man who wrote these words was the richest and wisest who ever lived. You could not imagine him being without hope, but clearly having everything at your ready disposal does not necessarily supply one with hope.

I still remember vividly our mission team delivering a box of groceries and some blankets to a lady in Brazil. She had at least six children in her home. In appearance, she looked every bit 60 years old. The missionary told us she was not yet 40. Her oldest daughter was in prison at the age of 16 and two of the children in our midst were hers. The home they lived in had a dirt floor. The only thing the children had to cover with at night was pieces of used carpet padding she had salvaged from a dumpster. I have a picture of her as she received the gifts and it records a faint smile upon her face. I think of her often especially when I throw the word hope around casually.

Solomon said that when the desire of our hope comes it is like a tree of life. This phrase lends the idea of stability and long lasting benefit. When hope is delayed in its fulfillment the human soul becomes sick. The word he used is translated "deferred." It means to be drawn out or stretched. In the Brazilian lady's case, hopelessness had stretched to the next generation. She now was rearing grandchildren in the same squalor that she and her children had experienced. It's enough to make the heart sick. The word sick means to rub raw like a grievous wound. Truly this is the pain I still remember in the Brazilian woman's face.

Would you join me today in this prayer? Lord, help me to be the answer to someone's hope today. Use me to bring health to a sickened heart. May my life be a tree of life to someone bent and broken. Father, you are my desire fulfilled! Let me not be guilty of hoarding that with which you have blessed me! In Jesus' name. AMEN!

02/26

The Missing Part

I grew up in a time when most every boy had a chance to get grease under his fingernails working on his older model auto. We kept them running by constant repair and tweaking.

One of the main parts that took a lot of tweaking efforts was the ignition system. I was constantly "fine tuning" the functions of the distributor. Here, I could adjust the points, set the timing, and try to make what was for the most part a piece a junk, a functioning mode of transportation.

Inside the distributor was a little part called the rotor. If this was removed, a person could attempt to start a car until they drained the battery of all power, but to no avail. Without the rotor in place, you could do nothing.

If Jesus had been speaking to a bunch of us boys from the 1960's in John 15, He might have used just such an illustration. He was, however, speaking to those who understood farming. Therefore, he said, "I am the vine, you are the branches. He who abides in Me, and I in him, bears much fruit; for without Me you can do nothing." ~ John 15:5

Like the rotor that distributes an electrical current to each cylinder of an engine and thereby provides the spark needed for combustion, Jesus is the missing part that brings us to life. Without Him, we may have everything that makes us look like a Christian, but we are going nowhere, because He alone distributes the power.

The great majority of people who drive an automobile today think little about what is taking place under the hood. All of the electronics that work together to make an auto function are remarkable to say the least.

The day of the "shade tree mechanic" has nearly concluded. Self-service gas stations allow people to just keep putting gasoline into the tank with little thought about maintenance. The vehicle just runs until it doesn't. Only then do we stop.

Your Christian life is not possible without Jesus in His rightful place at the center of all that will be distributed through you today. Don't wait until you are stranded along life's highway. This is not something you can fix or tweak. It is surrendering to the reality that without Jesus there is nothing you can do.

02/27

Hungry?

A dog, her puppies, a couple of chickens, and I sat down to eat a meager meal situated on a plate near the center of the table. All that would feed the pastor, his wife, their seven children, and me was on that one plate. I was considered the "honored" guest and I would eat alone. Well, alone with a dog, her puppies, and a couple of chickens. The place was Nigeria. This was my first mission trip. It changed me forever.

Most of us have complained at some point about being hungry. Usually, at the first little rumble in our stomachs we search out something to soothe our appetites. Few of us in America have ever truly been hungry, though there are some who experience real hunger each day even in this land of plenty.

Not only do we fill our plates and our stomachs, we then throw away what would be a sumptuous meal to many in this world. And then we find ourselves with an unresolved longing for something else to satisfy. This condition is not isolated to America, nor is it anything new. The Israelites fit this model perfectly as they traversed the wilderness that lay between them and the Promised Land.

God had provided manna for them each day. This bread from heaven appeared at each daybreak and lay upon the dew, ready for them to gather and prepare. But they grew tired of God's provision and soon complained to God. They cried out for meat and with disdain for God's provision developed a loathing for the bread which came down from heaven. The Psalmist compressed this incident in the wilderness into a single sentence: "And He gave them their request, but sent leanness into their soul." ~ Psalms 106:15

A literal storm of quail rained down upon the Israelites. And they ate. And they ate. And they ate. They ate meat to the point that the Bible tells us they had quail running out of their noses! (Numbers 11:20)

It is perfectly right to make your request known unto God, but beware when you ask for that which is outside of His will with a spirit of complaining. It is possible to have your request fulfilled and still be starving.

Remember that somewhere there is a dog with her puppies and a couple of chickens and a host of humanity that would be very glad to have what you are complaining about today. Make it a daily practice to be satisfied with what's on the table and with what's at your feet.

Tough Row to Hoe

There is a saying that I use a lot when I am speaking about a hard situation. You will hear me say, "That's a tough row to hoe." Unless you grew up in the country, you may not know exactly what this means. It is an idiom that was used a lot in the early 1800's when our country was agrarian. And to answer your question, "No, I was not a farm boy in the early 1800's!"

Perfection is a tough row to hoe and the idea of perfection keeps many from following Christ. It is a trick of the devil to tell a person that he can be a follower of Christ and then remind him that he can't be perfect. That's a very long row to hoe!

But there is good news! God's not looking for a few perfect people. He's not even looking for a few good people. His desire is for a person who will seek His heart even with failures on his or her record.

David was just such a man. I thank God that his story is included in the Bible in all of its ugly detail. David was a man who had a tough row to hoe, but always was seeking God's heart. His testimony is recorded for us in Acts 13. God removed Saul from being king in Israel and "…He raised up for them David as king, to whom also He gave testimony and said, 'I have found David the son of Jesse, a man after My own heart, who will do all My will.'" ~ Acts 13:22

Now we know David was not perfect. Some of his rows were very crooked. His sins included what we would call "biggies" like adultery and murder. But even in the midst of his failures he was constantly seeking after God's heart. David's conscience was always working to draw him back. We see this in big and little ways.

Once David caught Saul in a cave. Saul was unaware of David's presence. Saul was on the hunt for David. He had come to En Gedi with 3000 men to seize David. In a somewhat embarrassing predicament, Saul had entered the cave to answer the call of nature. While there David slipped up and cut the corner from Saul's cloak.

But we see immediately the heart of David. "Now it happened afterward that David's heart troubled him because he had cut Saul's robe."~1 Samuel 24:5 Herein lies the proof that David was a man after God's own heart. He could not get away with even the small stuff without conviction overtaking him.

Quit trying to be perfect! Quit trying to make every row tough to hoe! Give God all your best and when you fail repent quickly. You too can be a person after God's own heart!

Open Your Heart

These are amazing times in which we live. Especially, when one considers the advancements made in the field of medicine. I can still remember the day I went to the hospital to visit a man who had just undergone open-heart surgery. I had only recently surrendered to the ministry and hospital visitation was still a little nerve racking for me.

Having determined the correct room number, I made my way down the corridor and steeled myself in preparation for visiting a very sick man. I gently knocked on the patient's door, but heard no answer. Carefully opening the door, I discovered an empty room. I expected the worst.

A check at the nurses' station led to my discovery that this man, who had only a few hours before lay on an operating table, was now up and walking with assistance down the hallway. Amazing!

He informed me, though in pain, that the surgery had saved his life and he felt a renewed energy. Have you been spiritually worn out with no energy to perform God's will? Could it be that you need to have a spiritual open-heart surgery scheduled today?

The Apostle Paul spoke to the Corinthians about having an open heart. "O Corinthians! We have spoken openly to you, our heart is wide open. You are not restricted by us, but you are restricted by your own affections. Now in return for the same (I speak as to children), you also be open." ~ 2 Corinthians 6:11-13

Paul diagnosed severe blockages in the hearts of the Corinthian believers. Not only did he recommend that they have the blockages removed, he declared that he also had undergone a similar spiritual heart surgery.

Our hearts, like the Corinthians, can be constricted by our own selfish desires. It's time to place yourself under the knife of the Holy Spirit.

Only the Great Physician can restore your spiritual health. Make your appointment now!

· MARCH

Defining the Wind

The professor asked his students to define the wind. After many valiant attempts by the students, most of them could only define the wind relative to the response of some object to the effect of the wind. The wind itself was left without a definitive description.

One student rose to her feet and approached the professor. As she drew within inches of his face she blew gently creating a warm breeze that traversed his skin. She returned to her seat without a word spoken.

The professor applauded. This young lady had defined the wind by demonstrating the feeling that this unseen phenomenon created as it passed by without any other evidence of its existence.

There is much in the world that can affect our feelings. Most of it is unseen and for the most part undefinable, yet we describe these things not by their reality, but by the feeling that they leave behind.

Feelings rush into existence in the first few pages of scripture. Though the word feel is not used, we understand from our own responses that feelings were active. No sooner had Adam and Eve sinned than they felt ashamed and guilty.

The results: They hid themselves from the presence of God. Or so they thought, because God found them even as they cowered under the feeling of remorse. Without feeling we would have no response to the effect of sin. We would be like a paralytic who would not know the wind was passing over his skin since he could not feel its effect.

This danger of not understanding the effects of sin is described in Paul's letter to the Ephesians. He clearly defines what the end result is when a person moves past the point of feeling. "This I say, therefore, and testify in the Lord, that you should no longer walk as the rest of the Gentiles walk, in the futility of their mind, having their understanding darkened, being alienated from the life of God, because of the ignorance that is in them, because of the blindness of their heart; who, being past feeling, have given themselves over to lewdness, to work all uncleanness with greediness." ~ Ephesians 4:17-19

Ask God to renew your feeling today. Ask Him to make you super sensitive to the wind of sin as it passes by you. Like a cold wind leaves one shivering in response to its bite, so may we be quick to react when we are tempted to be blown off course by sin.

May the cold harsh wind of this world be replaced with the warm gentle breeze of God's Spirit upon your life. This is my prayer for you today.

03/02

Building Bridges

Time was when nearly everyone called me son. It would really aggravate me. As with all young folks, I was very sure that I knew everything that there was to know. The only question I had was why everyone else did not know that I knew everything. Then I had children and in particular I had a son. No one told me I should, but I found myself calling him son. I still do today, even though he is a grown man and probably thinks that he knows everything.

We live in a time that is sadly missing the element of respect between generations. What I perceived as a disparaging remark by older people when they called me son was actually a bridge between generations. But like all bridges, the road over them runs in both directions.

Paul had just finished exhorting the elders of the church at Philippi when he turned his attention to the younger people. He said, "Likewise you younger people, submit yourselves to your elders. Yes, all of you be submissive to one another, and be clothed with humility, for God resists the proud, but gives grace to the humble." ~ 1 Peter 5:5

The first thing that comes to my attention is that the terms elder and younger people do not come with age brackets. There simply is no time when we all wind up on the same end of the bridge. Even though I am a lot older now, there are still occasions where I am called son. Amazingly, it does not affect me like it did when I was a mere lad.

Secondly, Paul lumps everyone together and gives us the materials for building bridges in our lives. The framing of the bridge is submission. The idea of submission is not being under another person's control, but it is coming under an orderly process that leads to the success of the whole. It has a military connotation whereby everyone understands their rank and functions inside that rank. The results is a victorious army.

A bridge that only consists of framing may span a chasm, but it is useless without decking. There must be a secure surface for traffic to pass over from one side to the other. Paul tells us that we are to be clothed with humility. Humility then is the material for the deck of the bridge.

When we are humble then all can cross the bridges of our lives from generation to generation. More important than being called son or calling someone else son, you will make a way for others to cross the bridge of your life to find The Son. His name is Jesus.

The Day Missy Died

Missy was dead. Missy was the little rat terrier that we owned and she had made the mistake of grabbing the television plug that had just been pulled from the wall socket. The old tube-style televisions had high voltage capacitors which stored a lot of electricity. The moisture of her mouth was just enough to ground out this stored energy. There she lay, dead on the living room floor.

As you wipe your tears, let me tell you the rest of the story. My mother shouted for me immediately to go fill the bathtub with cold water. I did without question, since I was still in shock over seeing my dog get electrocuted. She picked Missy up into her arms and ran to the tub full of cold water. Then to my amazement, she immersed the little dog in the icy water. Even more amazing was the instant revival of what I was sure was a dead dog.

Missy was alive! I don't know if she had died or was just stunned, but I know for me she was as good as dead and I saw her come back to life.

When I think of revival, I cannot help but think about Missy. She was like many that are in the church today. There was a time when the believers frolicked in their new found joy and excitement of being born again. Then somewhere along the line they grabbed something that should have been left alone and in an instant they were stunned; shocked to near non-existence and lifelessness.

If you are in this condition today, why not cry out to the Lord? Join with the psalmist in praying, "Will You not revive us again, that Your people may rejoice in You?" ~ Psalms 85:6 Ah, like a cold splash into your soul you will find yourself living again.

By the way, Missy went right on living for many years, but two truths were evident in her little dog life. First, she never, ever grabbed another electrical plug laying on the floor. Once was enough for her! Second, she always bore the mark of her misadventure. That plug had permanently scarred her lip. I can still see that part of her lip hanging down curled and deformed.

God wants to revive you today so you can walk in fellowship with Him again. But remember…you may always bear the mark of the days spent un-revived.

Revive us again, O, Lord!

Cheap Hearing

The old gentleman decided that it was time to get a hearing aid. He had put it off as long as he could, so off to the hearing aid store he went.

He was shocked at the price attached to hearing well, as the salesman started to explain the value of his most expensive units. These were priced at $1000 per ear! The old man quickly decided that hearing was not that important and asked for a cheaper pair of hearing aids.

The haggling continued between the salesman and the man. The price of each set of hearing aids got cheaper and cheaper as the quality diminished. Finally, the salesman remarked, "I have a hearing aid that only costs $1.00" Now he really had the old man's attention.

"I'll take it!" he exclaimed with glee. The salesman then pulled a string with a button tied to one end out of his desk. "How does it work?" asked the customer. "You put the button in your ear and run the string down into your shirt. You will be amazed how loudly everyone will talk when they see you are wearing a hearing aid!"

All of us can be hard of hearing at times; especially when it comes to hearing what God has to say. The good thing is that it doesn't take a $1000 set of hearing aids nor does it take a button in your ear to hear God's voice. The secret to hearing God is really very simple.

When the boy Samuel was spoken to by God, he kept mistaking the voice he heard for that of Eli, the priest. Eli's instructions to Samuel for hearing were not difficult. He told Samuel to respond to the voice of God by saying, "Speak, for Your servant hears."

Samuel returned to his bed and waited for God to speak. Now the Lord came and stood and called as at other times, "Samuel! Samuel!" And Samuel answered, "Speak, for Your servant hears." ~ 1 Samuel 3:10

Not only did God speak, but Samuel heard Him perfectly.

The secret to hearing is wrapped up in the little word "hears." This word means that Samuel heard intelligently with a response of obedience. We can never really say that we have heard the Lord unless we have full intent of obeying.

If you desire to hear God's voice today, then stop right now and pray this little prayer: "Speak Lord. I obey." Be ready. God has much to say to the obedient ear.

From the Depths

"During a brief ceremony at 4 p.m., the family of 37-year-old Jeffrey Bush placed a teddy bear, a photo, notes and flowers into the bucket of a backhoe, which dropped them into the estimated 60-foot-deep hole in Seffner, about 15 miles east of Tampa. Then came a truckload of gravel, the first in the process of filling in the yawning hole that took Bush without warning." ~ U.S.A. Today

Jeffrey Bush went to sleep in his bed not realizing that while he slept his bed would become his coffin and the ground beneath his bedroom would be his gravesite. The site is now designated his permanent grave.

All of us can find ourselves suddenly sinking. What begins as a perfectly fine day becomes a tragedy. The ground that we trust to support us gives way and like Jeffrey Bush we leave our relative place of peace and safety with a scream.

Psalm 130 begins with a cry from the pit. We are given no information as to the cause. There is no indication of a warning; just a pitiful cry from the depths. "Out of the depths I have cried to You, O Lord; Lord, hear my voice! Let Your ears be attentive to the voice of my supplications." ~ Psalms 130:1-2

No one can begin to surmise the awful sensation of being swallowed by the earth. I can imagine many things, but I am sure that none of them would match those that you might conjure up when your mind is left to itself.

Somehow our psalmist has survived the fall. He now lies at the bottom of the pit. No, not the pit—his pit. Cold, damp, darkness surrounds him and he senses the full and horrible reality that he will not get himself out of this. Yet I can imagine that the walls of this pit are scarred with the deep scratches of the broken fingernails now on both his hands. In the loneliness of the pit you can hear his rasping breath as he begins to submit to the finality of his predicament.

But then, he looks up—way up beyond the gaping mouth of the hole that now keeps him prisoner and he cries. His cry courses its way up from the grave and to the ear of God Himself. His plea is both determined and direct.

"Hear *My* voice! Give Your attention to *My* cry!"

There was no physical rescue for Jeffrey Bush. I do not know if his cry was directed toward heaven, but yours can be. You need only look up, admit your inability to rescue yourself, and be sure that your cry will reach the ever-attentive ear of God. Then you will feel the warmth of His hand in yours as He guides you up and out of your sinkhole.

The Call

The old ox stood with the yoke around its neck. Time and again its master had come to attach the lines leading to the plow and with ready obedience the faithful animal had pulled the plow through fallow ground.

Now the ox stood in a place he had never before found himself. The plow lay on the ground and smoke rose from an altar. It was time for a new level of obedience. No longer would he pull; he would simply lay down to die.

Some old Roman coins that have been excavated show this scene impressed upon the coin's face. The inscription reads: Ready for either or both. This is the place of the obedient Christian. We stand between the plow and the altar ready to pull or die—or both.

As Elijah's ministry was coming to its end, he approached Elisha who was plowing with his oxen. His command was simple and direct and silent. "So he departed from there, and found Elisha the son of Shaphat, who was plowing with twelve yoke of oxen before him, and he was with the twelfth. Then Elijah passed by him and threw his mantle on him." ~ 1 Kings 19:19

Elisha's response was much as ours would be at the sudden call to ministry. He only requested that he might return and say farewell to his parents. Elijah's response was to the point, "Go back again, what have I done to you?" (1 Kings 19:20)

Clearly, the call was not coming from Elijah, but from the Lord Himself and Elijah wanted that point made. Elisha's response was dramatic. He slew the oxen that had been pulling his plow, used the wood from the plow to build a fire, cooked the oxen, served the meal to his fellow workers, and became the servant of Elijah. Elisha's actions remain as a hallmark of making a decision for God. His choice was final. He never looked back nor left an opening for returning to his former status.

But I cannot help thinking about his faithful ox. This beast of burden had faithfully pulled the plow for many seasons. He had never shirked his duty; always leaving behind him a straight row. And yet with all of this faithfulness, he was now called upon to be a sacrifice.

Never come to the place where you imagine you have arrived. As a believer you stand between the plow and the altar. Always be ready for either or both.

What's This For?

If you have ever gone to a museum, you might have come across a section of antiquities that displays tools. Sometimes it is difficult trying to determine what certain tools were used to accomplish. On the other hand, it is amazing what could be done with very rudimentary equipment. In our day of an invention a minute it seems like there is a tool for everything and you can get one if you call an 800 number in the next 10 minutes.

Did you know that God has a tool box? If you look into it you will find some strange looking tools. You will also be asking a few other questions. What are these tools used for? Why are no two alike? You will be amazed, because God's toolbox is indeed strange.

A list of these tools can be found in First Corinthians. "For you see your calling, brethren, that not many wise according to the flesh, not many mighty, not many noble, are called. But God has chosen the foolish things of the world to put to shame the wise, and God has chosen the weak things of the world to put to shame the things which are mighty; and the base things of the world and the things which are despised God has chosen, and the things which are not, to bring to nothing the things that are, that no flesh should glory in His presence." ~ 1 Corinthians 1:26-29

Notice how mysterious the tools are in the toolbox of the Creator:

- Those who are not too smart

- Those who are not too strong

- Those who are not well-bred

- Those who seem senseless

- Those who are weak

- Those who are of low status

- Those who are rejected

- Those who are unnoticed

God's toolbox has you in it. You and I can find ourselves in one or more of the tools listed above. As you look at the other tools in God's toolbox you probably are like a person peering at some relic in a museum as you wonder how God could ever use such a tool. But never forget: God uses tools like you and me so no person might ever glory in His presence. May God take you out of His toolbox today for His use and glory.

03/08

Speak, Your Servant Hears

Our day is so much like the day when Samuel served Eli in the temple. "Now the boy Samuel ministered to the Lord before Eli. And the word of the Lord was rare in those days; there was no widespread revelation."~1 Samuel 3:1 There are a lot of voices in the world today. Mine is one of them each day as I write a new devotional.

The opportunity to hear or read God's word is available in dozens upon dozens of ways. You can take your choice: radio, television, or Internet. Determining where you will listen to God's word is one step. But the greater question is whether what you are accessing is really a word from God or not.

Samuel was confused when God spoke to him as a young boy. This is the context in which we find the verse included in today's devotional. The word of the Lord was rare in Samuel's day. I believe it is just as rare today. Young Samuel was given by his mother Hannah, to serve the Lord, so he lived in the temple serving Eli, the priest.

You would think that a person living in the house of the Lord would be attuned to hear God, but Samuel was not aware of God's voice when He called. It is much the same today. Lots of folks spend hours in church or in contact with God's word, but seem to never hear God's voice.

Three times Samuel ran to Eli when God called his name. He assumed it was the priest calling him. Finally, Eli realized that God was speaking and he instructed Samuel to say to the Lord, "Speak, Lord, for your servant hears." (1 Samuel 3:9)

The real problem then, as today, is not that God is silent. It is a problem with our hearing. God has a word for you today. You can hear Him in any one of the ways listed above or through His word, or even through a still small voice.

Stop now and follow the instructions of Eli to Samuel. Quietly say to the Lord, "Speak, your servant hears." You will be amazed at just how much God really is saying today. Then having heard be ready to obey. Only then will God speak even more into your hearing. Are you listening?

03/09

Scaredy Cat

I have never been much of a scaredy cat, but we all have our moments when we would like to hide behind someone bigger than us. At least I like to think that way...it makes me less afraid of you thinking that I really am a scaredy cat.

The Psalmist must have been having a scaredy cat episode when he penned the words that we have recorded in Psalm 91. "He who dwells in the secret place of the Most High shall abide under the shadow of the Almighty. I will say of the Lord, 'He is my refuge and my fortress; my God, in Him I will trust.' Surely He shall deliver you from the snare of the fowler and from the perilous pestilence. He shall cover you with His feathers, and under His wings you shall take refuge; His truth shall be your shield and buckler." ~ Psalms 91:1-4

What can we learn from these verses about having a place to hide when we are afraid? First, this place of safety is not just a place to run to when we are afraid. The Psalmist dwelt in this secret place. The idea is to be permanently in this hiding place as we abide in the shadow of God. The word translated as *shadow* means to provide shade by hovering. The protection of God is no moving shadow like that which is cast by the passing day. We have a continual place of safety as we dwell in His protective cover.

This concept of safety is strengthened as the Psalmist declares that God is more than a shadow. He is a refuge and a fortress. God is a bulwark of hope and the Psalmist places his whole trust in this fact. God not only keeps us safe as we dwell in His protection, but when we stray from it and find ourselves entrapped and endangered He can and will deliver. We indeed are blessed!

Finally, we see God covering us like a bird spreading its feathers over its young. The word *cover* means to entwine as a thick hedge that has grown and thickened over time. It also has the idea of a screen. God will not allow anything to get to us without going through Him. We can trust Him to protect us like a shield and buckler. The thought here is to be surrounded by a thorny wall of cactus.

Nothing is going to get to us as we hide under His hand. Quit being a scaredy cat!

Rest in His shadow!

03/10

Where There's Smoke …

I smelled smoke, but I figured it must have been coming from one of the many fires burning in and around the homes of people along the highway we were traveling. I was mistaken. The smell of smoke wasn't coming from outside the vehicle I was riding in as we traveled from the meeting we had just finished in the front yard of a Nigerian preacher. The smoke was quickly filling the vehicle I was sitting in at the moment.

I can still remember casually remarking that I smelled smoke, but no one seemed to respond. Some of the reason for this was that I was the only person in the vehicle that spoke or understood English. The other was that I was not used to traveling with live coals of fire in the trunk of the car.

Wood is so scarce in that part of the country I was in, that the men had literally gathered up the smoldering remains of the fire we had been around in the yard, placed it on a piece of tin, and put it in the trunk of the car! Like I said, "I smelled smoke!"

I am afraid that we have put the fire out in our lives. We do not like the smell of smoke and we have a fear of fire breaking out in our lives. The writer of Hebrews tells us that "...our God is a consuming fire." ~ Hebrews 12:29

God's place in our lives is not the trunk of our lives where we only catch a scent of Him from time to time. His intent is to consume us. God wants to burn away all that is not real in our lives, so that all that is eternal will shine forth all the more brighter.

By the way, I finally got them to stop the vehicle. I quickly exited and the men opened the trunk. With the rush of fresh oxygen, the fire reignited. I stood there in utter amazement that just behind the seat in which I had been sitting a fire was ready to consume me.

In this case, the men extinguished the fire which was a good thing for me and the vehicle. Make sure, however, that you never allow the fire to go out in your life. It's a good thing to smell like you've been near or even in the fire of God.

May others always respond in your presence, "I smell smoke!"

03/11

When A Brave Man Takes a Stand

A medal hung about the neck of the cowardly lion was enough to muster all the courage he needed to stand against the wicked witch in the classic film, The Wizard of Oz. Nothing was changed. He was the same lion that had cowered at the slightest noise, but with the encouragement of his friends and the proclamation of the wizard, he was now brave.

All of us have had our moments when courage had to be summoned. Harold Wilson who served as the prime minister of England said, "Courage is the art of being the only one who knows you're scared to death." Courage is, however, contagious to some degree. Billy Graham remarked, "When a brave man takes a stand, the spines of others are often stiffened."

Courage is spoken of often throughout scripture. As Jesus neared the end of His earthly ministry he told His disciples, "These things I have spoken to you, that in Me you may have peace. In the world you will have tribulation; but be of good cheer, I have overcome the world." ~ John 16:33 Here the phrase, be of good cheer, is translated from the same word that we derive the word courage.

You may find yourself today in a place that calls upon you to act courageously. It may be a moment of solitude in which you will need to make a decision based on courage. Then again it may be quite public. Perhaps the actions of one relatively unknown general may be an encouragement to you. His courage began in the battlefield, but carried him into the king's court.

Frederick the Great was a scoffer, but his general, Von Zealand, was a Christian. One day at a gathering, the king was making coarse jokes about Jesus Christ and the whole place was ringing with guffaws.

Von Zealand arose stiffly and said, "Sire, you know I have not feared death. I have fought and won 38 battles for you. I am an old man; I shall soon have to go into the presence of One Greater than thou, the mighty God who saved me from my sin, the Lord Jesus Christ whom you are blaspheming against. I salute thee, sire, as an old man, who loves his Savior, on the edge of eternity."

With trembling voice, Frederick replied: "General Von Zealand. I beg your pardon. I beg your pardon! I beg your pardon!"

The company silently dispersed.

Now go out and quiet the maddening crowd! Be courageous!

03/12

When Daddy Put His Hat On

The Stetson hat was taken from the box that rested under my parents bed and situated with a slight tilt upon my daddy's head. This hat was only worn a few times each year. Each time it saw the light of day, it meant that some important event was about to take place in our family. On this day the wearing of the hat meant we would be going into Baton Rouge. Our destination: Furniture by Heck.

My father was going to buy a new stereo for our home. Wait, not a new stereo as in a replacement, but our first piece of musical equipment ever, other than a radio. We came home with the six foot long cabinet that allowed us to listen to 33 rpm long play records.

Wait, not records, record would be more accurate. We only had one. It was the record that was playing on the floor model we brought home with us that day. That one record was the beginning of my extensive music repertoire. That last statement is fully intended to be in jest!

Music has never been my thing. I enjoy it, but it does not rise to a high level of interest for me. I do, however, recall a song or two that have stuck with me over the years.

One of the songs on our only album was "Won't You Come Home, Bill Bailey". I don't recall who was singing it, but I heard it so many times that I still remember some of the words. Another song that has resonated with me over the years was sung by Johnny Nash. His number one hit was titled "I Can See Clearly Now".

When I think of the words of this song, I always remember the words of John as he spoke of how much the disciples remembered after the resurrection of Jesus. "Therefore, when He had risen from the dead, His disciples remembered that He had said this to them; and they believed the Scripture and the word which Jesus had said." ~ John 2:22

When the clouds and rain of everyday life are encircling our heads, it can be difficult to see clearly. But the day will come when it will all be blue skies again. The rainbow will be painted on the canvas of heaven and the promises of God will be sure once more.

If this is a difficult and dark day for you, then take out the Stetson, tilt it just right, and remember the old songs of God's faithfulness. Like Johnny Nash sang in his hit release: "Gone are the dark clouds that had me blind / It's gonna be a bright, bright / Sun-Shiny day."

03/13

My Money Manager

I had a money manager when I was a kid. No, I was not some Wall Street miracle boy who got rich successfully investing my money in just the right stock at just the right time. My money manager was my mama.

I worked at the Red & White. My first job there was bagging groceries and taking them out to the customer's vehicle. I was not hired by the owner, but by the clerk. I worked each day that she asked me to do so. My pay was $1.

That dollar was surrendered to my money manager who placed it in a mason jar in one of the kitchen cabinets. I can still see the exact shelf in that cabinet just to the right of the kitchen sink. All transactions were made through that mason jar. I guess for me it was the Mason Jar Bank & Trust.

One of the instructions issued forth by my money manager was the setting aside of my tithe from my huge salary. Each Sunday morning I withdrew ten cents from the mason jar and placed it in the envelope that I would carry to Sunday School. I never went to church empty-handed. My Bible and the envelope which held 1/10th of my salary were always with me. God instructed the Israelites also to never come before Him empty-handed.

"Three times a year all your males shall appear before the Lord your God in the place which He chooses: at the Feast of Unleavened Bread, at the Feast of Weeks, and at the Feast of Tabernacles; and they shall not appear before the Lord empty-handed. Every man shall give as he is able, according to the blessing of the Lord your God which He has given you." ~ Deuteronomy 16:16-17

At these three feast times God required an offering to be brought before Him. These three feasts are quite symbolic to us as believers. The Feast of Unleavened Bread is a picture of the haste by which Israel departed Egypt. So, our giving should be offered up in haste, lest we resist giving it freely.

The Feast of Weeks corresponds to the Day of Pentecost when the Holy Spirit was given freely to rest upon each believer. The promise of Jesus was that the Holy Spirit would guide us in all things. Without His presence we would not know how to manage all that has been given to us.

Finally, the Feast of Tabernacles is noted. This was the time of ingathering. It was held at the conclusion of the harvest. What better time to give to the Lord than when we are fully aware of all His blessings.

Is it time for you to open an account at the Mason Jar Bank & Trust? Decide today to never come before the Lord empty-handed.

03/14

That Smells Good

If you have ever had a severe cold, then you have lost your ability to smell and along with that your sense of taste. Amazingly, we do not really taste that much with our tongues. It is our noses that give us the great variety of what we describe as tastes. Our tongues can only detect sweet, sour, salty, and bitter. Our noses literally add the finesse to our sensory ability.

Scientists use this fact to trick our taste buds into tasting all sorts of flavors, when in actuality we are just smelling them. Various chemicals are used to create artificial flavorings. You will see this listed as an ingredient on most packaging labels. Nearly all artificial flavors are created to mimic something already found naturally. The chemical formulas are tweaked until they reach the closest approximation to the real thing.

For the most part people like scents that are known, but mistakes occur in the laboratory. Sometimes these turn out for the good. One example is Juicy Fruit gum. Juicy Fruit was the very first gum flavor offered by Wrigley in 1893. It is still their best seller and the secret of its uniquely unnatural flavor is strictly guarded.

Christians offer a unique flavor to the world. It is not natural. Perhaps this is why people react to us so quickly; or at least they should. We should be leaving a taste in their mouths that they have never sensed before. Hopefully, the scent we exude will be one that is attractive to all.

May we be like the oil that Mary poured on the feet of Jesus. "Then Mary took a pound of very costly oil of spikenard, anointed the feet of Jesus, and wiped His feet with her hair. And the house was filled with the fragrance of the oil." ~ John 12:3 May the scent of our broken and poured out lives fill the world in which we live.

In a similar account another woman broke open an alabaster flask of oil and poured it upon the head of Jesus (Matthew 26:7). In both cases there were some who resented what they considered a waste of valuable perfume, but Jesus highlighted the actions of these women and declared that wherever the gospel was preached this story was to be told.

Today, you will leave a fragrance in the room of your life. May it be as unique as Juicy Fruit and may it leave a desire in all sense it to taste and see that the Lord is good.

03/15

Bullies

Age is relative, but I am an old man. Well, at least I am older today than I've ever been. Being this old allows me to recall parts of a history that goes back—let's just say it goes back a long way.

One of the pages of my history has written upon it this little fact about me: R.E. Clark has never in all of his days ever struck another person. You read that right. I have never been in a fight where fists were thrown. I think I have been close a few times, but I have never been required to physically clobber another person.

I did have a bully or two that crossed my path as a kid. These were the days when kids took care of bullying all by themselves. Very seldom did parents or teachers get involved. I'm not saying that was good or bad; that's just the way it was.

Louis was one of those bullies. It was his goal in life to beat me up or at least that's how it seemed to me. He just did not like me—period. Each time our paths crossed, he was in my face with a verbal barrage and his fists clinched.

This confrontation went on for years, but neither of us ever exchanged blows. For some reason, I knew how to calm the beast in Louis. I would begin talking with him and after a few minutes, he would simply walk away. It was as if he could not remember the reason he had confronted me.

We have a bully that is always on the prowl, looking for an opportunity to threaten us. Of course, you know of whom I speak. Satan, like a roaring lion, is seizing every moment he can to accuse us and entice us into an altercation.

The good news is that we do not have to come out swinging, nor should we fall into the trap of thinking that we have a chance on our own. "But the Lord is faithful, who will establish you and guard you from the evil one." ~ 2 Thessalonians 3:3

Therein is our hope! It is the Lord who rushes in as our Defender. He is always looking over us like a big brother. He is ALWAYS on duty. He is always ready for Satan or any one of the Louis's that might cross our path.

No, I've never been in a fight, but I've never run either. The promise is twofold. He will guard, but He will also cause us to stand our ground. Something happens to bullies when we set our feet on the solid rock and they sense the shadow of our big brother falling over their shoulders.

Louis is out there, but it's okay. He's already whooped! He just doesn't know it yet!

03/16

Gleaning

A box of chicken nuggets made all the difference.

The young lady in front of me in the checkout line was pushing a double baby stroller. The children on board were both under two years of age. When the clerk told her the amount for the groceries, she paused, and almost it seemed without thought, took the box of chicken nuggets out of the bagged items.

She precariously loaded her bags onto the stroller and began making her way to the door. That's when God spoke. Not audibly, but in that still small voice: "Add the chicken nuggets to your bill."

I quickly told the clerk to scan the box of nuggets and handed them to my wife, who stopped the young lady as she was about to leave the store. Suddenly, a box of chicken nuggets was transformed into manna and a look of joy filled her face. Hopefully, when they got home the nuggets filled a couple of hungry children.

One of God's earliest instructions to the nation of Israel was concerning the poor. As they re-entered the promised land, God commanded that they leave a portion of their fields for the benefit of the poor.

"When you reap the harvest of your land, you shall not wholly reap the corners of your field, nor shall you gather the gleanings of your harvest. And you shall not glean your vineyard, nor shall you gather every grape of your vineyard; you shall leave them for the poor and the stranger: I am the Lord your God." ~ Leviticus 19:9-10

I have been blessed with harvest in my life. I don't ever remember having to leave a box of chicken nuggets behind to balance my budget. But I do not take for granted that it is God alone that has provided the harvest.

The seed is planted by us, but God sends the sunshine and the rain.

Few of us probably will ever harvest a huge crop in this life. But the size of a person's land is not mentioned in these verses. All of us can leave something behind for those less fortunate.

Each time that a gleaning opportunity arises stay alert to the privilege of leaving a box of chicken nuggets in the corner of your field. And never forget that He told us the real reason for doing so: "I am the Lord your God."

Happy planting!

03/17

Sit Down and Wait

The Lord of the Rings trilogy is my favorite movie collections. I simply never tire of watching it. We will have a marathon now and again where we watch all three. I always come away with a favorite character. The amazing thing is that my favorite character never remains the same. I seem to choose one based on what's happening at that moment in my life.

As I considered the scripture verse for today's devotion, Gandalf rushed in to be my favorite. Gandalf was a wizard. Not in an evil wizard sense, but a good wizard. He did not always have the answer to every situation. Sometimes he had to stop and wait just like you and I must do from time to time.

In Isaiah's prophecy, he speaks of the terrible choices that Israel had made in trusting the feeble strength of Egypt. They had rejected the word of God as well as the prophets and teachers God had sent them.

But God has mercy for His chosen people and says, "Your ears shall hear a word behind you, saying, 'This is the way, walk in it,' whenever you turn to the right hand or whenever you turn to the left." ~ Isaiah 30:21

Israel would make the right choice, though it would come after many heartaches and trials brought about by their disobedient choices of the past. How can we make the right choices from the beginning and avoid these times of despair? That brings me back to Gandalf.

In *The Fellowship of the Ring*, Gandalf is leading the nine who make up the fellowship through the mines of Moriah. He comes to a place in the deep recesses where he does not remember the way. His decision at this moment is one that makes him my favorite. He just sits down.

What a decision! He just sits down and waits. This is so contrary to most who would lead. After all, leaders ought to be forging ahead against all odds, but not Gandalf. He just sits down and waits!

Just prior to His words about hearing which way to go, God told Israel, "Therefore the Lord will wait, that He may be gracious to you; and therefore He will be exalted, that He may have mercy on you. For the Lord is a God of justice; blessed are all those who wait for Him." ~ Isaiah 30:18

Are you at a decision point in your life today? Take Gandalf's advice. Sit down and wait. The time will come that a breath of fresh air will sweep down the right corridor and you will find your way out to a right choice. Until then…wait!

03/18

No Place Like Home

If I had to choose a favorite shape it would be the circle. Perhaps it is the mystery of its beginning, for having been drawn no one can tell where it began nor where it ends. Its area is defined by using a mathematical formula that has in it a term that cannot be fully computed and is noted by the symbol π. Pi represents the ratio of a circle's circumference to its diameter.

Bored yet? I'm going somewhere with this, I promise.

This mysterious element in defining a circle has to be the reason I am so attracted to it. I even tend to travel in circles. Very seldom do I take a direct route to a place and then return the exact same way. I will usually figure a way to circle around on my journey.

One thing is always true, however. My circuitous route always leads me back where I began: home. As Dorothy said in "The Wizard of Oz", "There's no place like home, there's no place like home!"

The psalmist surely had a destination fixed upon his heart when he wrote, "Blessed is the man whose strength is in You, whose heart is set on pilgrimage."~Psalms 84:5 From the context of this verse, we know that his destination was the courtyard of God's palace. The Amplified Bible says that this man has the highway of God written upon his heart.

If I might take some liberty here, I would write this verse like this: The man whose strength lies in God will be happy, because in his heart he knows that the road he walks will lead him home to God's presence.

My journeys have taken me across five continents. I am grateful for the strength that God has given for each step. But no matter how short or long the journey, I am always glad to be back home—back home to complete the circle.

It does not take long though before I begin to feel the urge to travel again. It is as if my journey is not yet complete. Yes, another fold of the map has been disclosed and the road highlighted, but I still sense a few more miles untraveled. My heart is set not upon an earthly home to complete my circle, but a heavenly one where my possessions lie.

03/19

Brainy Men

Many years ago I was a cooperative observer for the National Weather Service. I would record the daily weather and submit monthly reports. All of my equipment for measuring temperatures and rainfall was located at my grocery business. Being located in the country meant that farmers would stop by my store for the forecast.

I wasn't always right, but neither are the guys on television with all of their fancy equipment. I did all of my forecasting the old fashioned way. I would watch the barometer and the clouds. I would oft times get it right.

We have seen a lot of storm clouds gathering on the horizon of our country lately. Flashes of lightning from an impending storm can be seen in the decisions being made daily by those who are our elected representatives. The Bible speaks about the effects of righteousness on a nation. "Righteousness exalts a nation, but sin is a reproach to any people." ~ Proverbs 14:34

R.A. Torrey wrote in his book, *Fundamentals*, a chapter entitled, "Tributes to Christ and the Bible by Brainy Men Not Known As Active Christians." One of the brainy men he quoted was Daniel Webster. Webster said, "If we abide by the principles taught in the Bible, our country will go on prospering and to prosper; but, if we and our posterity neglect its instructions and authority, no man can tell how sudden a catastrophe may overwhelm us and bury all our glory in profound obscurity. The Bible is the book of all others for lawyers as well as divines, and I pity the man who cannot find in it a rich supply of thought and rule of conduct. I believe Jesus Christ to be the Son of God. The miracles which He wrought establish in my mind His personal authority and render it proper for me to believe what He asserts."

These are the words of a man not noted as an outstanding Christian, but a well-known statesman. If he could clearly remark about the importance of the Bible being a guidebook for thought and rule of conduct, should we not as believers take our stand in its clear instruction.

To ignore its teaching is like forecasting a fair day when the barometer is falling, the wind is rising from the south, and clouds are thickening to the west. All indications point to a storm in the making. As Webster put it, "a sudden catastrophe may overwhelm us." Isn't it time to look to heaven again for the answer and begin to obey the instruction we have already been given? Perhaps we may yet avert a catastrophe. God helps us as a nation!

03/20

Brushstroke of His Touch

Painters are known by their technique. Their use of color, application of paint by certain brush stroke, or subtle blending of light and shadow. Other artists such as singers or songwriters are easily identified by their genre or lyrics. Even common folk who have not left huge marks in life can be singled out by tone of voice or a certain gait.

The Apostle John said twice in a matter of four verses that we know Jesus by two distinct markers. Take note of the phrase "by this we know" used in First John 2. "Now by this we know that we know Him, if we keep His commandments. He who says, 'I know Him,' and does not keep His commandments, is a liar, and the truth is not in him. But whoever keeps His word, truly the love of God is perfected in him. By this we know that we are in Him. He who says he abides in Him ought himself also to walk just as He walked." ~ 1 John 2:3-6

We can have certain knowledge of our knowledge of Him because we keep His commandments. This does not mean that we are without sin, but that we have the indisputable brush stroke of His touch in our lives and that we can note that touch by obedience to His command. As a matter of fact, to say that you know Him and not keep His command makes you a liar. In essence, like a copied masterpiece, you are a fake.

Second, we can have certain knowledge of our knowledge of Him, because the love of God is fully matured in our lives and this causes us to walk like Jesus in this life. To walk like Jesus is to bear His characteristics in our lives. Like the common man illustrated above, you are known as a follower of Christ by simple things like your tone of voice or your steady gait.

Certainly, you are thinking that it can't be this simple, but it really is. We know—that we know—that we know. We don't know because we know, but because we know Him, we know that we are in Him. This is not a riddle to confuse, but a reality to reveal. In Him, I am no longer known. Only He is known as others try to know us, because they see Him in our walk and our talk. And that is a masterpiece of His redemptive work.

03/21

The Board Road

I answered a dare many years ago that took me to the very edge of my strength. It was a challenge to join my brother-in-law to work on a board road. The pay was phenomenal for those days and I accepted the challenge.

Now a board road is literally what it sounds like: a road built by using thick, heavy oak boards. This particular road and the accompanying pad was huge. The road extended across a swampy area in south Louisiana. The pad was three football fields square.

Our job was to interlace three layers of oak boards and nail them together using long spikes. Thousands of boards and multiple thousands of spikes were assembled into a huge worksite above one of the salt domes that became part of the strategic oil reserve.

I had come from behind a grocery counter to answer the challenge of this work. I soon learned how heavy a single-blade ax becomes after it is swung overhead a few hundred times. I was stretched beyond my ability and to the point of agony.

The word agony is only used once in all of scripture. It is found in Luke's account of Jesus praying in the Garden of Gethsemane just before his trial and crucifixion. "And being in agony, He prayed more earnestly. Then His sweat became like great drops of blood falling down to the ground." ~ Luke 22:44

We cannot fully grasp the position from which Jesus was praying. He was aware of the fact that He would bear the full brunt and weight of the sins of all mankind. The penalty of sin was about to fall upon Him in the form of God's wrath outpoured. He would soon be deserted by all and forsaken by His Father.

There is a sense of increasing intensity in this word to the point agony is no longer felt, but instead it becomes a place. It is an existence which fills every molecule of space surrounding Christ to the point that the capillaries of His body burst under the pressure. From His skin the perspiration rains down red as it is mixed with His blood.

On that board road my hands trembled as the day stretched out before me. Each spike weighed heavier than the last. Each blow of the hammer brought shockwaves of pain into my joints, but at the end of the day I went home. My agony, or at least my idea of agony, came to an end.

It was not so with our Lord. The agony of the garden was only the beginning. The blows of the hammer upon the spikes were yet to fall. But…He met the challenge. He paid the price. He did not quit. He did not go home until the price was paid.

Hallelujah! What a Savior!

	03/22

To Tell the Truth

A message came to the classroom from the school office. I was to report immediately to the principal. Well, one of my friends and I were to go and face the charges that had been brought before the judge and jury that resided in the person of the principal.

There was no need for a plea of innocence that day. I was guilty. I knew it. There was only one course of action to be taken: confession. So, as I took the slow walk down the hall toward certain punishment, I decided that I would tell the truth.

The scene could have been worst. Thank goodness it was not. Sitting there in the principal's office was a kid with red marks on various parts of his body. It was evident that he had run into something. I knew what it was. Earlier that day I had taken part in a prank. We had found a spool of thin wire that had been discarded in shop class. With great care we had strung this wire like a spider's web across several doorways in the shop building. The kid in the office has been our "victim" of chance. He had run through one of the passageways and the results were the red marks now apparent upon his skin.

He was not seriously injured, but he had reported the results of our prank. Now I stood before my accuser and the judge who would most likely sentence me to corporal punishment.

I had made my decision on the way down the long hallway that led to the judgment chambers. I would simply tell the truth. I knew why I was summoned and I knew that I was guilty. So, when the principal asked if I had strung the wire in the doorways, I gave a one word response: Yes.

The principal seemed stunned at my response. There was a brief moment of silence as he contemplated my answer. Then amazingly he told us to go take it down. That was it; just take it down. I was guilty, but I went free.

It was not so with Jesus. He was asked a simple question. Are you the Son of God? (Luke 22:70) He answered truthfully that He indeed was, but results were not as it had been for me.

"And they said, 'What further testimony do we need? For we have heard it ourselves from His own mouth.'" ~ Luke 22:71

So began the day that we call Good Friday. Falsely accused, beaten, crowned with thorns, marched through the crowds, and nailed to a cross, Jesus died for me. He paid the price for me stringing wire across a doorway and hurting a boy I did not even know.

He died. I went free. It really was a Good Friday.

03/23

Denial

The room was still dark and only a few early morning sounds could be heard through the shuttered window. A man sat in the corner, his beard wet from a night of tears that had poured from his eyes. The source of his bitterness came from a single glance that had come from the Man who had been arrested just the night before in a lonely garden and the sound of a rooster crowing in the distance.

He could still hear his proclamation that he would never deny this Man. Boldly, he had challenged the prophecy and declared that he would even go to prison with Him. But now he sat alone in a dark corner, a denier of his Friend. Though he had followed away off, he still at the end cursed His name in denial.

"Then he began to curse and swear, saying, 'I do not know the Man!' Immediately a rooster crowed. And Peter remembered the word of Jesus who had said to him, 'Before the rooster crows, you will deny Me three times.' So he went out and wept bitterly." ~ Matthew 26:74-75

This was certainly the darkest day Peter had ever experienced, but in a few brief hours even the sun would refuse to shine as God's Son would hang suspended between heaven and earth. Peter must have thought all lost as he sat there alone, but he did not remember that Sunday was coming!

Are you in a dark corner this day? Do you think that you have crossed a line and there is no return to the side of your Friend? Listen! Sunday's coming!

Though the memory of your failure still looms big, Sunday's coming! Though the chants of the gathering crowds grow louder, "Crucify Him!", Sunday's coming! Though all hell rants against you declaring that you are unfit to be his friend, Sunday's coming! Even though the person you see in the mirror sneers back, "Denier!", SUNDAY'S COMING!

Don't give up! Don't give in! Don't turn away, because SUNDAY'S COMING!

It Can't Be Stopped

There is usually a focus at Easter on Good Friday and Easter Sunday, but what about Saturday? Much was happening on this day after the crucifixion. We can assume that the disciples were in hiding, awaiting their possible arrest. The crowds would have gone back to their regular routines. The Pharisees would be nervously awaiting Sunday.

It seems that the Pharisees believed the prophecy of Jesus more than the disciples. They at least feared the forced fulfillment of Jesus rising on the third day. To prevent it they sought assistance from Pilate.

"On the next day, which followed the Day of Preparation, the chief priests and Pharisees gathered together to Pilate, saying, 'Sir, we remember, while He was still alive, how that deceiver said, 'After three days I will rise.' Therefore command that the tomb be made secure until the third day, lest His disciples come by night and steal Him away, and say to the people, 'He has risen from the dead.' So the last deception will be worse than the first.'" "Pilate said to them, 'You have a guard; go your way, make it as secure as you know how.' So they went and made the tomb secure, sealing the stone and setting the guard." ~ Matthew 27:62-66

Not only did the Pharisees want to prevent the resurrection, Pilate hinted at the fact that it could not be stopped. He told them to make it as sure as they could. I wonder if Pilate was surprised when his seal was broken and his guards struck down as dead men. I think he might have expected it!

Here's the most amazing part of this Saturday's happenings. We know what happened on Sunday. We aren't hiding somewhere expecting arrest. We don't have anyone sealing the tomb. Yet we are silent.

The seal is not on the tomb today. It's on our lips and hearts. It's time to say to the world, "Go ahead, and make it as sure as you can, but death nor you can keep Him in the tomb!"

> Up from the grave He arose!
> With a mighty triumph over His foes,
> HE AROSE! HE AROSE!

Sunday's Coming!

The crowds were gone. Quiet replaced the tumult that had roared across Jerusalem like a low flying jet. All of the hate and spite that could be generated against one man had come and gone as if a tidal wave had washed ashore and simply swept it all out to sea. Jesus was dead.

Upon portals unseen to human eye and unrecorded for us to really know, I can imagine two scenes unfolding. In heaven there might have been an unusual stillness. The angels had folded their wings as if to wrap themselves away from what they had witnessed. They had stood ready for the command of God. A legion would have rescued Him from the cross, but the order never came. And now Jesus was dead.

Satan and his demonic forces must have thrust their proud chests forth and with ungodly cries of seeming victory marched through hell with their banner lifted high. Jesus was dead.

The disciples were now re-gathered. Huddled in their hiding place, they would have feared every move outside the door. They had all fled except John, but even he now cowered in the shadows with many unanswered questions. The women dried their tears, as they prepared the spices and ointments that would be used the next morning. There had been no time to properly prepare His body. It was laid in the coolness of a borrowed tomb. Jesus was dead.

Those in authority could not relax. They had heard His words. "On the third day I will rise again." Hurriedly, they sought permission from Pilate to prevent anyone from entering the tomb and creating the appearance that He was alive. They knew better. Jesus was dead.

The order was written. "Pilate said to them, 'You have a guard; go your way, make it as secure as you know how.' So they went and made the tomb secure, sealing the stone and setting the guard." ~ Matthew 27:65-66 The guards assigned this task had never had such an easy job to do. Everyone feared them who would think to approach. And as for the body in the tomb, Jesus was dead.

Who really knows what was transpiring in heaven or hell on the day after the crucifixion of Jesus. We have no eye witness account of what the citizens of Jerusalem were discussing. The words of the disciples are not recorded. We only know that Pilate's very command carried with it the hope of a day otherwise filled with grief and doubt. Make it as secure as you know how, opened a possibility to the dilemma that Jesus was dead.

It was Saturday. Jesus was dead. But Sunday was coming!

Never Alone

Passover had come and gone. Every Israelite who was an obedient follower of the commandments of God would have performed each detail of the occasion with precision. There would have been meticulous obedience. Each year the Passover served as a reminder of Israel's captivity and release from Egypt. Yet, somehow the rituals would leave the participant all alone.

This year had been no different, except for the awful, heartbreaking happenings of the past few days. Jesus had ridden into Jerusalem with all the grandeur of a king's arrival. He departed its walls without even the visage of a man. The same crowds that had welcomed Him railed upon Him in disdain and cried out for His crucifixion. He was all alone.

Both God and man had forsaken Him. He died alone on the cross. He lay alone in the tomb. And on this Sunday morning a few women came alone to finalize His burial. No palm branches were waving. No glad hallelujahs rang out from the masses. No kingly throne was His residence. Lo, in the grave He lay…alone.

As the night gave way to the breaking dawn, these women beheld a sight they could have never imagined. The guards at the tomb had fled. The stone was rolled away and the body of Jesus was not to be found. "And it happened, as they were greatly perplexed about this, that behold, two men stood by them in shining garments. Then, as they were afraid and bowed their faces to the earth, they said to them, "Why do you seek the living among the dead? He is not here, but is risen! Remember how He spoke to you when He was still in Galilee…"" ~ Luke 24:4-6

The women were perplexed. They could not run from the scene. They could not evade the truth. They were held captive as the moment unfolded around them. These who had just fulfilled the remembrance of the deliverance of Passover were now held like prisoners as they heard the voices of the angels in unison declare, "He is not here, but is risen!"

The first word they heard after the news of the resurrection was the command to remember. Perhaps on each Easter morning, it would be good to remember again. To stand with these women, trapped in utter amazement at the truth of the moment.

No matter your circumstance, let this day serve as a reminder that you are never alone. "He is not here, but is risen!

Tension

What is it that allows a water spider to walk across the surface of water and not sink? Certainly you are thinking, "Who cares?" But that is just the point of asking. The answer to this question is the reason you should care and it holds the answer to what you will face today. So, how can a spider walk on water? In simple terms: tension.

The spider carefully walks on the thin layer of tension that exists between his tiny feet (Do spiders have feet?) and the surface of the water. Without tension the spider would sink. Now this is interesting because we spend so much time trying to alleviate all of the tension in our lives that we become entirely tensed and ultimately the weight of all our tension sinks us!

What then are we to do about this? David H. Fink, author of *Release From Nervous Tension*, wrote an article for the "Coronet Magazine", as to how we can overcome mental and emotional tensions. Fink's work as a psychiatrist for the Veterans Administration gave him access to 10,000 case histories in this field.

Many patients had asked Dr. Fink for some short, magic-button cure for nervousness. In his search for such a cure he studied two groups; the first group was made up of thousands of people who were suffering from mental and emotional disturbances; the second group contained only those who were free from such tensions.

One astounding fact began to stand out: those who suffered from extreme tension had one trait in common—they were habitual faultfinders, constant critics of people and things around them. However, those who were free of most tensions were the least faultfinding.

What's the Bible's answer to life's tensions?

Here it is: "Finally, brethren, whatever things are true, whatever things are noble, whatever things are just, whatever things are pure, whatever things are lovely, whatever things are of good report, if there is any virtue and if there is anything praiseworthy— meditate on these things. The things which you learned and received and heard and saw in me, these do, and the God of peace will be with you." ~ Philippians 4:8-9

Now go walk on some water today. Be glad for the tension for it can be the very support that keeps you afloat!

The Old, Old Story

Returning home always leaves me in a reflective mood. In some ways there is regret that the journey is complete and in others there is the calming effect that your easy chair has upon wearied bones and tired flesh.

I recently visited Israel. I returned to the Holy Land after nearly 30 years of absence. It is amazing how quickly three decades have evaporated. These years seem long on this side of the ocean, but when I place them upon the time line of the Holy Land they just vanish.

After all these years a lot of excavation and archaeological digs have unearthed some new and interesting discoveries that date back over 6000 years. Interesting, though, is the fact that after 30 years, I felt like nothing had changed. Deep down under all of the new super structures, highways, and tweaks to the facade surrounding some of the biblical sites, there is the old, old, story still crying out from centuries long gone.

I have reflected upon the one place that I considered the most likely to be a place that Jesus actually walked. Now certainly I saw many places that could have been visited by the feet of Jesus, but with great assurance I knew that the Sea of Galilee was one of them.

Imagine with me the evening that Jesus and the disciples entered one of the boats as he said, "Let us cross over to the other side." (Mark 4:35) With the gentle rocking of the boat Jesus fell asleep in the stern as they rowed towards the opposite shore. But one of the sudden squalls arose, as so often occurs here, and the disciples fearing for their lives cried out to Him.

"Then He arose and rebuked the wind, and said to the sea, 'Peace, be still!' And the wind ceased and there was a great calm." ~ Mark 4:39

Our boat ride was a calm one, but all of the years that have passed since my last visit to this place have not been filled with peace. Tragedy, sickness, and sorrow have come rushing down from the seaside cliffs to rock my boat.

Times came when I forsook my faith and cried out with the disciples, "Lord, don't you care if I perish?" But He has been with me through it all. Faithfully, He has risen with a strong word and a move of His hand in my favor to calm my sea. One day this journey will end on the other side and I will be able to thank Him for being with me in the very places where my journeys took me across this globe.

Hear His voice today, "Peace, be still!"

Do You Have a Backup?

Catastrophes come in all shapes and sizes. Sometimes I think that we would like to know that they were coming. Our minds tell us that we would have prepared better if we had a little forewarning, but our hearts tell the truth: we usually don't prepare very well.

Case in point is the recent crash of my computer. I never saw it coming. I have been using computers since the days of the Commodore 64. These were the computers that you booted up on Tuesday so you could use it on Wednesday!

The saga of my catastrophe went like this. I was minding my own business (aren't we all) when everything came to a halt. No warning, no clicks, no rattle, no bits of data loss. Just sudden irreversible silence! That seems so strange to use an exclamation point after the word silence. It ruins the effect of the word. Silence is just that…silence.

Now you are thinking, "Surely, someone who had been using computers so long had an up-to-date backup?" Remember the part above about us minding our own business? Now would be a good time to practice that!

No! I did not have an up to date backup, because I had never had a hard disk failure that was not preceded by some warning. But isn't that the real malady of catastrophe? It comes without warning.

So it was for Hezekiah when Isaiah delivered a word from God. "In those days Hezekiah was sick and near death. And Isaiah the prophet, the son of Amoz, went to him and said to him, 'Thus says the Lord: set your house in order, for you shall die, and not live.' Then he turned his face toward the wall, and prayed to the Lord, saying, 'Remember now, O Lord, I pray, how I have walked before You in truth and with a loyal heart, and have done what was good in Your sight.' And Hezekiah wept bitterly." ~ 2 Kings 20:1-3

Hezekiah was like all of us; totally unprepared for catastrophe. He had been sick, but the news of impending death was overwhelming. He was told to set his house in order. In technological terms he was told to make a backup. If you are familiar with his life you know that God extended his life 15 years, but he still died due to some catastrophic occurrence.

The lesson is simple. Keeping your house in order is the best prevention against catastrophe. And ALWAYS create a backup!

At Wit's End

Have you noticed how much more likely we are to give praise to God when He has delivered us from some storm? It seems that I drift along paying a passing homage to the Lord while the sun shines and the blessing are unfolding regularly.

Consider these thoughts: "Oh, that men would give thanks to the Lord for His goodness, and for His wonderful works to the children of men! Let them exalt Him also in the assembly of the people, and praise Him in the company of the elders." ~ Psalms 107:31-32

He appears to be pleading with us to make it a full part of our lives to be thankful and exalt the name of the Lord publicly. Opportunities abound for us to have an attitude of gratitude. Of course, God can also arrange for us to experience a storm in our quiet and peaceful existence that will bring us to the place of praise. As a matter of fact, that is the very context of these verses.

The Psalmist described the storm like this: "For He commands and raises the stormy wind, which lifts up the waves of the sea. They mount up to the heavens, they go down again to the depths; their soul melts because of trouble. They reel to and fro, and stagger like a drunken man, and are at their wits' end. Then they cry out to the Lord in their trouble, and He brings them out of their distresses. He calms the storm, so that its waves are still. Then they are glad because they are quiet; so He guides them to their desired haven." ~ Psalms 107:25-30

Have you arrived at your wits' end? This is the place where hopes and dreams are swallowed up and despair sets in as our companion. Remember, it is the Lord who raised the wind and lifted the sea. It is God who uses the external to perfect the internal. His desire is to change us from the inside to the outside. Our praise and thanks will not flow from a hardened heart. The word picture of the soul melting is like a softening to the point of it dissolving. The troubles which come our way are not there to punish or to penalize. They are in our lives to perfect our praise and tune our thanksgiving.

As you ride the waves of storminess, remember that the calm will come and you will anchor your soul once again in the haven of rest. That will be a glad day of praise unto the Master of the storm.

Dogfight

A couple of days ago I watched a "dog fight" in a parking lot. No, I am not speaking of two dogs literally fighting one another. I am not even speaking of dogs. The "dog fight" was between a mocking bird and a moth. You are probably totally confused at this moment about this illustration and exactly where I intend to go with it. I don't blame you, but stay with me a bit and it will become clearer.

The *Oxford English Dictionary* gives the origin of the term dogfight. "The term dogfight has been used for centuries to describe a melee; a fierce battle between two or more opponents. The term gained popularity during World War II, although its origin in air combat can be traced to the latter years of World War I. The first written reference to the modern day usage of the word comes from *Fly Papers*, by A. E. Illingworth, in 1919, 'The battle develops into a 'dog-fight', small groups of machines engaging each other in a fight to the death.'"

What I saw in the parking lot was a dogfight between a mocking bird who was desperately trying to have lunch and a moth that was trying to get home to his wife and family. One was in hot pursuit and the other was fleeing for its life. The epic battle that I observed came to mind when I read this verse from First Timothy, "But you, O man of God, flee these things and pursue righteousness, godliness, faith, love, patience, gentleness." ~ 1 Timothy 6:11

We are in a dogfight as believers, but the battle is not with another; it is within ourselves. As in a classic clash between two aircraft or as in my illustration of a mocking bird and a moth, this conflict takes place in very close quarters.

Like the moth, we must flee with all diligence those things which will destroy our fellowship with God and our witness to others. Paul enumerates some of these in the preceding verses: strange doctrine, pride, arguments, chasing after riches, just to name a few.

Like the mocking bird, we are to pursue with faithfulness these things: righteousness, godliness, faith, love, patience, and gentleness. Both the words flee and pursue are written in a tense that demands immediate and continuing action. We are in this dogfight to the end!

I don't know what happened to the moth. If he made it home, he had a great story to tell about fleeing; if he didn't, then the mocking bird had a great story about pursuing.

Will you end this day with a great story?

I hope so…either way it goes for you.

• APRIL

Remember Your History

As Joshua neared the end of his days as the leader of Israel, he opened a discourse with the people about their journeys from Egypt to the Promised Land. Joshua 24 recounts this gathering of Israel to hear Joshua's farewell address. "Then Joshua gathered all the tribes of Israel to Shechem and called for the elders of Israel, for their heads, for their judges, and for their officers; and they presented themselves before God. And Joshua said to all the people, 'Thus says the Lord God of Israel: 'Your fathers, including Terah, the father of Abraham and the father of Nahor, dwelt on the other side of the river in old times; and they served other gods.'" ~ Joshua 24:1-2

These verses are not the most familiar of Joshua 24. Many can repeat the words of the fifteenth verse: "As for me and my house, we will serve the Lord." Many folks have this verse inscribed on a plaque or other wall hanging in their home. But how do you get to verse 15 and its sold-out commitment to serve the Lord. You have to begin where Joshua did with the people that day.

First, it is always good to remember now and again where God found us. I don't think we should dwell there. Paul made it clear that he had put things behind him, but his testimony always rang out clearly the truth of where God had called him. Joshua reminded the people of their history. They were not always the chosen people of God. Their ancestors were born on the other side of the river. In modern terms, they had come from the wrong side of the tracks. There was nothing worthy or extraordinary about their heritage. It was all grace that had brought their forefathers out of pagan worship.

Second, he reminded them of their covenant relationship with God. He declares that the words he speaks come from the God of Israel. They were in the Promised Land because of God's promise not because of their faithfulness. This is an important element for us to seize upon each day. I am who I am and where I am, by the grace of God.

Finally, he reminds them of God's provision. Note Joshua 24:13: "I have given you a land for which you did not labor, and cities which you did not build, and you dwell in them; you eat of the vineyards and olive groves which you did not plant." Here Joshua recalls to them the fact that the land they now possess is in its present condition by someone else's hand.

So, as you make your decision for yourself and your house to serve the Lord, remember how you got here and what keeps you here. It will make your commitment even deeper and your rejoicing even higher.

04/02

Speaking With An Accent

Years ago one of the members in my church became ill and was hospitalized in a northeastern city. I placed a call to the hospital to gather information on the man's condition. The switchboard operator at the hospital was very nice and referred my call promptly to the patient's room.

To my surprise, the man who answered said, "Hello, pastor." I, of course, was shocked that he would know that it was me calling. I inquired as to his ability to guess my identity. He told me that the operator had called the room to make sure that someone in the room was willing to accept a telephone call. I had not given her my name, but she told the patient that a Southern gentleman was on the other end of the line. He then said, "You were the only Southern gentleman that I could think of that would be calling me in the hospital."

My accent had disclosed my identity. It's not easy to separate a person from their heritage. We are who we are and it's difficult to disguise this fact. Paul declared that he had successfully disconnected himself from his heritage. It was not his Hebrew upbringing or his accent that changed, but his connection with the world that had been severed. "But God forbid that I should boast except in the cross of our Lord Jesus Christ, by whom the world has been crucified to me, and I to the world." ~Galatians 6:14

It was the cross that allowed Paul to live a life without a worldly accent. He had already declared in this same letter to the Galatians that it was no longer he that lived, but Christ that lived in him. (Galatians 2:20)

Have you noticed that very few people who take part in commercials speak with an accent? This is no mistake on the producers part. They want to appeal to as many people as possible with little or no stereotyping. Paul had a similar desire to be all things to all people, but he clearly drew the line at acting like the world. He made sure of this by placing the cross of Christ distinctly between himself and the world system.

Ours is not an acting job of disguising our heritage. We are not making a commercial for Jesus. We can be witnesses for Christ in this world even though we might have a strong Southern accent.

Let the cross set the parameter of your life and speak out for Christ every chance you get.

Made Acceptable

I'm not sure if I was the first person, but those who had invited me to their club were shocked when I told them that I did not want to join. It was the Beta Club that I had qualified to be a part of by maintaining an exemplary scholastic average. But I refused to join. I don't really know why. I think it had something to do with being more widely accepted. This club seemed to me at the time to be a hindrance to my goal of acceptance.

I suppose that everybody is a little concerned at times with being accepted. This is perhaps one of the biggest reasons why some people will not attend a church. They fear rejection and thereby create the very thing they thought would occur: non-acceptance.

We carry this idea with us as we approach a relationship with God also. We imagine that God will accept us if we come before Him with our very best side showing. We contrive all sorts of religious antics to prove to Him that we are acceptable in His sight.

The reality is, however, that we have nothing to offer to Him. He is perfect in every way. We are fallen creatures, tainted by the effects of sin, and without hope of repairing ourselves to the point of acceptance.

This is why Jesus came to die for us. He makes us acceptable. So the Apostle Paul declares concerning who we are in Christ, "to the praise of the glory of His grace, by which He made us accepted in the Beloved." ~ Ephesians 1:6

Therein lies our hope of acceptance. We have not become acceptable because we have done anything. We have not performed at a certain level. Our spiritual grades did not average correctly. He MADE us accepted in Christ.

All who come to Christ by simple faith are accepted. From that moment on, God no longer sees us in our imperfection, but sees the perfection of Christ wrapped around us by His work of grace.

Acceptance in Christ is not like an invitation to join the Beta Club. My rejection of that invitation cost me nothing in the long run. Rejection of Christ has eternal consequences.

I'm inviting you today to be accepted. All who come in faith are guaranteed acceptance in the Beloved. Welcome to the club!

The Present Truth

I have the uncanny ability to remember many tidbits of information that are for the most part of no value to anyone else. These memories often come rushing forth and form a launching pad for one of my daily devotions.

I have a better recollection of the good things than I do the bad, though the dark memories will invade from time to time as well. It was the 15th century philosopher Leon Battista who said, "A well-trained memory is one that permits you to forget everything that isn't worth remembering." My memory is not that well trained, but I do try to focus on the good things that have occurred in my life.

The Apostle Peter was in a mode of recollection as he neared the end of his journey here on earth. In his second letter he speaks of encouraging his fellow believers to be active rememberers. "For this reason I will not be negligent to remind you always of these things, though you know and are established in the present truth." ~ 2 Peter 1:12

The best place to start a good memory is in the here and now. Peter told his readers that his intent was to first remind them of that which they presently know. This is excellent advice for us all. Cling tightly to the truth that you know already lest it becomes buried under the overload of information that pours into our lives daily.

Peter continues his focus on remembering the truth by declaring that as long as he lived he would be busy reminding others of the truth. There is a tendency for us to fabricate the truth the further we move from the actual occurrence of it. How many times have you told a story from childhood as true, only to discover later in life that it never happened as you imagined?

We need to be retelling the story over and again to all who will hear us. Begin with your children and grandchildren. Continue to stretch the links to the truth until you have recounted to everyone how it actually happened. I am speaking, of course, of the story of our salvation and the finished work of Christ on the cross.

Not only did Peter intend his readers to know the truth in the present, but he concluded that they should have a constant reminder even after his decease. His concern was that the story never change over time.

When I am gone, I certainly hope to be remembered. But more than that, I hope that folks remember my Savior, the One who changed my life forever.

That's my story and I'm sticking to it! How about you?

Saved By a Tree

As I looked out the window of the vehicle, the next stop was several thousand feet down. The tree now resting against my door was holding us precariously to the side of the mountain. Here's how the story unfolded.

Jasmine lives in the village of Tesanj (pronounced *Teshan*) in the northern part of Bosnia. Each time we visited him he would insist that we go with him to the top of the mountain to see his getaway. It was nothing fancy. Just a block building where some of his friends would spend weekends. It was a Bosnian man cave.

The road, if you could call it that, to the top was treacherous. It was washed out in several places and nothing less than a four wheel drive vehicle could make the journey. As we crept up the incline, we struck a particularly rough spot where water had coursed a deep rut across the path. The vehicle lurched sideways and deposited us at a steep angle against a small sapling. That little tree was our savior. The next stop was a long rolling way to the bottom of the mountain.

I'm not sure how many times God has delivered me from death, but this was certainly one of them. I can join with the psalmist in proclaiming "For You have delivered my soul from death, my eyes from tears, and my feet from falling." ~ Psalms 116:8

This particular psalm begins with deliverance from death and concludes just a few verses later by saying that the death of a saint is precious in the eyes of the Lord. Imagine that! We win whether there is a sapling to catch us or not!

Now I am glad to be here. I rejoice in the fact that I did not spend my last moments in life tumbling down a mountainside. But I know that it would have been alright if God had chosen to take me home that way.

In between these statements about death and deliverance the psalmist asks a question, "What shall I render to the Lord for all His benefits toward me?"~Psalms 116:12 The question is not asked believing that he could ever fully repay God for all He had done. The word render holds the idea of returning, but not to the starting place. We simply could not ever repay God for we can never fully know all that He had done for us.

I was delivered by a tiny tree that suspended me from ultimate harm. That day I saw the hand of God; many days His hand is there and I just don't see it.

Why not take a moment right now and thank Him for deliverances both seen and unseen? Thank God for things like saplings that can become our saviors.

Disguising the Gospel

Underwear is certainly a strange subject to consider for a devotion. Actually, it is not the underwear, but the selling thereof, which I speak.

I have told you from time to time of my days in the grocery business. To understand my grocery store you must get the vision of a multi-aisled supermarket out of your mind. My store was deep in the rural parts of the parish (that's county for everyone not from Louisiana).

The legal name of my business was Clark's General Merchandise. I sold everything from fresh vegetables to cattle feed. I hand sliced bacon and if I wasn't too busy inside, I would pump your gas for you. The signage read Clark's A.G. Grocery, but I always sold general merchandise. That gets me back to the underwear.

I got a great deal once on men's underwear. So, I bought a few cases and set up a display right next to the ice cream case. There was no connection between ice cream and underwear. It was just the only open floor space I had.

Needless to say, I sold all of the underwear super-fast. It was amazing how a display of men's underwear in a grocery store caught so much attention. But then again, why not? It was so out of place that it could not be ignored.

As Paul traveled about on his missionary journeys, he carried with him the message of the gospel. This revolutionary good news was sweeping the known world. Thousands were accepting the truth that Jesus saves and their lives were being radically changed. But like all successful ventures some will attempt to replace the original with a substitute and offer it as an alternative.

Paul's second letter to the Corinthians addressed those who were marketing the novelty of the gospel, but not the full unadulterated truth of it. He wrote, "For we are not, as so many, peddling the word of God; but as of sincerity, but as from God, we speak in the sight of God in Christ." ~ 2 Corinthians 2:17

We are in a time where offering the staple of the gospel message is not so appealing. Many are trying to disguise the gospel or otherwise water it down. Some try to display it like underwear next to an ice cream counter. But the gospel is good news. It doesn't need a new wrapper. It can't be improved. It is the truth and its display is accented by the light of heaven.

We are not gospel peddlers. We are not hawking heaven's hardware. We need only offer it to all, knowing that some will accept it freely.

Obedience...In Spite Of

Plans have a way of changing.

I began my first pastorate with every intention of remaining there for the rest of my life. Three and one-half years later God moved my family and I to a church in Oklahoma.

The life of a preacher goes something like this: You surrender your plans to His design. You go where and when God directs. You can expect the blessings of God to be found, but you can expect obstacles also.

When I drove out of the parsonage driveway everything my family owned was in the back of a rented U-haul. Our possessions were once again reduced to the capacity of a truck body. I sensed I was fully in God's will, yet the obstacles began immediately. Within the first hour of travel, the truck broke down abandoning us on the highway. The repairs took hours and only lasted for another few miles down the road. U-haul towed the truck and we spent two nights less than two hours away from where our journey had begun.

All of our goods were trans-loaded to another truck by men who had no concern for a lifetime of gathering. Upon arrival we discovered missing boxes, broken furniture, and scratched appliances.

My youngest child was less than one month old. Time, distance, and cold rainy weather left him ill. Not long after arriving he was diagnosed with pneumonia. Sounds like fun, doesn't it?

Now imagine the apprehension in the children of Israel as they camped on the edge of the promised land. The spies returned with this news: "'We went to the land where you sent us. It truly flows with milk and honey, and this is its fruit. Nevertheless the people who dwell in the land are strong; the cities are fortified and very large; moreover we saw the descendants of Anak there.'" ~ Numbers 13:27-28 Do you see it? It was a land of milk and honey and GIANTS!

When we obey God it is only natural to assume that everything will be milk and honey. But the truth is, there will be giants in the land also. Obstacles will arise that will threaten our commitment to follow Him wherever He leads.

The children of Israel only faced giants as they moved forward into the promised land. They never faced giants retreating into the wilderness. This is not a description of life set aside just for preachers of the gospel. God calls all believers to walk in a state of ready obedience.

So, load up!

Why The Fence?

Never tear down a fence until you find out why it was built.

It's an old saying, but it sure sounds like a good idea to me. Somebody at some point in time must have thought it was necessary. A time may come to tear it down, but it might be the perfect time to strengthen it, raise it higher, and make sure that the fence continues to serve its purpose.

David may not have had a fence in mind when he wrote what we know as the 40th Psalm, but his words hold a clear picture of a fence securely in place. He said, "Do not withhold Your tender mercies from me, O Lord; let Your lovingkindness and Your truth continually preserve me." ~ Psalms 40:11

This psalm begins with David rejoicing that he had been saved from a horrible pit. This deep hole in the ground would have been used to extract the clay used for pottery and other sculptures. It was dark, damp, and its sides so slick that a man who was found at the bottom without a rope or ladder would not be able to rescue himself.

I must wonder if David's thoughts about that horrible pit brought forth from his heart the plea that God would preserve him from ever falling therein again. He prayed, "Let Your lovingkindness and Your truth preserve me."

These words form the picture of a fence protecting someone from ever falling into the pit. Consider them in reverse and the picture becomes even clearer. The word *truth* holds the idea of stability. Truth is like the fence posts. Without truth it will not matter what material you use for the fencing. The fence cannot withstand the elements without sturdy upright supports.

Lovingkindness is the material used to create the fence. Most fences are built with the pretty side facing outward. No one sees the posts. Lovingkindness represents the beauty, favor, and mercy of God.

The next time you see a fence, stop and ask why it was built before you start tearing it down or climbing over it. There may be a deep, slimy, horrible pit on the other side. May God in His lovingkindness keep us on the right side of the fence of truth.

The Evidence of Unforgiveness

I carried the slip of paper in my wallet for months. It was a cash register receipt with a person's name scribbled across the back of it. I have forgotten the exact total printed on the receipt. I think it was $27 and some change. I also remember the day I removed it from my wallet, crumpled it, and threw it away. That was the day I was set free.

The receipt was for a bill of groceries that had been purchased. The lady whose signature was written on the back had promised to pay me for the groceries on a certain date. Not only did she not pay, she quit shopping in my business. I carried that slip of paper in my wallet, but it was like a weight around my neck. Each time I saw her at some other store shopping, another pound was added to that little piece of paper.

The amazing thing was that the day I destroyed the evidence of the debt, I never saw the lady again. That was over 35 years ago. As far as I know, I've never seen her again to this day.

Unforgiveness is like that slip of paper in my wallet. It did not affect the lady who had charged the groceries or promised to repay—it was my burden of debt until I laid it to rest.

King David was a man after God's own heart, yet he struggled with sin and unforgiveness in his life. He was overcome with happiness when his sin was forgiven. "Blessed is he whose transgression is forgiven, whose sin is covered. Blessed is the man to whom the Lord does not impute iniquity, and in whose spirit there is no deceit." ~ Psalms 32:1-2

Sometimes we carry the slips of others in our pockets; sometimes the name scribbled on the charge receipt is our own. We all need to be forgiven. We all need to forgive. In either case, unforgiveness becomes an anchor dragging down our souls.

Marghanita Laski was one of England's best-known secular humanists and novelists. A few days before she died in 1988, she noted in a television interview, "What I envy most about you Christians is your forgiveness; I have nobody to forgive me."

God is ready to forgive. His wallet is empty. The receipt with your name on it was nailed to the cross.

Now go forth and forgive—it's time to empty your wallet.

Up the Down Escalator

My brother and I were lost. We were not desperately lost; just lost. We were not in the forest or some strange location, but we were lost. We were lost and we did not even know it. We were lost and our mother was looking for us.

We had gotten lost in the new Sears and Roebuck store. Most of you do not remember the "Roebuck" part of this department store's name unless you are as old as me. It was a two story building. We had asked our mother if we could go and look at the most amazing thing we had ever seen. I can still remember us standing there marveling at the shiny set of moving stairs. We were totally enamored as we watched people ascending on the escalator.

Of course, curiosity soon got the best of us and looking was not enough. We had to take a quick ride for ourselves. Little did we know that once we got to the top floor that the down escalator was located in another section of the store.

Hence, we were soon lost; not because we did not find the down escalator, but because our mother began her search for us evidently about the same time we had ascended. As she ascended, we were descending on the down escalator. This began an up and down search, as mama went down, we were on our next ride up on the greatest invention we had ever seen. Our mother was worried. We were just having a fun time on a ride that didn't cost us a penny. She was searching for us; not the other way around.

We were lost and didn't have the sense to know it. Many are like that today. Just enjoying what they think is a free ride, but all the while lost. You may be one of the lost ones. Stop the joy riding and begin your search for the only One who can save you. God says, "And you will seek Me and find Me, when you search for Me with all your heart." ~ Jeremiah 29:13

Did you know that there are five times as many verses in the Bible that speak about finding than there are those that refer to searching? God had made Himself extremely easy to find. Seek Him with your whole heart and you will find Him immediately.

If my brother and I had just stopped riding the escalator our mother would have found us quickly. If you will stop for just a moment today, you will find God faithfully waiting, because He alone knows your every up and down.

Falling Into Disrepair

My journeys have taken me far and wide. A lot of the miles I have traveled along highways and byways in an automobile. You get a totally different perspective of the landscape while traveling in this manner. Unlike traveling by air, you see the scars of time painted along the roadside as you study life through a windshield.

One of the sights I sometimes come across is an abandoned home site. What surely was once a beautiful place to live has been overtaken by the ravages of time. Lack of care has brought down once strong buildings. Roofs are caved in and trees now protrude through places where windows once guarded against the cold wind. You have to wonder how it all happened. When did someone no longer care enough? What tragedy caused the owners to disregard the inevitable march of time?

We must be just as careful in the upkeep of our hearts and minds. There is a constant threat of deterioration that swirls around us. Left to ourselves, we quickly fall into disrepair. We all have the potential of being like an old homestead abandoned to the elements.

The good news is that God had planted in the heart of man a moral law that cannot be denied. Paul spoke of this in his letter to the Romans: "…who show the work of the law written in their hearts, their conscience also bearing witness, and between themselves their thoughts accusing or else excusing them…" ~ Romans 2:15

All mankind has a moral conscience and without this basis for knowing what is right and wrong everything collapses like an old barn left to the wind and rain. Why then doesn't everyone take care of their own hearts, minds, and souls? Wouldn't we be better off if everyone did?

The answers to these questions and others like them can only be resolved when a person admits the full effect of sin in the human life. Sin only destroys. It brings ruin and decay. It leaves testimony of lives once lived in joy and hope, but now abandoned and dilapidated.

Turn the keys of your life over to Jesus today. He alone can maintain your life against the storm of sin and degradation. Not only can He prevent you from becoming an abandoned shell of your former self; He can restore your life to livability. Surrender the deed of your life into His hand today.

How Big Is Your Cup?

It is very easy to get distracted by a world that operates in numbers that start with a "t." You and I have a difficult time even wrapping our minds around a trillion. If you count really fast you might be able to count up to 200 in a minute. Then if you had the stamina to keep counting at the same rate it would take you 9500 years to count to one trillion. With trillions being thrown about like confetti it is easy to get sidetracked.

David put his life in perspective because he did not focus on the world around him, but on the heaven above him. He said, "O Lord, You are the portion of my inheritance and my cup; You maintain my lot. The lines have fallen to me in pleasant places; yes, I have a good inheritance. I will bless the Lord who has given me counsel; my heart also instructs me in the night seasons. I have set the Lord always before me; because He is at my right hand I shall not be moved. Therefore my heart is glad, and my glory rejoices; my flesh also will rest in hope." ~ Psalms 16:5-9

Notice how David measured his life. He began by confessing that the Lord was the portion by which his inheritance was determined. Imagine that! David did not use any measure found on the earth; he let the Lord be the size of his cup.

It is one thing to receive an inheritance; it is another to keep it. David concluded that his inheritance came from the Lord, but his inheritance would also be maintained by God. What a blessing! He declared that God Himself would sustain the value of all David possessed. But it gets even better…

Where some might gain a huge inheritance, how many would then find their life ruined by the riches? David answers this dilemma. He announces that it is the same Lord that gives and maintains which also gives counsel. No sleep is lost over wealth for God instructs in the night as well. My old uncle used to say that he never lost sleep due to worry. The way he figured it, God never slumbers nor sleeps, so why should both of them stay up.

David concluded that he simply would not be moved with God at his side. He would be glad and rest in hope. By the way, if David had started counting to a trillion in his day and was still alive and counting today, he would still have over 600 billion to go! Quit counting and trust the One who maintains your life.

Go Ahead...Taste It

Sometimes it's a good thing to revisit. You can revisit an old friend that you haven't seen in a while or visit a vacation spot once again. I have left a problem or concern unsolved only to revisit it and see the answer almost immediately.

Today I'm going to revisit a previous devotion that I wrote many months ago. It spoke to me in a brand new way today. I hope it does you as well. By the way, this devotion and others like it are available in my devotional, *Glasses in the Grass: Devotions for My Friends*. Get your copy here: http://amzn.to/155MYoI

Good is a very small word, but have you ever looked it up in the dictionary? It has a very big definition. We use the word good all the time. We can have a good time, eat good food, see a good movie, or go to a good friend's home. What does God have to say about good?

The Psalmist stated it this way. "Oh, taste and see that the Lord is good; blessed is the man who trusts in Him! Oh, fear the Lord, you His saints! There is no want to those who fear Him. The young lions lack and suffer hunger; but those who seek the Lord shall not lack any good thing." ~ Psalm 34:8 10

Scripture makes a couple of interesting comparisons here as we think about what is good. First, finding the goodness of the Lord involves trust. The Psalmist tells us that we can show our trust by tasting. This is a great illustration. How many times has someone offered you a taste of something with the assurance of these words, "Go ahead, taste it...it's good!" No one has ever suggested that I should taste something because it tasted awful.

The second comparison has to do with the satisfaction that comes from having good things. Here the verse compares those who seek the Lord to the young lions. The young lions in the pride get the leftovers after the dominant males have had their fill. God says that those who seek the Lord shall lack no good thing. We are not subject to the rules of the pride. We do not find ourselves making do with leftovers.

What a promise! But here's the caution! Don't define good with a worldly definition. God's good for you may not always appear as such at the moment, but it never fails to reveal His eternal purpose for your life. Have a *good* day!

Unsinkable

On April 14, 1911, just minutes before midnight the Titanic struck an iceberg. This magnificent piece of engineering slipped beneath the icy waters of the north Atlantic in less than three hours. Estimates are that on April 15, 1911 at least 1514 persons entered eternity in the wee hours of that day. To date this is the most people ever lost at sea in a single incident.

One cannot help but think what these travelers faced in those last minutes. How many held sharp regrets over the life they had lived? How many gave their spots in a life boat because their eternity was settled? How many cried out for mercy in the waning moments of life and found Christ faithful to save to the uttermost? Questions like these will never be answered on this side of eternity and these same questions won't matter on the other side.

As the cold waters enveloped those who were believers on that dark night, what did they see when they awoke on the other side of this life? I must believe that they saw just what John saw in his vision from the Isle of Patmos.

"Then I turned to see the voice that spoke with me. And having turned I saw seven golden lampstands, and in the midst of the seven lampstands One like the Son of Man, clothed with a garment down to the feet and girded about the chest with a golden band. His head and hair were white like wool, as white as snow, and His eyes like a flame of fire; His feet were like fine brass, as if refined in a furnace, and His voice as the sound of many waters; He had in His right hand seven stars, out of His mouth went a sharp two-edged sword, and His countenance was like the sun shining in its strength. And when I saw Him, I fell at His feet as dead. But He laid His right hand on me, saying to me, "Do not be afraid; I am the First and the Last. I am He who lives, and was dead, and behold, I am alive forevermore. Amen. And I have the keys of Hades and of Death." ~ Revelation 1:12-18

Imagine that! From darkness to the light of seven lampstands; from cold to the warmth of His eyes like a flame of fire; from the sound of rushing water filling a sinking ship to the sound of His voice like a flood of grace and mercy; from the weakness of hypothermia to the strength of His right hand; from the fear that death's grip lays on us all to the assuring words, "Be not afraid!"

Those who slipped to watery graves that night saw Jesus high and lifted up as the One who lives forevermore. He was there at the first and at the last, because He is Alpha and Omega, the beginning and the end. Never sail without Him.

If you have never trusted Him as Savior, do so today…ICEBERG! Right ahead!

More Than A Zettabyte

Recess in the library is probably not what most kids would think of as fun. I spent lots of recesses in the library; especially when I had a question. And I always had lots of questions!

For me, the library held all the answers. When an adult would not give me what I thought was a straight answer, I would head for the books. I have often wondered just how weird I would be if I would have had the Internet to access with the push of a button.

The first hard drive I purchased for my computer was 20 megabytes. You read that correctly! Hard drives today regularly surpass a terabyte. These storage devices are over 5000 times bigger that my 1980's device. I can still remember how remarkable I thought my hard drive was and the assumption that I would never need to purchase anything larger.

George Gilder wrote in a 2008 article about the future of data storage that by 2015 we would face a zettabyte flood. He missed it by a little bit. The National Security Agency is building a facility that will house 5 zettabytes of information. This facility will be able to hold the contents of all the information in the Library of Congress repeated over 250 times!

Yet with all of this data, one would still be unable to answer the questions asked by one of Job's friends. "Can you search out the deep things of God? Can you find out the limits of the Almighty?" ~ Job 11:7

Job's friends were not well meaning in their questioning, but God used their challenges to reveal some amazing truths about Himself. This friend, as much as he can be called such, asked Job two questions that leave us with but one answer. No, we absolutely cannot understand the deep things of God nor determine the extent of which God exists.

The idea of searching out the deep things of God is one of enumerating. It would be like making tally marks; one for each concept or truth about God that we could think or imagine. Suppose we could mark down a zettabyte of facts about God. How many tally marks would that be? You would have a number represented by 10 with 21 zeroes following it! If you thought of one fact a second, it would take you 31 trillion years to think of a zettabyte of unique concepts about God!

If you plan on finding out the limits of who God is, you had better get started now or just admit that all of your questions will never be answered—not even if you spend every recess in the library.

Porch Swing Banking

I have never personally known many men who would be considered rich with this world's goods. I know they are out there and that their riches have surpassed any possibility of my achievement in this life. This does not make me feel slighted in the least, nor do I begrudge their success. I am blessed beyond measure and have no complaints.

My daddy told me a story many years ago about a man he knew. He was, as the story went, the richest man in town. My dad arranged a loan from this man to help meet a shortfall in his life. The man instructed daddy to come to his home at a certain hour and the money would be in a brown bag on the porch swing. No papers to sign, no lawyers to pay, just two men making an agreement. Repayment was to be monthly in the same manner. My father left each month's note in a brown bag on the porch swing in front of this rich man's house.

Let me repeat, I don't know anybody like that, but I do know how rich my Father in Heaven is and how much of His riches He laid down because of His love for me. "But God, who is rich in mercy, because of His great love with which He loved us, even when we were dead in trespasses, made us alive together with Christ (by grace you have been saved), and raised us up together, and made us sit together in the heavenly places in Christ Jesus, that in the ages to come He might show the exceeding riches of His grace in His kindness toward us in Christ Jesus." ~ Ephesians 2:4-7

God is rich beyond measure in His mercy and those riches cannot be measured with dollar signs, but in the value of His love for us. And it only gets better! God arranged to give His riches to us while we were yet dead in sin and trespasses. He then made us alive in His Son Jesus. He then lifted us out of our spiritual poverty and gave us equal status with Christ. And even more than we have experienced is yet to be revealed in the endless ages to come!

Our rich God did not provide all of this in a mysterious transaction of brown paper bags on porch swings. He did it openly on a cruel cross in public view for all the world to see! Truly, I don't personally know any super rich folks, but I have been adopted into God's family where all that is His is mine. It can be yours too! Join me today in a living relationship with Jesus and experience riches untold!

Unexpected Falls

One moment I was standing; the next I was flat on my backside. Worse than the fact of my fall was the reality that my stupidity had all been recorded.

My "accident" occurred in Colorado many years ago. Being from the deep South, I had little to no experience in walking on icy surfaces. I was sure that I was walking carefully, but I was fooled concerning my footing. I still remember zipping my jacket and placing my hands in my pockets to guard against the cold. The next step was my undoing. As my feet went out from under me and with my hands secured deeply in my pockets, it was a micro-moment from vertical to horizontal.

Of course, all of this was being recorded for perpetuity. That home movie is still around the house somewhere. My kids wanted to send it to *America's Funniest Home Videos*; I did not.

We all have moments that get recorded in our minds. Many of these seem to be like the Boston Marathon bombing. The tragedy and horror cause the scenes to be burned into our memories. We mark these moments in time and space. We are able to remember exactly where we were and what we were doing when these historical moments transpired.

When tragic events occur we need to find a way to bring balance back to our lives. The word of God supplies us with the ability to right ourselves again after the unexpected fall. The Bible can help us frame times like these.

Jesus said, "But why do you call Me 'Lord, Lord,' and not do the things which I say? Whoever comes to Me, and hears My sayings and does them, I will show you whom he is like: He is like a man building a house, who dug deep and laid the foundation on the rock. And when the flood arose, the stream beat vehemently against that house, and could not shake it, for it was founded on the rock." ~ Luke 6:46-48

We must understand that the storms will come. We simply will never be able to stop them. The floods of hatred are here and they come roaring into our lives in a flash. Since we cannot prevent the onslaught of terror, we must do what we can. Dig deep and find the bedrock for a foundation that cannot be shaken.

Only when our foundation is sure will we be able to face the unexpected falls of life. When the storms come, don't listen to the thunder; listen for the voice of God. The difference between ruin and resilience is found in the hearing and doing of God's word.

God Cares

Sometimes it is easy to feel a little boxed in by this life. This world is not our home as believers and we can begin to feel like prisoners with no hope of escape. But God had extended His grace and peace toward us that we might have the hope of deliverance.

Paul tells us in Galatians, "Grace to you and peace from God the Father and our Lord Jesus Christ, who gave Himself for our sins, that He might deliver us from this present evil age, according to the will of our God and Father, to whom be glory forever and ever. Amen." ~ Galatians 1:3-5

The story is told of a Frenchman named Charney who was put into a dungeon by Napoleon. He was forsaken by his friends and forgotten by everyone. In loneliness and despair he made a pen of a stone and scratched on the wall of his cell, "Nobody cares."

Time passed and one day a green shoot pierced one of the cracks in the stone floor of the dungeon. It began to reach up toward the light in the tiny window at the top of the cell. Charney reserved drops of the water brought to him each day and poured it on the tiny plant. It grew until at last it became mature and brought forth a beautiful blue flower.

As the petals opened in full blossom, he crossed out the words previously written on the wall and above them scratched, "God cares." News of Charney's little plant touched the heart of the Empress Josephine, who persuaded the emperor to set him free.

We too will be delivered from this worldly prison one day soon. It will not be because we cared for a lonely plant or because of the kindness of an earthly ruler. Our deliverance will come because it is God's will to do so. With the voice of the archangel and the sound of the trumpet we shall be caught up into His presence.

This is the literal meaning of the word deliver. We will be rescued, plucked from this prison and like the old song says, "Like a bird from prison bars has flown, I'll fly away!" No matter the height of your prison wall scratch these words deeply upon its surface:

GOD CARES AND WILL DELIVER!

Tying Up Loose Ends

Have you ever spent time tying up loose ends? You know what I mean…taking care of little things that never got fully finished or other things that just got put on the back burner. We all must do this from time to time, but there are spiritual matters that must be finished also.

In First Peter we read, "Therefore gird up the loins of your mind, be sober, and rest your hope fully upon the grace that is to be brought to you at the revelation of Jesus Christ;" ~ 1 Peter 1:13 Since this verse begins with the word "therefore" we need to determine what it's there for. Peter had just reminded his readers that their faith would be tried, but their faith would take them to the end with no loose ends left untied. "In this you greatly rejoice, though now for a little while, if need be, you have been grieved by various trials, that the genuineness of your faith, being much more precious than gold that perishes, though it is tested by fire, may be found to praise, honor, and glory at the revelation of Jesus Christ, whom having not seen you love. Though now you do not see Him, yet believing, you rejoice with joy inexpressible and full of glory, receiving the end of your faith—the salvation of your souls." ~ 1 Peter 1:6-9

We are to tie up the loose ends of our minds as it relates to our faith. The first loop in this knot is to be sober. This has nothing to do with drunkenness. It means to keep our minds within moral boundaries. The second knot used to tie up our loose ends is to rest in the hope of His grace. Resting holds the idea of setting our hope wholly and unchangeably on the grace of God.

This is an act of faith based on the promise of His second coming. Peter tells us that we believe that which we cannot see. This is the essence of faith. But we rejoice as if we have received the end of our faith—the salvation of our souls. And this my friend is joy unspeakable and full of glory!

Less Than Perfect

Several of my friends and I worked together on a project for our high school literature class. We had received permission to complete the project as a group. We clearly understood that we would receive a grade on our work as a whole. Everyone had to depend on each other to pass the test.

We chose to recreate the home of Silas Marner, the main character in the book titled the same, and written by George Eliot. We built the scaled down home in my driveway and then transferred it into the back of Mrs. Speight's classroom.

We had all the features of a real home. Walls, doors, windows, thatched roof, and furniture. We even had installed a chimney. That's where we lost some points in our final grade.

While we were building the house one of us moved a vehicle and ran over our cardboard chimney. The tire imprinted a perfect tread imprint down the length of the chimney.

Short on time, we painted over it, turned it towards the rear of the house and assumed that it would never be noticed. We were one set of proud boys. I still remember going to the school on that Sunday afternoon and reconstructing the house in the back of the class.

On Monday morning there sat Silas Marner in his house, counting his gold pieces at his kitchen table. Everyone marveled at our ability to get such a structure inside the classroom, including Mrs. Speights.

A few days later, we received our grade—a 97%. We could not believe that we had not received a perfect score. We had poured our hearts into this project. Mrs. Speights, however, discovered the tire track imprint on the back side of the chimney. She deducted three points.

Thankfully we serve a God that is working to eradicate all of the tire tracks of life from us. David said, "The Lord will perfect that which concerns me; Your mercy, O Lord, endures forever; do not forsake the works of Your hands." ~ Psalms 138:8

We will receive a perfect score one day. Not because we built a perfect house, but because we trusted a perfect Savior. As God looks at us, He will see us through His perfect Son, Jesus Christ.

Don't try to paint over the tracks that have been left upon your life. Don't try to tuck them away out of sight. Believe me, if Mrs. Speights could find them, God surely can. Thank God for His perfecting mercy!

04/21

When Disaster Strikes

When tragedy strikes it seems to squeeze out of us what is really at our core. This has certainly been true as the events of the last few years have unfolded before our eyes. No matter how close or far removed you might have been to the bombings at the Boston Marathon, the collapse of the World Trade Center, or a myriad of other events, each affects us all in deep, lasting ways.

I, like so many others, have found myself glued to the media reports. In this world of instant reporting, we are wafted away and dropped into the battle zone whether we wish to be there or not. It is in all of this instantaneous reporting that we often get a view into the responses of those who are living out the news in their own backyards. I am amazed at the wide specter of responses that come pouring out of people. Some fall to their knees and begin to pray as we saw in footage from the bombing site while others have the audio portion of their videos bleeped out just to be able to play them on the airwaves.

The book of Job unfolds like the scenes of a tragic explosion. Families are ripped apart; possessions are vaporized; and disease disrupts the ability to cope. Job experienced not just a week of tragedy, but month upon month of disaster as he witnessed a lifetime of faithful service race away from him like sand falling through an hour glass.

Imagine, if you will, a reporter interviewing Job about all that had transpired. His possessions had been obliterated by storms; his children had all died; his body was riddled with burning boils; and his wife was demanding that he turn his back on God and all that He represented.

The reporter asks the question that we all want answered, "How are you holding up, Mr. Job, with all that has happened to you?" Job's answer needs no editing. Nothing has to be bleeped out to air it on the evening news. Job lifts his eyes toward heaven and says, "For He performs what is appointed for me, and many such things are with Him." ~ Job 23:14

And we sit fixated on his every word. How can a person go through such tragedy and still give God all the glory? Only when you have a personal relationship with the God who holds all in His hands is this possible.

A loving wife from East Baton Rouge parish, known only by the initials L.F., wrote this last stanza of a poem to her husband as he fought in the Civil War:

> Then go to him with praying heart,
> Oh! be but faithful on your part,
> To God and to yourselves be true,
> Your battles he will fight for you.

The poem is dated March 5, 1862. What was true in 1862 is still true today. When tragedy comes your way, what will be squeezed out of you? Now is the time to determine your answer.

What's That I Smell?

Of the five senses there is none stronger than the sense of smell. How many times have you smelled the slightest hint of an aroma and long forgotten memories are stirred? The sense of smell quickly attracts or repels us according to how pleasant or unpleasant the scent is.

The Apostle Paul spoke of our scent as Christians. "Now thanks be to God who always leads us in triumph in Christ, and through us diffuses the fragrance of His knowledge in every place. For we are to God the fragrance of Christ among those who are being saved and among those who are perishing." ~ 2 Corinthians 2:14-15 We are like the reeds that are used to diffuse scented oil into a room. The reed is used because of its design. The cellular structure of each reed divides it into 20 or so tubes. Like micro-straws the oil is drawn up through the reed and evaporates into the air filling the room with scent. The reed works because there is nothing blocking the flow of the oil.

What does God do in our lives to promote the flow of His scent up, through, and out of our lives? These verses give us the answer. God leads us into triumph in Christ. We literally break out into a celebration of victory and from that celebration the fragrance of Jesus is diffused through us. To believers it is the sweet smell of victory and life, but to the unbeliever it is the smell of death and defeat.

Is your life filled with the scent of Christ? Is it easy for folks to know whose you are? If not, remember the fault lies not in the fragrant oil, but in us as the diffusing reed. Something must be preventing the oil from flowing freely up, through, and out of us. Try this. Begin singing the words of this old favorite hymn. "Oh, victory in Jesus, my Savior forever! He sought me and He bought me with His redeeming blood. He loved me 'ere I knew Him and all my love is due Him. He plunged me to victory beneath the cleansing flood!"

There now! I can sense the sweet fragrance of Christ flowing freely from you already. Go! And make your world smell like Jesus today!

In The Cross of Christ I Glory

Music has never been one of my strengths. Not only do I struggle to carry a tune, I have little desire to invest much time with it. For a long time I owned one CD. I kept it in my vehicle and would listen to it from time to time. My solo CD was a big joke around the house.

Music is just fine; I just lack an aptitude for it. I can still remember taking those generic tests in school to help a student realize what their strengths and weaknesses are. I don't remember what scale was used for scoring, but I do remember my score in music. I rated a whopping one point.

Even though I am not musically inclined, every now and again I come across a piece that really speaks to me. Many of those that grasp my attention are several hundred years old. Perhaps my vocal chords are just time warped.

The song that recently caught my attention was written in 1825 by John Bowring. The tune for the words was written 26 years later in 1851. One interesting fact is that the tune is named for a lady named Beriah Rathbun.

This lady was the only soprano that showed up for choir one particular Sunday. Mr. Ithamar Conkey, the choir director, went home discouraged, but in the midst of that discouragement found hope in the words of the hymn, In the Cross of Christ I Glory. He wrote a tune for it and named it after Mrs. Rathbun.

The song is based on Galatians 6:14, "But God forbid that I should boast except in the cross of our Lord Jesus Christ, by whom the world has been crucified to me, and I to the world." ~ Galatians 6:14

Here are the words of that old hymn. I hope they bless you today.

> In the cross of Christ I glory,
>   Tow'ring o'er the wrecks of time;
> All the light of sacred story
>   Gathers round its head sublime.
> When the woes of life o'ertake me,
>   Hopes deceive, and fears annoy,
> Never shall the cross forsake me,
>   Lo! It glows with peace and joy.
> When the sun of bliss is beaming
>   Light and love upon my way,
> From the cross the radiance streaming
>   Adds more luster to the day.
> Bane and blessing, pain and pleasure,
>   By the cross are sanctified;
> Peace is there that knows no measure,
>   Joys that through all time abide.

Defenders of the Innocent

When our country is attacked, we usually take ownership of the attack as a nation. This is a good thing, since we are the United States of America. There is, however, more than just a patriotic response to attacks which have occurred. We must be careful to not only respond to these attacks out of our own strength and resilience. If we are not sensitive to God's hand at work, we will attempt to shake these episodes off and all of us will pick up slogans which dare to expound our own perceived strength. We will be saying things like, "American Strong", but our real strength lies beyond ourselves.

Now before you start declaring me unpatriotic or uncaring, please hear what I have to say. Although we should make a strong stand against those who try to harm us, we should not let some sense of our own self-reliance hide what God is saying to us as a nation through these incidents.

It is clearly evident that we, as a nation, have turned away from the Lord. We reel in horror at the death of those killed at the marathon, while we dismiss a doctor who left breathing babies to die after botched abortions. For those little ones, being wrenched from their mother's wombs was just as much an act of terror as a bomb exploding at the feet of unsuspecting spectators.

My only question is, "Where are the defenders of the truly innocent?" There is no greater sense of being strong than when we protect those who have no strength.

It is fine to hold up a sign saying, "American Strong", but we will never really be strong until our self-reliance ends. Oswald Chambers said: Complete weakness is always the occasion of the Spirit of God manifesting His power. The Apostle Paul said, "I can do all things through Christ who strengthens me." ~ Philippians 4:13 Jesus said, "I am the vine, you are the branches. He who abides in Me, and I in him, bears much fruit; for without Me you can do nothing." ~ John 15:5

America, it is time to realize that the real terror is not a bomb blast. The real terror is a nation that forgets that their real strength lies not within themselves, but in their God.

"Blessed is the nation whose God is the Lord, The people He has chosen as His own inheritance." ~ Psalms 33:12

Holding God's Hand

Anyone who has held the hand of a child can relate to the moment of pure reliance that comes in that simple act. A tiny hand enveloped by the hand of an adult provides a sense of safety and security to the one whose hand is being held.

As children grow they come to the time when they decide that they want to hold your hand. The act is prompted by their own will, but the reality is not changed. They can never really hold our hand. Our size and strength always tips the scale toward us. Even though they initiate the act, it is the adult that does the holding.

God spoke to the children of Israel as He promised their ultimate restoration. The picture quickly develops of an adult holding the hand of a small helpless child. "'Fear not, for I am with you; be not dismayed, for I am your God. I will strengthen you, yes, I will help you, I will uphold you with My righteous right hand.' For I, the Lord your God, will hold your right hand, saying to you, 'Fear not, I will help you.'" ~ Isaiah 41:10,13

H. W. Webb-Peploe* perhaps said it best when relating the truth of these verses: "Don't try to hold God's hand; let Him hold yours. Let Him do the holding, and you do the trusting."

Don't waste your energy trying to hold onto God. By faith, simply place your hand in His and let Him hold you. Neither struggle as is the case with children at times. Every child reaches the age where they resist having their hand held. They will pull away and even attempt to separate themselves from a parent.

Then there are the moments, especially in a crowd, when a strange child will reach up and grab your hand. All is fine until they look up and see that they have taken the hand of a stranger. If this has ever happened to you, you can remember the look of fear that strikes their face when they realize their mistake.

It's time to submit your hand into the strong grip of the Lord. Don't resist. He has your best interest at heart. And always take a glance upward from time to time; especially when your life gets crowded. Be sure your hand is truly in the hand of God.

*H.W. Webb-Peploe was an Anglican minister. He was born in 1837 and was a contemporary of some of the greatest preachers of the last two centuries such as: F.B. Meyer, G. Campbell Morgan, W. Graham Scroggie, W.H. Griffith Thomas, A.T. Pierson, C.I. Scofield, James M. Gray, R.A. Torrey, A.C. Gaebelein, H.A. Ironside, etc.

God In A Box

Many people have compartmentalized God. This begins when we isolate God to certain areas of our lives. Ultimately, we begin to visit God at His house (church) and walk away leaving Him at the altar.

Now you and I both know that God cannot not be "housed", but it seems that this is how many live their lives. God has no place in the home, the school, the business, or the workplace anymore it seems.

There is an Old Testament account that parallels this mindset. The Philistines had once again come against Israel. The Israelites brought the Ark into the battle. The Ark was supposed to reside continually in the Holy of Holies in the Tabernacle, but Israel was convinced that they had God in a box.

Apparently, the Philistines thought so too, for when the soldiers began to shout upon the arrival of the Ark in the Israeli camp, the Philistines began to fear. They thought God resided in a box as well. First Samuel 4 tells us that Israel was defeated and the Ark fell into the hands of the Philistines.

"Then the Philistines took the ark of God and brought it from Ebenezer to Ashdod. When the Philistines took the ark of God, they brought it into the house of Dagon and set it by Dagon. And when the people of Ashdod arose early in the morning, there was Dagon, fallen on its face to the earth before the ark of the Lord. So they took Dagon and set it in its place again. And when they arose early the next morning, there was Dagon, fallen on its face to the ground before the ark of the Lord. The head of Dagon and both the palms of its hands were broken off on the threshold; only Dagon's torso was left of it. Therefore neither the priests of Dagon nor any who come into Dagon's house tread on the threshold of Dagon in Ashdod to this day." ~ 1 Samuel 5:1-5

This account shows us that God can't be housed, boxed, or captured. His omnipotence bursts forth in all of its glory. The Philistine idol could not stand before God. This idol of stone bowed before God and then fell losing both its hands and head. The effect was so dramatic that the followers of Dagon no longer entered this house of idol worship.

How has God in all of His power affected your life? Are you trying to box God into a package that you think you can handle? Listen, you cannot downsize God to fit into your life.

Take down the walls; destroy your container; experience God in all of His awesomeness!

He's Got Talent

A parade of people marched across the stage. A group of judges watched as these folks performed before them in an attempt to put on display their talent. I use the word talent very loosely. I can still remember such acts as the man who could make disgusting noises with his belly button!

The program was aptly named The Gong Show. At any moment in the act one of the judges could rise to sound the huge gong located near the stage. Some people did not last long to the relief of all.

The Gong Show was the grandfather of many such amateur talent shows that have come and gone over the years. Amazingly, out of all the bad stuff, a rising star or two have been revealed.

One of the parables told by Jesus was of a man who gave three men some money. The currency of the day was the talent. There is no connection to the abilities of a person which we label as talents and the money of this parable. These men possessed nothing until the gifts were placed in their hands. Each received a different amount and each was commanded to invest the sum until the man returned to collect the profits from his investment.

The man with five talents returned to the master five more; the man with two returned two additional talents; but, there was a third man also. "Then he who had received the one talent came and said, 'Lord, I knew you to be a hard man, reaping where you have not sown, and gathering where you have not scattered seed. And I was afraid, and went and hid your talent in the ground. Look, there you have what is yours.'" ~ Matthew 25:24-25

Each of the men received a proportional sum and each had opportunity to invest the gift that had been bestowed upon them. The first two men did so, which resulted in them receiving the consummate praise of well done.

The last man was careful to guard his responsibility. There was no failure in his part to protect the gift, but in doing so, he missed the whole point of stewardship. The giver of the talents expected a return on his investment. The French protestant pastor, Adolphe Monod said, "Between the great things we cannot do and the small things we will not do, the danger is that we shall do nothing."

Every believer has been made steward of the gifts of God. Will you bury your talents or bankroll the sum in faithfulness to the One who entrusted you with the gifts?

Be ready! He is coming to collect…

Secret Thinking

Oswald Chambers gives an excellent exposé on human character in his book entitled *Our Portrait in Genesis*. He looks at the biblical characters of Genesis 12-25 and makes several insightful conclusions.

One of those revelations is about the inner working of the mind and in particular about the thought processes. He writes, "Beware what you brood on in secret, for the fateful opportunity will come when God and the devil will meet in your soul, and you will do according to your brooding, swept beyond all your control. This is a law as sure as God is God....Beware of saying, 'Oh well, it doesn't matter much what I think about in secret'; it does, for the opportunity will come when what you think about in secret will find expression and spurt out in an act."

Indeed the human mind is an amazing gift from God. As our minds function, we can use the mind to remember the past, mull over the present, or project "what-ifs" into the future. We are able to use our thoughts to lift our minds into the very throne room of heaven or cast ourselves into the pit of despair.

The mind is a battlefield. It is the place where the inner struggles of our being take place. Though Satan cannot read our minds, he certainly uses the gates of the mind to influence our thinking. These gates, of course, are the five senses that we use to relate to the world around us.

As we receive input from these senses our minds roil in a struggle to process the information. This battle is especially keen for the believer, since we are affected by the input of our flesh and the input of the Spirit of God.

"For those who live according to the flesh set their minds on the things of the flesh, but those who live according to the Spirit, the things of the Spirit. For to be carnally minded is death, but to be spiritually minded is life and peace. Because the carnal mind is enmity against God; for it is not subject to the law of God, nor indeed can be. So then, those who are in the flesh cannot please God." ~ Romans 8:5-8

This battle of the mind is unending. It yields either the stench of death or the joy of life and peace. When you find yourself thinking wrongly and focusing on fleshly things, purposefully yield your mind to godly thoughts. Don't be guilty as Zig Ziglar always said of "stinking thinking." Remember, what you spend your day thinking about will eventually find its way into an outward action.

Killing Time

When Edison was a train newsboy he would experience lay overs between train departures in Detroit. Many people would have gone to a ball game or to the movies or something to kill time, but Edison went to the library and spent his time with books that gave him further information and education. Many great discoveries have come out of a hobby or avocation outside of the regular routine of living.

Some examples of this are: the father of photography was an army officer; the inventor of the electrical motor was a bookbinder; a portrait painter perfected the telegraph. The inventor of the typewriter was a farmer; a carpenter invented the cotton gin; and the locomotive was invented by a coal miner. The telephone came from the after-school work of a schoolteacher, and a physician invented the pneumatic tire.

How do you use your spare time? Or a better question, how do you redeem the time given you each day?

Redeeming time is the phrase used by the Apostle Paul. "Walk in wisdom toward those who are outside, redeeming the time." ~ Colossians 4:5 The idea is of a person rescuing time from loss. None of us can add a nanosecond to our day, but all of us can use every nanosecond for His glory.

The word Paul uses and is translated as "time" is not, however, the tick-tock kind of time. The word he uses is "kairos." This is a descriptive word for time that speaks of an opportune time, a set time, an appointed time, in due time, a definitive time, a particular season of time, or a proper time for action. Where we usually think of time in quantity, Paul refers to it in terms of quality.

Few of us will probably ever use our time to invent anything that will make a significant splash in the ocean of time, but we can redeem every moment we have in making sure that our testimonies are pure. We need to make especially certain that we are walking with wisdom as we interact with our family, friends, and acquaintances that do not know Christ as their Savior.

Time is quickly passing for all of us. Its value is too high to simply squander. Would you make a commitment today to never spend time killing time?

04/30

Unmeasurable

David was weary from being chased and accused falsely by his enemies. Yet he concluded that God was still on his side and ever ready to bless him. "Oh, how great is Your goodness, which You have laid up for those who fear You, which You have prepared for those who trust in You in the presence of the sons of men!"~Psalms 31:19

This verse describes the magnitude of God's provision. The goodness of God is measured by the word "great." The idea is that of a multiplied myriad; literally unmeasurable. This provisional blessing has been ordained by God to belong to those who fear Him.

One of the most amazing elements of God's provision is that He has every intent of publicly blessing us. As much of a blessing this is, it is at the same time the very downfall of some. We accept God's blessed gift and then forget the Great Giver. Martin Luther said, "If in his gifts and benefits [God] were more sparing and close-handed, we should learn to be thankful.... The greater God's gifts and works, the less they are regarded."

An unknown poet wrote:

> God made the sun—it gives.
> God made the moon—it gives.
> God made the stars—they give.
> God made the air—it gives.
> God made the clouds—they give.
> God made the earth—it gives.
> God made the sea—it gives.
> God made the trees—they give.
> God made the flowers—they give.
> God made the fowls—they give.
> God made the beasts—they give.
> God made the plants—they give.
> God made man—he ...

Let us never forget the Great Giver and the result be that we become unthankful. May God unleash in a public manner the unmeasurable volume of stored blessing and may we be both thankful and ready to be a conduit of blessing to others.

· MAY

Between Heaven and Earth

I suppose that there may be some person who has navigated life without experiencing the tolling of the bell marking the departure of a loved one from this life, but I would be hard pressed to find them. Death approaches with quiet steps and visits unexpectedly. We find ourselves caught off guard by it time and again, but scripture is plain on this subject. "It is appointed for men to die once, but after this the judgment."~Hebrews 9:27

It would seem that we would eventually grow more comfortable with the reality of death, especially since we know that scripture is true, and we experience the departure of one loved or friend after another. It always catches us by surprise and we realize anew that we can only travel so far together down the road of life. At some point the separation comes and we are left behind once more.

Charles Spurgeon who was known as the prince of preachers addressed the subject of what seems an extensive chasm between heaven and earth. I hope that his words can close the gap a little if you are experiencing the reality of death's appointment today.

Here are his thoughts:

> Do not think that heaven and earth are divided. They are but two ships moored close to one another, and one short plank of death will enable you to step from one to the other. This ship, having done the coasting trade, the business of today, and full of the blackness of sorrow. That ship, all golden, with its ensign flying and its sails all spread, fair as the angel's wing. The ship of heaven is moored side by side with the ship of earth. Though this ship may rock and careen, yet the golden ship of heaven sails by her side, never separated, always ready, so that when the hour comes, you may leap from the dark ship and step on the golden deck of that happy one on which you will sail forever.

Indeed, it is appointed unto each person to die, but God in His matchless mercy has provided the plank that connects heaven and earth. That plank is constructed from an old rugged cross that stood on a hill.

Come to the cross today and you can face tomorrow's appointment without fear or sadness. May the ship of Zion draw near to you today as you place your trust in the One who holds eternity in His hands.

05/02

Standard Parts

Have you ever noticed that when you go to purchase a replacement part that the model you have demands a special order? It's as if all of these products come off this huge factory line exactly the same, then suddenly a worker decides to substitute a part in the very item that winds up in your possession. Whammo! Your equipment cannot be repaired without the special part instead of the standard part that every other person on the planet gets to use. Does this just happen to me? I didn't think so!

I have good news though. There is a standard when it comes to the subject of love. However, the standard is so extraordinary that it most likely will seem like it is special. And truthfully, it is very special indeed.

John tells us the standard for love and also tells us that we can actually know this love as our own. He says in his First Epistle, "By this we know love, because He laid down His life for us. And we also ought to lay down our lives for the brethren. But whoever has this world's goods, and sees his brother in need, and shuts up his heart from him, how does the love of God abide in him? My little children, let us not love in word or in tongue, but in deed and in truth." ~ 1 John 3:16-18

Now that had to be the most special standard set ever! The standard of God's love is established in the giving of His own Son. Here's the paradox that is revealed. If we are to live up to the standard of love set before us in Christ's sacrificial death then we must be willing to die for our brothers and sisters in Christ. We must die to live! We must die to love!

But you are saying, "Wait just one minute! I didn't sign up to die! No one told me this would be the cost of discipleship." You are so right. Few could say that they knew up front that serving Jesus would mean death, but it is happening all around the world. Thousands are dying for us as a testimony and as a declaration of love's standard.

We are blessed here in America and will most likely not have to lay down our lives, but we do not escape the standard of love. Our love is to be acted out as we meet the needs of brothers and sisters in need. No doubt in this very day you will have the opportunity to demonstrate the standard of love by meeting a need. In doing so we join the Apostle John by loving not in word or tongue, but in deed and in truth. So, go be a standard bearer for the love of Christ today!

God's Open Hand

Consider this list:

- The near miss of an accident.
- The birth of a child.
- Finding employment after months of no work.
- A verse of scripture that speaks to you at just the right moment.
- Rain after a drought.
- Car keys found.
- The Red Sea opened and the Egyptian army drowned in the aftermath.

What does it take for you to recognize God at work?

The Israelites were so much like us when it comes to recognizing the works of God. It was only after the entire Israelite population had passed through the Red Sea that scripture records these words, "Thus Israel saw the great work which the Lord had done in Egypt; so the people feared the Lord, and believed the Lord and His servant Moses." ~ Exodus 14:31

The history of Israel was filled with the mighty works of God. If one only goes back as far as the arrival of Israel into Egypt, the list of God's great work would fill volumes. God had prepared the survival of His chosen people by placing Joseph in a ruling position in Egypt. He had blessed Israel even during centuries of slavery. As the time of their exodus transpired, God showed Himself mighty as He decimated the Egyptian nation through a series of plagues. Time and again He placed Israel in the safety of His hand.

It is interesting that this verse tells us that Israel recognized the great work of God only after the miracle that delivered them through the Red Sea unscathed. The words "great work" come from a Hebrew word that means the open hand.

The same hand of God that had been closed around Israel in safety was opened in a full slap of retribution against Egypt. It was this open-handed work of God that brought Israel to the place of belief.

Here's where it gets really interesting! Today's verse says Israel saw the great work of God and believed. The word "believed" means to move to the right; especially to move into the right hand. Israel for over 400 years had been protected in the hollow of God's hand. They experienced the power of God's open hand against their enemy and this prompted them to run into the protective right hand of God's mercy and grace.

Go back over the opening list again. What will it take for you to recognize the open hand of God? See His great work and run into the safety of His strong right hand. You will never see anything as inconsequential again.

05/04

No Plans

Life rushes past us at an amazing speed. This globe upon which we reside is spinning somewhere around a thousand miles per hour. The earth itself is traveling around the sun at a rate of some 67,000 miles per hour. More amazing is that we never think about it. It's just happening and we are enjoying the ride.

The believer rests in the pure fact that God is holding it all together. The person who has placed their faith in chance doesn't want to think about it, because it might all come crashing down and then where would that person be?

There are moments though when we must stop for just a second or two and realize that God really is in control of everything. One of those moments happened recently for my son-in-law. He wasn't thinking about the earth's rotational speed nor its journey around the sun. As a matter of fact he was barely thinking about the 70 miles per hour that he was traveling up I-55. Few of us do. We just get on our way and with little thought head along a given route.

Kevin's thoughts about speed, direction, and other forces beyond his control came rushing to the forefront when the left front tire of a 63,000 pound test truck blew apart and sent him careening into the median. He had no time to think of the particulars of that moment. He could not have planned for the left lane to be clear of traffic as he was catapulted from the right lane. He could not have planned for the median to be elevated at that point which kept him from crossing into oncoming traffic. He could not have planned for heavy rains the night before which softened the median and that mud and water would act like a giant catcher's mitt. He could not have planned…but God did!

Kevin is safe though the truck was destroyed. Not a scratch on his person! This is why we should follow the advice of the psalmist: "For this cause everyone who is godly shall pray to You in a time when You may be found; surely in a flood of great waters they shall not come near him. You are my hiding place; You shall preserve me from trouble; You shall surround me with songs of deliverance. Selah." ~ Psalms 32:6-7

Kevin testified to the state trooper that just "happened" to be a few cars behind him that his eternity was settled before the tire blew. How about yours? Life happens really fast.

Be prepared. Trust Christ today…

Look!

Nothing in this world is more powerful than one's personal testimony concerning salvation. The moment someone comes to know Christ is indelibly inscribed upon the heart and mind.

Scripture describes it as the quickening of a child in its mother's womb. Life springs forth seemingly from nowhere and there is a full realization that once you were dead in your sins and trespasses and now you are living.

God makes it clear that there is no salvation to be found apart from him. He not only is our salvation, but He clearly declares it for all to hear and to find. Isaiah records God's words: "Tell and bring forth your case; Yes, let them take counsel together. Who has declared this from ancient time? Who has told it from that time? Have not I, the Lord ? And there is no other God besides Me, a just God and a Savior; There is none besides Me. "Look to Me, and be saved, All you ends of the earth! For I am God, and there is no other." ~ Isaiah 45:21-22

This was the very section of scripture that Charles Spurgeon heard for the first time on the morning he trusted Christ as his Lord and Savior. Here are his own words as he tells his personal testimony:

> I sometimes think I might have been in darkness and despair until now, had it not been for the goodness of God in sending a snowstorm one Sunday morning, while I was going to a certain place of worship. I turned down a side street, and came to a little Primitive Methodist Church.

> The minister did not come that morning; he was snowed up, I suppose. At last a very thin-looking man, a shoemaker, or tailor, or something of that sort, went up into the pulpit to preach. Now it is well that preachers be instructed, but this man was really stupid. He was obliged to stick to his text, for the simple reason that he had little else to say. The text was— "LOOK UNTO ME, AND BE YE SAVED, ALL THE ENDS OF THE EARTH" (Isa. 45:22)

> The man began thus: "This is a very simple text indeed. It says 'Look.' Now lookin' don't take a deal of pain. It ain't liftin' your foot or your finger; it is just 'Look.' Well, a man needn't go to college to learn to look. You may be the biggest fool, and yet you can look. A man needn't be worth a thousand a year to look. Anyone can look; even a child can look."

"But then the text says, 'Look unto Me.' Ay!" he said in broad Essex, "many of ye are lookin' to yourselves, but it's no use lookin' there. You'll never find any comfort in yourselves."

When he had managed to spin out about ten minutes or so, he was at the end of his tether. Then he looked at me under the gallery, and I daresay with so few present, he knew me to be a stranger.

Just fixing his eyes on me, as if he knew all my heart, he said, "Young man, you look very miserable." Well, I did, but I had not been accustomed to have remarks made from the pulpit on my personal appearance before. However, it was a good blow, struck right home. He continued, "And you will always be miserable—miserable in life and miserable in death—if you don't obey my text; but if you obey now, this moment, you will be saved." Then lifting up his hands, he shouted, as only a Primitive Methodist could do, "Young man, look to Jesus Christ. Look! Look! Look! You have nothing to do but look and live!"

I saw at once the way of salvation. I know not what else he said—I did not take much notice of it—I was so possessed with that one thought. I had been waiting to do fifty things, but when I heard that word, "Look!" what a charming word it seemed to me. Oh! I looked until I could almost have looked my eyes away.

If you've never looked to Jesus for salvation, do so today. If you have, then tell your story to someone else who needs only "Look!" to be saved.

Time For The Harvest

Our mission to the Dominican Republic is called *NW2NW*. This acronym reflects our partnership. It represents the geographical tie between the northwest Arkansas and the northwest parts of the Dominican Republic. This area has some evangelical work, but there is a need for new churches and strengthening those that exists.

Amos recorded the words of God to the people of his day and they remind me of the areas our association ministers to in the Dominican Republic. "I also have given you cleanness of teeth in all your cities, and lack of bread in every town; yet you haven't returned to me," says Yahweh. "I also have withheld the rain from you, when there were yet three months to the harvest; and I caused it to rain on one city, and caused it not to rain on another city. One place was rained on, and the piece where it didn't rain withered. So two or three cities staggered to one city to drink water, and were not satisfied: yet you haven't returned to me," says Yahweh." ~ Amos 4:6-8 (WEB)

These judgments of God were sent to draw the people back to Himself. All of these can be seen in a spiritual and sometimes physical sense in the Dominican Republic. There are those who are hungering for the Word of God. They are like the people described in these verses. Their teeth are clean because they have no food to chew.

God had withheld the rain from these people at the moment it was most needed. With only months to go before the harvest, the rains had ceased and the crops had withered. The few places where rain had fallen crowds gathered to the point that there was not enough water to satisfy.

Oh, that God might open the heavens and rain down His salvation blessings as we scatter the seed. Oh, that we might be aware of the harvest. May Jesus open our eyes like He did the disciples in John 4, "Don't you say, 'There are yet four months until the harvest?' Behold, I tell you, lift up your eyes, and look at the fields, that they are white for harvest already."

As Jesus said, "man shall not live by bread alone, but by every word that proceeds from God." (Luke 4:4) Would you pray that our ministry to the Dominican Republic would be blessed so that we may be bearers of the bread of life so the spiritually hungry may be filled? Pray that our eyes are open and that the scythe of heaven sweeps across the fields of the Dominican Republic.

Restoring Focus

We have great responsibilities and privileges as ministers of the gospel. Some of you will fulfill your calling daily in your home or perhaps in a small circle of influence. Others like myself have experienced the discovery of God's will by serving in places far and wide. I could never have imagined traveling to places I never knew existed when I first came to know Him as my Lord and Savior.

You may not be able to travel to other lands, but you can be obedient to serve Him right where you are. Second Chronicles 18-20 tells us of a portion of King Jehoshaphat's rule as King of Judah. One verse summarizes the type of ruler he was: "Behave courageously, and the Lord will be with the good." ~ 2Chronicles 19:11

Jehoshaphat served the Lord well in contrast to the rule of Ahab in Israel. He removed the places of idol worship and restored the people's focus on Jehovah. The Lord strengthened Jehoshaphat's rule and the fear of God fell on all the enemies of Judah.

His biggest error in judgment came when he aligned himself in battle with Ahab. Even here, he sought counsel of God's prophet, but still went to war alongside Ahab.

The prophet Micaiah warned that Ahab would die in battle and so he did at the hand of an unnamed warrior that shot an arrow at random. This arrow found the breast of Ahab.

It is no mistake that God will protect us even when we err, but we must return to his will and follow closely His ways. In chapter 19 Jehoshaphat set up godly judges across Judah. He commanded them that they should judge faithfully and with a perfect heart. He concluded with the verse noted above about behaving courageously.

These men were to deal courageously when passing judgment on the matters before them. He instructed them to execute their roles in such a way that they would have the Lord with them in all of their business.

Make it your desire to deal with people in such a way that they conclude that God is with you and then they may have a desire to follow the Lord as their Savior.

Over and Under

When my girls were little, I used to plait their hair before they made their way to school. I don't think I could plait hair today if you threatened me with severe consequences. As much as I can remember, it was not really difficult. After learning the over under routine, I would soon have their hair looking very pretty, if I must say so myself.

Psalm 40:17 uses the idea of plaiting when it speaks of God's concern for us: "But I am poor and needy; Yet the Lord thinks upon me. You are my help and my deliverer; do not delay, O my God." ~ Psalms 40:17   The word translated as "thinks" holds the concept of God being so involved in our affairs that it is as if He is plaiting our existence into His eternal Being.

Imagine God's hands busily at work taking all that comes our way and weaving it into His everlasting purpose and plan. He has never come to the place where he needed to say, "Now, what do I do with this piece of hair?" Over and under, over and under, over and under…God is plaiting what appears a tangled mess into a masterpiece.

This verse begins by declaring the desperate condition that prevailed. The words poor and needy can mean just that, but if you look at them just as economic words you will miss the deeper meanings. The psalmist is confessing that he is depressed and destitute. His life looks like my girls' hair did some mornings when they had evidently tossed all night in their sleep. No plaiting could begin until the tangles were combed out completely.

With tired, droopy eyes my girls would stand with their back towards me while I combed through their hair and prepared it for my "finesse". How many times has your situation seemed completely tangled to the point of crying out, "Lord, I am poor and needy; depressed and destitute!"

It is at these moments that we need to declare in spite of the tangles, that God is our deliverer. Indeed, we may be in our tangled situation just so we can only call out to Him as our Deliverer. Note that desperation prepares us for the hands of God to work His de-tangling miracle. We then proclaim, "O, God do not delay in making my situation beautiful."

It's time to submit your tangles to the Master's hands. Let Him work out His plan as He plaits your tangled ways into His will.

Doctor in Residence

As much as I can remember, I never went to the doctor much as a child. I remember going once when I was five. I had cut a corner too closely and nearly scalped myself. Ask me sometime and I can show you the scar!

The next time I remember going to the doctor was when I was about 14 or so. I had been injured playing soccer and the school sent me to get my wrist examined. All of the years in between I was pretty much treated by the doctor in residence—my father. He believed that all things could be cured with *Dr. Tichenor's* antiseptic and his sanitized pocket knife. So far his treatments have lasted for nearly six decades.

I am sure that many would grimace at some of the archaic treatments provided under the care of my dad. For the most part, he simply was practicing the medicine he had learned from his parents. And of course, they had learned it from theirs as well.

There are some old-timey practices that don't really cause any harm; they may not particularly help, but they won't kill you. When it comes to spiritual matters, however, we need to take extra care.

Paul instructed his young student minister Timothy to be on guard against spiritual practices that had no real basis for faith. "But reject profane and old wives' fables, and exercise yourself toward godliness." ~ 1 Timothy 4:7

This verse comes as a warning about the danger of believing something just because it keeps being repeated as truth. Sooner or later the dabbling in fables becomes the doctrine of the day. The word translated as fable could also be translated as myth. Paul told Timothy to outright refuse or shun these mythical concepts.

We protect ourselves from bad spiritual practices by strengthening ourselves in godly matters. The idea is to place oneself inside the daily regimen of gospel truth and to never cross the threshold laid down by God's word.

My father's intent in practicing bad medicine was not to cause me harm. Thank God I was a healthy kid who could be "healed" with *Dr. Tichenor's* and a pocket knife. Neither my dad nor I knew any better and I lived to tell the story.

It's not so in the spiritual world. What you don't know can kill you and it's your responsibility to live in the godliness of truth.

Water of Life

During one of my mission trips I had the privilege of preaching to an overflow crowd gathered in and outside of a little wooden building. We were packed in place and were blessed by the glorious praise of the born again believers as they rejoiced together.

My understanding of Spanish is better than my speaking of the language. I understood enough that I knew the first song was about the water of life. I was overcome with a sense of God's presence and an assurance that I was preaching exactly what needed to be said that evening.

My text was John 4. My subject was the Samaritan woman at the well of Jacob and her interaction with Jesus.

Here are a few of the verses that begin with the woman's amazement that a Jewish man would ask her for a drink of water. "A woman of Samaria came to draw water. Jesus said to her, 'Give Me a drink.' For His disciples had gone away into the city to buy food. Then the woman of Samaria said to Him, 'How is it that You, being a Jew, ask a drink from me, a Samaritan woman?' For Jews have no dealings with Samaritans. Jesus answered and said to her, 'If you knew the gift of God, and who it is who says to you, 'Give Me a drink,' you would have asked Him, and He would have given you living water.'" ~ John 4:7-10

I preached of this woman's loneliness. This was evidenced by her coming to the well at midday and her coming all by herself. She was an outcast among the outcasts. She was despised by the Jews because of her race and despised by her own Samaritan people because of the life she was living.

If there is one thing that I have learned as I have preached on five of the seven continents, it is that loneliness is common to all. No matter the color of a person's skin, or their status in life, or the size of the community in which they live, all people find themselves with one common malady at some point in life: loneliness.

After telling this crowded audience of the loneliness of this woman, I told them how that this same Jesus who had passed through Samaria to keep an appointment with one woman was now passing through their community. The result: Five people gave their hearts, and hopes to Christ and had their loneliness erased by His eternal presence. And that is why I go on mission trips!

Provision for the Work

Rains can be very beneficial. They provide life sustaining qualities. Many who live where water flows freely from the faucet take a simple downpour for granted. I have been on mission trips where rains are scarce and I have been on some where there was just too much rain.

In the northwest part of the Dominican Republic too much rain can be a problem. Heavy rain means there will be lots of runoff into the river. The river water will become very muddy. The community we minister in draws its water directly from the river. The pumps cannot handle the muddy water. When this happens, the pumps are turned off and we will not have water for a period of time. Therefore, the joy of the cooling provided by the rain comes with a cost: no running water.

Provision has been made though. There are barrels in the kitchen with water that has been collected prior to the rain. Because someone took the time to fill the barrel, we have water to use for necessities. I am thankful for this provision.

David also made provision when he was king of Israel. His desire was to build the Temple, but God would not allow him to do so. God's plan was for Solomon to be the builder. This did not discourage David. He began to make provision for his son's work. "Now David said, 'Solomon my son is young and inexperienced, and the house to be built for the Lord must be exceedingly magnificent, famous and glorious throughout all countries. I will now make preparation for it.' So David made abundant preparations before his death."

What forethought! David was thinking about God's will being fulfilled even after he was no longer on the scene. What provision are you making to carry out God's mission for your life? Like David, you may not live to see a dream fulfilled, but you can make provision that will extend beyond your life.

My journeys to foreign fields began before time began. God had made provision. Before time was, God saw His only Son dying on the cross for the people that would live in my time. He made provision for their sin debt to be paid in full through Christ's death.

The delivery of that message of hope is to be carried out by your mission to the world. Imagine this: You too are part of the Great Provider's provision!

Send Her Away

There are no greater heroes in life than mothers. Mothers are the defenders of the home and none can contend with a mother that has had one of her children placed in harm's way. Time and again stories are written of mothers who sacrificed themselves to spare the life of a child.

One such account can be found in Matthew 15. This account begins with a mother approaching Jesus. "And behold, a woman of Canaan came from that region and cried out to Him, saying, 'Have mercy on me, O Lord, Son of David! My daughter is severely demon-possessed.'" ~ Matthew 15:22 One of the amazing things about this story is the response of Jesus. He answered her not a word (15:23.)

Taken at face value one would have to wonder at Jesus' response to this woman's great need. It appeared to be callous toward her pain. Thankfully we have the whole story and can clearly see that Jesus was both instructing the disciples and allowing her faith to reach maturity. Here is another example of God's ways being beyond our ways and His thoughts beyond ours.

The silence of Jesus did not lessen her pursuit for His help. The disciples were so aggravated with her cries that they wanted her sent away, but she pled all the more. "Then she came and worshiped Him, saying, 'Lord, help me!'" (15:25)

Jesus answered her cries by saying, "It is not good to take the children's bread and throw it to the little dogs."(15:26) Wow! First silence and now Jesus refers to her and her people as dogs. Don't get angry here! This ends well!

And she said, "Yes, Lord, yet even the little dogs eat the crumbs which fall from their masters' table." (15:27) This was the moment of truth! She confessed her condition and in contrition asked for crumbs. This is exactly the place you and I must come to before we can accept by faith the work of salvation. Yes, Lord, I am a sinner and only one crumb of salvation will be enough to save me forever!

And as promised, here's the good news! Then Jesus answered and said to her, "O woman, great is your faith! Let it be to you as you desire." And her daughter was healed from that very hour. (15:28) There were only two times in the gospels that the phrase "great faith" was used. Both times it refers to Gentiles just like me and you. In both cases someone was healed at a distance.

As we celebrate mothers each year in May, remember that God can meet your need whether it be for you or a loved one. It only takes a crumb of His grace and as with this woman, healing can take place this very hour! Cry unto Him!

R.E. Clark

Voices

I hear voices. Now before you call the men with the funny clothes that zip up in the back, hear what I have to say. In other words, hear my voice.

It seems that everywhere I go there are voices. All sorts of electronics have been given human voices that are constantly giving us direction. GPS devices tell us when and where to turn. Elevators announce that we have arrived at our floor. Microwave ovens tell us our food is warmed. Our phones ring with voices that tell us who is on the other end before we have answered the call.

It seems we hear every voice except the inner voice that all of us have. We call it our conscience. This gift from God sets us apart from all of creation. It is the voice of self that reports the condition of our souls in relation to that which we know. Paul put it this way: "To the pure all things are pure, but to those who are defiled and unbelieving nothing is pure; but even their mind and conscience are defiled." ~ Titus 1:15

An old American Indian legend defined the conscience as a three sided object that resides in the chest of man. When a man does wrong his conscience turns and the sharp corners jab him on the inside prompting him to acknowledge his guilt.

The legend goes on to say that there is a problem with the conscience, however. If it is spun enough times the corners are worn away, and though it spins, there is no longer a response deep within the soul. The conscience is silenced in effect.

Recently, we have experienced one horrible act of mankind stacked upon another. Each time we gasp at the depravity put upon display for all to see. Each time we remark that it certainly cannot get any worse and then to our amazement it does.

How can all of this be happening? The answer is not that men are more wicked today than ever. The problem is not that men have access to evil more readily today. The spiral towards total degradation began when the conscience of mankind was silenced.

Conscience was described as an inhibitor. It was relegated to a particular era of piety. The guardian of the soul was bombarded until its corners were worn away. Now smoothed and polished, we see the results in the faces of men and women who are charged with the most heinous crimes. They stand before us with empty eyes and solemn, uncaring expressions.

We ask again and again, "How could this happen?" And the voice of conscience speaks quietly from the shadows, "It happened because you muted my voice."

I hear voices and it's a good thing. How about you?

Not Ashamed

We take a lot of things for granted in our everyday lives in America. The poorest person in our country would be considered rich in most of the world. It is not just money or other possessions that I speak of here. We are blessed with all sorts of conveniences, such as, water that always flows from the faucet and electricity that does not work only a few hours a day. These are just two of the items that you do not miss unless they are not at your ready disposal.

Unlike electrical power which can never be fully trusted to be available at all times, God's power is 100% trustworthy. Paul described God's power as the gospel of Christ released in the form of salvation. "For I am not ashamed of the gospel of Christ, for it is the power of God to salvation for everyone who believes, for the Jew first and also for the Greek. For in it the righteousness of God is revealed from faith to faith; as it is written, 'The just shall live by faith.'" ~ Romans 1:16-17

Luke records an incident in his gospel about the power of God being released into the life of a leper. "And it happened when He was in a certain city, that behold, a man who was full of leprosy saw Jesus; and he fell on his face and implored Him, saying, 'Lord, if You are willing, You can make me clean.'" ~ Luke 5:12

This man saw Jesus as the answer to his illness. Jesus was the source of power needed to heal him and in a demonstration of complete humility he fell on his face and asked for the power to be released. The response of Jesus was like flipping the switch for the power to be turned on: "Then He put out His hand and touched him, saying, 'I am willing; be cleansed.'" ~ Luke 5:13

This man's leprous condition is reflective of our sin-filled condition. We can no more save ourselves than we can keep the electricity on without fail, but God is willing that the power of the gospel be released and men be saved. It matters not if they are Jew, or Greek, or whatever your nationality might be.

When that power is turned on I always stand amazed. Praise God! He is still willing to save again by the power of the gospel!

Shelf-Stretchers

My first real job was in a supermarket. I had been working for several years, but this was a job where I actually received a paycheck. I still have fond memories of my first days stocking shelves with various canned goods and other items.

As a newbie in my position as stock clerk, I went through an initiation prompted by the more experienced clerks. All new guys would be sent to the warehouse to locate the shelf-stretcher. This errand was made necessary when a few items would not fit into the allotted space. Without a thought and wishing to impress, off I went in search of the elusive shelf-stretcher.

Returning without the non-existent shelf-stretcher would bring hilarious laughter from the rest of the crew. They had each experienced the same joke played harmlessly upon them. And yes, I asked the next new guy to scurry back to the warehouse to get a shelf-stretcher also. It was simply a rite of passage.

Life is a lot like stocking a grocery shelf. It seems that we always have a few items that just don't quite fit. Though we know better, we are always looking for a shelf-stretcher to make room for a little more.

It may be more time that we try to cram into a day. It could be that we attempt to over-reach our abilities. We may even be guilty of hoarding heaven's blessings, believing we can protect ourselves when a rainy day comes.

Perhaps the one place we seek to stretch our shelves is when it comes to the length of our lives. We are not alone in this dilemma. The Apostle Paul spoke of this stretching time as he wrote to the church at Philippi: "For I am hard-pressed between the two, having a desire to depart and be with Christ, which is far better. Nevertheless to remain in the flesh is more needful for you."~Philippians 1:23-24

I have witnessed this stretching time many times in the years of my ministry. It is always the same. The shadows grow long. Visions of eternity flash before the weary traveler. Remembrances of days long ago spent are relived. Joys of life's victories flash across the mind like the stretching of a runner for the finish line.

But there is always that moment when you realize that there are things that just would not fit. Some things are never meant to be. No matter how much we search the warehouse, there is no shelf-stretcher.

For each of us there is a limit. Live your life to the full for God's glory and when you've reached life's capacity scurry not in search of a stretcher. Rest in the assurance of a life well-lived.

Never Saw That Coming

I think that it is sometimes difficult for us to fully fathom the overwhelming protection of God that is precipitated by His foresight. Simply put—God is never caught off-guard. You and I might say things like, "Well, I never saw that coming!" But it is not so with God. Nothing slips up on Him and nothing gets past Him. God doesn't need peripheral vision. He sees 360 degrees and as far into the past or future that is needed.

To be perfectly honest I rarely concern myself with God seeing very far into the past. Even though the past attempts an intrusion into my present, I am reminded of the Apostle Paul's words, "Brethren, I do not count myself to have apprehended; but one thing I do, forgetting those things which are behind and reaching forward to those things which are ahead, I press toward the goal for the prize of the upward call of God in Christ Jesus." ~ Philippians 3:13-14

It is not so much the distant future that I am often concerning myself. I am comforted by the fact that God knows all of that, but more so that He knows what is just around the next corner.

I became ill in the Dominican Republic while on a mission trip with our association of churches. I was caught totally by surprise. I had already been ill for over two days and assumed that I was over the worst of it. That's when I has the severe pains in my stomach and made a hair-raising trip to the hospital via pickup truck. God was right there when the attack happened and along for the ride to the hospital.

No, that's not correct. He was walking just ahead of the vehicle all along the way. The driver had his foot through the floorboard; God was taking a walk in the park just a few steps ahead of every hole in the road or oncoming vehicle!

This experience reminded me of these words from David in Psalm 55: "Cast your burden on the Lord, and He shall sustain you; He shall never permit the righteous to be moved." ~ Psalm 55:22 Whatever you are going through today just remember as you scramble to get all your ducks in a row that God is right there, because where you are is where God has already been—waiting for you to arrive!

The Straw Bridge

Michael P. Green in his book, *Illustrations for Biblical Preaching*, tells the following story:

> There once was an ant who felt imposed upon, overburdened, and overworked. You see, he was instructed to carry a piece of straw across an expanse of concrete. The straw was so long and heavy that he staggered beneath its weight and felt he would not survive.
>
> Finally, as the stress of his burden began to overwhelm him and he began to wonder if life itself was worth it, the ant was brought to a halt by a large crack in his path. There was no way of getting across that deep divide, and it was evident that to go around it would be his final undoing.
>
> He stood there discouraged. Then suddenly a thought struck him. Carefully laying the straw across the crack in the concrete, he walked over it and safely reached the other side. His heavy load had become a helpful bridge. The burden was also a blessing.

Now I'm not certain about an ant's ability to reason, but God has given His creatures amazing abilities to display wisdom. Man is included here. As a matter of fact, there is a strong connection between trials and our finding wisdom in the midst of troubles and burdens.

James wrote about this when he said, "My brethren, count it all joy when you fall into various trials, knowing that the testing of your faith produces patience. But let patience have its perfect work, that you may be perfect and complete, lacking nothing. If any of you lacks wisdom, let him ask of God, who gives to all liberally and without reproach, and it will be given to him. But let him ask in faith, with no doubting, for he who doubts is like a wave of the sea driven and tossed by the wind. For let not that man suppose that he will receive anything from the Lord; he is a double-minded man, unstable in all his ways." ~ James 1:2-8

Like the ant, who probably never thought about a straw bridge until he faced the insurmountable crack in his world, we will seldom seek out answers of wisdom until we are under the weight of a trial or tribulation.

Whatever chasm you are facing today why not let your burden become a blessed bridge. You may find yourself closer to completing your God-given task by applying His wisdom to your situation.

The Lie of Deception

Today's devotion requires a few more verses than I would normally include, but the subject demands it. The subject is the deception of deception. You see the very danger of being deceived is that you will not know it—the moment you know it the deception will be ended.

"But you have an anointing from the Holy One, and you know all things. I have not written to you because you do not know the truth, but because you know it, and that no lie is of the truth. Who is a liar but he who denies that Jesus is the Christ? He is antichrist who denies the Father and the Son. Whoever denies the Son does not have the Father either; he who acknowledges the Son has the Father also. Therefore let that abide in you which you heard from the beginning. If what you heard from the beginning abides in you, you also will abide in the Son and in the Father. And this is the promise that He has promised us—eternal life. These things I have written to you concerning those who try to deceive you. But the anointing which you have received from Him abides in you, and you do not need that anyone teach you; but as the same anointing teaches you concerning all things, and is true, and is not a lie, and just as it has taught you, you will abide in Him." ~ 1 John 2:20-27

These verses give us the antidote for deception. It is the anointing of the Holy Spirit. The word "anoint" carries the idea of being smeared. Like applying sunscreen to protect your skin from the unseen harmful rays of the sun, the anointing of the Holy Spirit protects you from the lie of deception.

And what is the greatest deception of all? It is to claim a relationship with God apart from a relationship with Jesus. Many claim to know God, but they are deceived. Their lives clearly deny any knowledge of Jesus. This scripture teaches that to deny Jesus is to have the deception of Antichrist in your life. The anointing of the Holy Spirit brings you into truth. Remember Jesus plainly said, "I am the way, the truth, and the life. No one comes to the Father except through me."

Be not deceived! There is no way to God except through Jesus.

Miserable People

Misery loves company. At least that's what I've always heard (and sometimes practice.) But honestly I think that miserable people love to be around miserable people. Misery feeds upon itself. It cares not if the misery is perceived or real. It cares not if it consumes others. It just loves company.

Now there is a fine line between comforting someone who is miserable and joining in their misery. We can see this happening in John 11. The friends of Jesus were grieving the death of their brother, Lazarus. Both Mary and Martha had concluded that Jesus could have helped their brother if He had just come to their aid sooner. They were even bold enough to say so to His face when He drew close to Bethany on the fourth day since Lazarus had died.

As was the custom of that day, people had gathered to "help" the sisters mourn their brother's death. There was even some entrepreneurs who had mourning businesses. You could hire them to come and wail with you. Now these folks had to have really loved misery! It appears that many were on site at this occasion whether they were friends and family or professional misery maintenance folk. Martha had already gone to meet Jesus while He was a ways outside of Bethany and had sent for Mary to come. So scripture says, "Then the Jews who were with her in the house, and comforting her, when they saw that Mary rose up quickly and went out, followed her, saying, 'She is going to the tomb to weep there.'" ~ John 11:31

But to their surprise, it was not a sepulcher, but a Savior that she sought. They sought the company of misery; she sought the company of the Messiah. Note the response of Jesus, "Therefore, when Jesus saw her weeping, and the Jews who came with her weeping, He groaned in the spirit and was troubled. And He said, 'Where have you laid him?' They said to Him, 'Lord, come and see.' Jesus wept." ~ John 11:33-35

Jesus was not joining in their misery by weeping. He was weeping because they still did not understand the hope and assurance that could be found in Him. They were looking for an opportunity of misery instead of a miracle. And as Paul Harvey always said, "Now, for the rest of the story!"

The stone was rolled away and Lazarus lived again! The believers rejoiced; the company of misery-lovers reported their loss of revenue to the Pharisees and from that day they sought to kill Jesus because of the resurrection of Lazarus. Some people just can't be happy unless everyone is miserable. Don't be one of those people today. Rejoice in the resurrection!

Cut Off

Every now and then a person can have dreams that are very vivid and detailed. I had just such a dream that led me to the writing of this devotion. It was about a church named Cut Off. I'm not sure about the denomination, but since I'm Baptist, I'll just add that to my dream story. The church was Cut Off Baptist Church. It was located on Cut Off Street, of course.

In my dream I thought about a town in Louisiana named Cut Off. I'm not sure how it got its name, but one would have to assume that it was its location that played an important part. It may have been a turn off of a main road or more likely with all of the waterways of south Louisiana, it was a place that got cut off when the bayou changed its course. At any rate, the name lends all sorts of conjecture about being separated or disconnected from the surrounding area. Please note that this has no ill meaning toward Cut Off, Louisiana. I'm just tying up the loose ends of my dream.

The people in the Cut Off Baptist Church were dying. One by one, they were slowly slipping into non-existence. I found them in my dream meeting to talk about the old days—the days before things changed and the street where their church was located had been a thoroughfare. These folks had simply forgotten what the message of their church was all about and how it affected their existence. Actually, it had nothing to do with location or accessibility. It had everything to do with a Savior.

As dreams go, here's the twist in mine. While I met with these folks, I saw Jesus hanging on the cross and I heard Him speaking. His words were from John's account of the crucifixion. "After this, Jesus, knowing that all things were now accomplished, that the Scripture might be fulfilled, said, 'I thirst!'" ~ John 19:28 Two little words. But how did they tie into my dream?

After I awoke, this thought occurred to me. Hanging on the cross the Creator who spoke every ocean, river, and stream into being, chose to fulfill scripture by becoming thirsty. He who flooded an entire world had not one drop of water for our sakes.

He was cut off by choice to give us the message of hope found in the One who is our living water! You or your church may feel like the flow of life has been redirected and you have been left cut off, but here's the good news. Your message has not changed. Jesus is still thirsting today. Not for a cool taste of water, but for you to come with your empty cup and drink deeply of Him.

There's no reason to be cut off. He has made a way to the river of life and you have a message to tell!

It's All Good

The sticker on the back glass of the truck read: IT'S ALL GOOD! Now that struck me as funny, because I knew that most likely the person who owned the truck did not really mean it. Now before you judge me for judging the owner of this truck and its attached sticker, give me just a moment to explain.

Knowing how skewed our sense of goodness is in this world today, I just had to assume that the sticker was true conditionally. I wonder if it would have been all good if I had let the air out of his tires or if I had stolen his truck? You see, our measure of goodness comes from a defective sense of good that has been marred by the effects of sin.

Imagine God ending each day of creation by slapping stickers all over the world saying: IT'S ALL GOOD! Well, in a sense that's exactly what He did as each day's creative acts were crowned with the words, "And God saw that it was good." God concluded the sixth day of His creative works and these words that are recorded in Genesis 1:31, "Then God saw everything that He had made, and indeed it was very good. So the evening and the morning were the sixth day."

How did He conclude that it was all good? His evaluation was not based on what a competitor had done. He had no other universe to measure His work against. He was not reading the latest opinion poll. God simply determined that it was all good because He had done it!

We can join the Psalmist in declaring, "Oh, how great is Your goodness, which You have laid up for those who fear You, which You have prepared for those who trust in You in the presence of the sons of men!" ~ Psalms 31:19

Now back to the guy with the truck and the "IT'S ALL GOOD" sticker: there is a possibility that it is all good for him, but only if he has a relationship with the one and only good God.

Is it all good with you today? Do you have a living relationship with my good God? Like the old preacher used to say to his congregation, "God is good!" and his congregation would reply, "All the time!" Then turning it around he would say, "All the time," and the people would shout, "GOD IS GOOD!"

With God: IT'S ALL GOOD! Have a good day!

Change

It had been said that as much as things change they are always the same. Recently, while I was traveling Interstate 40 across Arkansas, I had to traverse several construction zones. I found myself complaining that crews were involved again in repairs and requiring everyone to slow down accordingly. Then reality stuck me.

I had been living in Arkansas for 14 years. When I moved there those many years ago the entirety of Interstate 40 was under construction. I just couldn't imagine repairs had begun again, but time had taken its toll. And now, as much as things had changed over these years, they were just the same.

We are always hearing news accounts as they burst forth with one scandal after another taking front page priority. Witnesses are summoned to tell the truth, the whole truth, and nothing but the truth. But if you are like me, you have to wonder if the truth can ever be reached.

Incredibly, person after person responds almost in chorus when questioned about one event or another. Each witness reaches back 6000 years to take the same defensive stance that was taken near the beginning of time. Each gives a similar answer to questions posed by those trying to get to the truth about the scandals that seem to be everywhere.

Their defense was formed in the heart of the first son of Adam and Eve. His name was Cain. He had brought an unacceptable sacrifice before God and it was rejected. His anger was apparent for all to see and for God to know.

But God showed kindness in His response toward Cain. He said, "If you do well, will you not be accepted? And if you do not do well, sin lies at the door. And its desire is for you, but you should rule over it." ~ Genesis 4:7

Cain had every opportunity to do the right thing, but as in all scandals one ill deed leads to another. Instead of remedy, he sought revenge. His response was to kill his brother Abel, then intensify the scandal by hiding the body and attempting to lie to God.

When God asked Cain where his brother Abel was, Cain responded, "I do not know. Am I my brother's keeper?" ~ Genesis 4:9

And there is the answer we have heard to so many questions lately: I DO NOT KNOW! As much as things change, they stay the same.

Scandals cease where truth begins. It's time for folks to stop acting like Cain!

Avoidance

There is one agency of the government that most would like to avoid at all costs. I speak, of course, of the Internal Revenue Service. Some of you may have had a scrape with this agency of the government. I remember learning a little axiom about taxes years ago. It goes something like this: What is the difference between tax evasion and tax avoidance?

The answer—about 20 years!

It is perfectly legal to avoid paying taxes. It is perfectly illegal to evade paying taxes and the consequences of doing so is a paid vacation to the Federal Prison in Leavenworth or accommodations of similar quality.

There is a parallel between taxes and evil. Now before I hear a collective, "AMEN!", let me explain. Though taxes seem evil, I am not trying to make that connection. My focus is on the subject of avoidance. We cannot evade evil in this world, but we can avoid it.

The wisest man in the world, Solomon, King of Israel, put it in these terms: "Do not enter the path of the wicked, and do not walk in the way of evil. Avoid it, do not travel on it; turn away from it and pass on." ~ Proverbs 4:14-15

Solomon did not declare that the path of wickedness or the way of evil should be barricaded. He did not suggest that we send in heavy equipment and eradicate the passageway of sin. He gave instruction on living with its existence.

He said that we should avoid this way all together. We are to refuse the temptation to travel upon this smooth, broad way that leads to certain destruction. As a matter of fact, he warned that we should turn away from it and use another route to reach our destination.

Many GPS devices now offer a feature called traffic avoidance. Satellites are constantly monitoring traffic flow looking for bottlenecks or accidents that would cause delay in your travel. If you use this service, it will recommend an alternate route that will allow you to avoid the troubles that could be just around the next bend in the road. It will not, however, force you to take the new road.

As you begin your day, why not ask God to show you how to avoid the evil-congested road? Avoid the way of evil with the passion of avoiding taxes. You cannot evade taxes or bad roads in this life, but with God guiding your life you can avoid purposefully traveling the way of evil.

Showers of Blessing

All who are seeking a blessing from the Lord, please raise your hand. I see that hand. One thousand one, one thousand two, one thousand three…wait…I'm still counting hands. Yes, if I asked who would like to be blessed today, hands would go up immediately.

The assumption would then be that there are many various needs that can only be remedied by God's hand. It would also be assumed that equal to the count of raised hands would be the potential blessings of God. We would naturally think in plural terms, because there are many needs. The key word here is NATURALLY.

How many of you have sung the old gospel hymn, "Showers of Blessing," and without a thought pluralized the word blessing? Go ahead, hum it to yourself and if you're alone sing it out loud. I have done it and I have heard it sung:

> There shall be showers of blessing(s):
> This is the promise of love;
> There shall be seasons refreshing,
> Sent from the Savior above.
> Showers of blessing(s),
> Showers of blessing(s) we need:
> Mercy-drops round us are falling,
> But for the showers we plead.

Did you throw the "s" onto the end? We just think if there are showers (plural), then there must be blessings (plural). The hymn was written correctly based on Ezekiel 34:26: "I will make them and the places all around My hill a blessing; and I will cause showers to come down in their season; there shall be showers of blessing."

I think that this is really more than a matter of grammar. You see, there will be many showers, but there will only be one blessing. There can only be one blessing, because there is only one *Blesser*. God will always bless according to His purpose and that is singular.

Certainly you feel at this moment that your need is unique. Remember, I saw that hand! But truthfully, all of our needs (plural) require the showers (plural) of His blessing (singular). The blessing of God is sufficient to meet every diverse need scattered across the globe today. It can be divided into individual droplets falling in downpours miles apart and yet each has the common source of God's merciful heart revealed in His singular purpose.

Dear God, let it rain! May Your blessing meet the needs of all my readers today.

Choosing Rightly

Vanilla. There would not be Baskin-Robbins if vanilla was the only choice of ice cream flavor available. I know some people prefer vanilla, but I don't understand them very well. It's just so…vanilla!

I, on the other hand, prefer choosing. And that is where a lot of my troubles begin. Choosing is never easy. I have a sincere desire to choose rightly, but I often find myself blindly making decisions and then hoping for the best. Right now, I'm just hoping some of you are sympathetic with my condition.

I read a few thoughts by Oswald Chambers recently on the subject of choosing and it left me with no choice. I had to stop and really listen while contemplating how many bad choices I have made in life. Not particularly bad in a moral sense, but bad, because I had chosen only the good instead of the best.

Chambers said concerning right choices, "Whenever [your] right [to choose] is made the guidance in the life, it will blunt the spiritual insight. The great enemy of the life of faith in God is not sin, but the good which is not good enough. The good is always the enemy of the best. It would seem the wisest thing in the world for Abraham to choose, it was his right, and the people around would consider him a fool for not choosing. Many of us do not go on spiritually because we prefer to choose what is right instead of relying on God to choose for us. We have to learn to walk according to the standard which has its eye on God."

Abraham was noted for his faith. He lived a life of belief in which he allowed God to make the choices. Did he ever fail at this? Yes, he did. He made lots of choices and each time he did, he suffered the consequences of HIS choice.

It may take us, like Abraham, most of our lives to get this choosing thing right. "When Abram was ninety-nine years old, the Lord appeared to Abram and said to him, 'I am Almighty God; walk before Me and be blameless.'" ~ Genesis 17:1

Life is full of choices. It's not a vanilla world in which we live. If it were, then faith would not be necessary. Walk in step with God through each choice that life brings your way. Surrender your right to choose, so God can reveal the right choice for you.

In Control

Man in all of his wisdom and cunning still finds himself totally under the control of one element of creation. God gave Adam the command to subdue the earth and all of its wild creatures. There are few animals that have not been controlled to some degree by man's ingenuity. There are still a few depths of the sea or a peak or two that have not been visited by man, but for the most part we have fulfilled that command given to Adam. But there is still that one elusive quantity that has never been fully understood nor controlled: the weather.

We have tried to make it rain and only succeeded in flooding some small area while leaving other places high and dry. A few years back the Chinese tried to wash the air before the Olympics to impress western dignitaries and guests. All of our efforts are to no avail. When it comes right down to it, we are not in control at all.

I can still remember as a young boy when my mother would get me up out of a sound sleep to sit up with her during the night. These times would be during a nighttime storm. I would sit there half-awake thinking to myself how silly all of this was. Our being awake was not going to redirect the power of the wind and rain, but I sat obediently with my mama and listened to the storm howl in the dark.

God has used the weather as an instrument of His judgment and blessing over centuries and I think He still does so today. See His power in these verse from Psalm 107. "He turns rivers into a wilderness, and the watersprings into dry ground; a fruitful land into barrenness, for the wickedness of those who dwell in it. He turns a wilderness into pools of water, and dry land into watersprings. There He makes the hungry dwell, that they may establish a city for a dwelling place…" ~ Psalms 107:33-36

It certainly seems that God is using what we would call "weird" weather to get the attention of our land. Take a moment this morning and read all of Psalm 107. Then you will understand the final verse of this Psalm, "Whoever is wise will observe these things, and they will understand the lovingkindness of the Lord." ~ Psalms 107:43 Though it be stormy or dry open your eyes and you will see God bending down in mercy to reveal His lovingkindness.

Rewinding Today

When my son was just a little boy, he had a favorite comment he would make when he had experienced a particularly good day. He would say with tired eyes, "I wish we could rewind today!"

These were the days ruled by the VCR. Incredibly, I risk writing to some who will have a difficult time remembering what a VCR (video cassette recorder) even is. Our memories are very short. Everything changes so fast that it has little time to take very deep root in our minds.

David wrote what we know as Psalm 38. This psalm is noted as a song of remembrance. Its words recount a dark and wearisome time in David's life. Is it not true that we both remember and refuse to remember those times that are the most troubling?

On this occasion the past came rushing in upon David like a flash flood. The psalm opens with a plea for relief from the rebuke of God. David senses the very hand of God pressing down upon him. He is reminded of his sin and takes full responsibility for the anger of God that is consuming him like a festering disease.

His predicament has left him all alone. Even his friends have forsaken him and his enemies are using this calamity to openly attack him. This is a dark day. This is a day that one desires to forget, but cannot be relegated to the realm of forgetting.

If this was a movie, the music would have reached crescendo. The camera would be focused upon the anguished face of David. Flashbacks would come roaring from off-screen into the present and the groans of a crushed spirit would be heard as they escaped from deep within David's heart.

But then, with utter amazement, we would hear the words that seem totally out of place in this moment. David's eyes turn toward heaven and with creased brow, he proclaims, "For in You, O Lord, I hope; You will hear, O Lord my God." ~ Psalms 38:15

WOW! What a scene! That which should have crushed the man forces from him a word of hope! A memorial to the faithfulness of God is poured out like a drink offering. There is no doubt of David's guilt and failure. There is no confusion as to the impossibility of escaping this tragedy. But he remembers that God is faithful to hear in the midst of the deepest trial. God can be trusted even when we cannot be.

Rewind the tape and be reminded that you can have full assurance of hope in the God who hears!

Scratch-and-Sniff

Our world is flooded with multi-sensory stimuli. I can still remember when the newest fad was scratch-and-sniff. Companies were pasting little decals in magazines and advertisements that allowed you to scratch the surface and have a delightful moment of sensing the smell of their product.

One of the most disgusting uses of this I ever came across was a book we purchased for our children. All throughout the story there were little spots on the pages where you could scratch the picture and get a whiff of the item. This particular book had a skunk as one of the characters. I can still remember getting sick to my stomach when I smelled the scratch-and-sniff of that little skunk. Some things you just don't need to smell!

We are most wonderfully made by God to be highly sensory. We have five senses by which we interact with the world around us. If we lose even one of these we are seriously handicapped.

We use these senses to gain insight into our world and thereby we marvel at God's creation. The end result is that we seek after the God of creation. It is possible though that our senses can trick us.

We can become de-sensitized. We need more and more stimuli to sense anything at all. Finally, we seek the sense itself as an end and lose the genuine purpose of the sense as it was given.

Solomon said, "A fool has no delight in understanding, but in expressing his own heart."~Proverbs 18:2 Here is the terrible end of a person who becomes senseless. He no longer finds understanding in that which exists outside of his own consciousness. He becomes an answer unto himself.

I am afraid that we have almost reached this point in society today. We think that we have solved all of the quandaries of life. We have answered the ultimate questions of who we are and why we are here. Or at least, we think we have.

We have been fooled into thinking that the answer lies within ourselves. But take another look. See that little dot on your heart. Go ahead and scratch it. Now take a deep whiff. It smells a whole lot like a skunk doesn't it?

Don't be foolish! Your delight cannot be found in your own heart. The answers you seek are found in Christ alone.

Loss of Appetite

I have overheard folks who work in a restaurant say that the last thing they desire to eat is that which is the most popular on the menu. Having served that particular item all day and going home with the scent of food embedded in their clothing, they just do not have an appetite for the special of the day.

Sometimes it seems that believers are a bit turned off by the smell of Jesus. We go to church, hang around other believers, partake of the sermon (that day's special), then we go home, and simply don't have an appetite for things of eternal value.

The Apostle John said in his first epistle that he could prove who Jesus was, because he had literally handled Him. He stated it this way: "That which was from the beginning, which we have heard, which we have seen with our eyes, which we have looked upon, and our hands have handled, concerning the Word of life— the life was manifested, and we have seen, and bear witness, and declare to you that eternal life which was with the Father and was manifested to us—"~1 John 1:1-2

Something tells me that as John wrote this he might have taken a deep breath. In doing so, he must have imagined again the scent of Jesus as he leaned upon Him at the last supper. He would have caught again the fragrance of the oil that Mary had poured upon His feet and wiped with her own hair.

He would have also breathed in the smells of a bloodied and bruised body that he had helped place in a borrowed tomb. He could still remember the cool damp scent of the empty tomb and he must have remembered the scent of heaven upon the resurrected Christ as He stood before them.

John smelled like eternity, because he spent time in the presence of Jesus. He declared the manifestation of Jesus in the life of the believer. This temporal ever-changing world should know Christ because we smell like Jesus. The evidence of the eternal should fill the room when we enter it.

Have you been handling Jesus? Is He the special of the day in your life? Never lose your appetite for Him and always be ready to tell others by your very life what's on the menu today.

Time For Cleaning

Many years ago when I was a young inexperienced pastor, I learned what to say and not say when visiting in someone's home. One example of my newness to the ministry happened as I dropped in for a visit in the home of one of our members.

I had been a pastor for less than a year. I'm trying to set the stage here and make this not appear as bad as it really was! After knocking on the door, the lady of the house invited me in and asked me to take a seat, which I did after clearing a spot on the couch. The lady's first remark after I was seated went something like this, "Preacher, if I had known you were coming I would have tried to clean the place up a bit."

As I looked around I honestly thought to myself that a three month notice would not have been sufficient. I knew that I needed to say something in response to her statement about a warning before my appearance at her door. So, being of quick wit and assuming that the preacher should never be at a loss for words, I said, "Don't be concerned about it." This is where I should have stopped, but being a man of many words, I continued, "If you can live here, I certainly can visit here!"

You guessed it! I immediately wished that I could take my words back, but it was too late. To my surprise the lady just smiled and said, "Yes, preacher. I guess that's true." It was a VERY short visit.

Paul was preparing to visit the church at Corinth and being a better pastor than I sent a warning that he was coming. Like this home I visited in my earlier days, the church at Corinth had a lot of stuff piled up and in need of cleaning. Paul wrote, "For I fear lest, when I come, I shall not find you such as I wish, and that I shall be found by you such as you do not wish; lest there be contentions, jealousies, outbursts of wrath, selfish ambitions, backbitings, whisperings, conceits, tumults…" ~ 2 Corinthians 12:20

How about it? Is it time for some spiritual house cleaning? It's not the preacher you have to worry about dropping by for a visit. It's the fact that the Holy Spirit is already dwelling in our house and is fully aware of all the junk. Ask Him to turn the light on brightly and identify the stuff that needs to be cleared away.

Did you hear that knock? Jesus is at the door…

Yes!

My children have always said with tongue in cheek that I never denied any request they made of me. The reason they give is not based upon my graciousness, but instead it rests upon their assumed ability to only ask questions that I would answer in the affirmative.

They were convinced that the best way to get a yes out of me was to only ask a question that could have yes as an answer. Their logic was sound. I only wish that I knew how to apply the same process to my prayer life.

So often I approach prayer with a hope that I can somehow convince God to say yes to my request. When His answer fails to meet my expectation I then fall into the trap of my own making. Disappointment in God and even despair of life can quickly overrule the facts of my request offered in prayer.

I blame God for the "wrong" answer, when it was my question that was really wrong. So how do we correct our prayer life to reflect who God is, and like my kids, expect the answer to be yes?

Return to the basics. Hear the words of Jesus as He taught the disciples to pray. The foundation of asking correctly begins with a recognition of God's holiness. Jesus said, "In this manner, therefore, pray: Our Father in heaven, hallowed be Your name." ~ Matthew 6:9

God will never say yes to anything that would violate His holiness. A.W. Tozer remarked in his devotional, Renewed Day by Day, "At the base of all true Christian experience must lie a sound and sane morality. No joys are valid, no delights legitimate where sin is allowed to live in life or conduct."

Never expect God to say yes, no matter how good your request is, if the result would violate His holiness. Tozer went on to pray these words: "Oh, God, let me die rather than to go on day by day living wrong. I do not want to become a careless, fleshly old man. I want to be right so that I can die right! Lord, I do not want my life to be extended if it would mean that I should cease to live right and fail in my mission to glorify You all of my days!"

I think that God could say yes to such a prayer. May your prayers always be answered with the Father's "YES!"

· JUNE

Your Day In Court

The last few years have given us opportunity to examine the sordid details of lives gone awry. I speak, of course, in reference to the strange courtroom exhibitions that have been published for all to see.

The newspapers and television have been filled with the exploits of those who were well known and of those who became well known simply because they were accused of breaking the law. Of course, they all are "innocent."

Some have been introduced to the swift hand of justice and our system of laws has prevailed to what seems to be the correct end. However, there are cases that simply allowed the guilty to escape the justice that they were due.

Amazing to me are the defense attorneys who must somehow believe that their client is innocent in the face of overwhelming evidence that proves otherwise. There is thankfully a court of higher justice in which all truth is revealed.

David found himself unjustly accused in Saul's court by a man named Cush. This man had told Saul that David could not be trusted as a friend and that David's intent was to bring harm to the king.

David's appeal was not to the judgment seat of men, but to the highest court which has as its judge the Ruler of the universe, God Himself. David proclaims, "My defense is of God, who saves the upright in heart." ~ Psalms 7:10

We do not hear David offering lame excuses. He is not placing blame on others. He is not creating sufficient doubt to sway a jury. He simply declares his defense to be in God.

Literally, God is his alibi. This is true because God knows his heart. There is no dishonesty before God. Excuses and pseudo-sorrow will not carry the day as we stand before God's justice.

God saves only the upright in heart. This has nothing to do with perfection or purity. This is not the sinless heart in full view of all. It is the honest heart.

153

Bring your case before the Lord today. Do not come with your attorney of pride nor your councilor of deceit. Come with the full acceptance of knowing that God knows all the secrets of your heart and fall forthrightly on the mercy of the court.

Only then can you hear the sweet words of grace, "Case dismissed!"

06/02

My Sister

This devotion was written to honor the life of my sister:

My sister died yesterday. How is it that we can encapsulate an entire life in four little words—one short sentence? Scripture tells us that our lives rush past us like the shuttle of a weaver's beam. Our lives are summed up like a tale that is told.

But when we take just a moment to consider a life, then the story lengthens, and we remember again that one life is really a series of moments. Every incident of life does not rise to the pinnacle of prominence in our feeble minds, but some do. And like all of us, we forget much more than we could ever hope to remember.

I awoke this morning reflecting upon my sister and our relationship. Marie, or Wee, as I remember calling her for years, was 12 years my senior. She had been adopted by my parents when it had been concluded that my mother would bear no children.

I can only imagine the shock and perhaps the horror in Wee's mind when it was disclosed that I was on the way. But, I would prefer to think that she was delighted at the prospect of a baby brother, although I surely must have been a pain to her at times.

This morning's thoughts of Marie took me to an unexpected place. Way before she taught me to blow bubble gum into giant elastic pockets of air that would burst and have to be peeled from my face. I even went back prior to the time she guided me in the fine art of riding a bicycle without training wheels.

I was reminded this morning of a time along the Nile River in Egypt. No, it wasn't Marie and I, but a maiden called Miriam and a baby brother named Moses.

Moses' mother had placed him in a basket and set him afloat upon the Nile in an attempt to hide him from Pharaoh. The order had been given that all male babies born to Israelites were to be killed.

If this had been me floating down the river, I think I know where Marie would have been—exactly where Miriam was: "And his sister stood afar off, to know what would be done to him." ~ Exodus 2:4

It was Miriam that ran along the bank of the Nile to watch over her baby brother. It was Miriam that would have placed her brother in the arms of Pharaoh's daughter. It was Moses' sister that would have recommended his own mother to be the nursemaid hired to feed her own son.

Thank God for a sister who loved her brother. I'll miss you Wee! Thanks for watching from a distance all of these years! See you soon!

06/03

A Reproach

There are times when I am at a loss for words or action. Just such an occasion transpired recently. I was in a place of business when I heard the faint sound of someone shouting. At first I thought it was kids playing, but as it continued I went to the place where I thought the noise was coming.

As I peered out the display glass of the business I saw the end of a very heated argument. It really was no contest. A man was shouting just inches from the face of a lady that I assumed was his wife. She stood there. It seemed that she had experienced this behavior more than just this time.

I wish that I could tell you that I stepped between them and stopped what was clearly verbal abuse, but I did not have that opportunity. Moments later he was hugging her as she cried on his shoulder. I don't think that there was resolution. I think she was using the only defense she had. They walked away as others arrived. I have no names, but God knows who they are. Join with me in praying for her protection and their salvation.

Here's the real twist to this story. The man doing all of the screaming was wearing a "Christian" t-shirt. Now the t-shirt may have been more of a "Christian" than he, but nevertheless he was wearing it. It may have been from a garage sale. Who knows?

I could not help, but be reminded of a portion of Daniel's prayer. Here's just one little part of that prayer: "O Lord, according to all Your righteousness, I pray, let Your anger and Your fury be turned away from Your city Jerusalem, Your holy mountain; because for our sins, and for the iniquities of our fathers, Jerusalem and Your people are a reproach to all those around us." ~ Daniel 9:16

Now I suppose that this couple had every right to argue in public. I am glad that we live in a free country that allows us to speak as we wish, although, I think that your right to use some language ends at the entry way of my ear!

All of these freedoms are precious, but we do not have the right to be a reproach to the name of Christ. Whether the man in this story is a believer is an unknown, but his outer garment became a reproach to Christ by his actions. How many times do our actions betray us and thereby we abuse the grace of God in our lives? Never let your life be a reproach to those around you.

06/04

Identity Crisis

You probably have noticed, but we are in a world that is suffering from an identity crisis. It's not a crisis of personal identity that I speak of here. The bookshelves are full of self-help instructions. You can read thousands of pages of stuff that is just that: stuffing. It fills the human mind and ego with a flood of hyper-importance about how significant man really is and how much more possibility exists for us if we just reach down and pull ourselves up by our own bootstraps.

No, the identity crisis I am speaking of is the lack of identifying who God is. This should not be a problem or a mystery that needs to be unraveled. God has been revealing His identity since the dawn of creation.

"The heavens declare the glory of God; and the firmament shows His handiwork. Day unto day utters speech, and night unto night reveals knowledge. There is no speech nor language where their voice is not heard. Their line has gone out through all the earth, and their words to the end of the world."~Psalms 19:1-4   God wants us to know Him personally, yet man spends hours trying to know the creation instead of the Creator.

When Moses was being commissioned to deliver Israel from Egypt he asked about God's identity. "Then Moses said to God, "Indeed, when I come to the children of Israel and say to them, 'The God of your fathers has sent me to you,' and they say to me, 'What is His name?' what shall I say to them?" And God said to Moses, "I AM WHO I AM." And He said, "Thus you shall say to the children of Israel, 'I AM has sent me to you.'" Moreover God said to Moses, "Thus you shall say to the children of Israel: 'The Lord God of your fathers, the God of Abraham, the God of Isaac, and the God of Jacob, has sent me to you. This is My name forever, and this is My memorial to all generations.'" ~ Exodus 3:13-15

So, God clearly gives us His name, I AM. He identifies Himself as the always present God who is not suffering from any form of identity crisis. He knows who He was, is, and always will be. He is the same yesterday, today, and forever and He wants you to know Him personally through His Son, Jesus Christ who multiple times used the same identifier to reveal Himself.

Over and again, Jesus said, "I am!" Now go live like He is who He is so you can be all that He has made you to be!

Values Driven

Why will you do what you do today? Some of you will do what the boss tells you to do…no more no less. Others of you will involve yourself with people in many different settings and will in those interactions both receive and give advice. Most of us will buy something today whether big or small and weigh the relative value of our purchase against some unseen standard. The list could go on and on, but the question still looms before us.

Why will you do what you do today?

The answer has little to do with society or peer pressure. Your particular upbringing has some bearing, but it will not be the deciding factor in your choices. The answer lies much deeper than these things. You will do what you do today, because of your value system. At some point you have formed a set of values that drives all of your decisions.

The dictionary begins defining value as relative worth or importance. But that's where most people let their value system rest—in the relativity of the moment. True foundational values are not moved or changed by the wind of circumstance.

A great example of value setting is demonstrated by the words of Jesus to the disciples as recorded in Matthew's gospel. "Therefore do not worry, saying, 'What shall we eat?' or 'What shall we drink?' or 'What shall we wear?' For after all these things the Gentiles seek. For your heavenly Father knows that you need all these things. But seek first the kingdom of God and His righteousness, and all these things shall be added to you." ~ Matthew 6:31-33

Jesus was realigning the values of the disciples from a temporal perspective to an eternal one. He knew that the disciples did what they did because their actions were driven by faulty values. Hence His statement, "For after all these things the Gentiles seek." The first word following this statement is key. It is the word, *but*. Our values must be based not on the things of this world, *but* those of heaven.

Alfred B. Smith said it best in the words of this old hymn:

> With eternity's values in view, Lord;
> With eternity's values in view -
> May I do each day's work for Jesus
> With eternity's values in view.

Now I'll ask that question once again. "Why will you do what you do today?"

Grace Period

It is interesting that nearly all debts have included with them a period of grace when it comes to repayment. The terms of this grace period are spelled out clearly in all of the tiny print that comes with your contract.

Now the very fact that an offer of grace would be issued in micro typesetting makes no sense. It is as if the lender is offering grace, but hiding the fact of it at the same time. In reality, that is exactly what is transpiring.

Furthermore, the grace being offered is filled with conditions. It is always limited in scope. There is a time when grace ends and, when grace is invoked, the interest and other charges related to the debt continue to accrue.

I am so glad that I am saved by grace. I entered the grace period over 33 years ago. All charges against me ceased, and my debt was paid in full.

Paul spoke of it in these terms. Note: none of it is in fine print! "For there is no difference; for all have sinned and fall short of the glory of God, being justified freely by His grace through the redemption that is in Christ Jesus, whom God set forth as a propitiation by His blood, through faith, to demonstrate His righteousness, because in His forbearance God had passed over the sins that were previously committed, to demonstrate at the present time His righteousness, that He might be just and the justifier of the one who has faith in Jesus." ~ Romans 3:22b-26

Wow! These are great terms of grace! These is no requirement on our part except to qualify. Qualification is simple—be a sinner. These verses declare all to be qualified for all have sinned.

There is no fine print. Grace was openly displayed for all to see on an old rugged cross nearly 2000 years ago. The debt was fully paid by Christ. His blood settled our debt and the books have been closed.

He became the justifier of His own justice because He is the Just One! A.W. Tozer said, "If God had acted according to justice alone, He simply would have pulled the stopper out and flushed us all down to hell and been done with it."

Thank God for unconditional, large print, never ending, saving grace! Have you applied? I know you qualify as all of us have. Enter the grace period today and be saved forever!

Foolishness

Stupid is one of the new words that most mothers go bananas over if they hear one of their children saying it. I grew up saying the word and at times acting the word out, but I guess it's okay to not want one kid calling another kid stupid. The truth is though that we all do some stupid things now and again.

Paul began his first letter to the Corinthians by reminding his readers that his message about the cross would seem very stupid to some. "For the message of the cross is foolishness to those who are perishing, but to us who are being saved it is the power of God." ~ 1 Corinthians 1:18

I know what you are thinking, "He didn't use the word stupid." Well, he did and he didn't. The word translated "foolishness" in the original could have been translated as silliness, block-headedness, moronic, or believe it or not, STUPID.

You see many are just fine with Jesus being a great teacher and a do-gooder, but they find it stupid to think about one man dying on a cross and that death being sufficient to save the whole world. It just blows their little pea-brains. By the way, we all have little pea-brains! It is only as we are saved that we can begin to comprehend the magnitude of Christ's atoning death on the cross.

So the writer of Hebrews says, "Therefore, when He came into the world, He said: 'Sacrifice and offering You did not desire, But a body You have prepared for Me. In burnt offerings and sacrifices for sin You had no pleasure.' Then I said, 'Behold, I have come—in the volume of the book it is written of Me—to do Your will, O God.' Previously saying, 'Sacrifice and offering, burnt offerings, and offerings for sin You did not desire, nor had pleasure in them' (which are offered according to the law), then He said, 'Behold, I have come to do Your will, O God.' He takes away the first that He may establish the second. By that will we have been sanctified through the offering of the body of Jesus Christ once for all." ~ Hebrews 10:5-10

It was God's will from the beginning to offer His Son as the atonement for man's sin. As these verses say, "By that will we have been sanctified." Hurry! Cover the kid's ears! Because it is just plain stupid to believe anything else! Amen!

Save Me!

One moment I was sitting on the bow of the boat—the next, I was under the water and desperately trying to breathe. It all happened so fast that I still to this day don't know what all transpired. I did conclude, however, that drowning is no way to leave this life.

I was fishing with a young man from the church where I was pastor. Paul and I had not been very successful in our attempt to entice the fish into the boat. The aluminum bateau was equipped with a very small motor. We were not moving along very quickly. I had no life jacket on as I sat on the bow looking back along the bank.

The top of the old sunken tree was barely above the waterline, but it was high enough to bring the boat to a sudden stop. When the boat hit the tree it was like we had struck a brick wall. I was ejected immediately backwards into the deep murky water.

The force of the boat was enough to push the tree up slightly, depositing me underneath its entangling branches, and letting it come to rest over me. I was buried instantly under a watery treetop. No bottom that I could find, no way up that I could see, and most importantly, very little air in my lungs.

In that moment I could relate fully with David as he cried out to the Lord, "Save me, O God! For the waters have come up to my neck. I sink in deep mire, where there is no standing; I have come into deep waters, where the floods overflow me." ~ Psalms 69:1-2

Needless to say, I wrote a devotion for today. You will have surmised that I did make it back to the surface that day, but I came very near to my death as I struggled to find my way through the tangled bough of that tree and finally take a deep gasp of air.

Perhaps today you are out of options. You have found yourself deep in the sea under a tangled mess of problems, trials, and tribulations. There is only one answer. It is the simple cry of David, "Save me, O God!"

Sing today the words of this old hymn:

> I was sinking deep in sin, far from the peaceful shore,
> Very deeply stained within, sinking to rise no more,
> But the Master of the sea heard my despairing cry,
> From the waters lifted me, now safe am I.
> Love lifted me!
> Love lifted me!
> When nothing else could help,
> Love lifted me!

A Samaritan Moment

The van was barely in the driveway of the parking lot. An incline was proving to be a formidable obstacle to the man who was clearly exhausted as he was pushing as hard as he could from the driver's side of the vehicle. I witnessed his struggle as I turned into the same store parking lot to get a cold Coca-Cola. I was in my dress clothes with a tie cinched tightly around my neck. My best shoes adorned my feet.

This was a Samaritan moment. You remember the story, don't you? A man was driving up to Jerusalem when his van broke down along the road. Just kidding…

A man was traveling along the road from Jericho to Jerusalem when he was attacked, robbed, beaten, and left nearly dead on the roadside. Three men passed by him that day.

One, a priest, passed on the other side ignoring what he clearly saw. The second, a Levite, took a look, but still passed on without offering aid. The third, a despised Samaritan, stopped and offered assistance.

Not only did the unnamed Samaritan bandage the man's wounds, he placed him upon his own donkey, transported him to an inn, made provision for his care, and offered to cover all charges incurred.

This parable was told by Jesus in response to the question a lawyer had asked Him. Jesus had just told this man that he was to love God with all of his heart, mind, soul, and strength. He also was to love his neighbor as himself.

The lawyer acted just like a lawyer. Luke tells us, "But he, wanting to justify himself, said to Jesus, 'And who is my neighbor?'" ~ Luke 10:29

It was at this moment that Jesus told the parable which we have labeled "The Parable of the Good Samaritan." He concluded the parable with a question to the lawyer. Jesus asked, "Which of these three men was a neighbor to the wounded man?

The lawyer responded, "The one who showed mercy."

The van was located in a parking lot 600 miles from here. It was hot and I was hurried. Helping the man push his van would provide no benefit to me. I will probably never meet him again. But Jesus' words sounded in my ear, "Go and do likewise."

I pushed and the man steered the big van into a parking spot. In an instant, a stranger on one of life's Jericho Roads became my neighbor.

Go and do likewise. Not because I did, but because Jesus said so.

A Look Into the Mirror

It had been said that when we look for praise we tend to look in the mirror; when we look for blame we tend to look out the window. I am guilty of this very process on more occasions than I wish to admit.

We may get away with this faulty line of thinking in dealing with each other, but it does not work with God. Hosea told the people of his day, "O Israel, return to the Lord your God, for you have stumbled because of your iniquity; take words with you, and return to the Lord. Say to Him, 'Take away all iniquity; receive us graciously, for we will offer the sacrifices of our lips.'" ~ Hosea 14:1-2

These verses are the Old Testament counterpart to the parable of the lost son in Luke's gospel. The young man took his inheritance, spent it in a frivolous manner, and found himself literally eating the leftovers of hog slop.

The story turns when the parable informs us that the young man came to himself and decided to return home to his father. He had his apology all ready by the time he arrived home. He had quit looking out the window and started looking into the mirror.

Hosea told the Israelites that they had stumbled because of their iniquity. Have you ever stumbled? Usually, you will look back to see what caused you to trip. Sometimes the stumble results in a fall that leaves you with cuts and bruises, reminding you for days that you had a serious misstep.

The Hebrew word that is translated as stumble in this verse does not speak of an external cause related to stumbling. The word points to an internal weakness of the legs and primarily a deficiency of the ankle. In other words, they did not stumble on something outside the window; they stumbled because of what was in the mirror.

The first step to recovering from a faulty ankle is to support it and take as much weight as possible off of the damaged joint. The truth is you are going to have to limp home when you've busted your ankle.

Like the young man in Luke's parable, it's time to limp home. It's time to offer to God as Hosea said, "the sacrifices of our lips." Take a long look into the mirror and then return to the Father. He is faithfully awaiting you. He will recognize you a long way off by your limp and with open arms say, "Welcome home!"

Come See

"Come see!" This is a very common phrase in the deep southern parts of Louisiana where I grew up as a boy. I understood completely what I was being commanded to do.

I still find it amusing to watch children here in this part of Arkansas respond to this statement. When you tell a child to come see, they will come, but it is usually followed with a question of their own—"See what?"

The two words, "come see" don't really mean come see something. They really mean come over here. There may or may not be anything to see. It is a command to come to this spot where I'm standing.

We have to be careful when we throw Christian phrases about and think that people know what we mean. We need to take the time to make sure that they really can see what we are saying.

When Jesus called Phillip to follow Him, Philip's response was to immediately find someone else to follow Jesus as well. John tells us in his gospel, "Philip found Nathanael and said to him, 'We have found Him of whom Moses in the law, and also the prophets, wrote—Jesus of Nazareth, the son of Joseph.' And Nathanael said to him, 'Can anything good come out of Nazareth?' Philip said to him, 'Come and see.'" ~ John 1:45-46

Philip offered the news of the Messiah's discovery to Nathaniel, but it must have been like a foreign language to him. It was clearly not what Nathaniel was expecting. Nathaniel resisted this news based on a well-known comment of disdain directed toward the residents of Nazareth. He might well have said, "Can anything good come from across the tracks?"

I like Philip's response to Nathaniel's curt remark—"Come and see." Or, as we would say in south Louisiana, "Come see!"

The word "come" is used over 500 times in the Bible. God in His mercy is extending His hands toward you today and saying, "Come see!" It's okay for you to come just as you are and it's okay for you to ask, "See what?"

It is in that moment that He will point to His Son, Jesus, and quote the final "come see" of the Bible, "And the Spirit and the bride say, 'Come!' And let him who hears say, 'Come!' And let him who thirsts come. Whoever desires, let him take the water of life freely." ~ Revelation 22:1

Framed

I enjoy visiting antique shops and taking a stroll back through time. Some of the items I discover are a mystery. At some point in time the old item served a vital purpose, but now it just sits on a shelf collecting dust.

Other items, I recognize immediately and often say out loud, "I used to have one of these!" Then reality sets in and you realize that there are items here that are as old as yourself. The word antique becomes very personal!

One of the things that I enjoy looking at are the old pictures. There will be a man or a lady, perhaps a couple, or maybe a baby in the photograph. The photos are usually very bland in color. Hardly anyone smiled for their photo.

The one thing that usually jumps out, however, is the frame. Most old frames were very ornate. A lot of craftsmanship had gone into carving intricate design into these pieces of wood that surround pictures of what appeared to be very sad people.

It was, as if, the owner of the photograph wanted to show off what bordered their life more than what their life was really like. The frame drew the viewer's eye away from the harshness of life to the outer edges where everything was beautiful.

These old photos and their frames give a wonderful insight into this world in which we live. The pictures we see are often sad. The images captured put on display the sheer desperation of fallen humanity.

Yet, if we look beyond the snapshot in time and take a look at the frame, we see that there is something beautiful holding this world all together. The writer of Hebrews said it this way: "By faith we understand that the worlds were framed by the word of God, so that the things which are seen were not made of things which are visible."~Hebrews 11:3

The next time you are strolling along and taking a review of this old world, remember the frame that holds life together is more important than the picture that you see of that day's happenings.

All of the tragedy, sadness, and despair of life is framed by the majesty of God's word. You see, people don't buy those old pictures because of the image seen in the photograph. They buy them for the frame.

Take your life and let it be framed by the word of God. It can make all things beautiful again.

A Pastor's Joy

Mission trips have become a central part of my life. I have the privilege of planning them and then participating with pastors and members of the Northwest Baptist Association churches. Often during one of these trips a real life story buries itself deeply in my heart. The following is just one of many of those stories.

I was preaching and teaching in a small Dominican Republic village on one of these trips. The pastor of the church in Los Almacigos is Raymundo Dominguez. My message was centered around the idea of joy. I could not have known how much the message was needed in this pastor's life nor how he would respond.

My text was 1 Chronicles 12. This chapter ends with these words: "...for there was joy in Israel." ~ 1 Chronicles 12:40   This was a time when the clouds of war were gathering on the horizon. The people were ready to install David as the King of Israel. Troops from all the tribes were volunteering to fight for David. They were described as being men who had loyal hearts and men that knew how to keep rank. These were men who lived orderly lives and had hearts that were not divided.

In the midst of impending trouble there was joy in Israel. A great feast was gathered and all of Israel was in unity of heart and mind.

I had no idea as I preached this text that the pastor had suffered a tragedy just days before our arrival. During a rainstorm, lightning had struck his herd of cows and six of them were killed. This was a severe loss to his family as they rely heavily on these cattle to sustain them.

Later I found out that his wife had been ill for two months and has lost her ability to hear in one ear because of infection. The pastor told our team after the services that God's word spoke to him about keeping his joy in the midst of these struggles.

This pastor's words convicted me of how quickly I complain and lose my joy over things that are merely inconveniences. I returned last year to visit Raymundo again. Since my first visit, he has suffered a debilitating stroke. Amazingly, his joy remains strong as he keeps his trust fixed on Jesus.

The needs of this family are tremendous and the family of God can surround them in care. Perhaps as you pray for this pastor and his family your joy will be restored also.

I'm Bored!

School's been out a few weeks now and you have very likely already heard summer's favorite exclamation, "I'm bored!" Children get bored and restless very easily. Some of it is because their attention spans are so short, but maybe more than that their time is so long. Since they have no real basis for evaluating time they conclude that there simply is too much of it. We, as adults on the other hand have seen our lives evaporate behind us and we see the value of time well spent. Or do we?

I know a lot of Christians who live bored existences as they serve the Lord. It seems to me at least that they spend day after day in menial service to the Lord, go to church for one hour on Sunday and watch time slowly tick by with little accomplished for the Kingdom. I'm tired just writing about it!

How different for the first disciples and the early church. Here were servants of God "…who have risked their lives for the name of our Lord Jesus Christ." ~ Acts 15:26 That surely doesn't sound boring. These men put it all on the line day after day.

The word *risk* means that they signed up for hazardous duty. The word lends the idea of giving oneself to adventure or to yield and offer one's life for the Lord Jesus Christ. How can this happen in your life? Most of the time it takes place unplanned. God simply intervenes and puts you into service. But you must be preparing yourself also.

I learned how to swim as a teenager. It was not by choice. I was with my friends at Magnolia Beach on the Amite River. My buddies were having a grand time in the water. I was sitting on the sandy beach watching. I wanted to swim, but I didn't know how nor was I willing to take the risk. My friends (I say that with a big question mark) suddenly grabbed me and carried me to the middle of the river with me kicking and screaming. There in the current with no place for my feet to rest… I SWAM!

I don't recommend this! It was dangerous! But I have to say that today I can swim. Have you been sitting on the beach too long? Is it time to yield to the risk and ask God to teach you how to swim? He will pick you up if necessary and drop you in the current, but always remember: He is a friend that sticks closer than a brother (Proverbs 18:24).

Language Barrier

I have enjoyed teaching ESL classes. This acronym stands for English as a Second Language. The enthusiasm of most ESL students is contagious. You quickly realize the teacher has the upper-hand in an ESL class. I understand the English language fully—they do not.

The first rule in the class is that their native language cannot be spoken. Everyone must speak English so that total immersion will take place. The students usually know a few words, but speak them with very strong accents. Instructions are given by pantomime or by pointing. It is amazing how fast the class learns and after a mere 90 minutes all can speak at least 25 new words as well as some short sentences.

Sometimes we are like these students. We need some help understanding God's language. We hear it, but we cannot make sense of it. Jeremiah was teaching God's language to the people of Israel when he spoke these words from God.

"Then came the word of the Lord to Jeremiah, saying, 'Thus says the Lord of hosts, the God of Israel: Go and tell the men of Judah and the inhabitants of Jerusalem, 'Will you not receive instruction to obey My words?' says the Lord.'" ~ Jeremiah 35:12-13

God wants to speak to us, but we must follow His instructions explicitly. We must learn to speak His language and obey His commands. At first we may struggle and it may seem that we will never learn to speak the language of heaven. But, as they say, practice makes perfect!

Repetition is used as a primary tool to teach the students English. If there is one thing I have learned about God is that He will repeat Himself over and again if we have a sincere desire to learn His language.

So says James, "If any of you lacks wisdom, let him ask of God, who gives to all liberally and without reproach, and it will be given to him." Thank God for His patience in teaching us His language.

Confident Boldness

Boldness is a characteristic that can easily go awry. It is easy, if boldness comes naturally to you, to be considered brash or impertinent. However, the person who is endowed with boldness has a real advantage when it comes to getting things done.

This word boldness is translated several ways at least 25 times in the New Testament. Sometimes it is translated as confidence. For example, in 1 John 5:14, John declares that this is the confidence or boldness that we have in prayer because we know that if we ask according to His will He hears and we have the petition of our hearts.

In Hebrews, we read, "Therefore, brethren, having boldness to enter the Holiest by the blood of Jesus, by a new and living way which He consecrated for us, through the veil, that is, His flesh, and having a High Priest over the house of God, let us draw near with a true heart in full assurance of faith, having our hearts sprinkled from an evil conscience and our bodies washed with pure water. Let us hold fast the confession of our hope without wavering, for He who promised is faithful." ~ Hebrews 10:19-23

These verses begin with a bold entry into His presence. This section ends by declaring that we should hold fast our confession without wavering. The idea is that of speaking a unified word that we boldly declare and will not back away from under any circumstance. How is such a bold stand possible?

First, because of His faithfulness, not ours. Second, because He made the way into God's presence by His own blood sacrifice. Remember how at His crucifixion the veil in the temple was torn apart from top to bottom. God reached down and opened the way into His Presence as He accepted the sacrifice of His Son. Third, we can be bold because He serves as our High Priest. He daily makes intercession for all believers.

You can be a bold witness today. You speak His words not your own. You stand in His faithfulness not your own. You are secure in His promise not yours.

As they always say at the opening of each Star Trek episode: "TO GO BOLDLY WHERE NO ONE HAS GONE BEFORE!"

Fly In the Ointment

In the diamond fields of South Africa a diamond was found and celebrated under the title of flystone. When placed under a magnifying glass, you can see enclosed in all its brilliancy a little fly, with body, wings, and eyes, in the most perfect state of preservation. How the fly came to be there no one knows, but no human skill can take it out.

Perhaps you have heard the expression: "That's the fly in the ointment." Did you know that it has a biblical source? "Dead flies putrefy the perfumer's ointment, and cause it to give off a foul odor; so does a little folly to one respected for wisdom and honor." ~ Ecclesiastes 10:1

Not a pretty sight! To understand this snippet of Solomon's wisdom you would need to read the conclusion of the previous chapter here in Ecclesiastes. The context is all about wisdom.

He tells the story of a city that was surrounded by an enemy, but was delivered by the wisdom of an unknown poor man. Solomon concludes, "Then I said: 'Wisdom is better than strength. Nevertheless the poor man's wisdom is despised, and his words are not heard. Words of the wise, spoken quietly, should be heard rather than the shout of a ruler of fools. Wisdom is better than weapons of war; but one sinner destroys much good.'" ~ Ecclesiastes 9:16-18

Who has not seen what a moment of folly can do to wreck an entire life? It really is like dead flies in the ointment. What should have been a sweet aroma coming from the jar now is repulsive and foul smelling. The diamond from South Africa is renowned for its fly, but not so with a fly in the ointment of the soul.

Those who look inside the flystone diamond don't know how the fly got there nor how to remove it without destroying the diamond. I, on the other hand, can tell you how to get the flies of folly out of your life.

Admit that the flies are there because of your sin nature. Believe that God has the power to remove them without destroying the heart that contains them. Confess that He alone is the sweet aroma of your life.

Like the flystone diamond people will speak of your life, not because of your flies, but because of the gift of faith found deep in your life. May every facet of your life shine with the light of Jesus today and may the sweet aroma of heaven be upon your life.

A New Cave

Are you tottering on the brink of decision today? Have you thought that maybe it would be best if you just stayed away from church? Perhaps the idea of people asking how things are just makes you want to hide?

What you need is a change of location; a new address; a different focus on life. You need to get out of your cave and find another one. Whoa! Another cave? Why change from one cave to another? I'm glad you asked!

For the answer, we will need to look back a few thousand years to David's time. He was in a real quandary. He had obediently served King Saul, yet found himself hated and hunted like a common criminal.

In 1 Samuel, we find him hiding in the Cave of Adullam. "David therefore departed from there and escaped to the cave of Adullam. So when his brothers and all his father's house heard it, they went down there to him. And everyone who was in distress, everyone who was in debt, and everyone who was discontented gathered to him. So he became captain over them. And there were about four hundred men with him." ~ 1 Samuel 22:1-2

We are not told David's mental state, but we can only assume that he was tired, lonely, and desperate. Just a little earlier in the previous chapter he had been feigning the part of a madman. Now his last escape from Saul had brought him to this cold, damp cave. The word cave in Hebrew means a place of darkness or to be naked. The picture is one of real heartfelt destitution. And then came the men from the countryside.

Not men of esteem, but the hurting. Those who were distressed, in debt, and discontented. They sought David in his cave of hardness and it became for them a cave of hope. So why should you climb out of your cave and find a church to attend? Won't church just be another cave?

Perhaps, but there are others who are waiting to gather by your side. Others who need hope in their distress, help in their indebtedness, and a hand out of their discontentment. God has had you in His hold all this time so you could help someone else in their time of need. We all need a change of caves now and again. Somebody's waiting for you to be a captain in their life.

Now get up and get out! See you at the First Cave of Adullam…

Too Many Words

The average person speaks around 371 million words in a lifetime. If you are like me, you may have been around people on both ends of that spectrum. I wonder if some folks have anything to say and others seem to never stop talking.

I know what you are thinking…"that's surely the pot calling the kettle black since you are a preacher!" Certainly there have been some times in my preaching days that I was long past being through before I ever shut up, but I think I'm getting better after a few thousand sermons!

Jesus delivered one of world's greatest sermons in barely 700 words as it is translated in Luke's gospel. Imagine that! The entirety of the greatest teaching of Jesus can be read in just a few minutes.

Yet we can sometimes get enamored over much speech. Though there are few words in the Sermon on the Mount or as they are better known, The Beatitudes, Jesus clearly warned of the danger of not hearing them. "Whoever comes to Me, and hears My sayings and does them, I will show you whom he is like: He is like a man building a house, who dug deep and laid the foundation on the rock. And when the flood arose, the stream beat vehemently against that house, and could not shake it, for it was founded on the rock. But he who heard and did nothing is like a man who built a house on the earth without a foundation, against which the stream beat vehemently; and immediately it fell. And the ruin of that house was great." ~ Luke 6:47-49

I'm not so sure that we think about the parable of the two builders in the context of hearing. Because the parable speaks so much about doing the building, we miss what is the foundational truth of the teaching. And I do mean foundational here!

Clearly, the foundations are laid in our hearing concerning what Jesus said nearly 2000 years ago in less than 700 words. The truths of the Sermon on the Mount are what dig deep to give us a sure footing for all that we will build with our own speeches throughout this life of 371 million words.

It's not that what we say has no importance; it's just that none of it will last if it is not built on the words of Christ. Words aren't tested in the moment they pass the lips, but when the storm comes into the lives of those to whom we have spoken.

Choose yours words carefully. Someone's building a foundation out of them!

Focused On Jesus

Is there a selection of scripture that has ever radically changed your life? Robert Morgan in his excellent devotional, *From This Verse*, tells the story of William Borden. Proverbs 24:11-12 was the catalyst that redirected Borden to a life surrendered to the call of missions and a world that does not know Christ.

William Borden was part of the Borden milk family. He had the family fortune at his disposal. He was handsome, extremely bright, and a gifted athlete. But he primarily focused on Jesus Christ. In 1906, as a freshman at Yale, he traveled to Nashville to attend a convention of the Student Volunteer Movement, which was devoted to overseas missions.

Samuel Zwemer, missionary statesman, was there with his maps, and his message melted Borden's heart regarding the Islamic world. Zwemer proclaimed: "Shall we stand by and allow these millions to continue under the curse and snare of a false religion, with no knowledge of the saving love and power of Christ? Of course it will cost life. It is not an expedition of ease nor a picnic excursion to which we are called...It is going to cost many a life, and not lives only, but prayers and tears and blood. We do not plead for missions. We simply bring the facts before you and ask for a verdict."

Zwemer then quoted the verses that seized the heart of William Borden. "Deliver those who are drawn toward death, And hold back those stumbling to the slaughter. If you say, 'Surely we did not know this,' Does not He who weighs the hearts consider it? He who keeps your soul, does He not know it? And will He not render to each man according to his deeds?" ~ Proverbs 24:11-12

William returned to Yale a changed young man and committed to reaching Muslims with the gospel. His commitment led him to give his fortune to Christian causes and leave the shores of America.

Borden never made it to the mission field, however. He died of spinal meningitis on board the ship bearing him to the foreign fields. Under his pillow was stuffed a last message: "No Reserve! No Retreat! No Regrets!"

His story was broadcast in newspapers across America, and his biography by Mrs. Howard Taylor resulted in numbers of young people offering themselves to missions.

"No Reserve! No Retreat! No Regrets!"

Power Belongs To God

Have you ever wondered if you heard correctly? It could be that you were not listening well enough or it might have been that the information was just so amazing that you could not believe what you just heard.

I think this might be the main two reasons that God repeats Himself so often throughout His word. For example, He says in three different places in scripture that the just shall live by faith. He knows that we need to hear something more than once at times to really hear it.

David said this very thing in Psalm 62:11, "God has spoken once, twice I have heard this: that power belongs to God." ~ Psalms 62:11 Literally, David said that God's word is always in unity. He speaks once, but He allows us to hear it again.

And what is it that David has been made sure of: the fact that power belongs to God. The word power here means strength of force, strength of security, and strength of majesty. Simply put there is no one stronger than our God!

Where does David gather this conclusion? He has carefully recounted God's previous display of strength. "He only is my rock and my salvation; He is my defense; I shall not be moved. In God is my salvation and my glory; the rock of my strength, and my refuge, is in God. Trust in Him at all times, you people; pour out your heart before Him; God is a refuge for us." ~ Psalms 62:6-8

Do you see how God repeats Himself to make sure we get it? Twice David says that God is his salvation. Twice he calls God his rock. Twice he uses the words refuge to describe his God. How then should we respond to the issues that confront us in this life? Find the truth and keep repeating it until you believe it! Trusting God totally comes when we open our inner most being (our hearts) before Him.

Now repeat after me, "Power belongs to God and He is my defense; power belongs to God and He is my defense!" Keep it up until you believe it; then you will begin to truly hear His voice and see His hand. Again, "Power belongs to God and He is my defense; power belongs to God and He is my defense!" I shall NOT be moved!

My Name Really Is Bob

Sometimes a word is not enough. Take for example my name. It seems simple enough to me. My name is R.E., but inevitably after I introduce myself, someone will ask, "Do you go by that?" I can be wearing a name tag and people will still ask if I go by R.E. I have begun a storyline now in which I tell people that my real name is Bob, but I work for the CIA and they require me to go by a fake name. Hello! My name is R.E. And yes, I go by that!

The same problem seems to exist with the simple message of the gospel. God could not have made it any simpler, but people just can't take it at face value. They want to make it hard. Paul described it this way. "For the message of the cross is foolishness to those who are perishing, but to us who are being saved it is the power of God. For it is written: 'I will destroy the wisdom of the wise, and bring to nothing the understanding of the prudent.' But we preach Christ crucified, to the Jews a stumbling block and to the Greeks foolishness, but to those who are called, both Jews and Greeks, Christ the power of God and the wisdom of God." ~ 1 Corinthians 1:18-19; 23-24

It's as if someone is asking God, "Did you really intend the gospel to be so simple?"

The answer, of course, is yes! Even though it is simple, however, it is profound. By its simplicity God destroys the wisdom that the wise claims to possess and the understanding of the overly cautious. In other words, the person who says I know better than to believe something so simple is the very candidate for the full benefit of the gospel.

What is it that releases the doubter or the defensive person? It is the message of the crucified Christ. There is no way to get around this one fact. As Paul stated in Romans 5:7-8: "For scarcely for a righteous man will one die; yet perhaps for a good man someone would even dare to die. But God demonstrates His own love toward us, in that while we were still sinners, Christ died for us."

When Christ is dealt with at the point of the cross, power and wisdom is released. You may know of Christ as a teacher, or good man, or even miracle worker, but only when you are confronted with the crucified Christ will your eyes be opened to the simple truth of the gospel: CHRIST DIED FOR US!

Like my initialed name, Christ died on purpose and for a purpose. He had no plan B for us to consider. God's plan was for His Son to die for a wicked world and that all who believe on Him as Savior would receive eternal life. Savior is on His name tag; and He goes by that! Simply believe and be saved!

Understanding the Cross

I had the opportunity to witness to a young lady on a recent plane trip. I was not supposed to be on this plane at all. I had missed an earlier flight and was placed on standby for this flight. Upon arrival the agent told me that the flight was oversold and my "chances" of getting a seat were slim to none. The call was made for interested ticketed persons to accept a voucher for a later flight due to the oversold condition. The plane was loaded and then they called my name. I had a seat, but it wasn't by chance.

As I took the last seat on the plane, I found myself next to a young lady who was of Hindu background. After takeoff, I continued reading a book by Jeff Simpson which I had begun earlier in the day. Her curiosity prompted her to ask me about the book. It is titled, *Active Believing*. Her questions gave me an excellent opportunity to ask her about her beliefs.

She told me that she believed in God, but did not understand too much about Jesus. She had been attending church with some friends and she was very interested in learning more. Our time was very short since we were already in our descent, so I offered her my copy of the book. She was very hesitant, but finally accepted the gift. You can join me in praying for her. You can just call her "A." God knows her and He will bring her path across the next Christian who can water the seeds I planted.

She is not so different than many today who think that their belief in God is enough for salvation. But scripture tells us that the demons even believe in God, and we know they will not be saved. "You believe that there is one God. You do well. Even the demons believe—and tremble!" ~ James 2:19

There must be a relationship with Christ for salvation to exist. "...let it be known to you all, and to all the people of Israel, that by the name of Jesus Christ of Nazareth, whom you crucified, whom God raised from the dead, by Him this man stands here before you whole. This is the 'stone which was rejected by you builders, which has become the chief cornerstone.' Nor is there salvation in any other, for there is no other name under heaven given among men by which we must be saved." ~ Acts 4:10-12

Unless a person deals with the reality of Christ's sacrifice on the cross there is no hope of salvation. P. T. Forsyth, a Scottish clergyman, wrote in the *Cruciality of the Cross*: "Christ is to us just what His cross is. All that Christ was in heaven or on earth was put into what He did there. Christ, I repeat, is to us just what His cross is. You do not understand Christ till you understand His cross." Pray for all those you know who need to know the *cruciality* of the cross.

Don't Leave Home Without It

Sometimes I get caught out of uniform. I will be somewhere in town and meet someone from one of the churches in our association. Many times they will not recognize me. They know me, but not in everyday attire. Inevitably, they will remark, "I didn't know you without a suit on!" I wonder how many of us are not recognizable as Christians without being dressed in our Sunday-go-to-meeting-clothes?

What exactly are the identifying characteristics that set us apart in our everyday lives? There are several, but I only want to speak of one here today: a heart of flesh. Israel had lost all of their testimony in the world. I do mean the entire world.

If you take the time to read Ezekiel 36 you will see that God had driven them out of their homeland because of disobedience. This did not change them, however. Every country into which they were driven saw them profane the name of God by their daily lifestyle.

But we serve a compassionate God! Here's what God did for Israel and this is what He will do for you. "I will give you a new heart and put a new spirit within you; I will take the heart of stone out of your flesh and give you a heart of flesh. I will put My Spirit within you and cause you to walk in My statutes, and you will keep My judgments and do them." ~ Ezekiel 36:26-27

The one identifying mark of a Christian that always distinguishes us from the world is this: the heart of flesh.

God told Israel that He did this not for their sake, but for His own. He desires that the world knows Him and He wants to display Himself in and through you. Only a heart of flesh will allow you to live in obedience and compassion. You may not always be in your Sunday best, but you can always have the heartbeat of God.

Like the old American Express commercial used to say, "Don't leave home without it!" Open your life today and let the world around you see the heart of God beating in you. When they ask why you are so different, tell them about the miracle of your life when God changed stone to flesh.

Remembering the Resurrection

If you knew you were going to die today what would you say to your friends and loved ones? What final remarks would you have? What would you hope they would reflect upon after you were gone? Paul must have been thinking along these lines when he wrote his last letter to Timothy. As far as we know these were some of his final thoughts before he was beheaded for the cause of Christ.

Paul's closing words to his young son in the ministry dealt directly with the subject of the resurrection. "Consider what I say, and may the Lord give you understanding in all things. Remember that Jesus Christ, of the seed of David, was raised from the dead according to my gospel." ~ 2 Timothy 2:7-8

Paul used two imperatives here as instructions to Timothy. One you might expect. The other seems strange in some ways, yet is very important to the effectiveness of Timothy's and our Christian lives.

The first word is *consider*. This word means to exercise the mind to the point of understanding. This ability to consider is unique to us as humans. Animals can think, no doubt, but only men have the ability to put the facts together or as Paul put it: to consider.

Unfortunately, a lot of Christians don't take into consideration the things of God. They act like there is a lid on their brains. Just open them up and pour stuff in until they are full. This is not what Paul meant as he spoke to Timothy.

The second word is *remember*. This means to exercise the memory to the point of recollection. Now this is an interesting thought. You would not think that Timothy would need to be instructed to remember the resurrection, but Paul thought it necessary to refresh his memory on this one very important topic.

Believers must remember the resurrection also. We have so compartmentalized the gospel that we forget one of the fundamentally simple truths about it. The gospel cannot be taken apart. The gospel is the birth of Christ, *and* the life of Christ, *and* the death of Christ, *and* the resurrection of Christ, *and* the second coming of Christ!

So, if you were going to die today, would you want just a piece of your life remembered? I don't think so! Our lives are a whole. The gospel is a whole. Keep considering it until you understand it. That will take you through to the end of your days. Then keep remembering each part of the whole until you can repeat it like it belongs to you. In essence, it does, because you are a new creation; created in Christ Jesus.

Is that true for you? Do you possess the gospel as your own? What exactly will you be remembered for after you spend your last day in this world? Consider Jesus and remember all He has done for you! Your life will begin to take on a reflection of Christ and you will be remembered for who you knew, not what you have done!

06/26

Exactly Where?

Years ago there was no subject called social studies. We took history, or geography, or civics as a course. I'm not sure why the change took place except that a title like social studies tells me that a lot of liberty can be taken on the supposed effects of history, geography, or civics with less focus on the facts of the subjects.

There is a lot of history in the Bible, but also a lot of geography. I think we gloss over a list of places sometimes thinking that it can't hold much spiritual significance for us. But we must ask why God included this detail if it wasn't for our edification.

Such a list is given in Numbers 21. "From there they went to Beer, which is the well where the Lord said to Moses, 'Gather the people together, and I will give them water.' Then Israel sang this song: 'Spring up, O well! All of you sing to it—the well the leaders sank, dug by the nation's nobles, by the lawgiver, with their staves.' And from the wilderness they went to Mattanah, from Mattanah to Nahaliel, from Nahaliel to Bamoth, and from Bamoth, in the valley that is in the country of Moab, to the top of Pisgah which looks down on the wasteland." ~ Numbers 21:16-20

What is the lesson for us out of this historical and geographical listing? First, the context must be considered. The children of Israel had just been judged for complaining again. This time they whined about the manna. God sent serpents among them and many died. Moses lifted a brass serpent on a pole and all who looked upon it were healed. This serpent on a pole is still the symbol seen today for a physician.

From this judgment and healing they journeyed and the places were recorded as part of a song and poem. They returned to the well which had been provided to satisfy their thirst. It is good to remember the first time you drank deeply of salvation. This well had been provided by godly leaders who acted as servants. The nobles did the digging. That is so different from today. In our day the powerful want to be served; not to serve.

Their journey took them from this well to a place called Mattanah. This word means gift. Upon our salvation we are given grace gifts to live and serve Him who saved us.

From there they went to Nahaliel. Notice the "el" at the end of this name. This tells us it has something to do with the name of God. This word means the valley of God. So, He leads us to the still waters which are always down in the valley.

From Nahaliel they traveled to Bamoth, the heights. Scripture tells us to be humbled and He will exalt us in due time (1 Peter 5:6).

Finally, they arrive at Pisgah. The meaning of this word is a cleft or a place of contemplation. God wants to bring us to the place of refuge, but it will always be a journey.

Instead of just rushing from place to place, why not stop long enough today to consider both the history and geography of your journey. God is speaking in all times for it is "His story." God is speaking in all places for all places belong to Him who promised to be with you at all times and in every place.

06/27

Brokenness

Time and again Israel departed from the strength and confidence that was found in the word of God. Not only did they not desire to hear the true Word, they implored the prophets to soothe them with lies.

When we continue in this mindset long enough then the only remedy is brokenness. "And He shall break it like the breaking of the potter's vessel, which is broken in pieces; He shall not spare. So there shall not be found among its fragments a shard to take fire from the hearth, or to take water from the cistern." For thus says the Lord God, the Holy One of Israel: 'In returning and rest you shall be saved; in quietness and confidence shall be your strength.'" ~ Isaiah 30:14-15

None of us enjoys brokenness. It is painful and costly, but necessary to being restored. Only God can so shatter us as to bring us beyond our own strength to stand. In these verses from Isaiah, we see that when God breaks, He breaks into tiny fragments. The pieces cannot even be used as a make do tool or even a small cup to drink water. In the deepest time of brokenness it can seem that you are beyond repair, but take heart!

There is a secret to restoration. It begins not with tape and glue, but with a gathering of the pieces and offering them back to God. The fable says that Humpty Dumpty could not be put back together after his fall, but we are not just some broken egg.

We are the children of God and we have the possibility of restoration. Notice that it is God who declares the way to restoration. It is two-fold.

First, there is the return to a place of rest. The idea here is that of retreat and recline. It is a coming down and descending to a place of safety. Restoration takes time. Second, there is strengthening that comes from quiet confidence.

179

Here is a trust that allows you to be still and relax in the assurance that God can and will put the pieces of your life back together again. Like a broken bone that is mended, the area around the break will be stronger than the part that has never been damaged.

Come down from your perch. Give the brokenness of your life to Jesus. Stay still in the confidence of His ability to repair your worst nightmare. He wants to do this today, but be warned. I purposefully left out the last phrase of the two verses from above: "But you would not."

Your shattered dreams have no hope of restoration until you turn to Him. Do it today!

06/28

Learning How To Rest

I learned how to work as a boy; not a teenage boy—A BOY! My daddy believed in hard work and shared his belief with me on a daily basis. He didn't ask me if I believed it or not. He never asked my opinion on what the job would be or how long we would work. I worked when he said and we quit when he said. I used to love it when our neighbor would call him over for a talk—that meant a rest for me!

Now if you think I am complaining then you've got the wrong idea. I am grateful for the education I gained as I worked alongside my father. His method was not through a lot of explaining. Instead, it came by my watching him do the work. I will be grateful until I die for this "work-release" program!

My upbringing has left me with some residual work habits that can, if left unchecked, be detrimental. I have not learned how to rest well. I don't think I am not alone here. It seems that many in our busy world find it difficult to find time to rest.

Jesus spoke about the need for resting in Matthew 11. "Come to Me, all you who labor and are heavy laden, and I will give you rest. Take My yoke upon you and learn from Me, for I am gentle and lowly in heart, and you will find rest for your souls. For My yoke is easy and My burden is light." ~ Matthew 11:28-30

This word from Jesus is not a suggestion, but an imperative. It is directed to those who labor, but also to those who have piled on the burdens. The word "laden" refers to the overburdening of an animal or ship, but also means to be weighed down with ceremony.

Wow! That hit me like a ton of bricks—no pun intended! It's not always the stuff that tires us, but the whys and what-fors that get us weighed down and burdened beyond despair.

The other word that is interesting here is *rest*. It is used twice, but comes from two different sources. The first time it is used it speaks of repetitive pausing. Jesus said, "Come to Me and I will allow you to pause regularly." That flies in the face of the idea of busy-ness being equal to spirituality.

The second time the word *rest* is used is when Jesus says you will find rest for your souls. This is deeper than a physical rest. This goes way down deep into the psyche. It comes from a word that means intermission.

Do you see that! God's plan for us is to take an intermission. A time when activity ceases. The movie stops playing. The noise quietens. Simply put: You rest. Like the neighbor talking with my daddy, you have a chance to catch your breath, regain your focus, and learn to lay some burdens on Jesus.

It's intermission time!

06/29

Listening With Your Heart

Celebrity worship is nothing new and you don't have to look very far to find a gathering. They come in all forms and styles of "worship." Some are found around music, some around sports, some around politics, but there is also the most dangerous of all—religious celebrity. With the effects of electronic connectivity, it is very easy to bring masses of people together. Today, people are connected across miles. Celebrants do not have to be in one building to be following the celebrity.

God spoke to Ezekiel about those who were gathering to hear his prophecies. "As for you, son of man, the children of your people are talking about you beside the walls and in the doors of the houses; and they speak to one another, everyone saying to his brother, 'Please come and hear what the word is that comes from the Lord.' So they come to you as people do, they sit before you as My people, and they hear your words, but they do not do them; for with their mouth they show much love, but their hearts pursue their own gain. Indeed you are to them as a very lovely song of one who has a pleasant voice and can play well on an instrument; for they hear your words, but they do not do them. And when this comes to pass—surely it will come—then they will know that a prophet has been among them." ~ Ezekiel 33:30-33

Clearly God is not impressed by a celebrity following. He tells Ezekiel that these people come to hear. They are willing to sit and listen with seeming intensity, but the proof of their intent is found in their lack of obedience. Their mouths speak well, but their hearts are self-seeking.

In John 2 the scripture tells us a large following had all but made Jesus a celebrity, but this did not impress Him either. "Now when He was in Jerusalem at the Passover, during the feast, many believed in His name when they saw the signs which He did. But Jesus did not commit Himself to them, because He knew all men, and had no need that anyone should testify of man, for He knew what was in man." ~ John 2:23-25

In this day of mega madness, make sure that you are really following Christ. Even if you are part of a small gathering that studies God's Word and seeks to know the fullness of Christ in your life, never let the outward ornament replace inward obedience. Beware the grand gathering that only bends the ear, but never bends the heart.

06/30

Numbers

Numbers are very important in scripture. For example, the number one always refers to God, the number two to witness (He sent them out two by two), the number three to the Trinity. This list goes on for a ways and seems to hold true for nearly every use of a number in the text.

In Matthew we read of the account where Jesus comes walking on the water. "Now in the fourth watch of the night Jesus went to them, walking on the sea. And when the disciples saw Him walking on the sea, they were troubled, saying, 'It is a ghost!' And they cried out for fear. But immediately Jesus spoke to them, saying, 'Be of good cheer! It is I; do not be afraid.'" ~ Matthew 14:25-27

Notice that Jesus came walking on the water in the fourth watch of the night. The number four is the number of creation. There are four primary directions: north, south, east, west. The scripture uses the phrase "four corners of the earth" over and again.

Many times when miracles dealing with creative powers are involved we see the number four. In the miracle of the seven loaves four thousand were fed. When the paralytic was restored it was four men who carried him to Jesus. When the woman at the well came back with the whole city following her, Jesus said, "Do not say there are still four months until harvest."

When it seems that the whole world is coming against you and the wind and waves are contrary, remember that He is the Master of the wind. He is Creator God. All things were created by Him, for Him, and through Him. This world belongs to Him and it is fully under His control.

So, when your world is coming apart at the seams, look for the One who comes in the fourth watch of the night. He is never caught by surprise by this old world. He spoke it into existence and He will one day speak it out of existence. In the meantime, live under the fullness of the number five. That's the number of grace and it's always one up on the created world!

· JULY

Dumb Sheep

Dorothy repeated over and again, when her greatest desire was to return to the little farm where she had been picked up by the tornado and carried to the Land of Oz, "There's no place like home, there's no place like home!"

Time and again over the last 20 years, I have returned from a mission trip to my home. Each time is always a joy to behold as I make the final turn toward home. Each time I return, I am like one of David's sheep that rested in the green pastures and drank from the brook that ran nearby.

Mission trips can be a harried experience, especially, if you are the team leader. The responsibilities for safety and schedules are unending. On the trip, I am the shepherd; at home I am just a sheep.

Sheep are a little dumb depending totally upon a shepherd to guide and protect them. They have no natural defense mechanism. In other words, wool is not very dangerous to an enemy!

David's words in Psalm 23 make this clear. "He makes me to lie down in green pastures; He leads me beside the still waters." ~ Psalms 23:2 This verse begins by declaring that the shepherd MAKES me lie down in green pastures. You would think that rest comes naturally, but the shepherd had to lead the sheep to the place of rest and then keep them there long enough to recuperate from foraging among less green and lush places.

Then the shepherd leads the sheep to a place where they can drink deeply from quiet, barely flowing water. There are lots of analogies about sheep and their need to drink from still waters, but these verses hold a fresh meaning for me today.

After days of hustle and bustle through airports and racing along busy streets in a foreign land, I need *STILL* water. I don't need to hear a bubbling brook. I don't need slippery rocks. I don't need murky water. I don't need a swimming hole.

I need to take a deep drink from clear, cool, refreshing water that may have begun along the rocky slope of the mountain behind me. It could have begun as an icy melt from a glacier bound summit. But today, a sip of cool water will do; then let me lie down and rest a while.

A trip to Oz can be exciting, but there really is no place like home.

07/02

It May Be A Cover-up

I wonder where God fits in? I'm not thinking about your daily schedule. I'm speaking about the worship services at your church. We have choreographed God out of much of what we call worship. We have everything precisely computed to the minute. God forbid that we should be asked to change the order of things. Who knows what might happen if heaven were to ask that a place on the schedule be reserved for the Holy Spirit to speak!

We have at our disposal every modern convenience to facilitate an aura of God's presence. Just don't let the electricity fail; we would be lost in the dark…literally.

I always come back from a mission experience with serious questions about worship. Not only what most of us experience week by week in our churches, but my own personal worship time. Having watched the people of the Dominican Republic scratch out a tune on a güira (pronounced: *qwira*), a tube shaped piece of perforated sheet metal played with a stiff brush, and to see their excitement to be in His presence, I have to wonder at what we produce with multi-person choirs and orchestra pits.

May I suggest what many might think an inappropriate answer? Noise. Now it sounds like music to our ears, but what does it sound like to God? Is it beautiful in His presence and does it invite His presence? I can hear the naysayers, "This is NOT the Dominican Republic!" I know that, but I also must conclude that some of what we do is NOT worship either.

In John 4, the woman at the well was asked by Jesus to go get her husband. When the truth was revealed that she had already had five husbands and was presently committing adultery, she tried to turn the subject to worship. Is some of our worship activity just a cover-up?

The woman tried to place worship upon a certain mountain. We try to place worship into a certain style. Jesus placed worship squarely into the context of the person worshipped. "Jesus said to her, 'Woman, believe Me, the hour is coming when you will neither on this mountain, nor in Jerusalem, worship the Father.'" ~ John 4:21

As you think about worshipping God this Sunday or any day, is it not time to ask, "Where does God fit in?"

Feeding On God's Word

Hunger is a reality that few of us here in America have ever faced. I know there are hungry people here, but in comparison to some of the places I have travelled hunger is of limited scope. I also know that for the hungry person, it matters not upon what country's soil they happen to be residing.

A more serious hunger problem exists in the spiritual lives of many today. If we were able to see the emaciated frames of those proclaiming to know the God of the Bible, we would stand aghast at the horror.

Two prophets of scripture were both told to take a portion of God's word and physically eat it. One of those was John in Revelation 10, the other was Ezekiel. John in his revelation saw many strange things, but Ezekiel *did* some strange things under the direction of God.

In the beginning of his prophecy God commanded him to eat a scroll that had been completely covered with writing. Ezekiel obeyed. "So I opened my mouth, and He caused me to eat that scroll." ~ Ezekiel 3:2

In both cases these men sensed a sweetness like honey in their mouths, but a bitterness in their bellies. So it is with the word of God, which we feed upon daily. The Bible can be a book of extremes to our natures. We can relish its words at the beginning, but complain as they settled deep into our souls.

Robert Morgan, in his book, *From This Verse*, tells the story of eight men who survived after they had ditched their plane in the vast reaches of the Pacific.

Captain Eddie Rickenbacker and seven crew found themselves stranded on three rafts with no water and only four oranges. They tied their boats together while they drifted day after day without food or water, sometimes delirious, and always tortured by the relentless sun.

Their amazing survival was credited to something in the pocket of Private Johnny Bartek—a New Testament. From the beginning, Bartek, maintained his morning and evening devotions. The men began joining him.

Starting in Matthew's Gospel, they soon came to 6:31–34. It immediately became their hope, inspiration, and prayer: What shall we eat? What shall we drink?—Your heavenly Father knows that you need all these things.

God miraculously provided food and water for these eight men and all were rescued. The word of God was their real sustenance. The birds and fish He provided were just dessert.

Are you starving? Not for a cookie or a hamburger, but are you "dying" to dine upon God's word. The table is prepared. Pull up a chair and dive in for a delightful meal!

07/04

Opportunity for Independence

Remember, the war had not begun when the Declaration of Independence was signed by those gallant men assembled together for one common purpose. They decided to lay all on the line. I am sure they could not have imagined the full effect of their decision to sign that document.

So often, we make decisions not fully understanding what the consequences will be. We don't even know what the journey will entail as we set out to act upon our choice to obey with heart, mind, and soul.

I have had the privilege of sailing upon the Sea of Galilee several times. The waters of this lake can range from tranquil to treacherous. I have sailed upon it when we were rocking back and forth being tossed by the waves. I was really happy when we got back to the shore.

I have also sat in a boat upon a glassy, tranquil surface and wished that I could just stay a while and imagine the disciples rowing to the other side.

Remember, when Jesus commanded the disciples to go to the other side of the lake, the waters were calm. They did not set sail into the teeth of a storm. Perhaps they relished this opportunity of independence. Jesus had given them the freedom to obey and they did just that.

Soon after the ink had dried upon their commitment to go to the other side, the conditions changed rapidly and drastically. The winds roared and the waves began to fill the boat to the point of sinking. A joyous, carefree, cruise became a cascade into danger and despair.

But Jesus…

How many times must our founding fathers have reached the point of despair as the storm of war robbed them of life and joy? But Jesus…

But Jesus came walking upon the stormy sea. "Now in the fourth watch of the night Jesus went to them, walking on the sea." ~ Matthew 14:25

The fourth watch is the last watch. It is the deepest, darkest part of the night. It was in this moment that Jesus showed up to save. "And when [Jesus] got into the boat, the wind ceased." ~ Matthew 14:32

America, it's time to get Jesus in the ship of state once more. This will never be done corporately. It will be done one heart at a time. Make your Declaration of Dependence today. Stop your attempts to sail the sea under your own strength.

Go ahead…sign on the dotted line and Jesus will be with you before the ink dries!

07/05

Able To See

A man stood on the curb with his elbow bent out to the side as he placed his hand on his hip. The man was blind and was awaiting the kindness of someone who would help him across the street. Sensing a touch from a stranger both stepped into street and were hit by a bus. What went wrong? They both were blind men!

Matthew gives us the account of two blind men who sought out Jesus for healing. "When Jesus departed from there, two blind men followed Him, crying out and saying, 'Son of David, have mercy on us!' And when He had come into the house, the blind men came to Him. And Jesus said to them, 'Do you believe that I am able to do this?' They said to Him, 'Yes, Lord.' Then He touched their eyes, saying, 'According to your faith let it be to you.' And their eyes were opened." ~ Matthew 9:27-30

Can you imagine the lives of these two blind men? Neither was able to describe the pink of a rose, the blue of a babbling brook, or the yellow of the sun, to the other. Neither could warn of a stone in the path. One man could not help the other find a coin that had been dropped. But together their voices sounded forth in a cry to Jesus for help. Perhaps they encouraged each other in their cry and determination. It might have been that they supported one another as they answered the question, "Do you believe I am able to do this?"

Just think how the scales fell from their eyes and suddenly they saw the face of their Healer and Savior. They must have marveled as they saw one another for the first time. Together they had survived blindness; together they had stumbled toward Jesus; together they had their faith stretched and rewarded. Together they were seeing.

You may have a spiritually blind friend that is waiting for you to bring them to Jesus. Both these men were blind—you are not!

You know the way to eternal sight and salvation. Take your friend by the hand today and tell them your story. Cry with them as you seek Jesus together. Rejoice as your faith is rewarded and their eyes are opened. Together you will see Jesus and each other as a brother or sister in Christ.

Together you can sing:

> Amazing grace, how sweet sound;
> That saved a wretch like me.
> I once was lost, but now am found;
> Was blind, but now I see!

07/06

Time for the Beach

Seashells, rocks, and even a clump or two of salt from the Dead Sea—these are a few of the remembrances that my wife has transported back home from our mission trips and other journeys that have taken us to the water's edge of many oceans and seas.

This collection is a good way to remember the places we have been privileged to visit and carry the good news of Christ. They are, however at best, just a small sampling of the vastness that has lain before our eyes. Truly, most of what we see cannot hold a glint of light to the full majesty of God's creation.

Yet, He proclaims that all of this is little more than His handiwork (Psalms 19:1). God in His infinite wisdom has declared Himself to all by things as tiny as a seashell cast upon a sandy stretch of beach.

John the Apostle in attempting to validate his authority to write his first epistle said, "That which was from the beginning, which we have heard, which we have seen with our eyes, which we have looked upon, and our hands have handled, concerning the Word of life…" ~ 1 John 1:1

This verse is like a seashell gathered from some distant shore and brought home to display in a jar filled with other shells. One seashell can never convey the entire story.

A.W. Tozer said in his book, *Christ the Eternal Son*, "This is what we will attempt to do: we will walk along the broad seashore of God and pick up a shell here and a shell there, holding each up to the light to admire its beauty. While we may ultimately have a small store of shells to take with us, they can but remind us of the truth and the fact that there stretches the vastness of the seashore around the great lips of the oceans—and that still buried there is far more than we can ever hope to find or see!"

Why not stop today and reflect upon the shells of truth that you have gathered throughout the days of your life? Better yet, take a stroll along God's beachhead, which is the Bible, and gather a few new choice shells for your collection.

And even more importantly, show off your collection. Tell all you meet what each shell of truth means for you and how each shell is nothing more than a small representation of the vastness of God's greatness.

Enjoy yourself on God's beach today!

07/07

Who's Counting?

Note: This devotion was written on my birthday in 2013. I include this notation so that many years from now when I'm already at home with Jesus, the reader will understand the computations included.

I was not supposed to happen. My parents had been told that children would not be born to them naturally. The report of a "dead rabbit" must have been a shock to both my mama and daddy and here I am on my birthday. I have expended a little over 1.8 billion seconds, but who's counting! I have pictures around the house that show my daddy holding me precariously. I also have pictures of him holding a lot of fish, since he was an avid fisherman. I'm very glad he wasn't holding me by the gills!

I would have never imagined that having lived 21,551 days would have left me as the lone survivor of this branch of the Clark tree. I am grateful for the many limbs now protruding from my branch. Children and grandchildren now are extending themselves from the little boy born to unsuspecting parents over 31 million minutes ago.

God is good! And the people said, "All the time!" He has been good to bring so many people into the life of an Eastern Louisiana boy. He has been good to allow me the privilege to pastor some of the greatest churches on the planet. He is so good to allow me to serve the churches of Northwest Arkansas Baptist Association and be a part of reaching the world in and from this tiny dot in the universe.

We serve a God who sees time, but does not exist in it. Of Him, it is said, "…A thousand years in Your sight are like yesterday when it is past, and like a watch in the night." ~ Psalms 90:4

These 59 years, 708 months, 3078 weeks, 21,551 days, 517,224 hours, 31 million plus minutes, and over 1.8 billion seconds seem to stretch out behind me like a carpet made of thousands of threads. Each thread, a moment in time, and each one a piece of the mosaic that is becoming me.

My days are limited. There is an appointment that lies before me that I will not fail to keep. But, there are yet a few more nano-seconds to live; a few more friends to gain and a few more enemies to lose.

I am a blessed man. Praise God for every heartbeat that He has blessed me with over these years. And if you are counting I have lived over 2.5 billion heartbeats since conception…but who's counting!

07/08

Too Comfortable

It was going to be a good flight. I had arranged my seating so that I would have the bulkhead window seat. There would be lots of room. At least some level of comfort compared to other sections in the economy seating of the airplane.

All went well until one of the last passengers arrived and took his seat next to me. I could not believe my eyes. I was going to spend the next ten hours on a flight from Brazil seated next to a seven foot tall basketball player on his way to join a college team in America.

Suddenly, my space evaporated. I felt very small sitting next to this giant and my space continued to shrink as he settled in for a long night's sleep. Even the bulkhead in a plane leaves no room for a seven foot tall man to comfortably position his legs. He should have been charged for another half ticket, because a lot of him rode to the U.S. on my side of the armrest.

King David would have understood my dilemma. His heart's desire was to build a temple for God; the Lord had other plans. It was to be David's son, Solomon, who would lay the foundation for the temple.

David did not let this truth stop him from gathering millions upon millions of dollars' worth of building materials. The list is extensive as it is recorded in First Chronicles 29.

It would have been easy for David to swell up in pride over his accomplishment of amassing such a storehouse of provisions. Precious metals and stones were heaped up in preparation for what would become the most magnificent temple ever built in Israel.

But God came and sat down next to it all. Not literally, of course, but evidently David saw all of this wealth in context. So he writes these words in conclusion to the in-gathering of materials: "Yours, O Lord, is the greatness, the power and the glory, the victory and the majesty; for all that is in heaven and in earth is Yours; Yours is the kingdom, O Lord, and You are exalted as head over all." ~ 1 Chronicles 29:11

Have you settled in and gotten comfortable? Have bragging rights become part of your vocabulary? Maybe it's time for God to take the seat next to you for the flight home. Suddenly, you will realize how small you and all that you have really are in the presence of heaven's Majesty. It's up to you to enjoy the rest of your flight home.

07/09

Undivided Attention

The television was turned off immediately. That was the rule in the house where I was raised.

When someone came to visit us, the television was silenced. The visitor had the full attention of my parents. We did not wait to determine how long they would stay or if what that had to say was important. When we heard the knock on the door, the television's ability to interrupt ended.

Now the television is the least of the interrupters. It is difficult to find anyone who will give you their full undivided attention. We smile and write it all off as multi-tasking, but we know better deep down where it counts. People are either partly acknowledging us or halfway ignoring us.

You can only imagine what Jairus, the ruler of the synagogue, must have thought on the day he sought help for his dying daughter. After appealing to Jesus for intercession in his little girl's life, Jesus is interrupted on his way to Jairus' home.

A woman with a long term illness touches the hem of Jesus' garment and is healed immediately. Jesus delays long enough to seek the woman out of the crowd. The results: the woman is not only healed physically, but spiritually as well.

Another result of this interruption is reported by a messenger from Jairus' home. "While He was still speaking, someone came from the ruler of the synagogue's house, saying to him, 'Your daughter is dead. Do not trouble the Teacher.'" ~ Luke 8:49

Being ignored by someone who is talking on their cell phone or texting the next viral blurb is one thing, but an interruption of this magnitude is beyond compare. This delay had cost the life of a little girl.

But we serve a God who is never late and One who gives us His full attention, even when we cannot see through the tears of tragedy. Not only did Jairus receive the report of his daughter's death, but so did Jesus.

"When Jesus heard it, He answered him, saying, 'Do not be afraid; only believe, and she will be made well.'" ~ Luke 8:50 And she was! (Luke 8:54-55)

If you've got the idea that God is distracted or that He is more concerned with someone else's problems, you are very mistaken. When it comes to your need, God always turns off the television. You've got His full attention!

Test Time

When I was in school test time always came around. I never feared it and I was blessed to not have to cram for the test either. I do not have a photographic memory, but I could in a pinch close my eyes and see the page in the book. I would look over it in my mind and could at times pick the answer from the page I was seeing. I was blessed.

Now, it's test time again. Can you tell me the first words of Jesus that we have recorded in the gospels? It's okay if you can't. Here's the answer: "And He said to them, 'Why did you seek Me? Did you not know that I must be about My Father's business?'" ~ Luke 2:49

Here is the second question on this test. What are the first recorded words of Jesus after His resurrection? Again, it's okay if you don't know. And again, here is the answer: "Jesus said to her, 'Woman, why are you weeping? Whom are you seeking?'"~John 20:15

Do you see the connection between these two verses? Twenty years had elapsed between these statements of Jesus. Yet there was still a seeking after Jesus. We can only assume that the disciples knew of His boyhood statement as recorded in Luke. They had walked with Jesus for over three years and heard His teaching about His own death, burial, and resurrection. And yet He asked the same question at the tomb that He asked Joseph and Mary as a twelve year old boy, "Why are you seeking me?"

Jesus was about the Father's business in the synagogue as a boy. He also was about the Father's business at the tomb. He had broken the hold of death and stood living and breathing before the women.

Many today will attend church. Most will attend out of what they think is religious duty. Some will attend out of a childhood memory. But I believe that deep down under all of the religious fervor is a seeking after Jesus.

Now here's the third question on this test. What are the last recorded words of Jesus that we have recorded? Here's the answer: "He who testifies to these things says, 'Surely I am coming quickly.'" ~ Revelation 22:20

You really need to find Jesus today because He is coming soon! He wants to be discovered, but you'll not find Him among the dead. He's alive forevermore!

Grace Upon Grace

Standing under the construction pavilion that had been erected by Samaritan's Purse, I had the opportunity to preach to the workers gathered there. Their responsibility was to pre-fabricate one-room homes that would be loaded as segments onto trucks. These pieces would then be assembled on site into residences for the devastated Haitian people.

We sang and prayed together. I then turned the attention of these men to God's word and to the grace that God offers. Grace is not an easy concept to grasp. Either we miss it all together, declare it unobtainable, or we over simplify it to the point that it is cheapened nearly out of existence.

To eradicate grace is to declare God non-existent. It is to proclaim that God has died and all men are miserably lost forever. Grace is more than an attribute of God that He exhibits at times. GOD IS GRACE!

God is grace and the full measure of His grace was revealed in His Son, Jesus. John said as he opened his gospel, "And of His fullness we have all received, and grace for grace." ~ John 1:16

When Christ came, grace walked among men. God's grace was revealed in the flesh. John said we were given grace for grace. This was not a new grace. It was a new layer of grace laid upon grace. A. W. Tozer wrote, "Before Moses came with the Law, men were saved only by grace. During the time of Moses, no one was saved except by grace. After Moses, before the cross, and after the cross, and during all of the dispensations, anywhere, anytime, no one was ever saved by anything but the grace of God!"

It always has been grace. Since God cannot change, then His grace cannot change. It was in Christ that it was fully revealed as He became the sin bearer and bore our guilt and shame.

I paused in my delivery of that message in Haiti. I called one of the Haitian workers to the front, as I picked up a board from the ground. I commanded him to lean across a table and declared that I would beat him. His eyes grew large, but on my downswing, I stopped, exchanged places with him, and told him that he could beat me instead. I would take his place and receive his punishment. I was affording him grace in mercy.

I was very happy that he understood the illustration and that he had not taken me literally as far as the board was concerned! I could never give those men the full picture of grace, but Jesus fully did for us on the cross.

Hallelujah, what a Savior!

Forty Brave Soldiers

The following story occurred in Armenia around 320 A.D. It is supposed to be true; if not, then stories similar to it have occurred time and again around the world. A song based on this account was written by Tom Green 30 years ago. I have included a link to it at the end of today's devotion.

A company of 40 Roman soldiers known as the Thundering Legion were discovered to be Christians. They were commanded to worship Caesar as a god, but refused the order. Promises of honor were given if they would deny Christ and offer sacrifices to the Emperor.

One responded, "You offer us money that remains behind, and glory that fades away." They told him that they would rather die than renounce their faith.

The ordered was given for them to die a slow painful death. They would be stripped of their clothes and placed upon the ice of a frozen lake until they froze to death. To entice them to deny the faith, the bathhouse was warmed, so that if any of them should renounce Jesus Christ, he might be taken from the lake and put into the warm water.

When these good soldiers were put upon the ice, they encouraged each other to not be afraid of dying. "One night of suffering," they said, "and then an eternity of happiness in Heaven." They prayed that their number would remain 40 and they could all persevere to the end.

They endured this torture for many hours and then the cold finally became too much for one of them. He asked for one of the soldiers guarding them to carry him to safety and the warm bath. No sooner had he been put into the bath than he died.

Forty brave soldiers for Jesus had become 39, but the faith of those remaining faltered not. Suddenly one of the pagan guards who had observed the soldiers, tore off his clothes and ran onto the lake shouting, "FORTY brave soldiers for Jesus!"

As the next day dawned, 40 brave soldiers stood before their true King and heard Him say, "Well done, my good and faithful servants."

The writer of Hebrews could have include these men in the hall of faith which we know as Hebrews 11. Verse 35 reads, "...Others were tortured, not accepting deliverance, that they might obtain a better resurrection."

Will you be number 41?

http://youtu.be/eo2oMlaIDos

The Potter's Hand

As believers it is important that we remember just exactly who we are. In Isaiah 64 we are described as clay: "But now, O Lord, You are our Father; we are the clay, and You our potter; and all we are the work of Your hand." ~ Isaiah 64:8

The first truth that we need to remember is that God is our Father. Like our physical fathers, God has brought us into existence. We have no life apart from Him. Ephesians 2 says that we are dead in our sins and trespasses. It is our heavenly Father that quickens us to life, but the work only begins there.

We are nothing but shapeless clay before His hands are placed upon us. He reaches down into this world and lifts us out of the cold, damp, miry pit. Only when we yield to Him as the potter can we hope to begin taking shape into a useful vessel.

The potter's hands squeeze and mold the clay into that which the potter has envisioned for it. He never asks the clay for an opinion or for advice. The clay's only response is to yield to the shaping process. The potter will center our lives on the wheel and only when all resistance is removed can He begin His work.

This is the moment when the transformation occurs. A lump of clay rises from the wheel and takes shape into a vessel that can be used. We become the work of His hand.

Is God your Father? If so, are you yielding to His hand as your potter? Are you willing to be used according to His design for your life? If your answers are all yes then you are blessed. If not, then ask the Potter to break you if necessary and begin again.

Ask Him to center your life and lift you up from the wheel unto a vessel that will bring glory to His name. Most of all remember that we are all just clay in need of the potter's touch.

Being Known

When my kids were growing up they would constantly come across folks who knew me. Their identities were attached to me. They were R.E.'s kids. I'm not sure how it had happened in my life that so many people have come to know me, but it has. Being known is alright I suppose, but it all means nothing if we are not known by Jesus.

Jesus said, "I am the good shepherd; and I know My sheep, and am known by My own. As the Father knows Me, even so I know the Father; and I lay down My life for the sheep." ~ John 10:14-15 One word in the Greek is translated as know or known in these two verses. All four times it means to be fully aware, to have knowledge of, to be sure of, or to understand.

It may be true that a lot of people know me, but none of these know me like Jesus knows me. There is an intimate quality to Jesus' knowledge. These verses equate Jesus' knowing us to His knowing the Father. More than once Jesus declared that He and the Father are one. He told Phillip that if he has seen the Son then he has seen the Father. The same intimacy that exists in the Trinity is the intimacy that exists between the Good Shepherd and the sheep.

These statements about the shepherd knowing the sheep and the sheep knowing the shepherd are preceded by these verses: "I am the good shepherd. The good shepherd gives His life for the sheep. But a hireling, he who is not the shepherd, one who does not own the sheep, sees the wolf coming and leaves the sheep and flees; and the wolf catches the sheep and scatters them. The hireling flees because he is a hireling and does not care about the sheep." ~ John 10:11-13

The evidence of Jesus knowing us and the depth of that knowledge is revealed in the gift of His life. As the good Shepherd, He cares for his sheep. He leads us, He protects us, and He will never leave us.

You may be asking how a person can be sure of all this. That leads us back to the first two verses mentioned. He knows His own and His own know Him. Even though my kids joked about having no identity of their own they knew that knowing me and being known by me meant protection and security.

How can I be so sure of my relationship with Christ? I know because I am known and that settles it for me!

07/15

Consider Your Ways

Mark Twain told a story once of stealing a watermelon from a wagon and running away to hide while eating it. He said, after breaking it open, that he considered what he had done. The result: He went back and stole a ripe one!

Now you and I know that he really had not considered his actions well. Evidently, the Israelites had not considered their actions very well either since God told them five times in the short book of Haggai to consider their ways. "Now therefore, thus says the Lord of hosts: 'Consider your ways!'" ~ Haggai 1:5 The word *consider* here means to commit or take to heart. This is no casual thought, but a deep serious gaze into a matter.

God told the people that their actions had brought about consequences that would only be corrected after they had considered their ways. When was the last time that you spent some time asking some hard questions about yourself?

Take time to do so today. Ask God what He would have you do to correct any consequences that are a direct result of your actions. I can tell you that stealing a ripe melon will not be an option!

07/16

Nothing Hidden

One of David's psalms that speaks of the absolute sovereignty of God is Psalm 139. David spoke here of the complete knowledge of God about his life even from the moment of conception. David knew that God had known him even while he was in his mother's womb. Since nothing was hidden from God, David knew that God was not shocked by anything that was in David's life.

Because of this David could say to God, "Search me, O God, and know my heart; try me, and know my anxieties; and see if there is any wicked way in me, And lead me in the way everlasting." ~ Psalms 139:23-24 Could you comfortably say to God today, "God look into my life and see me in all of your omniscience?" You must have an intimate relationship with God to invite Him into your life in such a deep way. A good definition of intimacy is "into me see."

This level of intimacy gives God freedom in our lives to do several things. David asked God to search him. This is a deep penetrating examination. He asked God to know his heart. This is an acquaintance by recognition. God's knowledge of David was like that which you have with a spouse or very close friend. There was nothing hidden.

David asked God to test Him so his inmost thoughts might be disclosed. Especially those thoughts that might lead to a divided trust. Then David asked God to see. He was asking God to gaze upon Him until his very nature was uncovered in God's presence. Finally, David asked God to lead him. Here David was asking for guidance. This was not a generic course that David sought, but specifically the road to eternity.

You can have this depth of relationship with God today. Simply open the door of your life and give God unbridled permission to walk in and stay. Remember, He already knows all. He will not be surprised by what He finds. That's Him at your heart's door now. Go ahead and answer Him with an open door policy and you will be surprised!

God's Station Wagon

Vacations always involved a road trip in our family station wagon when I was a boy. My brother and I would pile our pillows and blankets into the back of the car and sleep the night away as our parents drove us to our destination.

Safety was not one of our concerns. There were no seat belts. We romped all over the vehicle and we made up our games as we went along the way. No videos, no electronics, and we knew when necessary that one of our parents' arms would immediately fly out to catch us if a quick stop was necessary.

Those were the days!

Nobody ever thought of hand sanitizer or sneezing into the crook of your arm. Kids played outside until dark and your neighbor would correct you as quickly as your parents without fear of a lawsuit.

All of us need a little protection now and again, however. Even in this world where every precaution is taken to keep us from harm, we need to know that God is actively watching over us.

David was a man who understood the dangers that existed all around him. As the king, he had many who sought to do him harm. He had at his disposal a great army, but David always sought the Lord's protective hand.

It is not, however, those flagrant attempts to do us harm that we need protection from the most. We are most often surprised by the sudden, out-of-nowhere, attacks that come our way. David said, "You shall hide them in the secret place of Your presence from the plots of man; You shall keep them secretly in a pavilion from the strife of tongues." ~ Psalms 31:20

I cannot remember how many times I was riding in a car as a child minding my own business, when my mother's arm would be suddenly extended across my chest and press me back against the seat. She was always aware of the sudden unexpected danger that I was oblivious to at the moment. Just as David relied upon God to protect him from the unknown plots of men and the deceitful tongues of his enemies, so we must rest in the ever watchful presence of the Father.

We will never be totally safe in this world, but we can relax knowing that God keeps us protected even in a hostile environment. So, get your pillow and your blanket ready. Lay yourself down in the back of God's "station wagon" and enjoy the road trip to heaven.

Child-like Faith

Children and animals have a lot in common. Now, before everyone goes bananas, (no pun intended with the monkey food reference) let me explain.

Have you ever spoken to a child and their response is a blank stare? How about telling your dog to do something and the animal will tilt their head and look at you with questioning eyes? This is exactly why I have connected children and animals. Not that kids ever act like animals or vice versa, it's just that they both respond similarly many times to that which they cannot fully understand.

One of my favorite Old Testament accounts is when Balaam had been hired to curse the children of Israel. As he journeyed to meet the king of Moab, he had an eye-opening encounter with Jesus along the road.

Balaam could not see the Angel of the Lord, Jesus, standing in the road way with His sword drawn, but his donkey could. Three times she attempted to avoid the Man in the road. Each time she did so, Balaam beat her unmercifully.

Here's where the story gets very interesting. "Then the Lord opened the mouth of the donkey, and she said to Balaam, 'What have I done to you, that you have struck me these three times?'" ~ Numbers 22:28

Now that will get your attention! You don't come across talking donkeys every day! The amazing thing is that Balaam continues the conversation as if it is completely normal to converse with an animal. Not only does he communicate with his donkey, he tries to argue his point of view.

That's where I connect children and animals. Not in their behaviors, but in the simplicity of their belief. For Balaam's donkey, life was just one burden after another transported to a certain destination. He most likely took everything at face value. His motto could have been: It is what it is.

Jesus said that no one could come into the Kingdom of Heaven unless he received it like a child. Children hear the word of God and receive it without question. They see by faith, what we lose by reason.

Is it time to function in child-like faith again? Is it time to follow Balaam's donkey down the road and see Jesus in all of His glory? Yes, children and animals are a lot alike in their understanding of the infinite.

Oh, that believers might once again act a little more like children…or at least like Balaam's donkey.

Flavorless

Much focus has been placed on the middle east in the past few years. You may have noticed as you have watched the news how many times people have shown their hatred through the use of a shoe. Remember when Sadaam Hussein's statue torn down, the people hit it with their shoes and stomped on his picture. This is a common demonstration of disdain.

Jesus used just such a picture when He said, "You are the salt of the earth; but if the salt loses its flavor, how shall it be seasoned? It is then good for nothing but to be thrown out and trampled underfoot by men." ~ Matthew 5:13 He describes the believer as the salt of the earth. We are the very flavor of the world. Without the Christian influence this world simply is bland and tasteless.

But there is a strong warning to us as the influencers of this life. It is possible for us to lose our savor. We will still look like salt, but provide no flavor. This word translated "flavor" comes from a word that means foolish. When we lose our influence it is moronic or to use a word that folks don't like anymore: STUPID!

There is nothing to do with this flavorless salt, but to throw it out into the path to be trampled with disdain. Once salt loses its saltiness it can never become salty again! Influence that is lost may never be regained. This is a strong word of caution to guard our position of influence lest we become like a torn down statue left to the shoe of shame.

Stay salty. Add flavor to your world of influence until Jesus comes for His own.

Trusting God

The following story is not about me, even though I did own a grocery business once upon a time. A lady once entered a grocery store to buy a chicken for supper. These were the days when meat wasn't all out in display, but behind the counter.

She asked the clerk for one chicken. He took a chicken and laid it on the scale telling her it weighed three and one-half pounds. She then asked for a bigger chicken. When he looked in the case he had no more to sell, so he took the same chicken, laid it on the scale, and told her it weighed four pounds.

She then told him that was just wonderful, but she had changed her mind. She would buy both chickens! Something tells me that clerk wished at that moment he could be God and create a chicken on the spot.

Thankfully, we serve a God who can be trusted. The Psalmist said, "For the word of the Lord is right, And all His work is done in truth." ~ Psalms 33:4 Two words describe the trustworthiness of God in this verse. The words are "right" and "truth." These words mean that God carries out His business both straight and in faithfulness.

What God says never varies from its path or intended target. It is literally spoken as straight as an arrow. What God does can be trusted because it functions out of His faithfulness. So when God says let your yea be yea and your nay be nay, He is not requiring anything of us that He does not Himself perform.

Also, when He declares that without faith it is impossible to please Him, He does so based on His own standard of faithfulness. Simply put: You can trust God in all He says and does!

07/21

Coloring Outside the Lines

Everybody at some point has had a picture that has been gently torn from a coloring book prominently attached to their refrigerator door. Most of these early artistic attempts are no more than scribbles with a crayon across the illustration carefully drawn on the page.

The artist that drew the picture would have carefully done so with dimensions in mind. Everything would be proportionate. Lines were drawn to give clarity to the image. The intent of the artist was to lay down boundaries. Each person could color inside the lines as he or she so chose.

But children don't understand dimensions or proportions. Lines mean nothing when one is armed with a crayon. The only choice is what color or perhaps size of the crayon.

With gusto, a child can cover the carefully laid work of the artist in a few brief moments of ecstatic "coloring" and we reward the effort with prime real estate on the refrigerator door.

Now imagine God for a moment. I know. It's hard to keep Him inside the lines isn't it? David sang these words after the Ark of the Covenant had been returned to Jerusalem, "Honor and majesty are before Him; strength and gladness are in His place." ~ 1 Chronicles 16:27

This one verse from a chorus of praise speaks volumes about God. We understand that God is majestic, but have you considered that majesty is before Him? Everything that exists everywhere shines forth the honor, beauty, and glory of God. God simply cannot be described within lines.

Yet, God in all of His majesty became Immanuel, God with us. Jesus told His disciples time and again that the Kingdom of God was within them. The God of the universe who cannot be placed inside any imaginable set of lines has constrained Himself to live inside each believer!

David saw in the Ark of the Covenant the very presence of God, but his psalm could not keep God in a box. God resides inside the lines of the human heart, but the songs of our life should forevermore show forth His majesty.

In one sense God colors all over us. He will not stay inside the narrow confines of the human heart. And when He finishes the artwork of your life, He places your picture on His refrigerator door!

07/22

Reaction

Reaction is a common human trait. We all react in some way and if not, then there's something wrong with us physiologically. Doctors check a lot of reactions to determine what action to take when we are ill. Chemist create chemical reactions in hopes of finding new compounds. Chefs know that ingredients must be added in just the right order so that certain reactions take place or the cake will flop.

We live in a world of reaction.

One of the first actions of Jesus recorded by Mark was the casting out of a demon from a man. Guess what? There was quite a reaction! "Then they were all amazed, so that they questioned among themselves, saying, "What is this? What new doctrine is this? For with authority He commands even the unclean spirits, and they obey Him." And immediately His fame spread throughout all the region around Galilee." ~ Mark 1:27-28

Not only did Jesus' actions cause an immediate reaction, followed by questions, but the ripple effect of this one miracle spread throughout the region.

Is there anything that might happen today that would cause you to react like this? As you attend worship will it be so different that you will react? Will the preaching of God's word stir you to amazement? Or will it be one of those: been there, done that, got the t-shirt days?

I believe that God wants to amaze us still! He wants you to start asking questions and seeking answers. He wants you to test the authority of what you have seen and heard and TALK about it! If there is no reaction, then you are spiritually ill. You need a doctor.

The good news is, I know one. His name is Jesus and He's got an appointment open for you. No waiting!

Knowing Your Limits

I had seen the commercial many times. A 19¢ *Bic* pen was connected to an ice skate. The skater then took a few spins around the icy rink to demonstrate that a *Bic* ink pen would always write, "First time…Every time!"

That was good enough for me. I was going to prove that *Bic* pens really lived up to their claim. I took my pen from my pocket and with observers to document the historic occasion, I carefully placed the tip of the pen against the brick wall of the gymnasium. The seam of mortar between two runs of brick seemed just right to really find out what the limits were to *Bic's* claim of writing first time, every time. The wall was only about 150 feet long. The pen was about six inches long. It seemed a fair testing ground to me.

With cheers from my friends, I ran the distance from beginning to end, with my pen tip planted against the mortar. This was certainly less distance than the ice skater had travelled in the commercial.

Finishing my race to the end of the wall, I was ready to prove *Bic's* claim that there was no limit to their pen's ability to write first time, every time. I looked at the pen which had started the experiment so well. I now saw a pen barely three inches long. There was no point to write with anymore, half of the pen was melted away, and a streak of ink now graced the side of the gymnasium.

There are limits to *Bic's* ability to write first time, every time! I had surely proven that!

Limits are seldom looked upon favorably and testing the limits does not always end well. We live with limits all of our lives. We are placed in beds with walls surrounding us as babies. Our first playgrounds have sides that keep us limited.

We are told not to cross the street as children and what time to come home as teenagers. Adults must drive within the speed limit. Oft times we dislike limits, but they are there to protect us.

The psalmist said of a God, "You have hedged me behind and before, and laid Your hand upon me." ~ Psalms 139:5 These were not words of complaint, but of comfort. They were a reassurance that although God sets limits, He has none.

We are limited in our ability to relive the past and we have no way to jump into the future. His hand is upon us. He knows our limits and will never test us to the point that we only leave a trail of ink upon the wall of our life.

Thank God for limits!

07/24

Consecrated

In thirty plus years of ministry I have been to a lot of dedications. I have seen ground dedicated, buildings dedicated, Bibles dedicated, and of course babies dedicated. In each case the intent was to make sure that thing or person was wholly committed to the Lord's service. All of this is perfectly fine, but I am not sure that we fully understand the level of commitment that is demanded in such occasions nor can we be sure of their outcome.

The Old Testament used the words consecrate and sanctify many times. At other times acts of consecration take place. One such occasion was the setting apart of Aaron and his sons for the priesthood. A sacrifice of a ram was made with the following instructions: "Then you shall kill the ram, and take some of its blood and put it on the tip of the right ear of Aaron and on the tip of the right ear of his sons, on the thumb of their right hand and on the big toe of their right foot, and sprinkle the blood all around on the altar." ~ Exodus 29:20

Here we see a deep level of commitment represented by the blood upon the ear. The priest's hearing was to be attuned to God's voice. The blood was then touched to the thumb as a symbol of all that would be grasped by the priest being consecrated to the Lord.

Finally, the blood was place on the big toe as an indication that the walk of the priest was to be holy. The remainder of the blood was sprinkled around the altar as a warning against false worship.

If Aaron and his sons being under the law showed such a high level of consecration, how much more should we under grace? We have a Great High Priest who offered Himself as the sacrifice, rose from the dead, and is seated at the right hand of the Father.

May our ears be open to His command, our hands ready to serve, our feet always walking within the way of holiness, and our worship genuine. We need more than some outward dedication; we need deep inward consecration in our lives today.

07/25

Wet Paint!

One of the most dangerous signs that can be posted in my presence is one that reads, "WET PAINT!" Every fiber of my body immediately focuses upon the surface now glistening with a fresh coat of paint. My brain sends microbursts of energy down my arm and into my hand. Before I know it, my finger is reaching towards the object. I have to know!

Sometimes I am a rebel. No, in truth, I am most of the time a rebel. Even in my secure position of salvation, I find sin always slinking around in the shadows ready to seize the moment. I would have never desired to touch the surface of the above mentioned item, but the sign declaring, "WET PAINT!", provokes me to rebel.

God had brought the children of Israel safely to the border of the promised land. They were inches away from receiving the reality that had for a lifetime only been a story told by the elders.

Spies had been sent into the land to check the validity of their promised possession. Twelve went and twelve returned, but not in unity of report. Ten declared the land impossible to conquer; two proclaimed all to be as God had said.

Here they were within reach of the promise and a spirit of rebellion rose up to arrest their progress. Joshua and Caleb warned them, "Only do not rebel against the Lord, nor fear the people of the land, for they are our bread; their protection has departed from them, and the Lord is with us. Do not fear them." ~ Numbers 14:9

Rebellion can take place in our lives in two different ways. Sometimes God says, "Don't touch!" Our response is to rebel against His warning by touching anyway.

At other times, God says, "Go forward and possess!" Our rebellious reaction is to turn around and run in the opposite direction. Either way, we act like rebels. In both ways, we miss a blessing and experience the consequences of disobedience.

So, which sign are you looking at today? Is there a "wet paint" moment occurring for you? Walk away immediately! The sign is there for your protection.

Perhaps you are staring at a sign that says, "OPEN!" God has made a way for you to proceed. Walk forward immediately! The sign is there for you to possess all that God had provided.

07/26

Never Forget

How hard is it for you to remember things? Let me ask that differently. Have you ever been really embarrassed because you forgot? Those are the times that remembering really takes the front burner of our minds. Yet we can all forget things at times. And, no, I don't think that it's got a thing to do with age!

I visited a fellow once many years ago and asked him about coming to church. He told me he attended a certain church, but it had been a little while since he had attended. When I asked the pastor about this man he told me that the man had not attended in over 20 years! I guess he just forgot!

In Deuteronomy Moses reminded the people not to forget. "And you shall remember the Lord your God, for it is He who gives you power to get wealth, that He may establish His covenant which He swore to your fathers, as it is this day." ~ Deuteronomy 8:18

I simply cannot imagine forgetting the Lord. He fills my day with His presence. I see His handiwork all the time. However, God saw fit for this verse to be recorded for us and all of these Old Testament verses are for our instruction.

So, will you join me today in remembering God. When you pay for something today don't forget that He gave you the strength to earn and the wisdom to spend well as a steward. As you walk your way through this day remember His covenant of salvation which He confirmed on an old rugged cross through His Son.

Never forget that this is the very day that the Lord had made and rejoicing in it will help you remember the God who owns it. And, if you can't remember the last time you've been to church, then this Sunday is a perfect day to go again.

Don't forget!

07/27

Double Outcast

Most of us run in the same circles. We take the same route back and forth to work, to school, or to shop. Some of this is generated out of convenience. We don't need to think about where to turn or what sights are along the route. If you don't believe this, ask yourself the next time you get to your destination, "Did I stop at that last red light?" See, you are thinking about it now and you don't really know!

Jesus conducted His journeys with intentionality. It certainly would have shocked the disciples the morning He said, "I must go through Samaria." (John 4:4) This was way off the beaten path for Jews. The Samaritans were considered mixed-breeds. They were a despised people that the Jews considered ceremonially unclean; to all except Jesus.

Not only were the disciples amazed at His departure from routine by this side trip into Samaria, the woman He met there was also. This woman was a double outcast. She was hated by the Jews and evidently scorned by her own people. This can be surmised by the hour of the day she came for water and that she was alone.

To her surprise Jesus asked for a drink. Her answer reveals her utter amazement. "Then the woman of Samaria said to Him, 'How is it that You, being a Jew, ask a drink from me, a Samaritan woman? For Jews have no dealings with Samaritans.'" ~ John 4:9

She used the word *dealings* to convey her wonder. This word means to interact with, but it also means to do so much as to graze against accidentally. She was saying to Jesus, "You Jews won't even brush up against us Samaritans, much less drink after us!"

The rest of the story in John 4 tells of her recognizing who Jesus was and telling the people who had scorned her to come see the man who told her all things she had ever done (John 4:39).

Who will you brush up against today? Will they all be your regular acquaintances or will you have a need to go through Samaria? Someone's waiting for you at the well!

07/28

A Place of Safety

A few years back, the area where I lived was under the threat of tornadoes. I knew it was going to get bad quickly when we heard what we thought were horses running on the roof. It turned out to be softball size hail and the tornado following close behind. I still remember putting all of the family in the bathroom and piling a mattress on top of them.

Thankfully, it passed just south of our home.

Is there one among you who would not with all diligence put your family in a place of safety if you knew danger was coming? In the case of this storm we had a little warning. Sometimes there is none. What if you could keep your family safe all the time?

When the Hebrew spies went into Jericho, they were hidden by Rahab. She had heard that the storm of God was coming and asked that the life of her family be spared for her kindness to them.

The spies told her, "We will be blameless of this oath of yours which you have made us swear, unless, when we come into the land, you bind this line of scarlet cord in the window through which you let us down, and unless you bring your father, your mother, your brothers, and all your father's household to your own home." ~ Joshua 2:17-18

Can you imagine the days that followed? The days before the storm of God leveled the city of Jericho. Rahab must have gathered every family member she could. All remained in safety behind a scarlet cord as they waited. Here they stayed as the children of Israel marched around the city. Here they stayed while trumpets sounded. Here they stayed as the people shouted. Here they stayed as the walls came tumbling down in a heap.

And they were safe behind a scarlet cord of promise!

The best I could do was put a mattress over my family in the face of a tornado. But you and I can still put our families behind a scarlet cord that extends all the way back to an old rugged cross. That cord is scarlet with the blood of Jesus and all who hide behind it are safe from the storm of God's wrath.

Don't wait for the sirens. All the warning you need has already been given. Get your family to the place of safety under the scarlet cord of Jesus' blood!

07/29

Sometimes You Just Don't Belong

Few of us really enjoy taking orders. I don't mean waiting tables, I'm speaking of someone telling us what to do or where to go. Several years ago I was visiting in the Chicago area. I came up with the idea that my kids needed to go to the top of the Sear's Building, the tallest building in Chicago.

I will admit that I'm a country boy and I'm not apologizing for that, but country boys are quickly out of their element in really big cities like Chicago. I knew this, so I decided to go on Saturday. I figured nobody would be in downtown Chicago on a Saturday.

Wrong! Not only do people still go into the downtown area on Saturday, I chose the one Saturday that the Blues Festival was being held. On top of this several candidates for the presidential race were scheduled to speak that day. It was mass confusion. Especially for a small town person like me.

Evidently, my out of town character showed in my driving. A lady police officer whistled me to a stop. I rolled down my window thinking she would offer me some help getting to the Sears Building.

Wrong! First, she asked me what I was doing in downtown Chicago. Then she compelled me to leave. That's right! She told me to get out of there because I didn't belong in downtown Chicago!

I left! Being compelled, I had no choice! Paul told the Corinthians that he was compelled by the love of Christ to tell the news that Christ has died that man might live. "For the love of Christ compels us, because we judge thus: that if One died for all, then all died; and He died for all, that those who live should live no longer for themselves, but for Him who died for them and rose again." ~ 2 Corinthians 5:14-15

Are you where you are supposed to be? Is the love of Christ compelling you to get up and tell someone today that Jesus loved them enough to die for them? That whistle you hear is the Holy Spirit compelling you to follow orders. Do it today!

By the way, I still have never been to the top of the Sears Building!

Bragging On Jesus

In your everyday circle of friends and acquaintances you would be hard pressed to find a person that does not have some knowledge about Jesus. This is not to say that this person is a believer, but they cannot claim total ignorance. How can you make sure that the impact you have in these lives will have an eternal consequence?

When Jesus sailed over the Sea of Galilee with his disciples they came to the land of Gadara. Immediately they were confronted by a man known only as the Gadarene demoniac. This fellow lived among the tombs, would not wear clothes, could not be bound, and was a threat to all who passed that way. Change a few of the descriptives and he could be your friend or family member!

Even this man recognized Jesus, and the demons within begged for mercy. In the exchange Jesus asked the demon's name. The demon said, "Legion, for we are many!" Your acquaintances are also beset by many demons. Some of them are present and some are in their past. They are controlled by all sorts of influences. But Jesus can set them free even as he did this man.

Jesus commanded the demons to leave this man and scripture then gives this account: "Now the man from whom the demons had departed begged Him that he might be with Him. But Jesus sent him away, saying, 'Return to your own house, and tell what great things God has done for you.' And he went his way and proclaimed throughout the whole city what great things Jesus had done for him. So it was, when Jesus returned, that the multitude welcomed Him, for they were all waiting for Him." ~ Luke 8:38-40

So the answer to the question is simple. Return to your home (circle of influence) and tell what great things God has done for you! You will find that those who rejected you before now welcome the message of the gospel. Just brag on Jesus and watch what happens!

The Gentleness of God

You did not pick up your newspaper this morning to discover that all is right with the world. Good news doesn't sell. I don't even expect good news anymore and neither do you, but that doesn't mean there isn't any to be had. We need to start looking for the good news in the midst of the bad; not apart from it.

In Psalms 18 David is recounting his struggle with King Saul and other enemies he had encountered. He describes it as a near death experience, but quickly turns to God as his shield and Defender.

God is described in powerful words that would make you wonder why anyone would run to Him. He shakes the earth to its foundation and uncovers the depths. Smoke and fire come from his mouth and nostrils. He hides Himself and yet reveals His power in thunderings and lightning.

Where is the good news in all of this? As already said, you need to look for it in the midst of the fray. It is found is Psalm 18:35. As swords are clanging and shields are clashing, David describes God as gentle.

"You have also given me the shield of Your salvation; Your right hand has held me up, Your gentleness has made me great." ~ Psalms 18:35 This is the only time in all of the Bible that God is described as gentle. The word means to condescend. Imagine the God of heaven bending down to scoop you up out of the dust of battle and cover you with His hand.

Fanny Crosby might have been describing this scene as she wrote the refrain of her hymn, "He Hideth My Soul."

> He hideth my soul in the cleft of the rock
> That shadows a dry, thirsty land;
> He hideth my life with the depths of His love,
> And covers me there with His hand,
> And covers me there with His hand.

That's the good news in the midst of the bad! Look for the gentleness of God and you will find it was there all the time.

· AUGUST

King Ralph

I must admit that I am not the best fan that the royal family has. For those of you in the same camp with me, I'm speaking of the English monarchy with all of its pomp and circumstance.

Following all of these aristocrats just doesn't do anything for me personally. I suppose I've just never gotten completely over the Revolutionary War!

Though I do not follow very closely the business of the queen and her progeny, I am not beyond learning a thing or two. One of the interesting things that I learned, as it relates to the birth children related to the Queen is that names are very important for these folks.

The royal couple whose newborn child is the third in line to the throne did not just pick up a book of baby names and flip through it at night trying to come up with something unique. After all, who would want to be called King Ralph or something even more ridiculous.

Now, here's the really ridiculous part of the royal rodeo. After the names (up to four, all given to one person) are selected by the parents, the Queen, no less, has to approve. What? I think I would tell her if she comes over for the 2:00 a.m. feeding, then she can pick one of the four names. Take it or leave it!

In all of this, I'm really just kidding. They have their ways and I have mine. Their names are important just as ours are, though none of us will likely ever have Queen or King attached to the front of ours!

When Moses was being sent back by God to deliver the children of Israel, he asked God how he was to respond when people asked who had sent him. In other words, by what authority was he there to set the people free.

God gave him a somewhat strange answer. "And God said to Moses, 'I AM WHO I AM.' And He said, 'Thus you shall say to the children of Israel, I AM has sent me to you.'" ~ Exodus 3:14

We often take this response of God about His name and try to wrap our finite minds around it by adding a blank at the end. I AM _____. We can only process God's name by relating it to something He has created. But in reality, GOD IS, period. Thus, His name is I AM.

He does not have to be anything, because He is ALL! He does not have to wait for His turn to be the king. He always has been, He is, and He always will be KING. And, by the way, He's not waiting on the queen's approval.

08/02

Take Time Today

Space. The final frontier. These are the voyages of the star ship Enterprise…so began each episode of Star Trek. Would all of you Trekkies raise your hand? Yes, I see that hand!

Space is not really the final frontier. There is another virtually unexplored region that you are existing in right at this moment. It is the arena of time. It is happening to all of us and for the most part it is unexplored.

Oh, we have good times and bad times, but usually time slips past us totally unexplored. So much so, that at the end of our day we often exclaim, "I didn't have enough time to get everything done today!" In reality you had the exact amount of time that you have had in every other day of your life and you had the same amount of time as every other person that lived that day.

Solomon, the wisest man who ever lived, put it this way, "To everything there is a season, a time for every purpose under heaven…" ~ Ecclesiastes 3:1

So how shall we ever find time to study our Bible or pray? If time is virtually untamable and unexplored and we have no time machine to advance it or reverse it, then what are we to do? We can follow the advice of Paul to the church at Colossae. "Walk in wisdom toward those who are outside, redeeming the time." ~ Colossians 4:5

Paul did not use the word for time in general in this verse. He did not use the word for time in mass such as an age or eon. He used a word that means specific time, a segment of time, or if you please a special occasion.

Oswald Chambers spoke of time in his piece "Our Brilliant Heritage". He demonstrates effectively this idea of redeeming time as in an act of seizing a particular segment of it. He said, "Of course you have not time! Take time; strangle some other interests and make time to realize that the centre of power in your life is the Lord Jesus Christ and His Atonement."

We use this same terminology all the time. We say that we are going to take time, but we do not. Solomon said there is a time for every purpose under heaven, but that time must be taken and set aside. Take time today!

Time. The final frontier. This is the time of _____. Put your name in the blank. May your voyage through time be fruitful!

08/03

Profitable for the Kingdom

I have been on dozens of mission trips during the time that I have served as the associational missionary for the Northwest Baptist Association. All of these trips ended with me rushing back to my work in Arkansas. I never took any time off after the mission trip to unwind until a recent extended journey to the Dominican Republic.

We were blessed to stay along the Atlantic coastline of the country in an all-inclusive resort. Neither of us have ever stayed in such a place before this. We paid one price for the room and everything else was included. We never had to buy a meal, a Coca-Cola, or even a bottle of water. It was nice; especially the hot water and cold air conditioning!

We could not keep from thinking that just outside the confines of what we considered luxurious, all of the poverty of the country still existed. We rested and recouped, then boarded an airplane that would take us back to the land of plenty. A place where everyone has the chance, if they so desire, to get up and make something of themselves.

One question plagued me as I returned back to the ministry God had blessed me to be a part of here in America: "Had I been profitable for the Kingdom of God over these past few days as I have served the King of Glory?" Only time will truly answer that question, but I hope the answer is yes.

As the Apostle Paul concluded his letter to the Colossians, he followed a customary pattern of listing some of those who were working alongside him in the ministry. One of those mentioned was Onesimus; "…with Onesimus, a faithful and beloved brother, who is one of you." ~ Colossians 4:9 This is the same Onesimus of Paul's letter to Philemon. He was a runaway slave who had been saved and was now serving with Paul in the ministry. His name means useful or profitable.

I want to be an Onesimus for the Lord in all that I do. I don't need this for my own glory, but for His alone. I need to know that my time was well spent and the investment of body, mind, soul, and strength has returned a profit unto Him who deserves all the praise.

Note that Paul described Onesimus as "one of you." As I have served Him who saved me, I rejoice that each of you have been part of this work for I am "one of you."

Days Fly By

Happy Birthday! Well, it might not be *your* birthday, but it is someone's today and everyone feels at times that somebody has been messing around with the gears in their clock. It has to be some kind of sabotage. We just had a birthday and here it is again!

We can all join with Job in the midst of his suffering and say: "My days are swifter than a weaver's shuttle, and are spent without hope. Oh, remember that my life is a breath! My eye will never again see good." ~ Job 7:6-7

Now you may not be in the midst of suffering this morning, but you may be feeling a little on the old side. Just remember: It's a good day, because the Lord has made it, and is completely engaged in the fulfillment of it. Do not worry about the conclusion of this day, for He who rules the sun and the passing of years holds you and time fully and securely in His hand!

However, we do sense with each passing year how swiftly life rushes by us. They are like Job's weaving shuttle. Each minute flows by like a passing river's current and a new thread is laid in place. The only guarantee of our lives is the last exhaled breath, but we are not without hope as Job described his days.

We will see good again whether we see another birthday or not. Fully expect God to use you in His service as His bond servant. And if it is His will that you do not see the end of this birthday or reach another year on your birth calendar, be assured that you will see the goodness of His everlasting presence in glory!

Alexander the Great, Julius Caesar, and Plato died on their birthdays. John Huss, the martyr, was burned at the stake on his birthday. The first three of these men are noted in history for their power and wisdom. Alexander had a goal to conquer the world. Julius Caesar lost control of his rule as he was killed by his "friend." The axioms of Plato are quoted to this day, but he too died and passed into history.

I want to live and die like John Huss. Huss stood against organized religion and all of its fallacies. His stance cost him his life as he was burned at the stake for the cause of biblical truth.

So, on this day make a choice with me. Let us refuse the recognition of emperor. Let us reject the wisdom of philosophy. Let us stand each day of this coming year squarely upon the foundation of truth and if necessary live to die as a martyr for our great King who is ageless and will never die!

Happy birthday! Whenever it happens to be…

Benefits

We have experienced a prolonged season of conflict in our world over the past years. Many have given the ultimate sacrifice. We have much to be thankful for on this day. I am thankful in particularly for the privilege of writing these devotions with the knowledge that nothing I say will be censored. This freedom has been purchased by the blood of heroes and patriots.

In no way desiring to diminish this sacrifice of human life for our freedom, I hope that a few words today from Psalm 103 would also allow us to remember what God has done for us. As David began this psalm with the words, "Bless the Lord!," he implored us to not forget.

So he continues: "Bless the Lord, O my soul; and all that is within me, bless His holy name! Bless the Lord, O my soul, and forget not all His benefits: Who forgives all your iniquities, Who heals all your diseases, Who redeems your life from destruction, Who crowns you with lovingkindness and tender mercies, Who satisfies your mouth with good things, so that your youth is renewed like the eagle's." ~ Psalms 103:1-5

David reaches deep down within himself to the soul level to bless the Lord. He does not seek a blessing, but seeks to bless the Lord who had already blessed him in so many ways. He tells us to not forget, that is, remember and hold in memorial that which God has done for us.

He reminds us of the benefits that are ours. The word benefit speaks of the bountiful treatment that is ours at the hand of the Lord. Those benefits include the forgiveness of our iniquities. This is more than forgiveness of sin; it is a forgiveness of our very sin nature which prompts us to act in sinful ways.

He expands the benefits list to include the healing of diseases. All of us can testify of those times that He blessed us as the Great Physician. Furthermore, He has redeemed us by the shed blood of His own Son and crowned us with loving kindness and mercy. He has satisfied our hunger and renewed our strength to the point that we can only proclaim,

"BLESS THE LORD,
O MY SOUL,
AND
ALL THAT IS WITHIN ME
BLESS HIS HOLY NAME!"

Soon the day will come when our crown as a symbol of all these benefits shall be laid at His feet and we will join the innumerable host in unified chorus as we sing, "Bless the Lord, O my soul!" Sure hope to see you there...

The God Factor

From the very beginning God has been in the process of revealing Himself. Scriptures are replete with descriptions of Him. These often are found in the acts of God which give us insight into His nature.

Amos described God this way: "He made the Pleiades and Orion; He turns the shadow of death into morning and makes the day dark as night; He calls for the waters of the sea and pours them out on the face of the earth; the Lord is His name." ~ Amos 5:8

Indeed the heavens declare His handiwork (Psalm 19.) When I think of handiwork, I imagine that which is done in one's spare time. Since God is timeless, then His creative acts that we see all around us were brought into being in an instant. As the Genesis account proclaims, God said and it was.

The constellations mentioned by Amos have been shining forth over the millennia. Each night they proclaim God's glory. Their groupings and names are the feeble attempt of men with finite minds to understand the infinity of God.

The reporters recently proclaimed that astronomers have gotten a close look (now that's not meant to be funny, but it is) at one of the oldest galaxies in the universe. Scott Pelley on the CBS Evening News proclaimed with bated breath that it took the light from that galaxy 11 billion years to reach the earth.

Really? Here's what God can and did do: "Then God said, "Let there be light"; and there was light." ~ Genesis 1:3 The reporter had to state his report in such a fashion, because he was attempting to compress the infinite into the finite. His assumption is that a bunch of "well-trained" scientists who have determined the speed of light and the distance to this galaxy have made a "gospel-truth" calculation.

Their problem and his is that they forgot one key element in their equation. They did not factor in Amos 5:8. Here's the correct formula: The distance to the galaxy divided by the speed of light multiplied by Amos 5:8 equals Genesis 1:3.

Amos said, "the Lord is His name" not some Dr. Know-it-all.

So, when you look up at the night sky and see Pleiades or Orion shining forth remember what God said; not some reporter on the nightly news.

Going Prodigal

Luke 15 tells us the story which is known as that of the Prodigal Son. The younger son in this home is never named, yet by his actions have forever earned him the title of Prodigal. His identification as prodigal has become an everyday modifier of any person who has turned their back on home, family, heritage, or a way of life. Not only does it mark the stranger, but most of us know someone in our own family that has gone prodigal.

Many of you know this story well, but a quick recounting will help us focus.

This young man had everything going for him. He had a well-to-do family. His father loved him dearly. He certainly was respected in the community. But the morning came when he took a long look down the driveway and thought about which way he would go—to the left or the right.

I suppose it didn't really matter. He just wanted to be somewhere other than home. So, he asked for his portion of the inheritance and off he ran to a far-away country. As in all prodigal stories he blew all he had on the desires of his heart. He soon depleted his resources, friends left him, and he took a job slopping hogs.

Dirty, dejected, and disheartened, the scripture tells us he became hungry. "And he would gladly have filled his stomach with the pods that the swine ate, and no one gave him anything." ~ Luke 15:16

The next verse says that he came to his senses. Hunger awakened his slumbering conscience and he remembered how it was back home. You will need to read the rest of the story for yourself in Luke 15. I will tell you this. It has a happy ending!

But what about you? Are you running from God today? Are you living the life of a prodigal. It may be in secret, but you are a prodigal nevertheless. Is it time to go back home?

The real question is: Are you hungry enough?

I hope so. The Father is waiting for you!

Speechless

People sometimes through some disagreement, personal hurt, or breach of trust, have decided to not speak to another person. I have heard of instances where individuals have spent a lifetime avoiding someone, so as to not speak a single word to them. That thought leaves me speechless.

God in His sovereignty saw fit to make for Adam a helpmate. Out of Adam's side came forth Eve and they walked together through life. Eve's creation came from the fact that God had said, "It is not good that man should be alone." (Genesis 2:18)

This proclamation came not from a discovery made by God, but by Adam. Prior to this act of creation, God had brought all the animals before Adam. His responsibility was to name them all. In the process Adam would have discovered that all these animals dwelt together as male and female, but also in herds. Adam discovered his aloneness.

We have the privilege and the responsibility of community. We are to dwell together, because God said it was not good to dwell alone. We are to be in harmony as husband and wife, brother and sister, employer and employee, and as neighbor and neighbor.

In every aspect we are to avoid being separated, but there is one relationship that must be guarded as supreme—our relationship with God. Oswald Chambers said, "The main thing about Christianity is not the work we do, but the relationship we maintain and the atmosphere produced by that relationship. That is all God asks us to look after, and it is the one thing that is being continually assailed."

David gives us some of the best insight into maintaining a right relationship with God at all times. After his horrendous sins against Bathsheba and her husband Uriah, David came to understand his aloneness. His sin had severed his fellowship with God and he cried out, "Against You, You only, have I sinned, and done this evil in Your sight— that You may be found just when You speak, and blameless when You judge." ~ Psalms 51:4

Are there some relationships that need to be repaired in your life? Start with speaking to God again and then one by one reconnect every broken line of communication.

Jesus Equals God

I like math. I use it all the time when I preach, as an example, or as an illustration. For me, mathematical ideas are constant. I never have to wonder if the truths of equations, formulas, or theorems have changed over time. The same geometry problems I solved in high school can be solved in exactly the same steps today.

After days, weeks, and months of walking with Jesus and observing His miraculous ministry, the disciples were still looking for proof to settle the spiritual equation:

$$JESUS = GOD$$

In John 14, Jesus begins by declaring what should have been an axiom. An axiom is a self-evident truth that needs no proof. Jesus said, "'Let not your heart be troubled; you believe in God, believe also in Me.'" ~ John 14:1

In other words, quit trying to figure it all out for yourselves. You have believed in God. You have believed that God has done and can do miraculous things. I do miraculous things. Therefore, I am God.

Easy enough for me. Then again, I like a good, logical, mathematical way of looking at a problem. Jesus used what was known as true to prove what could be known as fact.

Jesus then declared Himself to be the way, the truth, and the life. To further emphasize the truth of His own deity, He said that no one could come to the Father except through Him.

Easy enough for me again, but Philip was having a little problem getting this all down where he could grasp it. Then, "Philip said to Him, 'Lord, show us the Father, and it is sufficient for us.'" ~ John 14:8

Philip was really speaking for all of the disciples and maybe for you today. He wanted physical proof. He wanted a touchy-feely kind of faith that required nothing on his part. Just show me God and you've made a believer out of me.

Thank God for the patience of Jesus with these disciples and with us. Jesus asked Philip to think for just a moment about how long they had been together and all that He had seen. The proof that JESUS = GOD was in the fact that everything Jesus did and said came from God and matched perfectly the God they knew.

Someday I will construct a geometric proof for the existence of God and that Jesus equals God—just kidding! There's not enough paper nor ink in the world to hold the formula that would be written. It just takes simple faith in this equation: JESUS = GOD.

Into His Image

I am not sure at what point in our existence that we come to the place of self-identity. It must be learned to some degree. I still remember holding my kids in front of a mirror and asking, "Who is that in the mirror?"

Either that was a teaching moment for my child or the kid was thinking to himself, "Boy, have I've got a dumb daddy. He doesn't even know his own child!" I sure hope it was the first scenario!

Identifying with Christ and understanding who you really are as a believer is a lifelong process. It is very much a part of sanctification. We don't instantly look like Jesus the moment we trust Him as Savior.

Paul said to the Romans, "For whom He foreknew, He also predestined to be conformed to the image of His Son, that He might be the firstborn among many brethren." ~ Romans 8:29

This verse tells us there is an ongoing process. We are being conformed into His image. At first, this may sound a little radical—even painful, but the idea here is that of metamorphosis. You know, the changing of a grimy, earth-bound, caterpillar into a beautiful lighter-than-air butterfly.

There is a slight difference, however. Metamorphosis takes place whether the caterpillar wants it to or not. The creature will spin a cocoon and it will become a butterfly. You and I, however, play an integral part in the process of growing into the image of Christ.

We will as believers be conformed, but the length and languishing of this change is determined by our relationship and identification with Jesus. He is the firstborn or prototype. All believers will be shaped to His form.

Our morphing into His image comes by spending more and more time in His company. Allowing Him to control greater and greater parts of our lives will facilitate the change into His image.

Take a long look in the mirror. "Who is it you see?" If it is still you, then you need to spend some more time with Jesus and check back with the mirror of your soul often.

One day either on this side of life or the other, you will take a look in the mirror and there He will be. You will have been conformed (morphed) into the image of God's Son.

God Has A Secret

Can I tell you a secret? I didn't think so. I knew you would not be interested. I'll just find someone else to tell my secret. Sorry to bother you.

The very fact that you think I know something that you don't has grabbed your attention. I hear you screaming, "Yes, I want to know! Please, please tell me!" You did not even care that I was going to tell you a secret in a book of all places. Remember the millions that buy this book will know the secret as well!

We all love a good secret whether we are good secret keepers or not. Just give me a juicy tidbit that will make me feel like I know something that no else does and you have made me happy.

Okay, here's the secret: "Who is the man that fears the Lord? Him shall He teach in the way He chooses. He himself shall dwell in prosperity, and his descendants shall inherit the earth. The secret of the Lord is with those who fear Him, And He will show them His covenant." ~ Psalms 25:12-14

God has a secret He wants to whisper into your heart. He wants to teach you how to walk along the path the He has chosen for you. This is a secret that many people miss. They want to choose a path and then ask God to bless it, but it does not work that way.

God will only bless as we walk according to His plan. And here is the result of walking upon a God-chosen pathway: You will dwell in prosperity and your descendants will inherit the earth!

Now before you go out and buy a new house or plan a world-wide cruise, you need to understand what this word prosperity means. Our thoughts always rush to riches, but the word best means to be at ease, to walk a path of good, to be glad, kind, loving, and joyful, or to be well-favored. These are things that riches cannot buy nor can your descendants spend in a hurry after your demise. This is the greatest secret that ought to be told to everyone we meet!

So, are you ready to get in on a really wonderful little secret?

You will never know the secret of God's blessing until you learn to fear Him rightly. We must hold Him in reverential awe and when we do He will show us His covenant. He will make a promise and since God cannot lie you can take that to the bank.

Surrender Is Your Only Hope

You have probably heard the proverbial statement about drawing a line in the sand. The idea normally reflects a point of resistance. One figuratively creates a border or a point of no return. Crossing this line usually carries dire consequences.

During World War I trench warfare became common, though field works have always been part of the scheme of war. Trench warfare occurs when competing armies reach a certain point in the battlefield where the ability to decimate the enemy out runs the ability of the army to advance. Both sides would simply dig trenches and wait each other out until the squalor of the trenches took its toll.

The history of God's chosen people, Israel, is one of constantly choosing to lean upon the arm of flesh. The prophet Isaiah tells of just such a time in Isaiah 30.

Israel had begun to lean upon the strength of Egypt. "'Woe to the rebellious children,' says the Lord, 'Who take counsel, but not of Me, and who devise plans, but not of My Spirit, that they may add sin to sin; who walk to go down to Egypt, and have not asked My advice, to strengthen themselves in the strength of Pharaoh, and to trust in the shadow of Egypt!'" ~ Isaiah 30:1-2

It seems that Israel could not learn that their help came from the Lord alone. But God is faithful even when we are not and He is willing to entrench Himself and let us fight our silly battle against the God of the universe. "Therefore the Lord will wait, that He may be gracious to you; and therefore He will be exalted, that He may have mercy on you. For the Lord is a God of justice; blessed are all those who wait for Him." ~ Isaiah 30:18

The word *wait* in this verse carries the idea of entrenchment. God could with a flick of His little finger take us out of the battle, but He does not. He simply waits. And what is gained by this waiting?

His grace and glory are all the more demonstrated when we finally surrender. He waits and as He does His grace mounts up like a flood behind a barrier. Then when the time is right and our full and unconditional surrender is imminent, He steps out of the trench of waiting and displays His mercy in all of its glory!

You are not going to win this battle against God. Surrender is your only hope and option. He is the God of justice. His blessing goes to the one who waits in surrender. Go ahead and wave the white flag in your heart today. May He reign sovereign in your life!

Are You Prospering?

Few people relish the idea of going to the doctor. Even when we are ill, we hesitate before making an appointment. Perhaps we think we will get better all on our own or maybe we fear that the report from the doctor will only make us feel worse.

Physicians serve their purpose. I am sure that I could never be one. I cannot imagine seeing one patient after another, all day long, knowing that the majority of them are there as a last resort. I don't think I have ever said to a doctor that I was glad to see him—at least while I was sick and undone.

When I finally do get around to seeing a doctor, I want a quick fix. I want an injection, a pill, an elixir, or something that will make be better NOW! After all, I finally got around to making an appointment after writhing in pain and despair for a week. This hyper-educated practitioner should have some magic spell that can be cast and will instantly make me better, right?

You and I both know that it doesn't work that way. We have to work our way back to health usually with the slow painful steps that took us down the road to illness. Of course, the best remedy is to not get ill. Stay fit. Do all of the things that will keep you out of the doctor's office.

A really good doctor doesn't want to see you. He prefers that you stay healthy and live in such a way that you never have to make an appointment—one less sad face to look upon when he opens the examination room.

John made an interesting statement as he greeted the recipient of his third epistle. Writing to Gaius, he began his letter by saying, "Beloved, I pray that you may prosper in all things and be in health, just as your soul prospers." ~ 3 John 1:2

The apostle opens his letter with a desire that the health and welfare of his friend will be of good report. John does not seek Gaius' prosperity simply based on the hope that he would be well and successful in a physical sense. He actually prayed that his friend's well-being would be adjusted to correspond to that of his spiritual condition.

Makes me wonder how many of us would need to make a doctor's appointment, if suddenly, we were all stricken with a condition equal to the report of our spiritual health. Just wondering…

Pity Parties

We had just finished the first week of our mission trip. Things were going great. Souls were being saved. We had experienced a wonderful four days of ESL classes with 60 or so students.

Then I became ill. It came out of nowhere.

My story reminds me of Elijah's encounter in the book of First Kings. Elijah was literally on top of the mountain. In this case it was Mount Carmel. Previous to his confrontation with the prophets of Baal, he had prayed. As an answer to his prayer God had closed the spigot of heaven and it had not rained for three and one-half years.

On Mount Carmel after a day of verbal barbs with the prophets of Baal, God answered Elijah again and fire fell from heaven consuming the sacrifice on the altar. Then Elijah personally oversaw the killing of the 400 prophets of Baal. To close the day, he told Ahab to get off the mountain for the rain was coming as a deluge and so it did.

This is when the sudden turn occurred. Elijah overheard Jezebel proclaiming that she had every intent of killing Elijah. At this announcement, he ran. He ran until he was exhausted and we find him complaining to God.

"But he himself went a day's journey into the wilderness, and came and sat down under a broom tree. And he prayed that he might die, and said, 'It is enough! Now, Lord, take my life, for I am no better than my fathers!'" ~ 1 Kings 19:4

I have never prayed for a drought or the relief thereof and had an immediate answer to my prayers. I have never spent a day battling the prophets of Baal, nor have I seen fire fall from heaven. But I have spent time under a broom tree complaining. It seems that it has always come right after the victory.

Beware of this journey into the wilderness! It comes upon you suddenly.

Keep a watchful eye on yourself. No one is ever invited to these pity parties, but me, myself, and I.

Enjoy the victory.

Cancel the pity party.

A Call To Arms

There is a call to arms for the Christian. Whether you own a gun or not in the physical sense is truly your own business, but in the spiritual sense it is useless to own a piece of steel that can project a bullet at remarkable speeds, if you are not armed on the inside spiritually.

Peter addressed this in his first epistle. "Therefore, since Christ suffered for us in the flesh, arm yourselves also with the same mind, for he who has suffered in the flesh has ceased from sin, that he no longer should live the rest of his time in the flesh for the lusts of men, but for the will of God. For we have spent enough of our past lifetime in doing the will of the Gentiles…" ~ 1 Peter 4:1-3

Peter clearly issues a call to arms. We are to arm ourselves with the mind of Christ. The idea here is full protection of self, but in a broader sense it is to be armed offensively, not just defensively. Notice that the weapon of this war against the flesh is formed in the forge of suffering. As much as we all hate times of suffering, it is this very instrument that God uses to steel us against sin.

Sometimes we see the results of sin at work in a horrible way like in the mass shootings of innocent people, but other times it is the effect of sin at work in us personally that reveals our own despicable nature. In these moments we must be fully armed with the mind of Christ, so we can fight against the lusts that well up inside of us.

Peter spoke plainly of the outcome of this struggle. We are to cease living like we did in the past "for we have spent enough of our past lifetime in doing the will of the Gentiles." Arm yourself as a soldier in the Lord's army and be trained to fight the good fight until the end.

Marking Days

There are times that God uses us to prepare the way for others to do great things. Such was the case of Solomon's Temple. It would seem strange to even say, David's Temple, yet it was deeply in David's heart to build it for God's glory. It really bothered David that he lived in finery while God's "house" was merely a tabernacle of cloth and skins.

The Lord had told David that it would not be he that built the temple, but his son Solomon, because David had been a man of war. This cannot be denied for it was David that fought many a battle throughout his life, yet all under the direction of God's plan.

Now his desire to build would not be and you would think that this would be a great discouragement to David, but it was not so. David set out to gather all of the materials and workmen that would be needed for the construction of the temple.

If he could not build, then he would not sit idly by and mark days off the calendar. He would make provision for his son to finish his dream. So we read in First Chronicles a portion of the prayer where David led the people in the dedication of the supplies for the building of the temple. These words speak volumes of the intent of this man who was known to be one after God's own heart.

Imagine David speaking these words, "'Blessed are You, Lord God of Israel, our Father, forever and ever. Yours, O Lord, is the greatness, the power and the glory, the victory and the majesty; for all that is in heaven and in earth is Yours; Yours is the kingdom, O Lord, and You are exalted as head over all. Both riches and honor come from You, and You reign over all. In Your hand is power and might; in Your hand it is to make great and to give strength to all. Now therefore, our God, we thank You and praise Your glorious name. But who am I, and who are my people, that we should be able to offer so willingly as this? For all things come from You, and of Your own we have given You. For we are aliens and pilgrims before You, as were all our fathers; our days on earth are as a shadow, and without hope.'" ~ 1 Chronicles 29:10-15

Remember today that all we have to offer is His already, so who are we to offer so willingly as this? Thank you, O Lord, for using us in your work and accepting our humble sacrifice. Amen.

08/17

Calamity

Nobody needs friends like Job's friends! It is difficult to even grace them with the title of friend, but be that as it may, they had been friends during the good times in Job's life. Now when things had really turned sour they came knocking on Job's door.

Truthfully, I believe they were still his friends. They unfortunately had jumped to the wrong conclusions about Job's calamity. These three friends were overflowing with advice. Some of it good and some of it bad, but all of it recorded for us as inspired scripture. So we need not discount what these men said just because they were not the best of friends during Job's down time.

One of Job's friends was Eliphaz. He outright accused Job of some undisclosed wickedness which was entirely the wrong conclusion concerning Job's time of distress. In the midst of his discourse of corrective advice he said at least two things that are good for us to note at all times. He said, "'Now acquaint yourself with Him, and be at peace; thereby good will come to you. Receive, please, instruction from His mouth, and lay up His words in your heart.'" ~ Job 22:21-22

The advise of Eliphaz was relative to the peace that he thought Job was missing. I suppose at the bottom of Job's calamity he too probably was wondering what had happened to his peace. Eliphaz told Job to acquaint himself with God. The advice was to get to know God. The idea of becoming an acquaintance of God is that of being familiar with or customary in one's relationship. It even goes as far as meaning that we should be ministering to God.

Now this must have seemed strange to Job. His friend was telling him that he ought to be ministering to God when he was the one on the bottom rung of the ladder of calamity. This advice was to get to know God better when it surely seemed to Job that his friends ought to get to know him better before they laid down any more accusations. But the words of Eliphaz are good to hear. We do need to know God better and then find His peace available for every situation.

And just how do we do this? Lay up His words in our hearts! The Bible is God's autobiography. When we know its words, then we know the author. Know God, know peace.

08/18

Teach Us To Pray

Can you imagine what it must have been like to walk with Jesus during His ministry here on earth? Each day would have been filled with anticipation as you wondered what might transpire. Miracles of healing, of provision, and power were everyday occurrences. The disciples must have sat in awe at His teaching. Yet when they got alone with Jesus they did not ask Him to show them how to do miracles. They did not ask that He would make them wise enough to teach at His level. They asked Jesus to teach them to pray (Luke 11:1).

The disciples had watched Jesus spend hours alone on the mountain and in the garden seeking the face and will of His Father. Though they were not theologians they realized that the power of His life was directly connected to His praying. They also knew that they were seriously lacking in the knowledge of this kind of praying.

Two verses from Psalms give just a little insight into this matter of prayer. Both of these verses are foundational to effective prayer. The first verse identifies trust of and openness with the Lord as essentials. "Trust in Him at all times, you people; pour out your heart before Him; God is a refuge for us." ~ Psalms 62:8

We must trust God. This may seem elemental, but you will not really begin to pray until you trust God to answer. Notice also that we are to trust Him at all times. I wonder if this might correlate with Paul's words to pray without ceasing (1 Thessalonians 5:17).

Then the psalmist declares that we should pour our hearts out before Him. If there is any place we need to lay down our facade it should be in prayer. Only in complete honesty can we expect to find a refuge in prayer. "The Lord is near to all who call upon Him, to all who call upon Him in truth. He will fulfill the desire of those who fear Him; He also will hear their cry and save them." ~ Psalms 145:18-19

Notice in the second verse from Psalms 145 that God is near to those who call upon Him in truth. Trust and truthfulness result in God fulfilling the desire of our heart. This does not mean that God will grant our every wish like a genie from a bottle. It means that trust will cause us to believe that God wants what is best for us and being truthfully honest before Him will guarantee that He hears us. Lord, teach us to pray.

08/19

Ocean In a Bucket

The room was filled with eager to learn Haitian pastors, church leaders, and other interested persons. I was teaching the book of Ephesians as part of a week-long pastor's conference. The notepads of these students were being filled with jewels of truth that we were uncovering together from the text.

Our study had brought us to the section of Ephesians that speaks of the fullness of God (3:19). Paul's prayer was that the Ephesians would be able to fully comprehend the fullness of all that God fills. Don't be confused by that last sentence. It's fully difficult to discuss the fullness of God!

As I was teaching, I noticed a bucket on the floor. As happens so often with me, I saw an immediate opportunity to describe in a tangible way the fullness of God and our inability to fully comprehend it. We were only a few yards away from the northwestern shore of Haiti. The vastness of the Atlantic Ocean was at our disposal. Picking up the bucket I instructed one of the students to take the bucket down to the beach and bring back to me the Atlantic Ocean.

One thing you must understand about Haitians is that they are a very obedient people. They will do nearly anything you ask of them. The young man took the bucket from my hand and headed out the door to bring back the ocean in a bucket—or at least he was going to try to do so!

I stopped him as he stepped through the doorway. My explanation to him and the group of students was that he could not possibly bring me the ENTIRE ocean in a bucket. He could bring me a portion of it, but not the whole. There simply is not a bucket big enough in which to fit an ocean nor our God.

Yet, God wants to fill us in such a way that we know fully the fullness of all that He fills. God said through the prophet Jeremiah, "'Am I a God near at hand,' says the Lord, 'And not a God afar off? Can anyone hide himself in secret places, so I shall not see him?' says the Lord; 'Do I not fill heaven and earth?' says the Lord." ~ Jeremiah 23:23-24

Wow! This statement of God contains an ocean of truth. God fills up everything to the full. You cannot go anywhere that God is not and everywhere you go God is already there. He is like the ocean into which we dip our tiny buckets. He is not diminished by our filling nor does He cease to be the Filler of all that exist.

Go ahead—fill your bucket—then fill it again and again!

08/20

Counterfeits

Hey! May I have your attention for just a minute? Have I got a deal for you! If you buy from me you will get a product that's just like the real thing...but a whole lot cheaper!

Interested? Been there and done that? Thought so...

It's amazing how attractive counterfeits are. To be honest it's really difficult to tell the difference sometimes. Well, at least for two or three days! Usually the counterfeits just will not hold up to the rigors of everyday use. They would be great if you just left them in the package, took a picture of it and posted it on Facebook. After all, as long as you don't touch it no one will be the wiser. But you would know, wouldn't you?

A lot of people have a salvation that is just like one of those counterfeits. It looks like the real thing. It sounds like the real thing. And as long as you stay in the safe confines of a church pew no one will ever know the difference, right? But you know, don't you? More importantly God knows and that's the most dangerous part of counterfeit Christianity.

The Lord spoke to His people through the prophet Jeremiah and said, ""For My people have committed two evils: they have forsaken Me, the fountain of living waters, and hewn themselves cisterns—broken cisterns that can hold no water." ~ Jeremiah 2:13

You see, we have a God-shaped void in our lives and if we do not allow God to fill that emptiness, then we will always get busy building a counterfeit. This is what Israel had done. They rejected God who was willing to be the ever-flowing fountain of their lives. Then they immediately began to attempt the construction of a counterfeit, but the best they could do was create a cistern.

Now a cistern is not a bad idea, but it cannot fill itself. It must be constantly maintained. Water has to be transported to it or drained into it for it to have any semblance of a fountain. But even with this attempt it is nothing more than a stagnant collection of water. Israel could not pull off the counterfeit fountain. Even their attempt was defective for the scripture says that they built a broken cistern that could hold no water.

Is there a fountain of living water springing up in your life? Are you the real thing or just a counterfeit?

It's time to stop playing games and place your full trust in the real God of the universe who can make you a real Christian!

Call on him today!

08/21

From Where Comes Courage?

I am not sure that anyone awoke this morning and remarked, "Wow, I really feel courageous today!" Courage simply isn't one of those characteristics that exists in reserve or that we can flippantly engage. Time and again we hear of courageous acts, but it seems that they are revealed in the face of extreme danger.

The soldier goes out on detail and rescues a wounded compatriot or charges an enemy post. Let tragedy occur in some form and the stories abound of those who did not run or freeze. Instead, they acted courageously even to the point of their own demise.

This does not discount the courage it may have taken for someone this morning to face a day of disease, a workplace that is contrary to your witness, or a continual struggle of some form or another. Courage simply functions in the arena of struggle and challenge.

It could have been a day just like today for Joshua. He had spent four decades walking beside and working with Moses. Somewhere in the back of his mind he must have thought about the day that Moses would no longer be the leader of the Israelites. Someday…but not today.

But as always happens in life that day comes and no matter how much we have tried to generate the courage to face it the news of that day catches us by surprise. It surely was like this the day God spoke to Joshua. "Moses My servant is dead. Now therefore, arise, go over this Jordan, you and all this people, to the land which I am giving to them—the children of Israel. Have I not commanded you? Be strong and of good courage; do not be afraid, nor be dismayed, for the Lord your God is with you wherever you go." ~ (Joshua 1:2, 9)

There it is! The shock and awe! The news that shakes us to the core!

I am so grateful that God shows us biblical characters who were just like us. Joshua suddenly was taken from the secondary position and thrust out front. The news of his mentor's death had no time to sink in or to be mourned. Moses is dead. Now arise and lead.

Instead of, "Wow, I think I'll be courageous today," he may have been saying, "Where is the nearest exit?" But God steps in and reminds him to be strong and courageous. Turn aside thoughts of fear and dismay. You can do this, because I AM WITH YOU WHEREVER YOU GO!

Go and be courageous! Not because you are a hero, but because He is walking with you!

08/22

Smoke Signals

Have you ever prayed and wondered if God was hearing you? Divine delay is difficult for us to decipher. We apply our reasoning in light of our limited view of the present, much less a completely unknown future, and come to the conclusion that heaven must not care. Maybe this story from Michael Green's book, *Illustrations for Biblical Preaching*, will shed some light on this subject.

In the days of sailing ships, a terrible storm arose and a ship was lost in a deserted area. Only one crewman survived and was washed up on a small uninhabited island. The castaway prayed every day to God for help and deliverance.

Each day he looked for a passing ship and saw nothing. Eventually he managed to build a crude hut, in which he stored the few things he had recovered from the wreck and those things he had made from the meager supply of the island.

One day, as the sailor was returning from his daily search for food, he saw a column of smoke. As he ran to it he saw his hut in flames. All was lost. Now, not only was he alone, but he had nothing to help him in his struggle for survival. Stunned and nearly overcome with grief and despair, he spent a sleepless night wondering what was to become of him and questioning whether life itself was even worth the effort.

The next morning, he rose early and went down to the sea. There to his amazement, he saw a ship lying offshore and a small boat rowing toward him. When the castaway met the ship's captain, he asked him how he had known to send help. The captain replied, "Why, we saw your smoke signal yesterday, but by the time we drew close the tide was against us. So we had to wait until now to come and get you."

Do not despair when delayed answers seem to turn heaven's doors into brass. Even when calamity strikes God is always able to bring a blessing out of what seems to be a curse.

The prophets of God also had to wait at times. Daniel had been seeking the Lord's face and no answer came. But to his amazement God sent His messenger to say, "Do not fear, Daniel, for from the first day that you set your heart to understand, and to humble yourself before your God, your words were heard; and I have come because of your words." ~ Daniel 10:12

Take heart! God has seen your signal of prayer rise on the horizon. Even now your answer is on the way! Do not despair no matter the circumstance. Pray on!

08/23

To Do Or Not To Do—That Is The Question

Christianity is a funny business. Not in the sense of ha-ha funny, but in the fact that folks who are not Christians think of us who are as some kind of monks who spend all of our days focused on what we are NOT supposed to be doing. Sometimes I think they are right! We can become so focused on the negative that we forget that God has saved us to be about His business and that is anything but funny.

Herschel Hobbs said, "Many people define religion in terms of the negative rather than positive expressions. To them a good Christian is someone who does not do certain evil or questionable things. By this definition a clothing store mannequin could qualify, for it does not do any of those questionable things! Christianity should be seen as positive in nature. A true Christian will do certain good things because he or she is a Christian. A clean heart results in clean conduct."

The Apostle Peter by the inspiration of God penned a well-balanced treatise on this very concept. He spoke in First Peter 4 of ceasing from sin, but also of conducting the Christian life in such a way as to align oneself with the will of God and thereby bring glory to Him.

"…since Christ suffered for us in the flesh, arm yourselves also with the same mind, for he who has suffered in the flesh has ceased from sin, that he no longer should live the rest of his time in the flesh for the lusts of men, but for the will of God. But the end of all things is at hand; therefore be serious and watchful in your prayers. And above all things have fervent love for one another, for love will cover a multitude of sins. Be hospitable to one another without grumbling. As each one has received a gift, minister it to one another, as good stewards of the manifold grace of God. If anyone speaks, let him speak as the oracles of God. If anyone ministers, let him do it as with the ability which God supplies, that in all things God may be glorified through Jesus Christ, to whom belong the glory and the dominion forever and ever. Amen." ~ 1 Peter 4:1-2, 7-11

Don't be a store window Christian. Nobody admires the mannequin—only what the mannequin is wearing. We wear Christ. Let Him be displayed in your life today. Be known for what you do in His name—NOT for what you don't do because of it.

A Wrong Response

Sometimes I write a devotional based on a current event in my own life. Sometimes I have to wait a few days and let the dust settle! This is one of those days. The dust has settled and I have your full attention as you are wondering what kind of calf scramble (this is a term my pastor always used) I've gotten myself into recently. Well, here's the story for your edification and my exposure.

It all began when I dropped off a piece of furniture for repair. I thought I was being wise in leaving it with the shop before our mission trip to the Dominican Republic. In doing so I figured that I would not be wondering when the work would be finished and the company would not be under any pressure to get it done in a hurry. It turned out that I didn't think about it and they didn't get in any hurry either.

I called after the first month to discover that the part had never been ordered. I was still okay since I hadn't really missed the furniture anyway while gone on our journey. It was only after the seventh week that I pressed for an answer and like so many times after the pressure was applied I got the furniture back repaired. Unfortunately, before it was all said and done, I got angry. I know that disappoints you, but not nearly as much as it does me.

As I was returning home with my repaired furniture and fuming over the treatment I had received, God inserted Himself into the story. I felt like Jonah grieving for his gourd (Jonah 4). It was as I began to write this day's devotion that God showed me how wrong my response had been. As He often does, He spoke through His Word. So I offer these words to you hoping that you will handle your next situation better than I did.

Here's what God said: "Rejoice with those who rejoice, and weep with those who weep. Be of the same mind toward one another. Do not set your mind on high things, but associate with the humble. Do not be wise in your own opinion. Repay no one evil for evil. Have regard for good things in the sight of all men. If it is possible, as much as depends on you, live peaceably with all men. Beloved, do not avenge yourselves, but rather give place to wrath; for it is written, "Vengeance is Mine, I will repay," says the Lord." ~ Romans 12:15-19

I stand guilty as charged and grateful for His mercy and forgiveness. Amen.

What Good Is Religion?

Man has a natural penchant toward religion. No matter how deep and dark the jungle nor how isolated the region you will find people who have created a religion to soothe their aching consciences. Religion might be defined as man's attempt to reach God, whereas Christianity is God reaching down to man.

When Christianity is seen as just one religion among many, then wrong conclusions can be reached. Thus the story of the preacher and the president of a soap company comes to mind.

A preacher and the president of a soap manufacturing company went for a walk together. The president said, "What good is religion? Look at all the trouble and misery of the world! Still there, even after years, thousands of years, of teaching about goodness and truth and love and peace. Still there, after all the sermons and teachings. If religion is good and true, why should this be?"

The preacher said nothing. They continued walking until he noticed a child playing in the gutter. Then the preacher said, "Look at that child. You say that soap makes people clean, but see the dirt on that youngster. Of what good is soap? With all the soap in the world, over all these years, the child is still filthy. I wonder how effective soap is, after all!" The president of the soap company protested, "But preacher, soap can't do any good unless it is used!" "Exactly," replied the preacher. "Exactly."

And herein lies the error of thinking that a good application of religion can really clean a person much less keep them out of the gutter. There is only one remedy for our filthiness and that is the blood of Jesus.

"But now in Christ Jesus you who once were far off have been brought near by the blood of Christ." ~ Ephesians 2:13 / "[H]ow much more shall the blood of Christ, who through the eternal Spirit offered Himself without spot to God, cleanse your conscience from dead works to serve the living God?" ~ Hebrews 9:14

If you are thinking today that a good hot bath using the soap of religion can make you right with God, you need to stop now and reconsider. God has chosen only one way for us to be made righteous before Him. That way is through the shed blood of His Son Jesus and thereby you become a Christian.

Believe and be clean!

The Scale of Giving

I have a son-in-law that works in the scale industry. All day long he is either installing scales or calibrating those already in service. The accuracy of these instruments are very important. There are few things that are manufactured without a scale being used somewhere in the process. All of these devices must measure to a standard and do so with very tiny variances. The manufacturer and the consumer depend on the trustworthiness of the scales that are used.

I read somewhere when Hershey began to market his chocolate candy bar that he did so with the intent that it would always sell for a nickel. Instead of changing the price, he would adjust the weight of the chocolate bar, thereby, keeping the price fixed.

That sounds like a good idea, but it has been taken to the extreme in our day. In an effort to keep prices somewhat stable, weights have begun to shrink dramatically in many items. I have noted reductions in size that are approaching 25 percent in some products.

This trend has spread to our giving as well. There was a time when nearly everyone understood the concept of a tithe. Today, many are still giving, but they are doing so with a new standard. It appears they are giving with full obedience, but the package is shrinking.

Jesus witnessed this one day as He stood near the Temple treasury. The Pharisees were making grand entrance to the Temple and giving out of their abundance with great fanfare. Unnoticed by the crowds, a little lady approached the place where she was to make her offering.

I can see her reach into her pocket and remove a discolored and misshapen handkerchief. Wrapped tightly therein were a few coins equaling her life's savings. Tall, pious men pushed and shoved their way past her as she quietly deposited her "fortune" into the treasury and slipped away undisclosed except to Jesus.

"So He said, 'Truly I say to you that this poor widow has put in more than all; for all these out of their abundance have put in offerings for God, but she out of her poverty put in all the livelihood that she had.'" ~ Luke 21:3-4 In a moment, Jesus re-calibrated the scale and the weight of this widow's gift over-shadowed the thievery of the religious.

Is it time today, to call in a spiritual scale technician? He's on 24 hour call and His name is the Holy Spirit. Now, go get your giving scale fixed!

What If Syndrome

I have never liked being in a church building alone in the dark. It gives me the heebie-jeebies. This term was coined in the 1920's to describe a condition of nervous anxiety. I know that the building is empty of any physical presence, but the darkness seems to release the spiritual entities that war against God and the church.

My fears are temporary and for this I am very thankful. For the most part, I do not have any long-term phobias. I know some people do and their fears can be completely debilitating. Most people create fears out of situations that simply are not as bad as they might appear. These fears bring about what I call the great "What-If Syndrome."

When this "disease" strikes, a person begins creating all sorts of scenarios that simply never come to pass. As the mind works out the pseudo-details of these horrors, the person simply freezes up and all progress ceases.

In First Samuel chapter 18 you can read of Saul's fear of David. Saul's fear was brought on by several responses to David's accomplishments, but the primary reason was David's relationship with the Lord. The scripture records, "Now Saul was afraid of David, because the Lord was with him, but had departed from Saul." ~ 1 Samuel 18:12

How often have you been afraid of someone or fearful of a certain situation you are facing? Never forget this truth: When you have a right relationship with God, it will be the world and the ungodly that will be fearing you. This fact will be a great confidence builder for you if you keep it firmly fixed in your heart.

Departing From the Faith

Few people would contend with the fact that these are indeed the latter days that scripture speaks of so frequently. It seems that one can hear the gears of some great clock slowly moving with a certain tick, tick, tick. Just when you think it can't get any worse it does and once again you see the hands on the clock face inch forward.

Paul spoke to his young fellow minister Timothy about such days. Certainly we are living them. "Now the Spirit expressly says that in latter times some will depart from the faith, giving heed to deceiving spirits and doctrines of demons, speaking lies in hypocrisy, having their own conscience seared with a hot iron…" ~ 1 Timothy 4:1, 2

The departure of many from the faith is evident today. But how did they get to the point in their lives that they just walked away? Paul told Timothy that they would depart and then steps back through the process of desertion. First, the conscience goes. Paul used the idea of the conscience being burned to the point that it no longer has any feeling. It stops functioning as a safeguard against error.

Native Indians described the conscience as a triangle shaped object that resided in the chest. Each time a person would do something that violated their conscience it would turn and poke the person. You have experienced that same tightening of the chest when you are about to go against your own better judgment.

The Indians went on to say that left unchecked the object would continue to turn until the corners were worn down. When this happened there would be no more sensation of wrong-doing and the conscience would fail. I think this is exactly what Paul was speaking of in these verses.

Is there a remedy? Can we guard against our own desertion? Yes! Paul told Timothy in the following verses that there are four watch words to keep us from falling away. They are believe, truth, sanctification by the Word, and prayer. He then told Timothy, "If you instruct the brethren in these things, you will be a good minister of Jesus Christ, nourished in the words of faith and of the good doctrine which you have carefully followed." ~ 1 Timothy 4:6

Strengthen your conscience today. Sit down and dine upon God's word. Believe the truth and be set apart for great things as you pray that His will be done in your life.

08/29

Dead-end or Runway?

The tarmac of an airport is an interesting place of busyness. There are many vehicles and lots of people milling about doing their various jobs. All of this equipment and the personnel maintaining and using them are earthbound. Although they are on or near a runway, they might as well be on a dead end street. They are not going anywhere. Only the aircraft will taxi and takeoff. For the pilots and passengers a runway is an access point to far-away places.

The children of Israel came to a similar place in their walk through the wilderness. As they approached the Promised Land, spies were sent out to survey the conditions on the other side of the Jordan River. In Numbers 13 the report was given by the 12 spies. Ten of them gave a negative evaluation of their potential to take the land. Only two spoke by faith of their assurance of victory.

The first verse of the next chapter is a very sad commentary of a runway becoming nothing more than a dead end. "So all the congregation lifted up their voices and cried, and the people wept that night." ~ Numbers 14:1 In that one sentence all possibility of taking off into God's great adventure ended. The people wept that night, but ultimately they all died in the wilderness with the memory of a dead end always haunting them.

Where are you in your journey today? Have you come to what seems to be a dead end? Is the runway of your life busy with people and equipment? Have you noticed those big machines with wings sitting there so invitingly?

It's time to get on board with God. Leave all of the stuff behind. Take your seat and leave the flying to Him. The only way to turn a dead end into a runway is to fly by faith. The moment you do the earth and its troubles and trials shrink away below your feet.

Now boarding…

08/30

Discovering Your Origin

The longest chapter in the Bible is Psalm 119. It is all about God's Word. That surely seems appropriate that the most words in one chapter would be set aside to talk about the Word.

The Psalmist understood the importance of God's Word in his life. "Your hands have made me and fashioned me; give me understanding, that I may learn Your commandments. Those who fear You will be glad when they see me, because I have hoped in Your word. I know, O Lord, that Your judgments are right, And that in faithfulness You have afflicted me. Let, I pray, Your merciful kindness be for my comfort, according to Your word to Your servant. Let Your tender mercies come to me, that I may live; for Your law is my delight." ~ Psalm 119:73-77

Interestingly, our government recently spent a couple of billion dollars (give or take a billion) landing a rover on Mars in search of the origins of life. NASA and JPL could have spent a few dollars on a Bible and read the words of the psalmist. They would have discovered with the psalmist that God shaped us by His own hands.

Believe me, I have no problem with us going to Mars. I'm just curious enough to make the trip if I could, but I would go knowing who made me and who holds me firmly in His grasp. We are being fashioned by God's Word, by God's affliction, and by God's mercy. As the scientists probe the surface of Mars they are going to do so with all sorts of assumptions. They will already have the answer they hope to find and will search for the right rock to turn over that reveals the question they have been looking for all this time.

They will explain some scratch in the dirt or crack in a rock face by their own limited understanding of the universe. On the other hand, you and I can look in the mirror and see the lines of time etched on our faces and be assured that we know how they got there.

It is God's Word that works like a sharp two-edged sword to carve away at our lives as He shapes us into the image of Christ. It is the pressure of His faithful affliction that conforms us to His will and the lines of a smile form as we once again experience the tender mercies of God's unchanging grace.

I do not need a trip to Mars to discover my origins. I need only to open the pages of God's autobiography: THE BIBLE. Happy exploring!

08/31

Dangerous Instrument

There are many sayings that relate to the dangers of the smallest member of our bodies: the tongue. Besides a few birds that can be taught to mimic human speech, we alone have the gift of speech. Our words can either edify or destroy. The maxims of this little poem describe the tongue well:

"The boneless tongue, so small and weak
Can crush and kill," declared the Greek.

The Persian proverb wisely saith:
"A lengthy tongue, an early death."

Sometimes it takes this form instead:
"Don't let your tongue cut off your head."

While Arab sages this impart:
"The tongue's great storehouse is the heart."

From Hebrew wit the maxim's sprung:
"Though feet should slip, don't let the tongue."

A verse in Scripture crowns the whole:
"Who keeps the tongue doth keep his soul."

James used a large section of his letter to speak about the tongue. In our modern translation it constitutes most of the third chapter.

Here are a few verses that tell us of the importance of the tongue and its proper use. "For we all stumble in many things. If anyone does not stumble in word, he is a perfect man, able also to bridle the whole body. Out of the same mouth proceed blessing and cursing. My brethren, these things ought not to be so. Does a spring send forth fresh water and bitter from the same opening? Can a fig tree, my brethren, bear olives, or a grapevine bear figs? Thus no spring yields both salt water and fresh." ~ James 3:2,10-12

Clearly it is our words that trip us up most often. James uses the word stumble. It means to trip, but not just to trip ourselves. The idea here is to offend in such a way as to cause others to stumble to the point of falling.

James gives us many descriptions of the tongue, such as, the rudder of a ship, a fire, and poison. Yet there is nothing more descriptive of the tongue than its hypocrisy, for with it we both bless and curse. James says, "My brethren, these things ought not to be so."

As you begin this day why not take a moment to put a spiritual bridle upon your tongue. Ask God to give you divine control over the one member of your body that is most likely to cause you difficulty today.

What will it be: freshness or bitterness that people find coming from you? For truly, he who keeps his tongue doth keep his soul!

• SEPTEMBER

Remember God Today

Ah, youth!

Those glorious carefree days of splendor when everyday held its own little piece of mystery and excitement. Is there a better way to live those days of youth so to better prepare for the latter days of our lives? And is there a way to rectify miss-lived days and enjoy "old age"? I think the answer to both is yes!

Someone said that Solomon must have written the Song of Solomon as a young man, the book of Proverbs as a middle aged man, and the book of Ecclesiastes as an old man. The last chapter of Ecclesiastes certainly bears evidence of this as Solomon wrote, "Remember now your Creator in the days of your youth, before the difficult days come, and the years draw near when you say, 'I have no pleasure in them'" ~ Ecclesiastes 12:1

Here is good advice to you if you are young and reading this devotional. Remember God today. This does not mean just some reflective moment and then you get back to life. It means a decisive contemplation that leads to action and as we all know action comes a lot easier when you are young.

But this leaves no room to become old and lazy. We all are living longer and we all can be active for Christ for many years. Remember Caleb. He decided to take the mountain for his family in his eighties! (Joshua 14:12) In his book entitled *We Americans*, George Gallup presented some interesting statistics on the demographics of our country:

- If your grandfather was born in 1900, he could expect to live for forty-four years.
- If your father was born in 1940, the life expectancy had increased to sixty-three.
- If your son was born in 1980, he can expect to live to be seventy-five years old.
- Presently, there are twelve thousand-plus Americans over the age of a hundred.

The difficult days will come, but until they do serve Jesus well. Stay with the stuff. Go find a mountain to climb and claim as your own. Above all, remember your Creator as each day begins and act quickly upon His command.

Restoring Fellowship

It is very difficult when we experience disappointment at the hand of those closest to us, but it seems that if we live long enough it will happen. The Apostle Paul was not immune to disappointment either. Persecuted and imprisoned, we find him nearing the end of his earthly life as he pens his final letter to Timothy.

As he draws his letter to a close we read, "Be diligent to come to me quickly; for Demas has forsaken me, having loved this present world, and has departed for Thessalonica—Crescens for Galatia, Titus for Dalmatia. Only Luke is with me. Get Mark and bring him with you, for he is useful to me for ministry." ~ 2 Timothy 4:9-11

Here was a man who had poured his life out for the cause of Christ and now only had one friend remaining by his side. As many would have done, he requests that Timothy come quickly to his side. Not only was he needing Timothy's fellowship, Paul certainly knew that his days were coming to an end as he would be soon martyred.

Paul names some of those who had been with him and in particular mentions a man named Demas. We do not know all of the circumstances, but Demas departed from Paul's fellowship. One thing is certain for Paul states it clearly; Demas left because he loved this present world more than the ministry to and with Paul.

One could surmise that Paul was speaking out of anger or overwhelming disappointment, but there is a clue that this is not so. It is found in his request for Timothy to bring Mark with him when he comes.

If you remember, Mark had been a deserter also. Early on in Paul's ministry Mark had become homesick and left for home. This brought great contention between Paul and Barnabas to the point that they went separate ways. But now, in this moment of yet another desertion by a comrade in the work of the gospel, Paul asks for Mark to rejoin him.

What does this say of Paul and of what benefit is this lesson to us?

We have all been disappointed by someone and that incident may have even brought about separation for a time, but never let it be said that we would not forgive and even forget those moments of disappointment and weigh them against the greater benefit of a person being restored to fellowship and usefulness in the Kingdom's work.

Can you imagine the excitement that Mark felt when Timothy told him that Paul wanted him at his side once again? Be a restorer today. Bridge the chasm that may be separating you from fellowship with a brother or sister in Christ.

Your Full Attention

Pssst! Pssst! Have you heard?

Your ears are pricked up now aren't they? We just love a juicy piece of news.

No, that's not right. Let's call it what it really is: gossip. Now before you turn the page on today's devotional there is good news. It is not about gossip. I was just trying to get your full and undivided attention. Now that I have it, we can proceed…

Paul had heard some good stuff about the Colossians. Epaphras had delivered to Paul a report on the welfare of the church at Colossae. The word was good. It was better than good; it was a blessing to Paul's ears. The Christians at Colossae were living a life of faith and it was being evidenced by their deep love for all the saints. (Colossians 1:4) Paul went on to declare that there was a definite basis for their acting like this and it was literally out of this world.

The very next verse tells us that their faith was functioning because they understood that they had a hope laid up in heaven which had been revealed to them in the good news of the gospel. Here is a key piece of evidence that proves the power of the gospel.

When a person truly hears the gospel and its power is released, then a complete change of focus occurs. The eye now sees a future hope in heaven. The mind is filled with the assurance of faith in Christ and the heart overflows with love. But there is more…

Paul then says, "For this reason we also, since the day we heard it, do not cease to pray for you, and to ask that you may be filled with the knowledge of His will in all wisdom and spiritual understanding; that you may walk worthy of the Lord, fully pleasing Him, being fruitful in every good work and increasing in the knowledge of God; strengthened with all might, according to His glorious power, for all patience and longsuffering with joy…" ~ Colossians 1:9-11

When Paul heard the report of Epaphras about the progress of the church at Colossae, it was not enough to just say, "Well done. You have arrived!" Paul prayed that these Christians would grow in their faith and be more fruitful as they fully understood God's will. He prayed that they would know more and more of God's glorious power and be strengthened thereby.

Pssst! Pssst!

What's being reported about your walk with Christ today? Know this. I'll be praying Paul's prayer for you as I wait to hear good things about your life in Christ.

Mentors

Note: This devotion was written on the day of my son's ordination to the gospel ministry.

My father died when I was a young man. I was only 22 years old at the time. The day of his death is still as vivid in my mind as if it had occurred at this writing.

Among many of his attributes was an ability to mentor. Now, he did not call his actions toward me mentoring, nor did I. As a matter of fact, this concept of mentoring has really just come into vogue recently. Everyone seems to be a mentor today or they are desperately in need of one. My daddy nor I understood that part of our relationship.

I guess the majority of his mentoring was silent. His actions spoke more loudly than words. Decades after his death, his influence still bears witness in my actions as a father.

He did not live to see my surrender to the gospel ministry. He never heard me preach. I don't think he ever heard me pray. He knew only two of my four children and he never held one of my grandchildren. All of them would have benefited from his mentoring.

On this day he would have been humbled, as I am, to see the son of his son ordained to the gospel ministry. The effects of his mentoring, carried down to the next generation, prove once again that fathers do not have the luxury of abdicating their God-given roles.

My son in obedience to his heavenly Father follows a parallel path to his earthly father on this day. His calling comes not from his heritage. It comes not from the prompting of flesh and bone, but from God Himself. So Paul said, as he wrote to the Corinthians, "God is faithful, by whom you were called into the fellowship of His Son, Jesus Christ our Lord." ~ 1 Corinthians 1:9

It is out of this calling into a living and eternal relationship with Christ that my son joins thousands who have trodden before him in answering a call to serve in the gospel ministry. Because this call comes from above, then nothing here below can ever hinder the effect of it.

Today my son becomes a partner in the ministry as he answers God's call: a call that comes from eternity past; a call that is lived out in eternity present; and a call that provides the opportunity to effect eternity future.

My daddy would have stood an inch or so taller today as does the father of my son. Thank God for the call and those who still answer.

Thank you, son!

Anniversaries

Today is my anniversary. My wife and I have eight children, seventeen grandchildren, and one great grandchild. For those of you who know us, you are familiar with our story. For those who do not know us so well, I'll attempt to catch you up a little.

First, let me remind you that anniversaries as far as marriages are concerned cannot be found in the Bible. This doesn't mean that they weren't observed; we just do not have any record of them. The principle of an anniversary being a time of remembering is very clear especially in the annual feasts that were kept by Israel.

Even while the Hebrews were captives in Egypt God was reminding them to remember from where He had rescued them. "Now the Lord said to Moses, 'Go in to Pharaoh; for I have hardened his heart and the hearts of his servants, that I may show these signs of Mine before him, and that you may tell in the hearing of your son and your son's son the mighty things I have done in Egypt, and My signs which I have done among them, that you may know that I am the Lord.'" ~ Exodus 10:1-2

Did you see the anniversary aspect? "…that you may tell in the hearing of your son and your son's son the mighty things I have done in Egypt, and My signs which I have done among them, that you may know that I am the Lord." Now that brings me back to my anniversary story.

My wife and I bring into these few years nearly 80 years of marital experience. On our anniversary many memories flood our minds. I was Trudy's pastor over 31 years ago. Her husband, David, and my wife, Kay, knew each other. Our children played in each other's homes. I moved from what was my first pastorate and our lives continued along separate paths for over three decades.

All this time God was doing mighty things which we could never understand fully. In 2007 Trudy's husband, a police officer, was killed in the line of duty. In 2008 my wife was stricken with Lou Gehrig's disease and went home to be with the Lord that year.

God used Trudy to guide me along the path she had already been on for many months and from that God delivered both of us from the Egypt of grief and loneliness. And that's an overview of how we have a clan after only three years!

So, anniversaries are important. They allow us to remember. They allow us to take another small piece of our life's mosaic and place it in just the right spot. Anniversaries allow us to say, "I love you," with new meaning and to know that He is Lord.

Happy anniversary, Trudy! I LOVE YOU! God has done great things!!!

Foibles and Failures

It is incredible to read the words of David in the Psalms and from those words peek into the intimacy that existed between Him and God. David was far from being a perfect man. He was filled with foibles and failures, yet he was confident in who God was and is. He did not lean upon the arm of flesh; not even his own.

David declares in one of his many psalms, "Your mercy, O Lord, is in the heavens; Your faithfulness reaches to the clouds. Your righteousness is like the great mountains; Your judgments are a great deep; O Lord, You preserve man and beast. How precious is Your lovingkindness, O God! Therefore the children of men put their trust under the shadow of Your wings." ~ Psalm 36:5-7

In these selected verses David gives us an overwhelming picture of who God is and how David trusted Him. He begins with the mercy of God appearing like the overarching canopy of the sky. He saw the mercy of God extending from horizon to horizon. It would not matter how far one travelled there would constantly be God's mercy framed by the horizon.

For David, the clouds would have been extremely high and he used their height to express the faithfulness or security and trustworthiness of God. He said that God's fidelity reached higher than would ever be necessary in his life.

He then brings the attributes of God down to earth, yet still he can only measure them in majestic terms. He relates the righteousness of God to the greatness of the mountains. He even uses the Hebrew term, *el*, to describe the mountains. *El* always refers to deity and is used over and again in the descriptive names of God, for example, *El Shaddai*.

He then brings us from the heights of the mountains to the depths of the seas. God's righteousness is bordered by the highest mountain while His judgments or verdict is as deep as the ocean floor. Certainly neither are limited by height or depth, but David is trying to help us get a grip on the majesty of God in this way.

Just when one might imagine God as being too big to relate to in a personal manner, David tells us that we can find rest under the shadow of His wings.

Incredible!

We are being protected by a God so big that He cannot be framed by our limited minds. Like David, we can only make feeble attempts to describe Him. Don't try to…just curl up in the coolness of His shadow and rejoice.

Easter In September

My morning walks often bring about moments of great discovery. Even though I traverse the same course each morning, I see and hear new things constantly. Sometimes the discoveries are quite wonderful. The title of my first devotional book, *Glasses in the Grass*, came after I found a pair of glasses lying in the grass along the sidewalk.

I have probably picked up more than one whole dollar in change through the years of my morning stroll! Most of the time, I pick up nails and such that I disposed of before they flatten someone's tire. Who said I didn't have an exciting life?

When God speaks along the way, I am especially glad that I took my walk. So it was on this fine September morning.

As I walked, I heard the voice of a child singing. Finally reaching the home where the voice originated, I saw the little girl happily walking in her yard as she sang her little tune. In her hand was an Easter basket which she was using to pick up things in the yard. Nothing being placed in the basket appeared to be an Easter egg, but maybe she had found them all already!

Remember, this is September. Easter baskets are not very stylish in late summer, but she was oblivious to what was fashionable. She was content to place all of her efforts into the collection of her valuables. The Easter basket worked just fine for the task at hand.

Now back to God speaking, which He did, when I came across this parable of life being lived out before my eyes. I remembered another parable. One told by Jesus in Matthew 13.

"'Again, the kingdom of heaven is like a merchant seeking beautiful pearls, who, when he had found one pearl of great price, went and sold all that he had and bought it.'" ~ Matthew 13:45-46 This particular parable comes without explanation from Jesus, but is easily understood when applied to life.

The one pearl is the Church. The merchant is none other than Christ Himself. He laid down all of the riches of heaven to secure the greatest prize: The Church. Not the building, but the people who are the living Church.

Like the little girl singing her way along as she gathered her treasure, Jesus walks the paths of life seeking all who are lost. With great care and with total abandon, He will not rest until all are found.

Do you hear that singing? Amazing grace, how sweet the sound…

Refusing To Be Found

My youngest daughter and I have something in common. I am not sure if she even knows this or not. We both had a similar incident as a small child where we hid ourselves and refused to be found.

The experience I had (at least as it was told to me) was when my parents lived on a lake in Louisiana. The house was built on piers and provided a wonderful place for a little boy to explore—which I did.

When my parents discovered that I was missing they began to call for me as parents do in those moments. I, on the other hand, was very happy under the house and simply refused to answer. Of course, living on a lake left the obvious conclusion looming in everyone's mind; I had fallen in the lake and drowned.

Since I'm writing this today you can assume that was not the case. I was found and though I don't remember the punishment for not answering the call of my parents, I never refused to be found again.

My daughter's hiding story happened in my first pastorate. We had guests in our home and after a while we noticed that she was missing. I can still remember being frantic as we searched everywhere inside and outside the house. We called, but no answer was heard. The happy ending is that we found her asleep in one of the closets! She had gotten tired of the noisy visitors, found the only quiet place left in the house and refused to be found just like her father did once.

These two incidents in my life are in stark contrast to God's desire not to be hidden, but to be found by all. Two sections of scripture speak to this. One is from the Psalms and the other from Acts.

"God looks down from heaven upon the children of men, to see if there are any who understand, who seek God." ~ Psalm 53:2 / "Then Paul stood in the midst of the Areopagus and said, "Men of Athens, I perceive that in all things you are very religious; for as I was passing through and considering the objects of your worship, I even found an altar with this inscription: TO THE UNKNOWN GOD. Therefore, the One whom you worship without knowing, Him I proclaim to you: / so that they should seek the Lord, in the hope that they might grope for Him and find Him, though He is not far from each one of us;" ~ Acts 17:22, 23, 27

The good news is that God is not hiding! He wants to be found and is very close to you today.

Reach out! The hand you feel is His. It is not God that is refusing to be found, but us.

Opportunity

Opportunities to do good present themselves every day. Sometimes we will have to wait a long time to see a few seeds dropped in the ground, sprout, blossom, and produce fruit. Other seed planted will never break forth in our lifetimes. Solomon said it like this: "Cast your bread upon the waters, for you will find it after many days." ~ Eccl. 11:1

I read an interesting story from Virgil Hurley's, *Speaker's Sourcebook of New Illustrations* across it and thought you would enjoy it as well to illustrate Solomon's wise words.

> While walking outside a Vienna hotel in 1938, a Polish pilot was nearly upended when a man fleeing his pursuers rushed headlong into him. The pilot noticed he was overflowing with terror. Panting heavily, he kept repeating "Gestapo! Gestapo!" The man quickly hid him in his hotel room. Unaware of his guest's identity, but anxious to help him elude the Nazis, he flew the fugitive to Poland, landing in a meadow outside Cracow to protect him from arrest.

> The Polish pilot went on to fly in the Polish, French, and British Air Force. In June 1940, after being wounded in a dogfight over the English Channel, he nearly died when he suffered a severe skull fracture while landing his plane. The hospital considered surgery useless and only changed their minds when a respected brain surgeon arrived by plane and doggedly insisted they allow him to operate.

> When the pilot regained consciousness, the first face he focused on was the white-smocked Jew he had saved from the Gestapo two years before. When the officer weakly asked what he was doing there, the man told him his story. He had slipped into Cracow and, though pursued by the Nazis, had fled to Warsaw and then to Scotland. The surgeon told him that he had noticed the pilot's name on the plane's map and committed it to memory, vowing to repay the debt if an opportunity came.

> When he heard that a Polish squadron had distinguished itself in the Battle of Britain, he found that his friend was involved. Discovering that his friend had been critically wounded in combat and nearly killed in a crash landing, he asked to be flown to him. "But why?" the pilot whispered. "I thought that at last I could show my gratitude. You see, I am a brain surgeon—I operated on you this morning."

You may not have the opportunity to help the person today who may save your life years later, but you just may be able to restore someone's hope today and maybe even a life by a simple deed. The opportunity is yours…take it!

Living Sacrifice

Part and parcel to religious activity is the tendency to think that we can appease the wrath of God with some sacrificial offering. It seems prevalent among all people groups that have any concept of a god that the only way to have a relationship with their god is to make a due and diligent payment. Thus you can find offerings of all sorts from the gifts of fruits and vegetables all the way up to the offering of human life.

Micah's prophecy God recalls to his people the story of Balaam. Remember, Balaam was the guy whose donkey talked. You can find the whole story in Numbers 22-24.

The condensed version is that Balak, the king of Moab, sent for Balaam. He wanted Balaam to curse Israel, but in the end all Balaam could do was bless them. As this encounter unfolded seven altars were built and sacrifices made on each, but to no avail. It was in this setting that God reminded Israel where He had brought them from, how He had protected them, and how He was not impressed with the conniving of men.

So Micah responds, "With what shall I come before the Lord, and bow myself before the High God? Shall I come before Him with burnt offerings, with calves a year old? Will the Lord be pleased with thousands of rams, ten thousand rivers of oil? Shall I give my firstborn for my transgression, the fruit of my body for the sin of my soul? He has shown you, O man, what is good; and what does the Lord require of you but to do justly, to love mercy, and to walk humbly with your God?" ~ Micah 6:6-8

When we attempt to satisfy God with our own feeble attempts at righteousness we can only offer that which we can wrap our fingers around. Truthfully, this is the easiest thing to do. Build an altar. Kill a calf or two. Pour oil until it flows like a river. Promise a child in our place. This is not the end of the list, but the beginning.

God clearly defines what His requirements are. They are not easy; yea, they are impossible without divine assistance. He requires that we conduct ourselves justly—in a right and lawful manner; to love mercy—in a kind and pity-filled fashion; and to walk humbly—in a lowly state placing others before ourselves. None of this is possible apart from the indwelling of God's own Holy Spirit.

It's not a calf on an altar that God seeks, but you on the altar as a living sacrifice.

Never Forget!

I am not sure about other people around this world, but I do know this about Americans: We have very short memories! I can still remember signs everywhere after the terrorist's attacks of September 11, 2001. In some form or another they read, "NEVER FORGET!" Like signs that have been taken down, we have all but forgotten.

Forgetting is not all bad. We do need to move on, but I am afraid that we forget too quickly sometimes the commands of God and then somehow believe that He too has a short memory. Not so!

As Israel was making their way out of Egypt towards the promised land, the Amalekites rose up against them. Even though Joshua prevailed in battle against them, God never forgot that day.

During the reign of King Saul, God spoke. "Thus says the Lord of hosts: 'I will punish Amalek for what he did to Israel, how he ambushed him on the way when he came up from Egypt. Now go and attack Amalek, and utterly destroy all that they have, and do not spare them. But kill both man and woman, infant and nursing child, ox and sheep, camel and donkey.'" ~ 1 Samuel 15:2-3

As harsh as this proclamation might sound, remember that God is just and righteous. Amalek may have forgotten that day when they had attacked God's people, but God had not.

What exactly can we gain from this account of God exacting retribution upon Amalek? We need to remember that the same God who holds the Amalekites accountable also holds you and I accountable. Saul understood that God remembered the outstanding account He had with the Amalekites, but reasoned that God would not function at the same level of austerity with him.

Saul decided to disobey the command of God. "But Saul and the people spared Agag and the best of the sheep, the oxen, the fatlings, the lambs, and all that was good, and were unwilling to utterly destroy them. But everything despised and worthless, that they utterly destroyed." ~ 1 Samuel 15:9

When Samuel came to the battle site to confront Saul's disobedience, Saul acted as we do at times. He attempted to justify his actions making his disobedience sound spiritual. But he forgot that God always remembers.

That day God removed His hand from Saul's kingship and a downhill slide began in his life. What has God commanded in your life today? NEVER FORGET! Return now in obedience and fulfill His direction for your life. NEVER, EVER FORGET!

Forgiveness

There is no sadder story in the Bible than that of Saul, the first king of Israel. Here was a man chosen by God to lead Israel yet because of jealousy and spite he came to a disastrous end.

Saul's hatred of David literally consumed him to the point that he sought to kill David. The entire account found in First Samuel makes for very interesting reading and holds much insight for us into what happens when a man turns from seeking God's direction and leans on his own understanding.

As Saul continued seeking David throughout the land, David fled to the land of Moab. Scripture tells us that 400 men came to join David as a ragtag army. It would have made sense for David to assume several things since people were following him and declaring him their captain.

He could have marched on Saul's army or made a brazen declaration of his kingship. After all, he had already been anointed by Samuel, but he did not. "Then David went from there to Mizpah of Moab; and he said to the king of Moab, 'Please let my father and mother come here with you, till I know what God will do for me.'" ~ 1 Samuel 22:3

Here is the mark of a man after God's own heart. He did not make a decision based on circumstance or a pros-and-cons list. He decided to wait until he knew God's will. How I wish I could learn to fight the tendency to do something even if it's wrong. How many times has this led me down a troublesome path? Don't ask!

Because Saul was not walking in God's will nor seeking His wisdom, he had come to an awful conclusion. He not only assumed David to be his enemy but everyone in his company to be so.

"'All of you have conspired against me, and there is no one who reveals to me that my son has made a covenant with the son of Jesse; and there is not one of you who is sorry for me or reveals to me that my son has stirred up my servant against me, to lie in wait, as it is this day.'" ~ 1 Samuel 22:8

There is a valuable lesson here. When we decide to harbor ill will toward someone it never stops with just one person. Like a cancer it spreads until we are left alone to suffer the consequences.

As Matthew West sings in his song "Forgiveness":

> Help me now to do the impossible
> Forgiveness.
>
> It'll clear the bitterness away
> It can even set a prisoner free
> There is no end to what it's power can do
> So, let it go and be amazed
> By what you see through eyes of grace
> The prisoner that it really frees is you.
>
> Forgiveness,
> Forgiveness,
> Forgiveness,
> Forgiveness.

09/13

The Jesus Vaccine

I used to give blood donations regularly until I started making mission trips to lands that required a multiplicity of vaccines. Each time that my system has gotten over some dose of vaccine, it's time to go on another mission trip, and the folks who draw blood for donation disqualify me. I want to help, but my blood is useless to others since these vaccines are coursing through it.

Vaccines have saved millions of lives. The stories of how some of them were discovered is interesting. For example, the vaccine for yellow fever was discovered in West Africa in 1927. A blood specimen was taken from a native named Asibi, who was sick with yellow fever. A rhesus monkey which had just been received from India, was inoculated with the specimen. Asibi recovered, but the monkey died of the disease. The vaccine was named the Asibi Vaccine.

All the vaccine manufactured since 1927, derives from the original strain of virus obtained from this humble native. Carried down to the present day from one laboratory to another, through repeated cultures, and by enormous multiplication, it has offered immunity to yellow fever to millions of people in many countries. The blood of one man in West Africa has been made to serve the whole human race.

Every believer alive today or who has ever lived has been made well and protected by the blood of one man also. His name is Jesus. The Jesus Vaccine is available by faith in His shed blood.

By application, it removes the death sentence of sin that courses through our veins. It protects us from everyday contact with the virus of sin that is still rampant in all parts of the world. One day it will remove us from the very presence of sin and take us to a place called heaven where there is no sin, no sickness, and no death!

Diseases can require one to be quarantined; cut off from human contact. Sin does the same, but there is hope. "This is the message which we have heard from Him and declare to you, that God is light and in Him is no darkness at all. If we say that we have fellowship with Him, and walk in darkness, we lie and do not practice the truth. But if we walk in the light as He is in the light, we have fellowship with one another, and the blood of Jesus Christ His Son cleanses us from all sin." ~ 1 John 1:5-7

The line forms here.

If you have never been protected by the Jesus Vaccine, it is yours today for the asking. No need to roll up your sleeve.

Just ask in faith, believing, and the cure for sin is yours.

09/14

At The Cross

Each Sunday faithful preachers will expound from the pulpit the truth of Scripture. No matter where they begin their exposition, it will not be a complete message until it ends at the foot of the cross. God had the cross on His mind from eternity past as He looked ahead to the redemption of mankind. God, on the cross in Christ Jesus, had you and me on His mind as He longed for the day that we would believe and trust Him as Savior.

Paul said in First Corinthians that he had one purpose in his ministry and that was to preach the gospel. He then immediately connected the gospel to the cross for without that connection there can be no good news.

"For Christ did not send me to baptize, but to preach the gospel, not with wisdom of words, lest the cross of Christ should be made of no effect. For the message of the cross is foolishness to those who are perishing, but to us who are being saved it is the power of God." ~ 1 Corinthians 1:17-18

There is in Paris a famous picture by Zwiller named "The First Night Outside Paradise." The painting takes you to the time that Adam and Eve have been driven out of the Garden of Eden and are preparing to spend their first night in the desert beyond.

In the distance can be discerned the figure of the angel with the flaming sword, but the eyes of the exiles are not fixed on him. They are gazing far above his head, and there, outlined in light—faint, but unmistakable—the artist has painted a cross. In wondering awe their gaze is fastened on it.

Today may be a desert day for you. It may be a day of recalling the past and regretting the sin that has stolen your peace and safety. Like Adam and Eve you feel driven and separated, but lift now your eyes.

Don't focus on the closed gate to the Garden, but look above the fray. Let your gaze see, though faintly, the glow of a Cross. Peer closely at that Cross and see the blood stains.

These were left behind for a day like this. A day when the world calls the Cross foolishness, but you know it is the power of God to all who are being saved.

Take hope!

09/15

Get In The Boat

Have you ever gotten into trouble doing exactly what God told you to do?

Now that question is immediately going to raise an eyebrow or two and maybe cause a shiver to run up someone's spine. You know, at the least, you have thought about it. You have engaged a project or a relationship or a new job or you name it and suddenly in the midst of doing what you honestly and sincerely believed was the will of God a storm hits.

Take comfort. You are not alone!

We have the account of just such an occasion recorded for us in the gospels. The multitude had pressed upon Jesus and the disciples to the point that they had reached the shore of the Sea of Galilee. Jesus told the disciples to get in a boat and journey to the other side while he dismissed the crowds. He then went up to the mountain to pray.

We pick up the story at this point. The disciples were exactly where Jesus told them to be and, BAM!, the storm hit!

"Then He saw them straining at rowing, for the wind was against them. Now about the fourth watch of the night He came to them, walking on the sea, and would have passed them by. And when they saw Him walking on the sea, they supposed it was a ghost, and cried out; for they all saw Him and were troubled. But immediately He talked with them and said to them, 'Be of good cheer! It is I; do not be afraid.' Then He went up into the boat to them, and the wind ceased. And they were greatly amazed in themselves beyond measure, and marveled." ~ Mark 6:48-51

There now. My opening question doesn't seem disrespectful at all does it? You need to understand that being in God's will and doing God's will does not always mean smooth sailing. To the contrary God may be directing us right into the middle of the hurricane.

Here are a few jewels of joy for you just in case you are straining at the wind today.

- First, HE SAW THEM! Never think that you are out of God's sight.

- Second, HE CAME IN THE FOURTH WATCH! He didn't come in the first, second, or third; he came in the fourth watch. He came ON TIME! Not a bit early, but not a moment late!

- Finally, HE GOT INTO THE BOAT WITH THEM! He did not wait for the sea to calm itself. He climbed right up into the middle of their storm and calmed the sea.

Remember this: Sometimes God calms the storm. Sometimes God calms the servant in the midst of the storm. Get in the boat!

09/16

No Interference

I have mentioned in times past my interest in tracking the weather. I served several years as a volunteer cooperative weather observer. My curiosity with the weather has not waned over the years. I still have a weather station that I maintain from my home today.

When I first moved to my present location, I set up the weather station attempting to make everything as accurate as possible. That was a little over seven years ago. I have replaced several parts of the equipment over these years, but I had not done a full reset of the station since its installation.

The equipment was just fine. What had changed dramatically was the surrounding environment. I looked out one day to discover that several trees that were mere saplings when I installed my equipment had now grown to heights that were interfering with the station's ability to accurately record the weather.

The trees are not on my property. I had no way to change that which was affecting my equipment, but I could make changes to my weather station. I bought new parts, procured a pole that would raise the height of my anemometer, and made other adjustments that would remove the effects of the trees, etc.

With the interference removed, my equipment is now back up to par. How long has it been since you've checked for interference in your spiritual life? Just like the trees which slowly grew tall enough to block the wind from my weather equipment, things crop up in our lives which interfere with our relationship to Christ.

The Apostle Paul stated it like this: "Yet indeed I also count all things loss for the excellence of the knowledge of Christ Jesus my Lord, for whom I have suffered the loss of all things, and count them as rubbish, that I may gain Christ." ~ Philippians 3:8

Check your spiritual gauges today. Watch for those tiny inconsistencies that can be key indicators that something has grown up to interfere with your spiritual receivers. Remember you may not be able to remove the obstacle, but you can always relocate the equipment.

09/17

Lots of Pictures

We live in a world of over simplification. Nearly every item that you purchase has with it a quick start guide. These are meant to be simplistic, but I sometimes find them confusing. If you have one handy take a quick look at it: pictures. That's right pictures. Nothing but one diagram after another that is supposed to "help" you get your new gadget up and running.

I know that for most people it works and for me it does at times, but give me words! Just plain simple words. I don't want to have to match parts to some artist's rendering…just write it out for me!

Jesus spoke in word pictures also. They are called parables. The difference is that those who knew Him also knew the meaning of the parable. Matthew 13 is the parable chapter of the gospels. It begins, "On the same day Jesus went out of the house and sat by the sea. And great multitudes were gathered together to Him, so that He got into a boat and sat; and the whole multitude stood on the shore. Then He spoke many things to them in parables, saying: "Behold, a sower went out to sow." ~ Matthew 13:1-3

From here he launched into a series of parables, seven in all, that described the Kingdom of Heaven. This text then explains, "All these things Jesus spoke to the multitude in parables; and without a parable He did not speak to them, that it might be fulfilled which was spoken by the prophet, saying: 'I will open My mouth in parables; I will utter things kept secret from the foundation of the world.'" ~ Matthew 13:34-35

You may be thinking, "It sure doesn't sound like parables are meant to be easily understood." You would be right in your assumption except for the fact that God clearly is speaking through them. Parables reveal things that have been kept secret since the beginning of time. When I set out to write my first devotional, *Glasses in the Grass:*

Devotions for My Friends, I decided to parabolize the devotions. I am convinced that God is speaking through our everyday stories as He reveals the heavenly meaning of our otherwise common experiences.

Begin right now to look at your life through the lens of the parable. I think you will be amazed at what God is really saying. "Then He spoke many things to them in parables…"

09/18

It's Not All About You

It is a little bit funny to hear politicians and diplomats discuss how they are going to save us and straighten out this old crooked world. They are always looking for a utopia where, of course, their ideals are followed and their "man" sits upon the throne.

I would recommend as a daily reading for them Daniel 4. The chapter begins with Daniel being in the midst of interpreting some dreams for king Nebuchadnezzar. This was not a pleasant task for Daniel considering the fact that the news of this interpretation was not good for the king.

Nebuchadnezzar had become powerful and full of pride. He had imagined falsely that all that he had acquired was by his own hand. His dream foretold of his own demise. He would become mentally deranged and spend seven years living as a beast of the field. As he perused his kingdom and proclaimed his own abilities in obtaining and maintaining it the dream came true and he fell under the consequences of his own making. He spent seven years eating grass in the field. The dew of the night fell upon him. His hair grew out like feathers and his nails became like a bird's claws.

But God's mercy is never ending and Nebuchadnezzar recovered. "And at the end of the time I, Nebuchadnezzar, lifted my eyes to heaven, and my understanding returned to me; and I blessed the Most High and praised and honored Him who lives forever: For His dominion is an everlasting dominion, and His kingdom is from generation to generation. All the inhabitants of the earth are reputed as nothing; He does according to His will in the army of heaven and among the inhabitants of the earth. No one can restrain His hand or say to Him, 'What have You done?'" ~ Daniel 4:34, 35

Now back to the politicians and the diplomats. Take note that you might think that you are running this world, but you don't. Notice that Nebuchadnezzar's understanding returned to him and he concluded that God's dominion will never end. He functions according to His own sovereign will and no one has the right to say, "What have you done?"

By the way, this word is for you and your little universe also. It really doesn't all revolve around you! Lift your eyes to heaven. Bless, and praise, and honor the King.

Conducting His Business

Today we will take a look at a parable that is oft times overlooked. It is not shunned on purpose; it is overshadowed by its context and its similarity to another parable.

"Now as they heard these things, He spoke another parable, because He was near Jerusalem and because they thought the kingdom of God would appear immediately. Therefore He said: "A certain nobleman went into a far country to receive for himself a kingdom and to return. So he called ten of his servants, delivered to them ten minas, and said to them, 'Do business till I come.' But his citizens hated him, and sent a delegation after him, saying, 'We will not have this man to reign over us.'" ~ Luke 19:11-14

Just prior to Jesus speaking this parable was His encounter with Zacchaeus. This story is familiar to us. Some of you can even remember the little song you sang in Sunday School or Vacation Bible School. Remember: Zacchaeus was a wee little man, a wee little man was he... Following this parable is the Triumphal Entry into Jerusalem, just a few days before Christ was crucified.

Then this parable gets hidden away by a more familiar yet similar parable about three men receiving talents (money.) That parable tells how two of them returned the money with interest earned while one had hidden that given to him and was proven unfaithful.

Our text for today is a prophetic parable. It speaks of ten men receiving the exact same amount with the command to, "Do business till I come." Hopefully you will take a moment to read the entire parable, because it unfolds the whole of prophecy. Here's how it plays out for these servants.

The nobleman is informed by the citizens that they have no intent of allowing him reign over them and openly reject him. This prophecy would be fulfilled in just a few days as the crowds cried out, "Crucify Him!" But there is good news! The nobleman returns! At least two of the men did invest that coin given to them and returned to the owner all with interest. Others hid the treasure given and in the end had even that removed.

What can we learn from this parable? First, what we have has come to us from God. Second, what we have will be accounted before Him one day. Third, that day is soon approaching and He is coming again! Be ready! Whether you return unto Him ten-fold or five-fold matters not. Be faithful until He comes for He truly is drawing nigh!

No Cruise Control

Of all the modern conveniences placed on automobiles my favorite is the cruise control. With the push of a button the accelerator of a vehicle is set at a certain speed and you can at least let your foot relax while you zip down the highway. Neither hills nor valleys can affect your speed as the cruise control keeps everything set just so.

There is no cruise control on life. This is why the Bible speaks so much about self-control. Solomon who struggled in this area in his own life wrote: "Whoever has no rule over his own spirit is like a city broken down, without walls." ~ Proverbs 25:28

We are living in a day with little self-control. This is seen from the heights of government operating to the tune of multi-trillion dollar deficits, to the little child who is left to throw tantrums because he is not getting his way.

In 1942, when London was being blitzed, an article appeared in one of the British newspapers. It may not be out of place to take a look at this searching statement:

"We have been a pleasure-loving people, dishonoring God's day, picnicking and bathing—now the seashore is barred; no picnics, no bathing.

We have preferred motor travel to church-going—now there is a shortage of fuel.

We have ignored the ringing of church bells calling us to worship—now the bells cannot ring except to warn us of invasion.

We have left our churches half-empty when they should have been well filled with worshippers—now they are in ruins.

We would not listen to the way of peace—now we are forced to listen to the way of war.

The money we would not give to the Lord's work now is taken from us in higher taxes and high cost of living.

The food for which we refused to give God thanks—now is unobtainable.

The service we refused to give God is now conscribed for our country.

Lives we refused to live under God's control—now are under the nation's control.

Nights we would not spend watching unto prayer—now are spent in anxious air raid precautions."

You may be saying that we are not so out of control that those things are happening here, but neither was England just a few years prior to 1942. Someone said that we shall either learn from history or be forced to repeat it. Another said that self-control is the capacity to break a chocolate bar into four pieces with your bare hands—and then eat just one of the pieces.

The bar is broken. Now what?

09/21

The Old Days

Troubles, trials, and tribulations often bring us to the place of asking questions. One of the most common is why. We think that we want an explanation of the causation of our trouble. Somehow we become convinced that if God or somebody can tell us why that it will all somehow make sense, but in reality it is not the question of why for which we seek an answer.

The real question that looms in the background is how. I think that we know that troubles, trials, and tribulations are the inevitable result of sin at work in our world. What we really want to know is how could this happen to me? There must be some mistake. Sure, I'm a sinner and if I were to be penalized for my sin then all of this would be justified and make some sort of sense. We know why. We just don't understand how this could have happened.

There is an entire book in the Old Testament written about the how. It is the book of Lamentations. The title of this book comes from the opening word of this book as translated into English. "How lonely sits the city that was full of people! How like a widow is she, who was great among the nations! The princess among the provinces has become a slave!" ~ Lamentations 1:1 From this verse on to the end the book reads like a funeral dirge. There is weeping and wailing at the sight of Jerusalem fallen into disarray and abandoned. The question is formed early and it is not why, but how.

So, what is the answer when we find ourselves like Jerusalem? Where do we have to be so that God can bring back the glory days. As you draw near to the end of this book the answer is revealed. "The joy of our heart has ceased; Our dance has turned into mourning. The crown has fallen from our head. Woe to us, for we have sinned! Because of this our heart is faint; Because of these things our eyes grow dim…Turn us back to You, O Lord, and we will be restored; Renew our days as of old…" ~ Lam. 5:15-17, 21

There it is! It is not self-effort. It is not self-improvement. It is surrender! It is coming to the place of understanding that ONLY God can restore us from such a condition. Offer a lament today. Cry out to the Lord and ask Him to restore the days of old in your life.

Overlooking the Small Things

The white rabbit in Lewis Carroll's, *Alice in Wonderland*, said, "The hurrier I go, the behinder I get!" Richard Carlson titled his bestselling book, *Don't Sweat the Small Stuff…and it's all small stuff*. The subtitle is *Simple Ways to Keep the Little Things from Taking Over Your Life*. Well, I'm here to tell you this morning that we sometimes get so busy that we overlook the small things. Actually they are not so small. We have just made our own little world so big that they seem insignificant.

For example: "The heavens declare the glory of God; and the firmament shows His handiwork. Day unto day utters speech, and night unto night reveals knowledge. There is no speech nor language where their voice is not heard. Their line has gone out through all the earth, and their words to the end of the world. In them He has set a tabernacle for the sun, which is like a bridegroom coming out of his chamber, and rejoices like a strong man to run its race. Its rising is from one end of heaven, and its circuit to the other end; and there is nothing hidden from its heat." ~ Psalm 19:1-6

These verses clearly remind us to take note of God's handiwork. You know what handiwork is don't you? It is work done by hand and often done in one's spare time. God has set all around us little stuff that identifies Himself and we get so busy in our big world that we just ignore his handiwork.

A great illustration of getting refocused comes from Viktor Frankl's memoirs of his experiences in a Nazi prison camp. In his classic book, *Man's Search for Meaning*, he said deprivation made the eye more observant, the ear more attentive. He tells of the day a prisoner came running into the building as they were eating their customary evening soup and cried for them to rush out in the small yard to see the beauty of the sunset.

Tired as they were, they went out and stood in hushed silence watching the brilliant hues of the evening sky running the spectrum from red to steel blue. In fact, the rays of the sun on the muddy water standing in puddles on the ground looked beautiful. After several undisturbed minutes a prisoner said, "How beautiful the world could be."

Don't sweat the small stuff today, but don't ignore all of it either. You may just miss the wonder of His glory revealed on a grand scale.

Mother Boyd and Sister Irene

When I was a boy my brother and I worked each summer with our dad mowing lawns. Most people had large yards back then. We would mow and trim the entire place for $4.00.

One of the yards we kept up was that of Mother Boyd and Sister Irene. That's all I ever knew them by was those two names. They were missionaries to the native Indians out west. They would leave in May and not return until October or so, as they travelled the reservations teaching and leading Vacation Bible Schools. We mowed their yard all summer for free.

It seemed to me that Mother Boyd was 150 years old. I know better, but she sure seemed ancient to a nine year old boy. Her daughter, Sister Irene, was blind. I can still remember the stacks of long play records in their little mobile home that contained the entire Bible. This is how Sister Irene would "read". Together they journeyed in their jam-packed station wagon to bring the light of God's Word to a darkened world.

These two ladies remind me of Paul's commendation for the Ephesians: "Therefore I also, after I heard of your faith in the Lord Jesus and your love for all the saints, do not cease to give thanks for you, making mention of you in my prayers: that the God of our Lord Jesus Christ, the Father of glory, may give to you the spirit of wisdom and revelation in the knowledge of Him, the eyes of your understanding being enlightened; that you may know what is the hope of His calling, what are the riches of the glory of His inheritance in the saints, and what is the exceeding greatness of His power toward us who believe, according to the working of His mighty power which He worked in Christ when He raised Him from the dead and seated Him at His right hand in the heavenly places…" ~ Ephesians 1:15-20

Even though the Ephesians were faithful and certainly had in their midst a few "Mother Boyd's" and "Sister Irene's", Paul prayed that they would have even more understanding of Christ as their eyes were opened to truth.

As I think of those two ladies and the little that they owned in this life, I cannot help but smile thinking about them today. They have surely gone home to glory and are enjoying the riches of the glory of His inheritance. And Sister Irene doesn't need those records anymore. She is hearing the word right from the mouth of Jesus while Mother Boyd walks on the golden streets with Indian brothers and sisters.

Just remembering…

Bon Appétit

Google the words diet and blindness and you will get 7,830,000 hits! The responses to your query run the gamut from diets that prevent blindness to those that cause it. A common thread is blindness caused by a vitamin deficiency, in particularly Vitamin A.

The body uses vitamin A in the retina of the eye. Vitamin A is vital in the process that creates rhodopsin. These are the rod-shaped parts of the retina and are important in the way we see. Rhodopsin is needed to see black and white and also to see at night. Without them, a person suffers from night blindness. Our bodies use vitamin A in order to replenish the retinas' supply of rhodopsin.

That's why your mama always told you to eat your vegetables!

There is a spiritual application to the body's use of Vitamin A as well. Just as we are to eat a balanced diet to maintain proper vision, so we must consume the proper balance of God's word. We have a spiritual vitamin A called illumination. It is only available to the believer and to that person whom God opens the eye to His truth. The unbelieving person simply cannot see. The believer who has a deficiency of illumination will suffer "spiritual night blindness" and will not be able to distinguish black and white.

It is interesting that so many people prefer to live in the gray area of life. The problem is a spiritually unbalanced diet. Peter speaks of us consuming the word of God like a baby does milk. "Therefore, laying aside all malice, all deceit, hypocrisy, envy, and all evil speaking, as newborn babes, desire the pure milk of the word, that you may grow thereby, if indeed you have tasted that the Lord is gracious." ~ 1 Peter 2:1-3

Notice the unbalanced diet of malice, deceit, hypocrisy, envy, and evil speaking. These act as agents which destroy illumination, our spiritual Vitamin A. We are to be like babies who just hunger for pure milk. In our case, the pure milk of the word.

Have you ever tasted something really scrumptious? If so, no one ever has to beg you to eat it again. So as Peter says, "if indeed you have tasted that the Lord is gracious" you will always be ready for a full serving of God's Word.

Bon Appétit!

Here Am I...Send Me!

I think there are several responses that we might have when considering whether or not if God is speaking to us. The decision or should I say confusion comes not from lack of clarity on God's part, but instead from the fact that we are not in a position to hear.

For example, we can dismiss what we thought we heard by assuming that the message is for someone else. This might occur when we are in a church service where crowds have gathered to "hear" what God is saying. We simply pass the word to another like rain being displaced by an umbrella. We are standing in the rain, but we are not drenched by it since the umbrella leaves us in a field of drought.

We might, on the other hand, just not hear at all because we have tuned out the voice of God. All around you at this moment are various signals from radio and television stations, but unless you have a device to capture them and a tuner which can adjust to their frequency you remain oblivious to the sights or sounds.

God has a way of getting us alone so that the message is clear and there can be no mistake as to the recipient. This is exactly what He did with Isaiah. "In the year that King Uzziah died, I saw the Lord sitting on a throne, high and lifted up, and the train of His robe filled the temple. Also I heard the voice of the Lord, saying: 'Whom shall I send, And who will go for Us?' Then I said, 'Here am I! Send me." ~ Isaiah 6:1, 8

Isaiah was left alone in the presence of God and God dealt directly with him. These are the moments of great decision and radical change for us.

One such moment happened when Robert Moffat, Scottish missionary to South Africa, came back to recruit helpers in his homeland. Arriving at the church where he was to speak he noted that only a small group had braved the elements to hear his appeal.

What disturbed him even more was that there were only ladies in attendance that night, for he had chosen as his text Proverbs 8:4, "Unto you, O men, I call." Dr. Moffat, realizing that few women could be expected to undergo the rigorous experiences they would face in the undeveloped jungles of the continent where he labored, felt hopeless.

But God works in mysterious ways to carry out His wise purposes. Although no one volunteered, there was a young fellow assisting the organist who was thrilled by the challenge. Deciding that he would follow in the footsteps of this pioneer missionary, he went on to school, obtained a degree in medicine, and then spent the rest of his life ministering to the unreached tribes of Africa. His name: David Livingstone!

Are you listening today? Be quiet. Tune in. Will you respond? "Here am I! Send me!"

Telling The Story In Real Time

I remember seeing the old newsreel footage of the Hindenburg coming to its mooring position near Lakehurst, New Jersey on May, 6, 1937. In this age of reality television the final few moments of the Hindenburg's flight take the prize for really being real.

The reporters on sight ran out of words as they tried to tell their audience what was transpiring before their eyes. You can still watch the video of this terrible event. It is available at this location: http://www.youtube.com/watch?v=F54rqDh2mWA&sns=em if you are interested in seeing it in "real" time.

In Psalm 45 you can hear a Hindenburg-like response as the psalmist attempts to describe the King in His majesty. This psalm which is literally a love song speaks of the King in all of His glory and then of the queen in her beauty. The setting of the psalm is a wedding and most believe that it is a prophetic portrayal of the wedding of Christ to His Bride, the church.

"My heart is overflowing with a good theme; I recite my composition concerning the King; My tongue is the pen of a ready writer. You are fairer than the sons of men; grace is poured upon Your lips; Therefore God has blessed You forever. Gird Your sword upon Your thigh, O Mighty One, with Your glory and Your majesty. And in Your majesty ride prosperously because of truth, humility, and righteousness; and Your right hand shall teach You awesome things." ~ Psalm 45:1-4

The psalmist says that what he is viewing is more than he can contain and much more than he can translate from thought into pen and ink. Like the reporter at the Hindenburg disaster his words pour out so quickly that they cannot be controlled. His tongue is moving faster than his hands as he is overwhelmed with the glory and majesty of the moment.

Oh, what responsibility we have as those who know the truth. As John said in his epistle, "These things I have written to you who believe in the name of the Son of God, that you may know that you have eternal life, and that you may continue to believe in the name of the Son of God." ~ 1 John 5:13 The apostle John said he had seen truth with his own eyes (1 John 1). Because of this, he was fulfilling Psalm 45:17: "I will make Your name to be remembered in all generations; Therefore the people shall praise You forever and ever."

If you know Him, you have a story to tell. If you don't, you can call on Him today. It's time to make His name known and remembered.

An Awful Word

What is the one thing that people resist more than anything else in the world? Go ahead and take your time answering this question. I want to give you plenty of time to *CHANGE* your mind. While you are thinking, would you happen to have *CHANGE* for a dollar? Don't forget that it's only a few weeks until the season *CHANGES* and the leaves will all start to *CHANGE* colors. Whose turn is it anyway to *CHANGE* the baby's diaper?

Do you give up? You should know this. I've given you lots of hints. What is the one thing that people resist more than anything else in the world: *CHANGE*!

Someone said that the biggest room in the world is the room for change, but I think that few of us have ever spent much time in it. Jesus presented to His disciples principles that demanded radical change in their lives. They had spent years ingrained in rhetoric and religion. They had come to accept their position in life. They assumed that they were just part of the rank and file, but Jesus took them into the changing room as He drew near to the end of His earthly ministry.

Jesus called the disciples together into what is familiarly called the upper room. There they participated in the Passover meal. Then Jesus, "rose from supper and laid aside His garments, took a towel and girded Himself. After that, He poured water into a basin and began to wash the disciples' feet, and to wipe them with the towel with which He was girded.

So when He had washed their feet, taken His garments, and sat down again, He said to them, "Do you know what I have done to you? You call Me Teacher and Lord, and you say well, for so I am. If I then, your Lord and Teacher, have washed your feet, you also ought to wash one another's feet. For I have given you an example, that you should do as I have done to you." ~ John 13:4-5, 12-15

One of the greatest changes that takes place in a believer is the transformation to servanthood. G.T. Niles said, "It is easier to dole out services than to be servants." This is so true in our day. If we are not careful with our kindness and mercy, we can become just another welfare agency. Christ did not call us to be a service provider; He called us to be servants. "For I have given you an example, that you should do as I have done to you."

Now, go do it!

Don't Blame the Mirror

The only Jesus that folks will see today is you. For some of you that is an eye-opener; for others a ho-hum statement that you have heard hundreds of times. Nevertheless, it is true. Jesus clearly left His people, the church, here to be His representatives and with that representations of Him.

So, if you and I are the only Jesus that will be seen today, that forces a question to be asked. What will our friends and family see as they observe us in our everyday transactions?

Paul gave us some insight concerning the answer to this question in Galatians 5. "I say then: Walk in the Spirit, and you shall not fulfill the lust of the flesh. For the flesh lusts against the Spirit, and the Spirit against the flesh; and these are contrary to one another, so that you do not do the things that you wish. But the fruit of the Spirit is love, joy, peace, longsuffering, kindness, goodness, faithfulness, gentleness, self-control. Against such there is no law. And those who are Christ's have crucified the flesh with its passions and desires. If we live in the Spirit, let us also walk in the Spirit. Let us not become conceited, provoking one another, envying one another." ~ Galatians 5:16-17, 22-26

First, you need to understand that if you make the decision to really be the representation of Christ to those around you, then it will mean war. Every bit of you (that is the fleshly desires of life) will come racing to the forefront demanding prominence. Left unchecked, you will not be able to do the things you wish to do. Especially to be like Jesus.

You can counter this attack by allowing the Holy Spirit to produce in you the fruit of the Spirit. "But the fruit of the Spirit is love, joy, peace, longsuffering, kindness, goodness, faithfulness, gentleness, self-control."

There is no doubt that these are not natural to us. You only find this type of fruit in the follower of Jesus who is being controlled by the Spirit.

Finally, understand that we never fully arrive in this life. As the children's song says, "He's still working on me. To make me what I ought to be!" When we begin to see reflections of Jesus in our lives, be not conceited, filled with provocation, or envious.

Keep walking in the Spirit; marching in step with the Designer of our lives. And when you see a reflection that looks different from that of Jesus, don't spend time cleaning the mirror. The mirror is not where the distortion lies!

A Little Help From My Friends

Trampolines.

I still remember when our school got its first trampoline. The year was somewhere around 1967 or so. Most of us kids had never seen, much less had been on, a trampoline. The P.E. (physical education) teachers hauled the contraption into the gym and set it up right on the hardwood floor. Each of us took our turn bouncing up and down on the tightly stretched canvas hung between springs.

Here's where it got really interesting. Because none of us had any experience jumping on a trampoline, we usually could not maintain our balance or keep our trajectory centered. This could easily present a difficulty for the bouncer since flying off of the trampoline meant that the next stop was a hardwood gym floor.

P.E. teachers to the rescue! All of us watchers were required to ring the perimeter of the trampoline. When the bouncer approached our guarded position we would shove them back towards the center of the trampoline. As far as I know, nobody got seriously hurt on that contraption and we did it all without hundreds of dollars' worth of "safety" features.

We are to serve one another in a similar way in our relationship to one another as believers. We all have times when we drift toward the edge. Believe me. Flying off the edge results in a sudden hard landing. So, what can we do to help one another before tragedy occurs?

The writer of Hebrews gives us the answer. "Therefore strengthen the hands which hang down, and the feeble knees, and make straight paths for your feet, so that what is lame may not be dislocated, but rather be healed. Pursue peace with all people, and holiness, without which no one will see the Lord: looking carefully lest anyone fall short of the grace of God; lest any root of bitterness springing up cause trouble, and by this many become defiled…" ~ Hebrews 12:12-15

If you are on the trampoline of life rejoice that you have friends that will keep you centered. Make sure that they are in place before you start jumping and never ever bounce through life without your safety net of friends.

If you are one of those friends standing around the edge of someone else's life never forsake your position of guarding another's safety.

Have a great time on your trampoline and be safe!

In the Pit

Erma Bombeck wrote one of her classic books about life and titled it, *If Life Is A Bowl Of Cherries, What Am I Doing In The Pits?* Perhaps you can relate to her predicament today. You didn't ask to be in the pit, but here you are anyway.

You may have been minding your own business like Joseph. You were only doing the bidding of your father when suddenly you find yourself deep in a situation from which you cannot extract yourself.

Maybe you were walking in new territory and simply fell in unexpectedly. Or perhaps, if it were to be admitted, you purposely approached the edge, peered over into the deep, wondered what was down there, and with one slip here you are: THE PIT!

Now what?

David had an answer for us in his book of songs. "I waited patiently for the Lord; and He inclined to me, and heard my cry. He also brought me up out of a horrible pit, out of the miry clay, and set my feet upon a rock, and established my steps. He has put a new song in my mouth—praise to our God; Many will see it and fear, and will trust in the Lord. Blessed is that man who makes the Lord his trust, And does not respect the proud, nor such as turn aside to lies. Many, O Lord my God, are Your wonderful works which You have done; and Your thoughts toward us cannot be recounted to You in order; if I would declare and speak of them, they are more than can be numbered." ~ Psalm 40:1-5

In the pit? Wait patiently for the one who will bring you out and plant your feet again on solid ground. He wants to make your life a witness even after a stint in the pit.

This story from a Chinese Confucian scholar, converted to Christ, explains it better than I can: A man fell into a dark, dirty, slimy pit, and tried to climb out, but could not.

Confucius came along. He saw the man in the pit and said, "Poor fellow, if he'd listened to me, he never would have gotten there," and he went on.

Buddha came along. He saw the man in the pit and said, "Poor fellow, if he'll come up here, I'll help him." And he too went on.

Then Jesus Christ came. He saw the man and said, "Poor fellow!" then jumped into the pit and lifted him out.

In the pit? Cry out to Jesus and He will come in and lift you out, give you a new song, and a second chance to proclaim His wonderful saving work

• OCTOBER

The Unfinished Work

Patience is said to be a virtue and I suppose that some seem to have a better handle on it than others. The Apostle Paul certainly exhibited great patience with the church at Corinth. This was a church that was literally coming apart at the seams.

We have recorded for us in the Bible two letters that Paul sent to the Corinthians. The first letter dealt with a lot of deep-seated correction and evidently it was received well for the Corinthians made a lot of changes. In Paul's second letter he writes with some additional tweaks that he was hoping they would make.

One of the adjustments that the church at Corinth needed was in the area of giving. They had very good intent, but like many of us they lacked follow-through.

Paul wrote to the Corinthians in a challenging way, yet with a tone of kindness and clarity. Thus he writes, "So we urged Titus, that as he had begun, so he would also complete this grace in you as well. But as you abound in everything—in faith, in speech, in knowledge, in all diligence, and in your love for us— see that you abound in this grace also. I speak not by commandment, but I am testing the sincerity of your love by the diligence of others. For you know the grace of our Lord Jesus Christ, that though He was rich, yet for your sakes He became poor, that you through His poverty might become rich." ~ 2 Corinthians 8:6-9

The grace that Paul wanted to see matured in the Corinthians was in the area of giving. He had introduced the challenge by telling them about the Macedonian church who gave out of their poverty. You know the old axiom: You can't teach an old dog a new trick, but you can certainly make him jealous.

Paul was using the actions of another group of believers to prompt the Corinthians to step up to the challenge. But he takes it a step further in contrast. He reminds them that Christ who was never in poverty gave all and became poor for their sakes, so that they might become rich. That was a stake in the heart of the Corinthians selfishness and lack of commitment.

What do you need to follow through on today? It may not be in the area of giving, but right now God is showing you what it is that you are lacking in your Christian walk.

My prayer is that the unfinished work of grace might be completed in you to His glory. When it happens, be sure and have a grand opening to encourage others to finish the unfinished task of their lives as well.

10/02

Isn't A Circle A Direction?

Of course, it goes without saying that men simply do not ask directions. I'm not exactly sure where that attribute was attached to men, but it does seem a common trait. I have only two questions: Isn't a circle a direction? and Could you please repeat those directions one more time?

Now that the issue of directions is settled as far as geography is concerned, what about spiritual direction? How can we know that we are really walking in the direction God told us?

Sometimes God gives very clear directives. When God spoke to Isaac he told him where he was to not go. "Then the Lord appeared to him and said: "Do not go down to Egypt; live in the land of which I shall tell you." ~ Genesis 26:2 Clearly, it is just as important to know where not to go as it is where to go.

There have been times in my life that I simply have asked God to close doors. I tend to take note when I bang my head on a closed door! I may be a little slow, but after a few dozen closed doors, I tend to recognize an open one when I see it.

It is interesting that God told Isaac to remain in the land of His direction. In this case, it was the land of Gerar. If you take the time to read all of Genesis 26 you will discover what may appear strange to you.

We assume that being under God's direction means that everything will be peaceful and quiet. We tend to equate God's leadership in a certain area of our lives with a lack of struggle. But the opposite is sometimes true, as in this case of Isaac dwelling in the Philistine land of Gerar.

A look into the meaning of the word Gerar will help clear up the matter. Gerar is first descriptive of the landscape itself. It means rolling country. God will not bring us at times to a level plain, but instead to a roller coaster ride with all of its ups, downs, twists, and turns. Remember, God told Isaac to remain there. God also knew it would be a topsy-turvy ride.

Then the word means to drag off roughly or to work back and forth like the action of a saw blade. God will bring us to places where He can cut us down to size little by little.

Finally, the word, Gerar, means to ruminate. Like an old cow chewing the cud, we are brought to places where God allows us to fully contemplate what His intent is for us.

By the way, these thoughts are not just for the men, but for all. We all can use some direction in our lives. Just be sure you are where God told you to be and it will all work out for your good and His glory.

Excuse me, can you tell me…

10/03

Thirty Minutes Alone With God

Sacrifice is not an element to be found in abundance in our world today. Since the advent of Burger King's, "Have It Your Way" slogan back in 1973, there has been a general decline in people's attitude toward sacrificial living. Now before you go out and boycott Burger King, it's not their fault. The marketers simply took a good look at society and wrote a slogan that voiced its sentiment.

There have been, and I think always will be, bright spots here and there when it comes to living a life of self-sacrifice. Sacrifice is not relegated only to the Christian community as a whole, but we as individual Christians are indeed called to it: "I beseech you therefore, brethren, by the mercies of God, that you present your bodies a living sacrifice, holy, acceptable to God, which is your reasonable service." ~ Romans 12:1

Scripture makes it very plain that sacrifice for the believer is not an option; it is the only reasonable choice. An example of this comes from a student who was enrolled at the Baylor University School of Medicine. Rick Fox, a superior student and athlete at the end of his first year, was "top man" in his class. His dream was to be a doctor. During his second year he developed stomach pains, which led to a diagnosis of terminal cancer.

Upon hearing the news, Rick said to his doctor, "Let me have thirty minutes alone with God." At the end of the period, he called for the doctor and nurses and told them he wanted to offer himself "as a laboratory specimen," declaring he would keep notes of changes and reactions to treatments with the hope it might assist in learning more about the disease. Characteristically, he was always thinking of others.

Finally, Rick was told he had but a few days to live. He said he wanted to go home to see his family and the Colorado mountains. On the day of his departure sixty students from the medical school lined up to say farewell. From his wheelchair, he shook hands with each person, calling them by name. As he was taken up into the plane, he turned and said, "Remember, be good doctors."

In Rick's case, his sacrifice was an ultimate one. What about you? Are you willing today to make a decision to be a living sacrifice? God may never call upon you to make the ultimate sacrifice, but this much is true: If He does, it will be much easier to obey if your life is already on the altar. What will it be? "Have It Your Way" or "Have It God's Way?"

10/04

Falling Up the Stairs

Did you know that 63 percent of all accidents on stairways occur when people are going up the stairs? Why? It is simple really. People tend to be more careful with their steps as they descend a stairway. The perceived level of danger is higher, so they walk more carefully. We must be the most careful when we are on our way up in life. Time and again the stories are heard of folks at the pinnacle and climbing that fall to their demise.

I am useless for the most part in the dark. I can still remember times when for some reason the electricity would go off in the night. Somehow children immediately sense the total darkness and often they cry out for someone to come to their aid.

As a father and protector of the family, I would rise and begin to make my way in the night towards their beds to comfort them. For the life of me, I would immediately become disoriented in the darkness. My wife, on the other-hand, was out the door, down the hallway, by their bedside, and assuring them before I could find the threshold of our own bedroom door. So much for being the mighty protector!

Paul's challenge to the church at Ephesus was to stop walking like a person feeling their way through the night. "You used to be like people living in the dark, but now you are people of the light because you belong to the Lord. So act like people of the light." ~ Ephesians 5:8 (CEV)

It's time to come into the light. Easy now. Let your eyes adjust to the brightness. Now, act like people of the light! Other translations of this verse use the word *walk* instead of the word *act*.

I can relate to the interchanging of these two words. When I would find myself walking in the dark I sure acted differently! My steps are unsure, my hands are groping in front of me, and memories of stubbed toes haunt me.

In his inaugural address, October 13, 1961, Davis Y. Paschall, president of the College of William and Mary, recounted that as a boy he would often hear his father say as they entered the fields for a long day's work, "Today we shall walk humbly and plow a straight furrow." As you walk for Christ today, make sure you stay in the light and act like a child of the light. Walk humbly. Plow straight and lie down tonight satisfied with the Master's words, "Well done!"

Creator of Chaos?

I wonder how many of you could quickly respond to this question: Who was Johannes Kepler? Don't feel badly if you could not. Unless you are into astronomy you probably did not know the answer. Also, if you have been heavily schooled in secular education you would know little of this man.

Kepler was born in 1571 and died in 1630. He developed the primary rules of planetary motion and literally debunked the mystery that had been created by astrology. In his day astrology and astronomy were totally intermingled and much of the teaching was built on the basis of chaos. In other words, all that could be observed had come out a tangle of unexplainable occurrences.

Sound familiar? Sure it does. It's the very foundation of evolutionary theology. Notice that I did not say, theory; evolution is a theology. It supplants God as Creator and replaces Him with chaos.

Kepler's Christian faith brought him to a pattern of thinking which eventually enabled him to solve the riddle of planetary motion where so many other scientists had given up trying. Kepler had sought and found a simple logical pattern for planetary motion which reflected God's wisdom.

Kepler said: "We see how God, like a human architect, approached the founding of the world according to order and rule and measured everything in such a manner." He added, "Great is God our Lord, great is His power and there is no end to His wisdom."

The Apostle Paul said it this way: "For by Him all things were created that are in heaven and that are on earth, visible and invisible, whether thrones or dominions or principalities or powers. All things were created through Him and for Him. And He is before all things, and in Him all things consist." ~ Colossians 1:16-17

One of Kepler's friends believed avidly in the idea of everything coming out of chaos all by itself. In order to convince his friend, Kepler constructed a model of the sun with the planets circling round it. When his friend came into the observatory and saw the beautiful model, he exclaimed with delight, "How beautiful it is! Who made it?"

Kepler carelessly answered, "No one made it: it made itself." His friend looked at him and said, "Nonsense, tell me who made it." Kepler then replied, "Friend, you say that this little toy could not make itself. It is but a very weak imitation of this great universe which, if I understand correctly, you believe has made itself."

Now, what do you believe?

Quit Pinching God

If you have ever held a child you will know that it is easier to hold a very young child, such as a newborn, rather than a child that has developed a sense of fear. The newborn simply lies in your arms and trusts that you are holding them. There is no resistance, no clinging, or self-support. The older child will sometimes pull, pinch, and cling onto you causing both the "holder" and the "holdee" to be uncomfortable.

As much as I believe God wants us to grow up and be mature in our faith, I think that He wants us to be like newborns as we rest fully in His arms. This does not leave us without responsibility. We should be holding tightly to what we believe while trusting the One we believe to hold us.

So the writer of Hebrews exhorted the believers: "Let us hold fast the confession of our hope without wavering, for He who promised is faithful. And let us consider one another in order to stir up love and good works, not forsaking the assembling of ourselves together, as is the manner of some, but exhorting one another, and so much the more as you see the Day approaching." ~ Hebrews 10:23-25

We are to make sure that we cling to our confession of hope without wavering. The word confession means to say the same thing concerning our hope or expectation. We should not let circumstances dictate what we say about our belief in the One who holds us. Why? Because He who promised (that is the One holding us) is faithful. He is trustworthy. He will not drop you. You can securely rest in His arms not pulling up, clinging to, or grasping at self-support.

There is also direction in these verses that helps us understand the value of coming together as believers in an assembly. Simply put: Go to church! You need the support and exhortation gained thereby. In coming together we encourage each other to trust the One who holds us securely and through this challenge we stir up both love and good works throughout the assembly of believers.

Now settle down and quit pinching God. Your squirming is a sure sign of mistrust. You hold onto hope. He's holding onto you.

Silly Excuses

Silly are the demands that some place upon Scripture. It goes something like this: "I don't read the Bible because I don't understand it." Here's another, "Man wrote that book so I don't believe what's contained in it." Here's my favorite: "I don't read the Bible anymore because my parents made me go to church as a kid and I have just outgrown that stuff!"

This is not an exhaustive list of excuses for avoiding God's word. I suppose a devotional on the subject is like preaching to the choir, since you are reading this, and have at least some interest in knowing more of Him and His word. But we all interact with folks who use silly excuses. Perhaps we do as well at times!

Now I am not about to say that it's always easy to understand God or His word. As a matter of fact, scripture does not try to hide this truth. "The secret things belong to the Lord our God, but those things which are revealed belong to us and to our children forever, that we may do all the words of this law." ~ Deuteronomy 29:29 There it is. God said it and has let the proverbial cat out of the bag. There are some secret things that we just will never know.

I can hear the naysayers, "See, I told you so! Scripture is just too mysterious and I'm not going to even try to understand it!" You must finish the text before you offer your excuse too quickly. Not everything is hidden.

There are some things that God has revealed and those things we MUST do. The first excuse listed above is now removed. What you understand you must act upon since God reveals truth for that express reason.

The second excuse I have given deals with authorship. This is simple to deal with when considering The Bible. Man did write Scripture…as they were guided by the Holy Spirit. Again, I hear voices crying out, "I don't need to believe any book that a man wrote!" Your excuse dissolves by your own actions in other arenas. You use a phone book written by men and believe the numbers listed are correct. You take prescriptions written by a human hand and believe that the pharmacists will read it like the gospel so you can be healed. The second excuse is removed by your own actions.

The third excuse is also deleted by hypocrisy. We still do lots of things that our parents made us do as children. Hopefully, you still bathe! Surely, you still brush your teeth! With caution, you look both ways before crossing the street! How silly, indeed, for you to say you won't read God's word because your parents made you do it as a child!

So, what's your excuse for staying out of a daily Bible study? When you come to think about it, it's really silly, isn't it?

Hand Over the Remote

We have 3913 channels on our television. Not really. We do have several hundred; we watch about a half dozen. The choices are endless it seems and yet for the most part totally unfulfilling.

I think that we have brought the cable/satellite mentality into our worship. We are constantly seeking some new and exciting way to be involved in worship. Therein, lies the problem. We have made the content of worship equal to the activity of worship. Worship becomes relegated to a certain hour with particular actors and a well-scripted program. If we sit through one episode of worship and all of our buttons are not pushed just so, then we just change the channel, i.e., find another church, fellowship, or group.

Worship becomes man centered instead of God centered as it should be. Read slowly these words from the Psalms: "Oh come, let us sing to the Lord! Let us shout joyfully to the Rock of our salvation. Let us come before His presence with thanksgiving; let us shout joyfully to Him with psalms. For the Lord is the great God, and the great King above all gods. In His hand are the deep places of the earth; the heights of the hills are His also. The sea is His, for He made it; and His hands formed the dry land. Oh come, let us worship and bow down; let us kneel before the Lord our Maker. For He is our God, and we are the people of His pasture, and the sheep of His hand. Today, if you will hear His voice:" ~ Psalm 95:1-7

In these verses you can clearly see that worship is not prompted by our input or choice. It proceeds from the very revelation of God's presence and the firm evidence of His hand in and on all things. Worship leads the psalmist to confess that we are the sheep and He is the Great Shepherd of our souls.

William Temple once said: "Worship is the nourishment of the mind upon God's truth. Worship is the quickening of the conscience by God's holiness. Worship is the cleansing of the imagination by God's beauty. Worship is the response of my life to God's plan for my life."

Worship can and should take place everywhere and at all times. Lay down the remote control! Take time to experience the reality of true worship.

Shelter of Hope

"God is our refuge and strength, A very present help in trouble. Therefore we will not fear, even though the earth be removed, and though the mountains be carried into the midst of the sea; though its waters roar and be troubled, though the mountains shake with its swelling." ~ Psalm 46:1-3

I wonder when these words were penned by the psalmist? Were they recorded while troubles seemed to prevail? Or were they in response to some tragedy of the recent past? Surely they were written with expectation that sooner or later troubles would arise with a sudden and surprising explosion of fury.

The most violent volcanic eruption in recorded history took place on the island of Krakatoa on August 27, 1883.

At the beginning of that year, Krakatoa seemed an ordinary volcanic island, resting near present day Indonesia. Measuring 11 square miles in area, the island was dominated by a central peak 2,700 feet high. Few islanders worried about the volcano—there had been no sign of activity since the mountain had erupted two centuries earlier, in 1681.

As August 1883 approached, loud groans were heard deep underground like a giant beast awakening. Early in the evening of August 26, a deafening explosion rocked the island. The central cone erupted violently, throwing a column of dense ash and smoke 17 miles into the air.

At 10 a.m. on August 27, a cataclysmic explosion ripped the entire island apart. Two-thirds of Krakatoa simply ceased to exist. More than four cubic miles of rock were pulverized to dust and thrown into the air. Three hundred villages were destroyed and 36,000 people were killed. Houses were cracked open 100 miles away. The shock wave in the air blasted around the globe seven times.

A massive tidal wave, or tsunami, more than 100 feet high sped outward from the island at 700 miles per hour, almost the speed of sound. The dust remained in the atmosphere for many months afterward, creating beautiful sunsets and blue moons. All around the globe fantastic shades of red, purple and pink illuminated the night sky. It took three years for the dust to settle completely.

You may not ever experience a Krakatoan-like explosion of trouble, but just in case you do, never forget that God is a very present help. Never let the dormancy of trial lull you into a careless attitude. Though the earth shakes, the mountains melt, and the seas roar, fear not! God's shelter of hope is always open for the refugee.

R.E. Clark

10/10

Soul Craving

The longest fast that I have participated in was for 40 days. Now before you ooh and aah or before you decide in a brief moment that you will engage in an extended fast, STOP!

You need to make sure that you have clear directions from the Lord before you begin a fast of any length. Study the principles of fasting and then make sure that your purpose in fasting is to bring you into a closer relationship with the One whose you are and to the One who keeps you.

Fasting really awakens the body to the power of natural cravings. After a few days you experience real hunger. Even though it has been many years now since I entered into such a fasting time, I can still remember being really hungry. Few of us, I think, have ever known REAL hunger. The great thing is that the hunger subsides quickly and you discover that you won't really die without eating. Again, this must be under the Lord's full direction!

I am reminded of God's call in Isaiah 55: "Ho! Everyone who thirsts, come to the waters; and you who have no money, come, buy and eat. Yes, come, buy wine and milk without money and without price. Why do you spend money for what is not bread, and your wages for what does not satisfy? Listen carefully to Me, and eat what is good, and let your soul delight itself in abundance." ~ Isaiah 55:1-2

God is speaking to those who are trying everything to satisfy a craving of the soul. They may or may not have had anything to eat or drink. Perhaps they were like the rich man of Luke 16 and lived in opulence. But the truth is that all of us have a soul craving that only God can fill.

Oswald Chambers said in his book, *Approved Unto God*, "The gospel of Jesus awakens a tremendous craving…" Indeed it does, but just as in fasting, the gospel draws one to Jesus and then we stand fully exposed before His gaze. Chambers went on to say that not only cravings are awakened, "but also a tremendous resentment. People want the blessing of God, but they will not stand the probing and the humiliation."

Is there a God-sent craving in your soul today? Bring your hunger and thirst before Him who sees all and knows all. Wait before Him like one who is fasting until His presence is real and so are you. Then "eat what is good, and let your soul delight itself in abundance."

280

He Cannot Be Measured

How many of you have a door frame somewhere in your home where you have stood a child and meticulously marked off that child's growth? The child stands fully erect and if they can get away with it they will tip-toe hoping to gain an inch on the last mark.

Measurements are important to us as human beings. We mark off everything by precise increments. From weight to time, length to breadth, or height to depth, we have decided as humans to agree on certain quanitatives to take measurement of the world around us.

Perhaps this is why so many folks have such a problem in believing that God exists. He cannot be measured. He does not even attempt to describe Himself in such a way that measurements can be acquired. As the Bible begins, God is introduced simply as God in and the author of the beginning.

There is also difficulty when Jesus is considered to be equal to God in all ways. When the announcement came that the Messiah would be born, the angel Gabriel speaking of Jesus said, "And He will reign over the house of Jacob forever, and of His kingdom there will be no end." ~ Luke 1:33 Here again we see the impossibility of measurement. The kingdom of Christ surpasses the measure of time because its King is timeless.

Not only has Jesus been given a timeless kingdom as evidence of His deity, He was given the Spirit without measure. "For He whom God has sent speaks the words of God, for God does not give the Spirit by measure." ~ John 3:34

Now consider the fact that we as believers have also been given the Spirit of Christ as the very evidence of our salvation. "But you are not in the flesh but in the Spirit, if indeed the Spirit of God dwells in you. Now if anyone does not have the Spirit of Christ, he is not His." ~ Romans 8:9

A King of immeasurable reign and His Spirit which is given without limitation to believers, surely raises us to a higher mark as we attempt to fathom the fullness of it all. Without a measure of faith, we could never come close to comprehending these great truths.

So, stand tall as God places His mark in your life. You might even want to tip-toe a little as you peer into the great truth of an immeasurable God who sent the eternal Christ so that we could be filled with the limitless Spirit.

A Circus Act

I don't think that I could work in a zoo. It is not a lack of love for animals. It is not that I would have to feed and clean up after them. I just don't trust them. They are animals and given the chance I believe they will act like animals.

We have all heard the terrible stories of men and women who have worked closely with the animal world and then in a moment have suffered great harm from an animal "gone wild". These trainers have successfully taught a myriad of beasts to do remarkable things.

I have joined many of you in oohs and aahs as these wild animals perform before our very eyes. I think we are just as amazed at the talent of the trainers as we are the abilities of the animal.

But when the disciple of the animal is relaxed for any length of time then tragedy can occur. The wild beast will revert to its native character and a trainer can fall victim to the belief that a trained animal ceases to be wild.

We too must be on guard against the tendency to revert to our wildness. "For the grace of God that brings salvation has appeared to all men, teaching us that, denying ungodliness and worldly lusts, we should live soberly, righteously, and godly in the present age, looking for the blessed hope and glorious appearing of our great God and Savior Jesus Christ, who gave Himself for us, that He might redeem us from every lawless deed and purify for Himself His own special people, zealous for good works." ~ Titus 2:11-14

Now before you take my analogy of the wild beast too far, I hope you understand that I believe that there is a world of difference between us as humans and the animal world. However, we all have seen men who act very much like animals. We as humankind have the wonderful asset of God's grace that separates us from our wildness and strengthens us against reverting back to acting like we have never known His hand of grace.

Through Christ we have been redeemed. We are not captured and caged. We are not taught to do godly tricks. We are delivered from our wildness and set free to be His special people who now have the very nature of Christ within us. We do not perform good works for the tidbits of habit. We are now filled with a desire to perform for His glory and that is no circus act.

Never Look Back

I had butterflies in my stomach. I was 15 years old as I walked into the Western Auto in Denham Springs, LA. No, I'm not in some sort of trance! And yes, I REALLY had butterflies as I went into the Western Auto. The reason: I was about to go into debt for the first time in my life!

I had been saving for the newest gadget on the market to install in my 1963 Rambler American station wagon. This piece of technology was going to take me right up to the cutting edge. I was about to purchase an eight track tape player!

I had been saving, but I was still short about $85 if I remember correctly. So, with my mama standing beside me, I signed an agreement to pay the owner of the store $5 per week. I was now committed to make these payments under what I assumed was the penalty of death!
Yes, I had butterflies that day!

The Bible records a story of three men who had a desire to follow Jesus, but they lacked the commitment to do so. Luke records, "Now it happened as they journeyed on the road, that someone said to Him, "Lord, I will follow You wherever You go." And Jesus said to him, "Foxes have holes and birds of the air have nests, but the Son of Man has nowhere to lay His head."

Then He said to another, "Follow Me." But he said, "Lord, let me first go and bury my father." Jesus said to him, "Let the dead bury their own dead, but you go and preach the kingdom of God." And another also said, "Lord, I will follow You, but let me first go and bid them farewell who are at my house." But Jesus said to him, "No one, having put his hand to the plow, and looking back, is fit for the kingdom of God.'" ~ Luke 9:57-62

For the first man, the cost of commitment was too high because of the lack of convenience. The second man was not willing to commit, because he had prior commitments that overshadowed his desire to be a follower of Christ. The third man could not commitment because he had other relationships that took precedence in his life.

Jesus did not demand that any of them follow, but He did expose their lack of commitment. Ultimately, Jesus told those traveling with Him that it is better not to start plowing if you are going to spend the day looking back.

How can anyone make such a high level of commitment to be a follower? A.W. Tozer wrote, "Everything in life which we commit to God is really safe. And everything which we refuse to commit to Him is never safe."

I made a commitment that day in the Western Auto and I have never looked back. My commitment gave me the joy of listening to many an hour of music as I rolled along in my classic automobile. But greater still will be the joy of hearing Jesus say, "You've plowed a straight row. You've never looked back!

10/14

Protecting your Embassy

You probably haven't noticed, but the world seems to be coming apart at the seams. Especially bad has been the news about attacks and protests around the globe against our embassies. Perhaps a brief definition of an embassy would help here.

The term embassy actually refers to the diplomatic delegation itself, but is often used to define the buildings and grounds that have been set aside by the host country to house the ambassador and the staff, etc. Though these grounds are not technically sovereign territory of the government represented there, they reserve extremely protective rights and these grounds are to be guarded as such.

There is a spiritual application to the concept of embassies, diplomats, and protective rights. As believers, we become embassies the moment we trust Christ as our Savior. Our allegiance is transferred from this world to the Kingdom of God. He becomes the ruler of our lives and we are now his ambassadors in a foreign land.

It seems that we have forgotten as a nation that we have a right and responsibility to protect our embassies. I don't mean with threats or rubber bullets. Our nation's enemies are real and so are our spiritual enemies. They are bent on destroying the symbols of freedom. The world goes after a flag and desecrates it. Satan goes for the heart and destroys it.

When the children of Israel were coming back into the promised land God said to Moses, "Speak to the children of Israel, and say to them: 'When you have crossed the Jordan into the land of Canaan, then you shall drive out all the inhabitants of the land from before you, destroy all their engraved stones, destroy all their molded images, and demolish all their high places; you shall dispossess the inhabitants of the land and dwell in it, for I have given you the land to possess. But if you do not drive out the inhabitants of the land from before you, then it shall be that those whom you let remain shall be irritants in your eyes and thorns in your sides, and they shall harass you in the land where you dwell. Moreover it shall be that I will do to you as I thought to do to them.'" ~ Numbers 33:51-53, 55-56

We cannot appease those who would do us harm. If we offer even the smallest place for our spiritual enemies (and I think for our national enemies also), it will not turn out well. As with this account of Israel, those left to reside in sovereign territory may not kill us outright, but they will be like dust in our eyes and thorns in our sides.

The greater danger of not taking a stand is to fall under the judging hand of God. What God only thought of doing to our enemy he WILL do to us. God considers our bodies as embassies and our lives as ambassadors to be serious business. Shouldn't we?

10/15

Active Supporters

One very important ingredient to success in any venture is a solid base of support. The word support paints a picture of help, encouragement, and accomplishment. There may be one man out front, but he will not be there very long without supporters.

Often we don't take the time to fully consider just how much support we have or have had to get to the place we find ourselves today. We need to stop along the way and take an inventory of all the supporters who have helped us.

As I contemplated this, a scene from over 40 years ago came rushing to the forefront of my memory. I was in high school and a member of the basketball team. I was a starter for the junior varsity team, but I just didn't have what it took to be a starter on the varsity team. I played hard and was always excited when the coach would put me into the game.

It is from those days that I remembered my greatest supporters. My parents attended nearly every game. It did not matter if I was a starter or not. They were there anyway and they were not merely in the stands to make an appearance. They were active supporters. My daddy showed his support by bringing a cowbell with him to every game. I can still hear that bell clanging every time I was called up from the bench.

As Israel was making their way from Egypt back to the Promised Land, they fought many battles. One such battle occurred with the Amalekites. The battle went back and forth as we read in Exodus 17.

"And so it was, when Moses held up his hand, that Israel prevailed; and when he let down his hand, Amalek prevailed. But Moses' hands became heavy; so they took a stone and put it under him, and he sat on it. And Aaron and Hur supported his hands, one on one side, and the other on the other side; and his hands were steady until the going down of the sun."~Exodus 17:11-12

Aaron and Hur became the active supporters of Moses and Israel prevailed as the hands of Moses were held high. Thank God for the Aaron's, the Hur's, and the mama's and daddy's in our lives.

I don't think I ever thanked my parents for being there or my daddy for his cowbell. They are both gone now, but somehow I believe it's still right to say it: Thanks for the support! I couldn't have gotten here without you!

Searching For Truth

Truth is so important that people will pay large sums of money to procure it. For example, when we are ill the cost of the visit to a physician will not deter our search for truth. If we are seeking information relative to investments, we will not cut corners when attempting to discover the best return on our money.

It only seems that we are willing to compromise the truth when it comes to spiritual questions. People seem perfectly happy to set truth aside in order to feel good about their relationship with God and the outcome of their eternal destination.

Jesus left the question of truth fully disclosed as He prayed in John 17. This is truly the Lord's Prayer. In these verses, He spoke not only of the present day believers, but also of us who are living today. He asked God to—"Sanctify them by Your truth. Your word is truth." ~ John 17:17

Virgil Hurley in "Speaker's Sourcebook of New Illustrations" said:

> The search for truth [is] the irreducible fact that can judge all other matters because it is unimpeachably so! There must be such a source of authority in this world, beyond which we cannot go, beyond which we cannot appeal, whose word is final and perfect, whose judgment is infallible, whose decision is unassailable, which can discern between all the claimants to truth to ascertain the one, single truth that exists. For if truth exists at all in the parts, it must have its origin in the united whole. It is nonsense to say truth can exist only where we claim it. If there is truth anywhere, in anything, it came from Someone in particular, somewhere specifically.

The Someone Hurley speaks of is, of course, Jesus Christ and the foundation for all truth is the word of God. Why not seek the same degree of truth that you would from a medical specialist? You would never be satisfied with a diagnosis of a common cold if in truth you had a brain tumor.

May truth be your constant guide. Never settle for anything less…

Two Sides To Choose From

Demarcation is an interesting word. It is of Spanish origin. The word came into vogue between the years 1720-1730. It means to mark off boundaries and became the term used to literally divide the world between Spain and Portugal. Therefore, we speak today of a line of demarcation that separates any two distinct concepts, thoughts, people, or even nations.

There is clearly a spiritual line of demarcation as well. Many will try to make the line fuzzy and blur the clear distinctions of belief versus non-belief in Jesus as the Savior of the world. Because we try to erase denominational and religious differences, we sometimes forget that the world is only divided into two parts: the world of belief and the world of non-belief.

The obedience of Christ to His death on the cross leads to this conclusion: "Therefore God also has highly exalted Him and given Him the name which is above every name, that at the name of Jesus every knee should bow, of those in heaven, and of those on earth, and of those under the earth, and that every tongue should confess that Jesus Christ is Lord, to the glory of God the Father." ~ Philippians 2:9-11

Clearly one can see the line of demarcation. The line forms along the fact that there is only one name whereby men might be saved and that name is Jesus. The line itself extends from heaven to the earth and even under the earth. At this line all men will bow and confess Christ as Lord.

Oswald Chambers said in his book, The Psychology of Redemption, "The temptation to win and woo men is the most subtle of all, and it is a line that commends itself to us naturally. But you cannot win and woo a mutiny; it is absolutely impossible. You cannot win and woo the man who, when he recognizes the rule of God, detests it. The Gospel of Jesus Christ always marks the line of demarcation."

We must resist the belief that all religions lead to the same place and that God will accept good intentions. There is a line of demarcation not drawn by the fickle hand of men, but inscribed by the finger of God. Its origin was in the mind of God before time began. It can be traced squarely through the Cross of Calvary and ends at the door of your heart. Which side of that line are you on today?

Run Silent, Run Deep

I can sit and watch war movies over and over again. It does not matter that I know the ending, I still watch them with expectation. The great thing is since I know the ending, I can be assured of the outcome.

One of my favorite war movies is *Run Silent, Run Deep*. The two main actors are Clark Gable and Burt Lancaster. The movie is based on a 1955 novel of the same name and written by Commander Edward L. Beach, Jr.

As I thought of this movie and the stealth tactics portrayed in it, I thought of the many times it seems that God is running silent and deep. A submarine when trying to evade the enemy would stop all engines and settle to rest on the ocean floor. All onboard would be commanded to observe strict silence. Enemy destroyers would continue to search via sonar to detect the vibrations of the submarine's engines or even the voices and movements of those onboard.

It must have been a little like this when a pair of disciples were making their way to Emmaus after the crucifixion, burial, and what they supposed at that moment had been the resurrection of Jesus. As they left Jerusalem, they discussed together the happenings of the previous days. To them God was running silent and deep. As they walked, a third man joined them along the way.

"And He said to them, 'What kind of conversation is this that you have with one another as you walk and are sad?'" ~ Luke 24:17 The men were amazed that someone could not know what had transpired so openly over the previous three days. So, they filled this "stranger" in on all of the happenings.

"Then He said to them, 'O foolish ones, and slow of heart to believe in all that the prophets have spoken! Ought not the Christ to have suffered these things and to enter into His glory?' And beginning at Moses and all the Prophets, He expounded to them in all the Scriptures the things concerning Himself." ~ Luke 24:25-27

As they came to the end of their journey, this "stranger" acted as if He would travel on, but they implored Him to stay and eat. As the meal was blessed and the bread broken their eyes were opened to the fact that the "stranger" was none other than Jesus. "And they said to one another, 'Did not our heart burn within us while He talked with us on the road, and while He opened the Scriptures to us?'" ~ Luke 24:32

If today is a battle scene in your life, know this: Though it may seem that God is running silent and deep and you cannot sense His presence at all, be aware that He may come to walk along side you as a "stranger." Be patient and He will speak. When He does, your eyes will be opened and your heart will burn with His truth.

Call Him Up!

How many of you have ever gotten into your car, driven away, and then turned around to go back home—for your phone? Yes, I see those hands! I am old enough to remember NO cell phones; yikes, I even remember pagers! Those were the wonderful days when my trips to hospitals and other visits were undisturbed moments of peace and quiet. Now we are in constant contact with one another.

A relatively new phenomenon is texting. As a matter of fact, there are few times anymore that anyone answers the phone when I call them. I will get their voicemail and then wait for them to call me back or they will send a text in response to my call.

Hello! I would have sent you a text to begin with if I only wanted to communicate in a cryptic language.

Aren't you glad that God answers when we call? No time for thumbing a message on a tiny keyboard when troubles come. We join the Psalmist in saying, "Hear my prayer, O Lord, and let my cry come to You. Do not hide Your face from me in the day of my trouble; incline Your ear to me; in the day that I call, answer me speedily. For my days are consumed like smoke, and my bones are burned like a hearth. My heart is stricken and withered like grass, so that I forget to eat my bread. Because of the sound of my groaning my bones cling to my skin. I am like a pelican of the wilderness; I am like an owl of the desert. I lie awake, and am like a sparrow alone on the housetop." ~ Psalm 102:1-7

Imagine such distress as noted in these verses and hearing from heaven, "Hi, this God. Sorry I can't take your call right now. Leave a message and I'll get back as soon as I can. Have a great day!"

No sir, that will not do when your world has become a desert-like wilderness. When you can't sleep and loneliness consumes you, you need an answer in your day of trouble. Don't you?

Here's the good news from this same Psalm, "For He looked down from the height of His sanctuary; from heaven the Lord viewed the earth, to hear the groaning of the prisoner, to release those appointed to death." ~ Psalm 102:19-20

Can we be sure that God will be there? The Psalmist continues in this same line of thought as he concludes the verses of this song, "But You are the same, and Your years will have no end. The children of Your servants will continue, and their descendants will be established before You." ~ Psalm 102:27-28

God will not be trading up to the newest phone! He surpassed all technology before time began. Call Him up right now! He's always on the line!

Best Promise Ever Made

As much as I would like to name names I will not do so this morning. My desire is to distinguish the marked change in the premise of a promise from a mere 150 years ago to those who make promises today.

I recently heard a presidential candidate respond to a question about un-kept promises. The summary of his response was that he had indeed kept his promises because he had kept SOME of them. His conclusion was that no one could have realistically expected him to keep ALL of them.

Here is a story from the life of Abraham Lincoln as told by Martin M. Hyzer:

One day, President Abraham Lincoln was riding in a coach with a colonel from Kentucky. The colonel took a bottle of whiskey out of his pocket. He offered Mr. Lincoln a drink. Mr. Lincoln said, "No thank you, Colonel. I never drink whiskey." In a little while, the colonel took some cigars out of his pocket and offered one to Mr. Lincoln. Again Mr. Lincoln said, "No, thank you, Colonel." Then Mr. Lincoln said, "I want to tell you a story."

"One day, when I was about nine years old, my mother called me to her bed. She was very sick. She said, 'Abe, the doctor tells me that I am not going to get well. I want you to be a good boy. I want you to promise me before I go that you will never use whiskey or tobacco as long as you live.' I promised my mother that I never would, and up to this hour, I kept this promise! Would you advise me to break that promise?"

The colonel put his hand on Mr. Lincoln's shoulder and said, "Mr. Lincoln, I would not have you break that promise for the world! It is one of the best promises you ever made. I would give a thousand dollars today if I had made my mother a promise like that and had kept it like you have done. I would be a much better man than I am!"

Now I do not know what your definition of a promise is, but I prefer Mr. Lincoln's to the present day politician's. One thing is for sure—God keeps every one of His promises.

"Every word of God is pure; He is a shield to those who put their trust in Him. Do not add to His words, lest He rebuke you, and you be found a liar." ~ Proverbs 30:5-6

Finding God

Each Sunday the world today will be in one of two places: in church or not. That in itself is not a fantastic conclusion and there is no margin of error in my calculations.

What is the most incredible fact is that of those in and out of the physical church building today, there will be two general outcomes. In both cases some will come to realize fully who God is, while others existing in exactly the same situations will simply go through life oblivious to God's presence.

How can someone miss God? Certainly in a house of worship with songs about Him, speech that uses godly terms, and messages that are based on His own words being proclaimed, you would think that all would recognize Him.

Of those just out and about, one would think that nature itself, as it shouts forth the name of the Creator, would capture the attention of a few. But alas, many today will simply miss God all together.

The unknowability of God has plagued man for all time. At best, men are found groping after His mystery. "It is hard," said Plato, "to investigate and to find the framer and the father of the universe. And, if one did find him, it would be impossible to express him in terms which all could understand."

Aristotle spoke of God as the supreme cause, by all men dreamed of and by no man known. The ancient world did not doubt that there was a God or gods, but it believed that such gods as there might be were quite unknowable and only occasionally interested in mankind. In a world afflicted with sin and its blinding effect, God is a mystery and power, perhaps desirable, but never known.

The Apostle Paul declared, "However, we speak wisdom among those who are mature, yet not the wisdom of this age, nor of the rulers of this age, who are coming to nothing. But we speak the wisdom of God in a mystery, the hidden wisdom which God ordained before the ages for our glory, which none of the rulers of this age knew; for had they known, they would not have crucified the Lord of glory. But as it is written: 'Eye has not seen, nor ear heard, nor have entered into the heart of man the things which God has prepared for those who love Him.'" ~ 1 Corinthians 2:6-9

God wants to be discovered today. Seek Him and He will reveal Himself in all of His glory by the mighty working of the Holy Spirit. The world will go right on missing Him, but you can know Him. Seek Him early while He may be found (Psalm 63:1.)

Waiting For Something to Happen

Psychologist William Moulton Marston asked 3000 persons, "What have you to live for?"

He was shocked to find that 94 percent were simply enduring the present while waiting for the future. They would describe this as waiting for "something" to happen— waiting for children to grow up and leave home, waiting for next year, waiting for another time to take a long-dreamed-about trip, waiting for tomorrow. They were all waiting without realizing that all anyone ever has is today, because yesterday is gone, and tomorrow never comes.

The fact that Marston was shocked by the answers given is more interesting, than the very answers recorded of those interviewed. Marston died in 1947 just shy of his 54th birthday. Not only was he a psychologist, he was an inventor and a writer. He wrote several theories about feminism.

This is where his life gets really twisted. His invention of the systolic blood pressure test is still used today, but it came as a side note to him seeking a test to determine whether someone was telling the truth. It is still part of modern polygraph testing.

He wrote theories in feminism while living in a polyamorous relationship with his wife and two other women. He is credited with the creation of the Wonder Woman comic book series.

Indeed, he lived a very unusual life to say the least. His life brings to mind the scripture that Paul wrote to the Romans: "Likewise you also, reckon yourselves to be dead indeed to sin, but alive to God in Christ Jesus our Lord. Therefore do not let sin reign in your mortal body, that you should obey it in its lusts. And do not present your members as instruments of unrighteousness to sin, but present yourselves to God as being alive from the dead, and your members as instruments of righteousness to God. For sin shall not have dominion over you, for you are not under law but under grace." ~ Romans 6:11-14

Marston's life, like ours, could have been used for God's glory. But a decision must be made to use these bodies as instruments of righteousness instead of unrighteousness. The word instrument means a tool or implement primarily used as an offensive military weapon.

Each person's life has the potential for good or evil. Grace is the only difference. Marston's question needs to be asked again, "What have you to live for?"

Talking To the Television

I am a newshound. It takes an awful lot of news for me to get overwhelmed or tired of listening. And the answer is yes since I know what you are asking. You are thinking right now, I wonder if he is one of those people who talks back to the television? Duh? That's why they call it an opinion segment! Believe me, I have an opinion and I am more than willing to share it!

My talking back to the television is about like the world talking back to God. This is how the psalmist recorded just such an encounter in Psalm 2. "Why do the nations rage, and the people plot a vain thing? The kings of the earth set themselves, and the rulers take counsel together, against the Lord and against His Anointed, saying, "Let us break their bonds in pieces and cast away their cords from us." He who sits in the heavens shall laugh; the Lord shall hold them in derision." ~ Psalm 2:1-4

Seen here are the kings of the earth, the rulers of kingdoms, and the people of the nations, lifting their fists and voices toward heaven in an attempt to throw off what they perceive as God's restraint. God on the other hand watches all of their feeble attempts to declare sovereignty and rolls with laughter.

This may seem strange for us to consider God in this way. Because we are human, we reject the idea of being laughed at and made fun of strongly. But we see here the utter futility of man's attempt to overthrow God or to seize His rightful place as ruler of the universe.

Such attempts bring nothing but derision from God in response. Derision means that God mocks them like foreigners who are trying to speak His language, but their accents give them away as being just that: foreigners.

So remember the next time you are watching the news and hearing all of the grandiose plans that some politician has for getting us out of the mess we are in, that the noise you hear in the background is the belly laugh of God. I sure need to remember this. It will save me a lot of wasted conversation with the television!

The Full Benefit

Most of the time when I enter into a devotional time, I am doing so with one particular goal. I need something from the Lord. This is not out of selfishness. It is just a reality. I know that I lack so much in my walk with Him, so I go into a time of meditation with the assumption that it is all about me.

That's not a bad thing particularly, but it will always bring us short of the full benefit of a devotional time. As David drew near to the conclusion of what we know as Psalm 104, he said, "I will sing to the LORD as long as I live; I will sing praise to my God while I have my being. May my meditation be sweet to Him; I will be glad in the LORD." ~ Psalm 104:33

What brought David to this point in his devotional time? Why did he break out with singing and reach the conclusion that his desire was not what he would receive from his time with the Lord, but that his meditation would be sweet to God? If you read all of Psalm 104, which I highly recommend, you will find that David spent this devotional time reflecting upon all that God has done in His creative acts and in the maintenance of His creation.

As David was caught up in the glories of God's work, he said, "O LORD, how manifold are Your works! In wisdom You have made them all. The earth is full of Your possessions—" ~ Psalm 104:24

The idea of our meditation being sweet is that God would take pleasure in His communion with David. But there is a benefit for us also as we spend daily time with God in meditation. There will be gladness that comes our way. Here, the word glad means to brighten up, to become cheerful, to make merry.

Imagine that! The greatest benefit we can receive from spending time alone with God is that we will come away with a brighter outlook on life because our inner man has been lifted up into His presence.

So David concludes his devotional time with this statement: "May the glory of the LORD endure forever; may the LORD rejoice in His works. ~ Psalm 104:31 How much time will you spend alone with God today and what conclusion will you reach?

You can never be too downcast to approach Him. Just lift up your heart and begin to praise Him for all that He has done and soon you will find your load lightened and your spirit brightened.

10/25

The Aroma of Christ

One of the first stops that any missionary must make is to spend time in language school. Learning a new language for most of us is very arduous. I know pieces of several languages, but I am still not comfortable attempting a full blown conversation in any language other than English. What tools can we use to relax the learning curve a little? Here's a read a story that illustrates this very well.

A missionary to China entered her first day of language school. The teacher entered the room and, without saying a word, walked down every row of students. Finally, still without saying a word, she walked out of the room again. The students sat dumbfounded as to the reason for the teacher's behavior.

The language teacher then came back and addressed the class.

"Did you notice anything special about me?" she asked. Nobody could think of anything in particular. One student finally raised her hand. "I noticed that you had on a very lovely perfume," she said.

The class chuckled. But the teacher said, "That was exactly the point. You see, it may be a long time before any of you will be able to speak Chinese well enough to share the gospel with anyone in China. But even before you are able to do that, you can minister the sweet fragrance of Christ to these people by the quality of your lives. It is your lifestyle, lived out among the Chinese people, that will minister Christ to them long before you are able to say one word to them about personal faith in Jesus."

This is the very message that Paul was conveying to the Corinthians. We may not always feel that we have communicated the gospel clearly or that the mission was completed, but "…thanks be to God who always leads us in triumph in Christ, and through us diffuses the fragrance of His knowledge in every place." ~ 2 Corinthians 2:14

We may not be eloquent speakers. Perhaps you will never be able to walk foreign soil as a missionary, but you can make sure that everyone you encounter will be ministered to by the Christ-likeness of your daily life.

When you leave a room, may the sweet aroma of Jesus still permeate the atmosphere.

10/26

Hearing God

It is believed that hearing is the last sense that is still functioning as one nears death. Caregivers are often instructed to continue speaking to the dying person with the understanding that the dying do indeed continue to comprehend up to the the very point of death. I suppose we will never know until we too have crossed that threshold.

The Bible speaks often about the faculty of hearing; not only our hearing, but the hearing of God as well. David cried out to God in Psalm 28, "To You I will cry, O Lord my Rock: do not be silent to me, lest, if You are silent to me, I become like those who go down to the pit." ~ Psalm 28:1

David wanted desperately to hear the voice of God. He declared that without God's voice being heard he would be like a dead man.

Not only is it reassuring to hear God, but it is comforting to know that God hears what is going on as well. "Yet they say, "The Lord does not see, nor does the God of Jacob understand." Understand, you senseless among the people; and you fools, when will you be wise? He who planted the ear, shall He not hear? He who formed the eye, shall He not see? He who instructs the nations, shall He not correct, He who teaches man knowledge? The Lord knows the thoughts of man, that they are futile. Blessed is the man whom You instruct, O Lord, and teach out of Your law, that You may give him rest from the days of adversity, until the pit is dug for the wicked." ~ Psalm 94:7-13

God hears it all and loves us anyway! He is not like the elderly grandfather who was very wealthy. Because he was going deaf, he decided to buy a hearing aid. Two weeks later he stopped at the store where he had bought it and told the manager he could now pick up conversation quite easily, even in the next room.

"Your relatives must be happy to know that you can hear so much better," beamed the delighted proprietor.

"Oh, I haven't told them yet," the man chuckled. "I've just been sitting around listening—and you know what? I've changed my will twice."

God who made the ear also has a listening ear. Truly, this should bring us assurance. When we are falsely judged, God hears and avenges. When we speak foolishly, God also hears and correctly instructs us through His mercy and grace without changing His will for us.

Be grateful today for a God who both sees and hears.

10/27

Divided Devotion

Today's devotion is on devotion. The word devotion can be simply defined as ardent loyalty. It can be directed toward a myriad of object, ideas, concepts, or persons. Some of our devotion must be exclusive especially as persons are considered.

Our devotion to our wife or husband for example is to be in this exclusive realm. The accounts of many who have attempted divided devotion proves quickly that we are to be devoted to one another as husband and wife.

This same level of exclusivity exists in our devotion to God. Jesus said that a person cannot love God and money at the same time. As He spoke with Peter on the shore of Galilee he asked Peter three times if he loved Him. Jesus was specific in His question. He did not ask if Peter loved Him as one among others. There was a clear understanding that Jesus' question was exclusive.

Our devotion can be renewed and revived through a devotional life. David said, "Give ear to my words, O Lord, consider my meditation. Give heed to the voice of my cry, my King and my God, for to You I will pray. My voice You shall hear in the morning, O Lord; in the morning I will direct it to You, and I will look up. For You are not a God who takes pleasure in wickedness, nor shall evil dwell with You."~Psalm 5:1-4

Abstract devotion has little to no value. David spoke his devotion early in the morning and repeated it regularly. Don't be like the man who when asked why he never said I love you to his wife said that he had told her he loved her 40 years ago at the altar. He meant it then and had never changed his mind. If he ever did he would tell her.

Ridiculous! This is not a devotion that is being presented in an ardently loyal fashion. There is a clear need for us to direct our words unto the Lord. Does He know our hearts? Of course, He does, but the spoken words of devotion are really as much for us as Him. Notice that the result of the devotional time was that David looked up!

Are you downcast today? Do troubles seem to surround you? Do the thoughts of yesterday haunt you? Speak to God openly about it and before long your head shall be lifted up and you will look into His glorious face.

10/28

The Water Test

A jeweler gives, as one of the surest tests for diamonds, the water test. The jeweler knows that an imitation diamond is never so brilliant as a genuine stone. If your eye is not experienced enough to detect the difference, a simple test is to place the stone under water. The imitation diamond is practically extinguished, while a genuine diamond sparkles even under water, and is distinctly visible. If a genuine stone is placed beside an imitation one under water, the contrast will be apparent to the least experienced eye.

Is there a test that can be quickly performed on us as believers that will prove us to be genuine? Yes, there is and it is a paradoxical test. The test begins with a call to imitation and results in the proof of our relationship to Christ.

Here is the test: "Therefore be imitators of God as dear children. And walk in love, as Christ also has loved us and given Himself for us, an offering and a sacrifice to God for a sweet-smelling aroma." ~ Ephesians 5:1-2

This is how the test works. We are to be imitators of God in all of our lives like a child who mimics his parents. The more we are in God's Word and engaged in living out what we discover there the more and more we are like God. But this still is no proof to the world of our relationship to the God of heaven.

The water test for us is love. Like the diamond that is placed in water to prove its authenticity, when we are immersed in the love of God and carry out our lives with love as the parameter of living, we will prove our genuineness.

Interestingly, we will not pass the sight test, but the smell test. As we imitate God, we will take on the sweet smelling aroma of Jesus. All of us know very quickly when something doesn't smell just right. We don't have to see what stinks to know that something is rotten.

So it is with us as believers. It is not important for the world to see us. It is important that they sense clearly the sweet smelling savor of Jesus, however. What will it be today? Will those who get close to you sense Jesus or will they turn away because they smell something rotten?

10/29

Missing the Main Point

When I was a much younger preacher, there was one thing that would really bug me. I would diligently prepare my messages and preach them with my whole being only to have some well-meaning saint come to the door on the way out, shake my hand, tell me how good the message was, and then inform me of the real truths I had missed. Those were the days!

Now I'm older and so much more wiser. I sit under other's preaching all the time and sure enough I can think of half a dozen really good points they missed. But know this…I never shake their hand at the door and fill them in on the missing nuggets of wisdom that I have gleaned.

I believe this is what James was speaking of when he compared the wisdom of God to the wisdom of man. It is incredible how sin has even affected something as good as wisdom. Listen to his admonition.

"Who is wise and understanding among you? Let him show by good conduct that his works are done in the meekness of wisdom. But if you have bitter envy and self-seeking in your hearts, do not boast and lie against the truth. This wisdom does not descend from above, but is earthly, sensual, demonic. For where envy and self-seeking exist, confusion and every evil thing are there. But the wisdom that is from above is first pure, then peaceable, gentle, willing to yield, full of mercy and good fruits, without partiality and without hypocrisy. Now the fruit of righteousness is sown in peace by those who make peace." ~ James 3:13-18

The really wise person knows how to put a lid on his lips. Sometimes the smartest thing to say is nothing. Nobody appreciates a know-it-all. Spend a little time today gaining wisdom about being wise with the wisdom that comes from the One who is All Wise.

Let every word pass through the sieve of heaven's definition for wisdom. Are your words pure, peaceable, gentle, yielding, merciful, wholesome, and sincere? If so, then speak up. Otherwise, shut up. I've got nothing more to say!

10/30

Final Words

Final words can be very important. How many times have you heard someone repeating the final words that were exchanged between two people before some unseen tragedy occurred? A few words at a funeral or an epitaph inscribed on a headstone are used in an attempt to encapsulate an entire life.

Sometimes final words can be a bit funny. I read about the epitaphs of a husband and wife. They read something like this: On her headstone were the words, "She Died Wanting the World in a Hand Basket." On his headstone was written: "He Died Trying to Give It to Her." And so we see that a few last words can really tell a story.

As you read the closing words of Paul in his letters, much light is shed on his sincere desire to see those he ministered to become all that God intended. One example is the last words of 2 Corinthians. Remember, this had been a troubled and very immature group of believers.

Paul concludes his letter, "Finally, brethren, farewell. Become complete. Be of good comfort, be of one mind, live in peace; and the God of love and peace will be with you. Greet one another with a holy kiss. All the saints greet you. The grace of the Lord Jesus Christ, and the love of God, and the communion of the Holy Spirit be with you all. Amen." ~ 2 Corinthians 13:11-14

If you make a short list of Paul's final words to the Corinthians, you will discover his heart. He always desired maturity in the believers. Just as we tell our children as they depart from our sight to be good and to be safe, Paul wanted the Corinthians to no longer act like children.

The evidence of this behavior would be seen in their exhortation of each other in the faith. He told them to BE comforters; BE in unity; BE peaceable. This was not a DO list. It was a BE list. Remember, we are human BEINGS not human DOINGS!

The result of being like this was communion with God the Father, God the Son, and with God the Holy Spirit. His final words were bound in the presence of the Trinity! In essence, he was giving the Corinthians everything in a hand basket.

Have you ever thought about your final words? More importantly, have you thought about what final words others would have to say about you? Like Paul concluded, so will I, "AMEN!" So be it!

Black-tie Event

I have never been invited to a black-tie event. Come of think of it, I don't even own a black tie! Oh well, I'm not disappointed, nor will I check my mail today. I have no expectation that the fancy invitation with my name embossed upon it will be delivered.

Evidently Jesus had been invited to a black-tie event as Luke 14 unfolds. You can feel the tension rise in the room when a diseased man enters and Jesus graciously heals him. Problem: It's the Sabbath. Result: Jesus teaches a great lesson on grace and humility.

Jesus asked those offended at the healing of the man whether they would help an animal stranded in a ditch on the Sabbath and followed his question with a parable. I love Jesus' style! He had a way of messing around with black-tie folks.

First, he clarifies the importance of an attitude of humility when and if you ever get invited to a black-tie event. In essence, He told them to tie up their high horse outside before they enter. This may seem like a small thing, but for black-tie types it can be difficult to be humble.

Then just about the time the owner of the house thinks he's off the hook on this topic of graciousness and humility, Jesus turns to him and says, "'When you give a dinner or a supper, do not ask your friends, your brothers, your relatives, nor rich neighbors, lest they also invite you back, and you be repaid. But when you give a feast, invite the poor, the maimed, the lame, the blind. And you will be blessed, because they cannot repay you; for you shall be repaid at the resurrection of the just.'" ~ Luke 14:12-14

See there! Jesus left no black-tie untouched and none of us either. He instructs the one throwing the party to rework his invitation list. Invite those who could never ever invite him to their homes. Invite those who did not own any black ties.

Four types of people who should be on our invitation lists were mentioned: (1) The poor. These are the cringing ones. (2) The maimed. These are the constantly crushed ones. (3) The lame. These are the crippled ones. (4) The blind. These are the ones consumed by darkness.

Now before you go and garage sale all of your black ties, listen to me. There's nothing inherently wrong with a black-tie event. Just remember that this story ends with Jesus giving an invitation to The Great Supper to be held in the Kingdom of God. If you don't have an invitation to this gala event, it won't matter how many black ties you own.

• NOVEMBER

Show Me Myself

From time to time, I find a story that just cannot be improved upon with my own thoughts. Today, I give you this account as told by R.A. Torrey, the well-known evangelist, pastor, teacher, and author. Here is his account of one life changed by a look into the face of Jesus.

A minister was traveling in Scotland and stayed at an inn. At evening-time the landlord asked if he would conduct family prayer. He consented on the condition that all the servants of the household be summoned.

The servants came and when all seemed to be assembled, the minister asked, "Are all here?" "Yes," said the landlord. "Not one missing?" he asked. "Oh, well," said the landlord, "there is a poor girl we never bring in. She does the dirty work about the kitchen and is not fit to come in with the others." "Well then," said the minister, "I will not go on until she comes."

Seeing her neglected appearance, the minister took a peculiar interest in her. As he departed the next day, he called for the girl and said to her, "I wish to teach you a prayer, and I want you to pray it until I come back again. It is this, 'Lord, show me myself.'"

He left the inn, but returned in a few days. He asked the landlord, "How is that poor girl?" "Oh," replied the landlord, "she is of no use whatever now. She can do no work. She is weeping all the time. She mopes and is melancholy. I don't know what is the matter with her."

The minister knew, and asked to see her. The landlord brought her in and the minister said, "Now I wish to teach you another prayer. You have been praying, 'Show me myself?'" "Yes," she said, in deep distress, "and I am so wicked I can do nothing but weep over my sins." "Let me teach you another prayer, 'Lord, show me Thyself.'"

Years later the minister was preaching in Glasgow when a neat-looking woman came up to him at the close of the sermon and said, "Do you remember me?" "No," he said, "I do not." "Do you remember teaching a poor girl in an inn to pray?" "'Yes," he replied, "I remember that well."

"I am that girl. I prayed that prayer and got such a view of myself that I was overwhelmed with grief and despair. Then you taught me the other prayer, 'Lord, show me Thyself,' and He showed me Himself. I trusted Him and found salvation and He has made me what I am to-day."

This servant girl had learned the truth of Isaiah 35:5, "Then the eyes of the blind shall be opened..." It is a good prayer for us all to pray, "Lord, show me myself," and after He has shown us ourselves, let us go on and ask Him to show us Himself.

11/02

Fork In the Road

What path lies before you today? Is it a familiar one that leads to work and back again? Perhaps it is a path that diverges soon; you can see the fork in the road up ahead and you are wondering about the direction you should take. Then again, it may be a road that you have never traveled before. It may be a highway of suffering, doubt, or despair. Fear not! Your journey has not caught God by surprise.

As the children of Israel left the land of Egypt they went by a new and undiscovered course. For 400 years, this people had lived in Egypt—most of it as slaves. To leave the familiar, though it be the walk of a slave, must have been a challenge to the senses. But God was before and alongside them and that would make the journey safe.

"Then it came to pass, when Pharaoh had let the people go, that God did not lead them by way of the land of the Philistines, although that was near; for God said, "Lest perhaps the people change their minds when they see war, and return to Egypt." So God led the people around by way of the wilderness of the Red Sea. And the children of Israel went up in orderly ranks out of the land of Egypt. And the Lord went before them by day in a pillar of cloud to lead the way, and by night in a pillar of fire to give them light, so as to go by day and night. He did not take away the pillar of cloud by day or the pillar of fire by night from before the people." ~ Exodus 13:17-18, 21-22

The first few words of these verses should be noted. "Then it came to pass," are comforting words. Like the old gentleman who was always ready to quote these words as his favorite "verse" would say, "I'm so glad it came to pass and didn't come to stay!"

More comforting than the mere passing of events is the assurance that God has promised to go with us always. Though we may not experience a visible covering cloud by day or a pillar of fire by night, we can be sure that His presence is always with us and before us.

God led them on a journey that was longer, but also a journey that He knew would lead to success. Whatever your path today, be sure as a child of God that He walks every step with you. Soon you too will cross the river and enter a promised land.

More of the Same

You have certainly heard the expression, "Putting your best foot forward". The phrase has several connotations and linguists are not in agreement as to its certain origin, but generally one could say that it means to make a good first impression. As you walk into a situation, you would try your best to step into the scene in sync since there is no chance for a second first impression.

We probably do not see this lived out more than in the lives of those running for political office. Once every four years during the first week of November, we face the prospect of judging men, who are desiring to be president, based on this one fact: they have been putting their best foot forward. For the most part, we have only experienced men doing what they do best—stumble over their own feet!

The prophet Isaiah must have felt a little like many of us when we near the "finish line" of an election. With our best efforts to make the right choices, we are sure of the fact that we will have more of the same! Isaiah knew that the only answer for Israel's dilemma is the same answer for us in America.

Isaiah prayed: "Oh, that You would rend the heavens! That You would come down! That the mountains might shake at Your presence—as fire burns brushwood, as fire causes water to boil—to make Your name known to Your adversaries, that the nations may tremble at Your presence! When You did awesome things for which we did not look, You came down, the mountains shook at Your presence. For since the beginning of the world men have not heard nor perceived by the ear, nor has the eye seen any God besides You, who acts for the one who waits for Him." ~ Isaiah 64:1-4

Ask God to fold back the curtain of heaven and show Himself. May our people and elected officials all tremble like water boiling at the unseen touch of the fingers of fire. Ask God to do the awesome thing—the thing that is beyond our imagination.

Oh God of heaven, do that which no ear has ever heard nor eye has ever seen, so that, You may be glorified. We wait for you to put your holy foot forward…

Me…That Worm!

I am not sure that we fully grasp what was done for us at the moment of our salvation. This does not mean that we lack appreciation for our salvation or that we accept the gift of salvation by grace with callous disregard.

Though a person cannot be saved without fully accepting their lostness and confessing their sinful condition, we can, as we move away from that moment of salvation begin to forget all that was done for us.

Paul wrote his letter to the Ephesians as a reminder. He said, "And you He made alive, who were dead in trespasses and sins, in which you once walked according to the course of this world, according to the prince of the power of the air, the spirit who now works in the sons of disobedience, among whom also we all once conducted ourselves in the lusts of our flesh, fulfilling the desires of the flesh and of the mind, and were by nature children of wrath, just as the others. But God, who is rich in mercy, because of His great love with which He loved us, even when we were dead in trespasses, made us alive together with Christ (by grace you have been saved), and raised us up together, and made us sit together in the heavenly places in Christ Jesus…" ~ Ephesians 2:1-6

In these verses we fully see that our salvation is not the turning over of a new leaf. It is a full resurrection from the dead by the power of mercy and grace that has rescued us from the wrath of God. It is a powerful demonstration of God's love to lift us out of our sin and place us safely in Christ.

An old Indian, after living many years in sin, was led to Christ by a missionary. Friends asked him to explain the change in his life. Reaching down, he picked up a little worm and placed it on a pile of leaves. Then, touching a match to the leaves, he watched them smolder and burst into flames. As the flames worked their way up to the center where the worm lay, the old chief suddenly plunged his hand into the center of the burning pile and snatched out the worm. Holding the worm gently in his hand, he gave this testimony to the grace of God: "Me. . . that worm."

Rejoice today in your salvation and remember, "Me. . . that worm!"

11/05

Fixing Your Fickleness

Space would not allow me to include the entirety of Job 28, but I hope that you will take a moment to read the entire chapter. It is an incredible piece on the wonders of wisdom.

Here are a few select verses that tie the thoughts about wisdom together: "Surely there is a mine for silver, and a place where gold is refined. Iron is taken from the earth, and copper is smelted from ore. As for the earth, from it comes bread, but underneath it is turned up as by fire; its stones are the source of sapphires, and it contains gold dust. "But where can wisdom be found? And where is the place of understanding? Man does not know its value, nor is it found in the land of the living. The deep says, 'It is not in me'; and the sea says, 'It is not with me.' It cannot be purchased for gold, nor can silver be weighed for its price. "From where then does wisdom come? And where is the place of

understanding? God understands its way, and He knows its place. And to man He said, 'Behold, the fear of the Lord, that is wisdom, and to depart from evil is understanding.'"
~ Job 28:1-2, 5-6, 12-15, 20, 23, 28

Job describes the ability of man to open up the dark recesses of the earth and to bring forth every treasured stone and the precious ore that is held therein. By his own strength he can reshape the mountain face, re-channel the stream, and traverse the far reaches of the earth's surface, but he cannot discover wisdom on his own.

He can never amass enough wealth to purchase wisdom on the open market. It cannot be exchanged for anything that man might create. And so Job poses the question that all of us ask at some point in our lives. "From where then does wisdom come? And where is the place of understanding? (28:20)

Thankfully, Job answers his own question. But this in itself does not make him wise by natural extent. Job can answer this question because he had lived out the previous 27 chapters of his life. He had been in and under God's hand. He had been in the lap of luxury and languished on the ash heap. He had been loved and respected. He had been laughed at and rejected.

Only then could he answer his own question concerning the whereabouts of wisdom. "God understands its way, and He knows its place. And to man He said, 'Behold, the fear of the Lord, that is wisdom, and to depart from evil is understanding.'" (28:23,28)

If you are wondering about wisdom today, don't; in wondering you wind up in want. It is in the fear of God that your fickleness is fixed.

11/06

Seeing Through Walls

If you are like me you can still remember those times when you would be into something (usually mischievous) and you would hear one of your parents call from the other room, "What are you doing?" I never did figure out how they knew and even though I have evidently inherited the same ability to see through walls and hear unspoken conversations, I still don't really get it. Even though I don't understand the gift, I'm glad as a parent to have it.

Now God does not hear as a parent hears. He does not have to discern whether His children are up to something mischievous or not. He has given us His own Holy Spirit that dwells in us to bring about the full recognition of sin, righteousness, and judgment. He is with us always and it is comforting to know that He does hear us.

It is not a wall of dislocation that separates God's hearing from our voice. It is instead His own will that sets the parameters of hearing. "Now this is the confidence that we have in Him, that if we ask anything according to His will, He hears us. And if we know that He hears us, whatever we ask, we know that we have the petitions that we have asked of Him." ~ 1 John 5:14-15

God, who is omniscient in His ability to hear all, can at the same time not hear that which we ask outside of His will. It is like our parents asking through the wall concerning what we are up to at the moment. When we are not asking according to His will, He simply does not respond. If God is silent on an issue, stop now and re-evaluate your request. Does it match His will? If not, pray not for God to change His will, but that you can offer the right request.

On the other hand, we can be sure that even though we cannot see God in the room, He is hearing our petition when it is asked according to His will. You will find your prayer answered and like a child you will sit down and wonder, "How'd God do that?"

Thank God for answered prayer! May it always amaze us that God can see through the walls of our lives and hear our plea.

11/07

Prayer Effects

The disciples had the privilege of seeing all of the works that Jesus did while He spent a little over three years walking this earth with them. Imagine how many times one of the disciples might have said to another, "Hey, did you see what I just saw?" Or, "Man, I've never seen anything like this before!"

These were not the most amazing comments that the disciples might have spoken as they stood amazed at the supernatural evidence of Jesus' deity. Somewhere along the journey the disciples must have begun to notice a pattern in Jesus' life. Moments when He would simply draw away into solitude. Perhaps at first the disciples would have respected His space, but evidently one or more had crept up quietly to hear Him conversing with His Father.

Finally, they might have said to each other, "Did you hear that? He talks to God like He is in His very presence!" And then with great courage one of them said, "Lord, teach us to pray, as John also taught his disciples." ~ Luke 11:1

Jesus responded, ""When you pray, say: Our Father in heaven, Hallowed be Your name. Your kingdom come. Your will be done on earth as it is in heaven. Give us day by day our daily bread. And forgive us our sins, for we also forgive everyone who is indebted to us. And do not lead us into temptation, but deliver us from the evil one."~Luke 11:2-4

They did not ask to perform miracles. They did not ask to be kings or rulers. They did not ask for personal health or wealth. They asked Him to teach them the secret of His prayer life. How many times they must have watched Jesus enter a garden tired and burdened by the day's activity. How many times they would have seen Him return refreshed and renewed even after praying the entire night. Their request to learn the fine art of prayer was perhaps the most important request they laid before Him during His entire ministry on earth.

H.P. Liddon said, "Prayer is not, as it has been scornfully described, 'only a machine warranted by theologians to make God do what His clients want:' it is a great deal more than petition, which is only one department of it; it is nothing less than the whole spiritual action of the soul turned towards God as its true and adequate object."

Make a decision today that your life will be prayer-filled. So much so that others will not be saying, "Did you see what she did, but did you hear what was said while she talked with her Father?" Lord, teach us to pray!

11/08

Selling the Gospel

When I was a boy in elementary school, it was a lot like today in the sense that we were always being used as little salesmen. We were constantly dragging home magazine catalogs, book order forms, boxes of candy bars, or some other item to help offset the school's expenses and needs for basic items.

My favorite item to sell was boxes of seeds. I would always do well with these. They were cheap and easy to pawn off on the neighbors. My model was to go out on Saturday morning and catch ladies as they were heading out to go shopping. If I could get in the door and sit down, I knew they would buy a couple of nickel packs of seeds just to get rid of me! It worked! I was always winning the contests.

Unfortunately, we have a lot of folks today who think the gospel has to be sold. A variety of selling techniques are being used. Most of them are filled with glitz and pizzazz. These programs are a long way from the simplicity of the gospel. The god of pragmatism has been honored and the doctrine of whatever-it-takes has been processed. The assumption is that all that matters is that "seeds" are sold.

Here's what Paul had to say about his presentation of the gospel as he approached the Corinthians. Remember, the Corinthians were always ready for a show and they had already bought some strange seeds.

"And I, brethren, when I came to you, did not come with excellence of speech or of wisdom declaring to you the testimony of God. For I determined not to know anything among you except Jesus Christ and Him crucified. I was with you in weakness, in fear, and in much trembling. And my speech and my preaching were not with persuasive words of human wisdom, but in demonstration of the Spirit and of power, that your faith should not be in the wisdom of men but in the power of God."~1 Corinthians 2:1-5

The real danger of a pragmatic gospel is that it can be based on something less than Christ alone. In essence, if a person comes for a show, then they will only stay if you keep the show running at full steam.

We do not have a gospel of spinning plates. We have a gospel based on God's sovereign power and that's good news!

11/09

Everybody Wins! Really?

We live in a day of confusion. Our confusion is not that which comes from a lack of knowing what to do or even from an overload of information. I think we are confused by misinformation.

The best example of this is the mind warping misinformation that we are feeding children today. We are constantly involving kids in events where everyone is a winner. All the players get a trophy. Nobody loses because we don't dare keep a score.

This may seem "fair" at the moment, but I believe we are setting kids up for some serious problems later on in life, because the last time I checked everybody never wins. There will be losses in life.

Here's where the confusing part comes into the equation. We let everybody be a winner and then we challenge people to do their very best and prove their own self-sufficiency. My question is simple: Why should I pour my life into anything at all if I already am assured of the outcome?

If you take a look at scripture you find the correct model and balance to this equation of life. Paul remarked in 2 Corinthians 3 that he had so poured his life into the Corinthians that his epistle was written upon their hearts. Their lives spoke of the victory that had come through God's Spirit at work in their lives.

Now here is the balance to this statement of victory and success with which Paul begins. "And we have such trust through Christ toward God. Not that we are sufficient of ourselves to think of anything as being from ourselves, but our sufficiency is from God." ~ 2 Corinthians 3:4-5

That's what is missing in the psychology of victory and success today. Because God is left out of the equation, the extremes of pride set in. To counter that, we take away the possibility of personal success by making everyone equal and all a winner.

Winning is fine and success is an honor as long as you keep the source of your sufficiency firmly fixed in Christ. Now go out and be a winner! Be successful! And give God the glory for all of it!

11/10

How 'bout you, Gate Keeper?

Back in the ancient days of the 1970's, the craze was CB radios. These citizen band radios had been used for years by truckers and in other specific settings where people needed a way to communicate over distances of a few miles or less.

Somehow these devices became popular and lots of folks had a CB radio in their vehicle. You can probably still remember everyone that had one, because you remember those long whip-like antennas mounted on bumpers. I was one of those CB radio owners.

I had saved my money to buy a radio, antenna, mounts, etc. If I remember correctly, I had a couple of hundred dollars invested before it was all said and done. Most of the money I had raised by making fudge and brownies each night at home and selling it by the piece the next day in my grocery store. Ahh, those were the days!

You could not have a CB radio without a "handle." This was your radio name. It was how people called for you over airwaves that were jammed with talkers. It needed to be as unique as possible so you would stand out in the radio crowd. I chose "Store Keeper" as my handle. All the years I used a CB radio I only ran across one other guy using Store Keeper as his handle.

Keeping a store is what I did and it gave me a uniqueness. There were some men in the Bible who had the unique position of gatekeeper. They were so unique that some of their names are listed and their genealogies recorded.

"And the gatekeepers were Shallum, Akkub, Talmon, Ahiman, and their brethren. Shallum was the chief. Until then they had been gatekeepers for the camps of the children of Levi at the King's Gate on the east. Shallum the son of Kore, the son of Ebiasaph, the son of Korah, and his brethren, from his father's house, the Korahites, were in charge of the work of the service, gatekeepers of the tabernacle. Their fathers had been keepers of the entrance to the camp of the Lord. All those chosen as gatekeepers were two hundred and twelve. They were recorded by their genealogy, in their villages. David and Samuel the seer had appointed them to their trusted office." ~ 1 Chronicles 9:17-19, 22

Gatekeepers held a solemn and trusted position. So much so that they had been appointed by none other than the Prophet Samuel and King David. They guarded the tabernacle, its treasures, and the people as they watched by day and night.

God has appointed us as believers to be gatekeepers. We are to stand guard for our families, our congregations, the truth, and other treasures in the realm of our existence. This is a solemn duty.

What is your handle in the Kingdom's citizenry? Why not try Gate Keeper? I think it fits the Christian identity well. As I would say on the radio, "Breaker, breaker, how 'bout you, Gate Keeper? You got your ears on?"

11/11

Faithfully Waiting

Waiting is never much fun. Do you remember being a kid and waiting for your birthday to come? Kids nearly always will tell you their age by half years. Ask a child how old they are and you will get a response like this: "I'm nine and a half."

Children have a difficult time waiting, don't they? But we as adults don't do much better. Our waiting is not always for some event, but out of some frustration, because things didn't go as planned.

Worse than that is when we give up waiting. We spend time and effort in waiting and then bail out just before the event takes place.

Jesus said of waiting for the second coming: "But of that day and hour no one knows, not even the angels in heaven, nor the Son, but only the Father. Take heed, watch and pray; for you do not know when the time is. It is like a man going to a far country, who left his house and gave authority to his servants, and to each his work, and commanded the doorkeeper to watch. Watch therefore, for you do not know when the master of the house is coming—in the evening, at midnight, at the crowing of the rooster, or in the morning— lest, coming suddenly, he find you sleeping. And what I say to you, I say to all: Watch!" ~ Mark 13:32-37

Here is the key to faithful waiting. It is not in the time spent waiting, but in the attitude of watching. We are to spend our time with expectation like a kid waiting for some event to unfold, but we are to also be on duty like a guard.

He is coming! It is a sure event. Make sure that you are found faithfully watching as you wait!

Preserving the Fake

The world is full of substitutes, knock-offs, and fakes. I start every day with generic prescriptions followed by substitute sweetener in my coffee. I don't want to think about the rest of the day where I am accessing some store brand alternative to the real thing.

We have become very accustomed to this. It is not just here in America that we do this. A friend told me about a movie he found in another country. The owner explained that copyright in that country meant that you should always make sure that it had been copied right.

Sometimes we attempt to substitute the real thing with the fake when it comes to spiritual matters. This is what King Rehoboam did after he lost the treasures of the temple to the invading armies of the Egyptians.

"It happened in the fifth year of King Rehoboam that Shishak king of Egypt came up against Jerusalem. And he took away the treasures of the house of the Lord and the treasures of the king's house; he took away everything. He also took away all the gold shields which Solomon had made. Then King Rehoboam made bronze shields in their place, and committed them to the hands of the captains of the guard, who guarded the doorway of the king's house. And whenever the king entered the house of the Lord, the guards carried them, then brought them back into the guardroom." ~ 1 Kings 14:25-28

One of the first things seen as you entered the temple area would have been the golden shields held by the guards. When these were taken, Rehoboam commanded bronze replacements to be made and polished to look like the real thing.

The charade continued even after the fakes were manufactured. The king would require the guards to carry them when he entered the temple just as if they were real. Amazingly after this presentation, he would even have the guards store them safely in the guardroom.

Why is it that we often don't miss the authentic until it is gone? And why do we spend so much effort in pretending to the point of paying more attention to the preservation of the fake than we did to the real?

Guard the authentic in your life and never try to pretend. God is able to restore the gold of our lives if we lay it before Him instead of hiding it in the guardroom.

The Little Problems

Did you know that God cares about the little things that happen in your life? Not only does He care, He wants you to bring them to Him. Too often we miss an opportunity to see God work in a big way as He deals with our little problems.

The Bible tells us of just such an occurrence back in the days of Elisha the prophet. The students in the school of the prophets had engaged in building new facilities when a small tragedy occurred. The account is recorded for us in 2 Kings 6.

"And the sons of the prophets said to Elisha, 'See now, the place where we dwell with you is too small for us. Please, let us go to the Jordan, and let every man take a beam from there, and let us make there a place where we may dwell.'

So he answered, 'Go.'

Then one said, 'Please consent to go with your servants.'

And he answered, 'I will go.'

So he went with them. And when they came to the Jordan, they cut down trees. But as one was cutting down a tree, the iron ax head fell into the water; and he cried out and said, 'Alas, master! For it was borrowed.'

So the man of God said, 'Where did it fall?'

And he showed him the place. So he cut off a stick, and threw it in there; and he made the iron float. Therefore he said, 'Pick it up for yourself.' So he reached out his hand and took it." ~ 2 Kings 6:1-7

There are several truths hidden away in this little episode along the banks of the muddy Jordan River. First, we see the prophet of God walking alongside the workers. Elisha was God's representative here on earth and as a such a picture of God's presence in the midst of daily endeavors. God is interested in our everyday stuff.

Second, things happen. I know that doesn't sound very spiritual, but they do; things just happen. The loss of the ax head was not intentional. It was not particularly lost out of carelessness. It just happened and that is how lots of things come to pass...they just happen.

Third, the ax head was borrowed. Like everything in this life including life itself, it is all borrowed. We brought nothing into this life and we take nothing out of it.

Fourth, it is beyond our ability to restore the losses we incur. Like a heavy ax head, sin has carried us to the murky bottom and only a miracle can resurrect us to life again.

Fifth, there is a point of personal responsibility. The ax head floated by miracle, but the young man had to reach out and take it up for himself.

God is waiting for your cry today. He wants to hear you say that all is lost and then He will give you your miracle of the floating ax head. Reach out now and take it. It's yours today!

11/14

The End Is Near!

Ignorance is bliss. At least that is what they say and we all know that they know it all. Ignorance may indeed be blissful while you are in the state of ignorance, but reality and the knowledge thereof has a way of shocking us back into the truth.

Two men were standing on a road with a sign that read, "The end is near!" For hours they withstood the stares of passersby and in many cases outright insulting comments. Each auto that passed by them was followed by the screeching of tires and the sound of crunching metal.

One of the men said to his buddy holding the sign, "Maybe we should change our sign." "What do you suggest?" asked the other man. "I think something like, BRIDGE OUT AHEAD, might work better." There is the difference between the bliss of ignorance and the reality of truth.

David asked God to take him out of blissful ignorance and place him into the position of reality. David said, "Lord, make me to know my end, and what is the measure of my days, that I may know how frail I am. Indeed, You have made my days as handbreadths, and my age is as nothing before You; certainly every man at his best state is but vapor. Surely every man walks about like a shadow; surely they busy themselves in vain; he heaps up riches, and does not know who will gather them. And now, Lord, what do I wait for? My hope is in You." ~ Psalm 39:4-7

David asked God to *make* him to know the extent of his life. We are not eternal and we all have our limits. We just don't like to admit that. We prefer the blissful thought that we can do anything at any time.

Perhaps my age has something to do with it, but I am more aware of my limitations now than ever. Even with this truth in my pocket, I will need to pray as David did to keep myself in proper context.

The conclusion that David reached was that life is very short. All that we spend a life gathering will be consumed by others. But the brevity of his existence did not lessen his hope. He focused his hope in God alone.

Indeed, the end is nearer than you first thought and the reality is that the bridge really is out just ahead. The good news is this: God has built a new bridge. The bridge across the chasm of eternity is Jesus.

Here's my sign: THE END IS NEAR: SO IS JESUS! Drive carefully!

11/15

Keep the Lights Burning

Here are the words of an old hymn written by Phillip Bliss. Use the link at the conclusion of today's devotion for a video of Tennessee Ernie Ford's rendition of this old hymn.

The hymn is entitled "Let the Lower Lights Be Burning."

> Brightly beams our Father's mercy,
> From His lighthouse evermore,
> But to us He gives the keeping
> Of the lights along the shore.
>
> Dark the night of sin has settled,
> Loud the angry billows roar;
> Eager eyes are watching, longing,
> For the lights along the shore.
>
>
> Trim your feeble lamp, my brother;
> Some poor sailor, tempest-tossed,
> Trying now to make the harbor,
> In the darkness may be lost.
>
> Chorus:
> Let the lower lights be burning!
> Send a gleam across the wave!
> Some poor struggling, fainting seaman
> You may rescue, you may save.

Bliss wrote the words of this hymn after hearing the following story of a ship that had crashed on shore while traversing Lake Erie. The loss of life prompted him to challenge folks with the words of his hymn.

On a dark and stormy night, with waves piling up like mountains on Lake Erie, a boat rocked and plunged near the Cleveland harbor.

"Are we on course?" asked the captain, seeing only one beacon from the lighthouse.

"Quite sure, sir," replied the officer at the helm.

"Where are the lower lights?"

"Gone out, sir."

"Can we make the harbor?"

"We must, or perish," came the reply.

With a steady hand and a stalwart heart, the officer headed the ship toward land. But, in the darkness, he missed the channel and the vessel was dashed to pieces on the rocks.

You and I are the lower lights that guide our friends and family safe into the harbor of heaven. Jesus said, "Let your light so shine before men, that they may see your good works and glorify your Father in heaven." ~ Matthew 5:16

Do not grow weary in the stormy night of life. Ever keep the lower lights burning! You never know when a passing soul will be looking for the harbor entrance. Your light shining brightly through the darkness can lead them safely home.

Keep the lower lights burning, my friend!

http://bit.ly/17NpNLV

11/16

Looking Unto Jesus

Eyesight is a precious gift. It is a marvel of God's creative work in which the eye has the ability to focus readily upon multiple points laid out at various distances.

This ability to see far and close with clarity changes with age and many including myself are forced to wear some form of optics that corrects our inability to see clearly at one or more of these focal points.

When we focus too long on objects at one fixed distance, we can lose the ability to see at other distances. This is true in a spiritual sense also. We get our vision fixed on earthly things and we can no longer see things from a heavenly perspective.

The writer of Hebrews said, "Therefore we also, since we are surrounded by so great a cloud of witnesses, let us lay aside every weight, and the sin which so easily ensnares us, and let us run with endurance the race that is set before us, looking unto Jesus, the author and finisher of our faith, who for the joy that was set before Him endured the cross, despising the shame, and has sat down at the right hand of the throne of God." ~ Hebrews 12:1-2

We become so fixated upon this life with its trials that we can no longer clearly see the finish line and Jesus who stands there to welcome us. Charles Spurgeon illustrated it like this:

"Imagine that you are in a round tower with slits in the walls used for shooting through with guns. Now imagine that you are whirled around the inner circumference. Would you appreciate the beauties of the surrounding landscape? No.

But there are openings in the wall. Yes, but your eyes are set for objects near and do not have the time to adjust to distance as you are whirled past the slits. It would be as if the wall were solid.

So it is with earthly living. The near and earthly wall obstructs the view. An occasional slit is left open, perhaps a Sunday sermon or personal Bible reading. Heaven might be seen through these, but the eye which is set for the earthly cannot adjust itself to higher things during such momentary glimpses.

So long has the soul looked upon the world, that when it is turned for a moment heavenward, it feels only a quiver of inarticulate light. Unless you pause and look steadfastly, you will not see or retain any distinct impression of the things which are eternal."

Spend some time at the slits in the wall. Though small when compared to the entire wall they are there for us to look unto Jesus, the author and finisher of our faith. Precious, indeed, is a look into the face of Jesus!

11/17

Satisfied

As I begin to write today's verse into my devotional, you will recognize it immediately and will most likely finish it in your mind before you have read it with your eyes. Ready?

"The Lord is my Shepherd, I shall not want." ~ Psalm 23:1

You and millions of others know this text. People who rarely open the Bible can quote this verse, though many take no thought as to its real truth.

Elisabeth Elliot, the widow of Jim Elliot who was killed by the Auca Indians as he attempted to reach them with the gospel, often told the story of a toddler who was very ill. This child had learned to recite the Twenty-third Psalm on her fingers. Starting with her pinkie, she would grab a finger as she said each of the five words which begin verse one.

The—Lord—is—my—Shepherd.

As she said the word shepherd, she would clasp her thumb in recognition of the care God had for her.

One morning, after a long and hard fight against her disease, the little girl was found dead with one hand clasped around the other thumb. The Lord is her shepherd. He had made her to lie down in green pastures. He had led her to quiet waters. Surely she dwells in the house of the Lord forever.

Many believe that David wrote this psalm as an older man. Life's hard knocks had brought him to a full understanding of God's protection and provision in his life. With full assurance he wrote this verse in the present tense.

The—Lord—IS—my—Shepherd.

Some say that hindsight is always 20-20. I suppose that is true or at least it seems that way. We certainly have a clearer perspective on things when we look back over them. Experience had taught David that he could declare the Lord as his personal Shepherd.

It is one thing to think of God in some abstract impersonal way. A God who dwells on the other side of the cosmos and is only addressed on special occasions is one thing, but a God who leads as a Shepherd is quite another. David's relationship with the Lord was so personal that he could only say:

The—Lord—is—MY—Shepherd.

This deep interpersonal walk with the Shepherd led David to say at the very beginning of this well-known psalm, "I shall not want." As much as this sentence means without lack or failure it also means without grief. David concluded that a lifelong following of his Shepherd would never lead to regret or grief.

The—Lord—is—my—Shepherd. I—shall—not—WANT.

What about your walk with the Shepherd today? The best way to measure your walk is by measuring your want. Think of it like this: I am satisfied because the Lord is my Shepherd. Is this true in your life?

Abide With Me

In the fourteenth chapter of John, Jesus had informed His disciples of His soon coming departure. In this discourse He offers them the assurance of His return and of the provision of Himself as The Way, The Truth, and The Life.

I'm sure that you have taken note that nearly 2000 years have passed. At least you are aware of your small portion of that time. I hope that you can take heart in a couple of verses from the very next chapter of John. "Abide in Me, and I in you. As the branch cannot bear fruit of itself, unless it abides in the vine, neither can you, unless you abide in Me. I am the vine, you are the branches. He who abides in Me, and I in him, bears much fruit; for without Me you can do nothing." ~ John 15:4-5

The word abide means to dwell, stay, continue, be present. The idea is that of a permanent state in which the believer's existence is like that of a branch connected to the vine. We simply cease to exist without a connection to Him as our sustaining force.

This verse was on the heart of Henry Francis Lyte as he penned the words of his poem which became the hymn "Abide With Me." Lyre pastored among the seafaring folks around Devonshire, England until finally his strength gave out. In 1847 his doctor suggested he move to the milder climate of southern France.

Lyte could not leave without one final sermon to his church of twenty-four years. His health was so frail that his friends advised against it, but Lyte was determined.

Standing feebly, he said, "Oh, brethren, I stand here before you today, as alive from the dead, if I may hope to impress upon you and get you to prepare for that solemn hour which must come to all. I plead with you to become acquainted with the changeless Christ and His death."

After finishing his sermon, he served the Lord's Supper to his weeping flock and dismissed them. That evening, as his life's work drew to its close, he found comfort in pondering John 15: "Abide in Me, and I in you."

According to his gardener, Lyte wrote the following hymn after having walked down to the ocean and watched "the sun setting over Brixham Harbor like a pool of molten gold." Taking out a piece of paper, he wrote a poem and returned to his study to rewrite and polish it before giving it to his adopted daughter.

The next day he left for France. Reaching Nice, he had a seizure and passed away with the words, "Joy! Peace!" on his lips.

Validating Your Faith

Faith may be one of the most misunderstood doctrines of scripture. I find this keenly interesting since the writer of Hebrews makes us fully aware of this one fact: Without faith, it is impossible to please Him {God}. (Hebrews 11:6)

Is there a conspiracy of hell to keep God's people focused on some subject other than the very element that is necessary if we are to please the God we serve? Certainly, there is some trickery of satan at work here, but he is smarter than to just deny faith's existence or its importance. He is the master deceiver and it serves his purposes better to replace genuine faith with a fickle faith.

He prefers for God's children to claim a faith life, but in reality to hold nothing more than a shallow cup filled with best wishes for everything to turn out okay. Like a liquid spilling over the edges of their lives, many spend their days with a wary eye on what's left in the cup, hoping they will cross the finish line of life with a drop or two of faith in the bottom of their cup.

Peter explained it this way in his first epistle, "...that the genuineness of your faith, being much more precious than gold that perishes, though it is tested by fire, may be found to praise, honor, and glory at the revelation of Jesus Christ, whom having not seen you love. Though now you do not see Him, yet believing, you rejoice with joy inexpressible and full of glory, receiving the end of your faith—the salvation of your souls." ~ 1 Peter 1:7-9

Why could Peter express this concept of faith in such a manner? One word: EXPERIENCE. Peter's own faith had been proven as true in his life. He had gone through the rigors of seeing his faith exercised in episodes such as stepping out of the boat and making his way to Jesus out on the Sea of Galilee.

Peter had experienced the heartbreak of denial as he had gone so far as to curse the name of Jesus on the night of Jesus' mock trial and soon coming crucifixion. He knew what it was to lay faith aside and return to fishing again only to discover Jesus waiting for Him on the seashore.

Maybe these and other such experiences are why Peter could say, "Though now you do not see Him, yet believing, you rejoice with joy inexpressible and full of glory, receiving the end of your faith—the salvation of your souls." (1:9) So how's your faith? Is it genuine or fake? Ask God to give you the experience to validate your faith today.

Guard Your Smile

Few of us that can sit stone faced while we watch a video of a baby laughing uncontrollably. There is something about the purity of such joy. It matters not if the laughter is spontaneous or provoked, we will at the minimum break out into a grin and most likely join the little one in a good belly laugh.

I do not know if we fully realize how much we convey God's character when we make every attempt to wear a simple smile. All around us are people who only perceive of God as stern and unforgiving. I can only surmise that their opinion of God has come from those they have been in close contact with in their everyday lives.

The Bible speaks of the countenance of a man disclosing his heart's condition. Here are a few references to reflect upon:

"A merry heart makes a cheerful countenance, but by sorrow of the heart the spirit is broken." ~ Proverbs 15:13 / "A man's wisdom makes his face shine, and the sternness of his face is changed." ~ Ecclesiastes 8:1b / "Why are you cast down, O my soul? And why are you disquieted within me? Hope in God; for I shall yet praise Him, the help of my countenance and my God." ~ Psalm 43:5 / "But he (the rich young ruler) was sad at this word, and went away sorrowful, for he had great possessions." ~ Mark 10:22

Nothing is as simple to share as a smile, but nothing is as simple to detect as fake as a knock-off smile either. Those around us know when our entire countenance is involved in the upward curl of our lips into the form of a smile or whether we are simply painting light into the window of an empty house.

I read the story of a little girl who began to cry uncontrollably at church and ran into the arms of her mother. The pastor out of concern went to the mother after the service to inquire what had happened to the child.

The mother of the girl explained to the pastor that her little girl always looked forward to going to church because the pastor smiled at her. On that particular morning the pastor had not noticed the little girl smiling at him and without malice had overlooked her.

She was heartbroken because he had not returned her smile. She sobbed into her mother's ear in explanation of her crying, "God is angry with me; He didn't smile back!" For this little girl, the pastor was all she knew of who God was. Believe me, there are others in your life that you pass by each day that may think exactly the same thing. Be careful with your smile!

Digging Ditches

One of the more obscure miracles that Elisha performed was the miracle of the ditches. Technically, of course, as in all miracles, he did not do anything. It was all by the hand of God.

"And he said, "Thus says the Lord: 'Make this valley full of ditches.' For thus says the Lord: 'You shall not see wind, nor shall you see rain; yet that valley shall be filled with water, so that you, your cattle, and your animals may drink.' And this is a simple matter in the sight of the Lord; He will also deliver the Moabites into your hand."~2 Kings 3:16-18

The setting was an alliance of the three kings of Judah, Israel, and Edom. They had made a pact to fight against the king of Moab. The only king of the three who was attentive to the things of God was Jehoshaphat, the king of Judah. This coalition army found themselves in a dry valley with thirst about to destroy both the men and the animals.

Jehoshaphat inquired, "Is there no prophet of the Lord here, that we may inquire of the Lord by him?" So one of the servants of the king of Israel answered and said, "Elisha the son of Shaphat is here, who poured water on the hands of Elijah." ~ 2 Kings 3:11

After seeking a word from the Lord, Elisha commanded that ditches be dug in the dry valley in preparation for the miracle that God would give. Early the next morning water poured in from the east and the ditches were all filled to overflowing. What can be learned from this miracle?

First, sometimes God requires us to make preparation for receiving a miracle. Second, making preparation may not be easy. They had to dig ditches in a bone-dry valley. Third, God may ask you to do something that you consider beneath your ability. Elite fighting men were asked to become common ditch diggers.

Finally, as in many other miracles, the miracle was limited to the depth of the preparation. The water filled every ditch that had been dug. God is not limited by us, but there are times that He will go no further than we are willing to go.

What small thing is God asking of you in preparation for your miracle? Does it seem too hard? Have you thought it beneath your status to do as He has asked? Have you stopped digging too soon?

Listen! Is that the sound of rushing water? Pick up your shovel and dig your ditch. Joy comes in the morning along with the victory!

Walking Into A Miracle

"I don't think it can get any worse than this!"

Have you ever found yourself saying something like this? You feel like you have been the brunt of one cruel joke after another. Perhaps you had always wondered who the Murphy of Murphy's Law was and then you checked your driver's license. Somehow during the night your name had been changed to Murphy!

It was much like this for Samaria during the siege of the Syrians. Second Kings 6 reveals how intense the situation was for the Samaritans. The siege had brought conditions of mass starvation upon the people to the point that things like donkey heads were selling like rib eye steak and dried dove's dung was being sold as fuel.

It is at the height of this siege that four lepers reached a critical decision for themselves. "Now there were four leprous men at the entrance of the gate; and they said to one another, 'Why are we sitting here until we die? If we say, 'We will enter the city,' the famine is in the city, and we shall die there. And if we sit here, we die also. Now therefore, come, let us surrender to the army of the Syrians. If they keep us alive, we shall live; and if they kill us, we shall only die.'" ~2 Kings 7:3-4

These men concluded that they were going to die one way or the other, but perhaps they could find some mercy at the hands of the Syrians. God had other purposes at work, however.

As these four men approached the Syrian camp, God caused the soldiers to hear the footsteps of these men as if they were the clatter of an advancing army. By the time the men entered the camp, the Syrians had fled leaving all of their supplies.

The lepers opened tent after tent like little boys on Christmas morning tearing into presents. God had turned their misery into a miracle. You can only imagine them filling their pockets with the bounty when they came to themselves. "Then they said to one another, 'We are not doing right. This day is a day of good news, and we remain silent. If we wait until morning light, some punishment will come upon us. Now therefore, come, let us go and tell the king's household.'" ~ 2 Kings 7:9

Has this day broken with serious news for you? Are you thinking it cannot get any worse? Take heart! God is moving. If He could use four lepers to rout an army, He can use your situation to bring about a victory that will turn your life into a miracle. The questions are will you just sit and die or get up and walk into your miracle? Will you hoard God's blessing or pass it along? It is up to you...

Thankfulness

Consider these verses which demonstrate the fact that even our thankfulness can be warped when sin and self are involved.

Jesus spoke this parable to some who trusted in themselves that they were righteous, and despised others: "Two men went up to the temple to pray, one a Pharisee and the other a tax collector. "The Pharisee stood and prayed thus with himself, 'God, I thank You that I am not like other men—extortioners, unjust, adulterers, or even as this tax collector. 'I fast twice a week; I give tithes of all that I possess.' "And the tax collector, standing afar off, would not so much as raise his eyes to heaven, but beat his breast, saying, 'God, be merciful to me a sinner!' "I tell you, this man went down to his house justified rather than the other; for everyone who exalts himself will be humbled, and he who humbles himself will be exalted." ~ Luke 18:9-14

Exactly why are you thankful today? Not what are you thankful for, but why? Here's what happened to me just last night that helps me grasp this.

As I was attempting to scoop some very frozen ice cream the spoon slipped. It scooted the carton across the counter which struck the bowl which departed the counter top which hit the tile floor which shattered into a kajillion pieces. So why am I thankful for this?

I remembered that a pastor's wife in Nigeria has no freezer. She stores her food tightly in a plastic bag and submerges it in a 55 gallon drum of water at around 95 degrees in the shade. Her seven children have never tasted ice cream.

I have a countertop in a kitchen in a home filled with conveniences. In Bosnia Gypsy refugees are living in the shells of burned out buildings left over from a war they did not choose.

I have a bowl. Each of us have a bowl. A young lady in China crawls along the sidewalk pushing a small dish before her. The dish is there for someone to deposit a coin or two. Something tells me she will eat from that same bowl later tonight.

I have a tiled floor capable of shattering a bowl. I still see a grandmother with six children gathered in a lean-to home with only dirt to walk upon as they gather around her legs and peer up at us. Their blankets are used carpet padding found in a dumpster.

I could go on, but I do think this is sufficient to say that I discovered the why of my thankfulness in a shattered bowl full of Blue Bell pralines and cream ice cream. Now tell me again why your day is so bad…I didn't think so…

Light Friday

One day each year, shoppers flood storefronts to buy the unnecessary for those who are mostly unthankful, knowing very well they are most likely unable to afford any of what they consider to be the most unusual gift ever purchased. Ah, the joys of Black Friday!

The world is indeed in a state of blackness. As Jesus met with Nicodemus during the night (who knows, maybe it was a Friday) He told him that he must be born again.

Like the sounding forth of the best deal since creation itself, Jesus announced to Nicodemus that salvation was a gift (John 3:16). Amazing! The world is clamoring to find a deal and the best deal of all was announced in a night scene nearly 2000 years ago. There is no fine print, no limited supply, no first come first served, and no checkout lines.

But we should not stop too soon in our recollection of this night scene between Jesus and Nicodemus. Jesus continued to speak after John 3:16 as he said, "And this is the condemnation, that the light has come into the world, and men loved darkness rather than light, because their deeds were evil. For everyone practicing evil hates the light and does not come to the light, lest his deeds should be exposed. But he who does the truth comes to the light, that his deeds may be clearly seen, that they have been done in God." ~ John 3:19-21

Isn't it time to come out of the darkness and cover of night? It's time to receive the best gift you could ever have in your possession. It's the free gift of salvation. It matters not if it is Black Friday or not. Any day without Jesus is a day of blackness.

Here's a little more good news about this good news! This gift of salvation is for everyone. It is a one size fits all gift. Once received, you will never find a reason to return it. As a matter of fact, if it is truly received it is non-returnable. More than its non-returnability, I've never met a single person who has received the gift of salvation that was left wishing for something better.

Come home to Jesus! Leave your search for the perfect gift. It already awaits you. It's just a knee bend's distance from where you are right now.

Have a great Light Friday or whatever day you may be reading this!

When Desire Is Right

Desire is an item that can be frowned upon in the Christian community. Perhaps rightly so under some circumstances. We do have a tendency to unleash our desires and find them cascading down the slope into the lake of lust.

Somehow we humans have a propensity to function in extremes. We cannot seem to understand what the Apostle Paul meant when he declared that all things should be done in moderation. (1 Corinthians 9:25)

We must be careful then that we do not take what I believe is a God-given attribute of mankind and throw it under the proverbial bus. Remember that scripture commends desire in its proper place. "Delight yourself also in the Lord, And He shall give you the desires of your heart. Commit your way to the Lord, trust also in Him, and He shall bring it to pass. ~ Psalm 37:4-5

"You open Your hand and satisfy the desire of every living thing." ~ Psalm 145:16

It is also very easy to see that it was desire out of control that helped get mankind into our sinful condition in the beginning. "So when the woman saw that the tree was good for food, that it was pleasant to the eyes, and a tree desirable to make one wise, she took of its fruit and ate. She also gave to her husband with her, and he ate." ~ Genesis 3:6

Desires running amuck can also lead us into temptation and disruption of fellowship among brethren. "But each one is tempted when he is drawn away by his own desires and enticed. / Where do wars and fights come from among you? Do they not come from your desires for pleasure that war in your members? You lust and do not have. You murder and covet and cannot obtain. You fight and war. Yet you do not have because you do not ask. You ask and do not receive, because you ask amiss, that you may spend it on your pleasures." ~ James 1:14 & James 4:1-3

Don't be deceived by blaming so much on the poor devil. A lot of what goes on in our lives does not come from without, but from within. And like so much of what ails us, it is not bad that has gotten worse, but the good gifts of God that we have abused.

Never forget: "Every good gift and every perfect gift is from above, and comes down from the Father of lights, with whom there is no variation or shadow of turning." ~ James 1:17

Counting It All Joy

You may have noticed that sometimes God's word says some very difficult things for us to fathom. One of these hard sayings is: "My brethren, count it all joy when you fall into various trials, knowing that the testing of your faith produces patience. But let patience have its perfect work, that you may be perfect and complete, lacking nothing." ~ James 1:2-4

All of you have faced trials and troubles at some level. These times can range from mild inconvenience to outright misery and yet scripture is telling us to count such times as joy. This may produce a collective, "Wait a minute!" But a little deeper look into these verses will alleviate the misunderstanding.

The idea of counting trials as joy is made clear when you understand that this accounting takes place as a result of the trial. It is not the trial itself that you are rejoicing over or in, but as you look back at what God has done in you through the trial you cannot help but find joy.

The trial aligns us to the will of God. The adjustment is always in us. J. Vernon McGee said of these verses, "My friend, you are not reconciled to the will of God until you can rejoice—not for the trials, but because of them."

Another thing to note is that we fall into these times of trial. Simply put, things happen. They happen without notice for the most part. They happen to everyone and are as varied as are the people to which they happen.

Lastly, James instructs us as to the outcome of our trials. These times of testing produce in us a higher level of patience. Literally, each trial strengthens our endurance and thereby brings a deeper sense of joy as each wave of the trial passes over us. Then as patience is allowed to function in our lives we grow up in our Christian walk as faith, hope, and joy are fully matured in us.

Now the question is not if you will face some trial, but when. In a trial now? Then you are walking just ahead of others who will follow in your steps. God is at work. Ask Him to reconcile you to His will. Take out a pencil and paper and start counting it all joy!

The Wind At His Back

I am not a prophet, nor am I the son of a prophet. Sometimes I wish that I was. Then again, I'm glad I am not. The penalty for prophets getting it wrong was harsh. It might be better if it still was harsh. We all might be better off with a few less false prophets. But that is a story for another day.

I speak not as a prophet, but instead as a poor excuse for a historian. My reflection upon history does not lead me to look upon the happier or brighter days of a few decades past. To find some similarity to our day, I have had to go back over 3000 years.

My thoughts fell upon the rule of Solomon as king of Israel. Solomon came to the throne with the wind at his back. His father David had fought the wars, built a great country, and had gathered all that would be needed for his son to build the Temple. Simply put: Solomon had little investment in all that he inherited.

This lack of blood, sweat, or tears soon was revealed in his open disobedience to God's command. He gathered for himself chariots and horses. He allowed his lusts to consume him and went wild in his efforts to suppress his desires. He had nearly 1000 women in his life and spent his days appeasing all of their false religious ideals.

The amazing thing was that he did all of this as the wisest and richest man who has ever lived. Make no mistake. This wisdom and these riches had both come from the hand of God. Yet they were abused upon fleshly desire and resulted in a divided kingdom.

The end of Solomon's reign came like that of all men. "Then Solomon rested with his fathers, and was buried in the City of David his father. And Rehoboam his son reigned in his place." ~ 1 Kings 11:43 Soon afterwards the kingdom was divided between his sons and was never united again.

I think that our country is at the same crossroads. We now have a generation of electors who have no blood, sweat, or tears invested in this great country. Their votes are not cast on the basis of morality or even logic. They listen to the counsel of those who do not know the God of David. They have enjoyed the blessings of God both in wisdom and riches, but have no idea where all of these things originated.

I am no prophet. I do not know where our country is headed, but I do know this. United is not part of our future if we continue to go down this path. God help us all...

Mission Accomplished!

On May 1, 2003, George H.W. Bush became the first sitting President to make an arrested landing in a fixed-wing aircraft on an aircraft carrier. He landed on the USS Abraham Lincoln in a Lockheed S-3 Viking, dubbed Navy One, as the carrier returned from combat operations in the Persian Gulf. A few hours later, he gave a speech announcing the end of major combat operations in the Iraq War. Far above him was the warship's banner stating "Mission Accomplished."

All know now that this was presumptuous given the full display of history at our disposal. The President was not the first to mistakenly assume facts, nor will he be the last. I have also made such claims and then was forced to face the reality of my own jump to conclusions.

I often think about such times when I return from a mission trip. I wish that I could proclaim, "Mission Accomplished!", but I know that there is much more work to be done in the place I just visited and in other places around this world.

There are souls yet untouched by the good news of the gospel message. Our orders are still active and we have no choice but to return again and again until we will finally be able to sit at the feet of the only One who ever could say mission accomplished.

The grandest mission ever engaged was finished nearly 2000 years ago on an old rugged cross. It was not completed amongst fanfare or the lights of cameras. Its news was not instantly streamed around the globe.

It all occurred on a hillside outside of Jerusalem. Three men were dying on cruel instruments of death. Two were justly paying for their crimes. They hung on either side of a man who had nailed to His cross a placard declaring Him to be the King of the Jews.

All three men died that day, but only one said these words: "It is finished!" (John 19:30.) That man was Jesus. He truly is the Commander in Chief. He alone had the right, by demonstration of fact, to declare, "Mission Accomplished!"

So, as His servants, go forth with the message of hope. Be it across the street or across the wide expanse of the globe. Be faithful in the mission until you hear the words from Jesus Himself, "Well done, good and faithful servant. Mission accomplished!"

Turning Out the Light

As believers we experience lives of unfinished business. We turn our backs on an old life and set our faces toward a land we have yet to enjoy. We are pilgrims who, having heard the Master's call, now turn our attention to the journey of occupying the land until He comes for us or calls us home.

The writer of Hebrews speaks of others who have walked this journey before us. "These all died in faith, not having received the promises, but having seen them afar off were assured of them, embraced them and confessed that they were strangers and pilgrims on the earth. For those who say such things declare plainly that they seek a homeland. And truly if they had called to mind that country from which they had come out, they would have had opportunity to return. But now they desire a better, that is, a heavenly country .Therefore God is not ashamed to be called their God, for He has prepared a city for them." ~ Hebrews 11:13-16

Indeed we have been called out never to return. Our minds are made up and fixed not on our past, but on a bright future where a city is prepared and awaits our occupancy. The following story from the "Sunday School Times" illustrates this well.

A man whose youth and early manhood had been spent in evil ways, and who was converted to God, was one night giving his testimony. He had met an old drinking pal later that week who chaffed him for "getting religion".

"I'll tell you what," the man said to his friend, "you know that I am a lamp lighter; when I go around turning out the lights, I look back, and all the road over which I've been walking is filled with darkness. That's what my past is like."

The man went on to tell his former drinking buddy, "But, I look on in front, and there's a long row of twinkling lights to guide me, and that's what the future is since I found Jesus."

"Yes," said the other man, "but by-and-by you get to the last lamp and turn it out, and where are you then?"

"Then," remarked the believer, "when the last lamp goes out it's dawn, and there ain't no need for lamps when the morning comes."

Keep walking my friend. As you arrive at another lamp post reach up and turn out that light. Spend a moment in thanksgiving and then move on in the light of the next. One day soon you will extinguish the last lamp of your life; then you will be home where it's always morning.

Something Happened Here

Many years ago I stood overlooking the chasm that surrounds the Colorado Monument. Pinnacles of rock seem to shoot upward from the canyon floor. These rock formations did not grow out of the solid base of the canyon, however. Instead, the sandstone around these rocks have eroded away leaving them standing tall.

I still remember the words of my pastor as we stood there together overlooking the sights. He looked at me and proclaimed, "Son, something happened here!" Now his remarks were meant to be somewhat facetious, but nevertheless, they were true. Something had really happened there and we were left standing there to view the results.

Paul wrote to the Corinthians with an eye looking back over the history of scripture. He saw those whose lives had been recorded as standing tall in the face of a world that had eroded around them.

"Now all these things happened to them as examples, and they were written for our admonition, upon whom the ends of the ages have come. Therefore let him who thinks he stands take heed lest he fall. No temptation has overtaken you except such as is common to man; but God is faithful, who will not allow you to be tempted beyond what you are able, but with the temptation will also make the way of escape, that you may be able to bear it." ~ 1 Corinthians 10:11-13

How were they able to do this? They were not perfect people. Scripture records their failings and faults with no apology. Surely, this is an evidence of the infallibility and inspiration of the Bible. Few of us would have included such characters. We would have painted a picture of perfection. Instead, God saw fit to show us in these lives that temptation is common, but so is the way to escape the eroding consequences of it.

Know this: Temptations will come. Like violent winds and rushing waters they will over wash your pathway. As Paul said, these things happen. This word means to occur within the very steps you are walking. It's going to happen and there is nothing we can do about that.

So what will folks say as they look back over the history of your life? Hopefully, you will be left standing tall like the Colorado Monument and all will pronounce,

"Something happened here!

• DECEMBER

More Than a Gift Card

As December begins and the Christmas season gets into full swing, millions of gifts will be bought with the hope that the buyer will have found a unique item that will be just perfect for the recipient.

Then there are the millions of others who have reasoned that there is no unique gift and most recipients will not be that enamored with the gift nor appreciative of the efforts in finding just the right bobble. These folks will do what many do each year. They will buy a gift card!

Thank goodness God does not have a gift card mentality when it comes to salvation. He has set forth strict parameters on the gift of salvation. So much so that He has declared that there is no other name under heaven whereby a person can be saved (Acts 4:12.)

The book of Hebrews describes the gift giving required as part of the ministry of Jesus as He serves as the Great High Priest. He is actively presenting gifts before the Father as prescribed and described.

"Now this is the main point of the things we are saying: We have such a High Priest, who is seated at the right hand of the throne of the Majesty in the heavens, a Minister of the sanctuary and of the true tabernacle which the Lord erected, and not man. For every high priest is appointed to offer both gifts and sacrifices. Therefore it is necessary that this One also have something to offer. For if He were on earth, He would not be a priest, since there are priests who offer the gifts according to the law; who serve the copy and shadow of the heavenly things, as Moses was divinely instructed when he was about to make the tabernacle. For He said, 'See that you make all things according to the pattern shown you on the mountain.' But now He has obtained a more excellent ministry, inasmuch as He is also Mediator of a better covenant, which was established on better promises." ~ Hebrews 8:1-6

If you are a believer, you have been offered before the Father as a gift. You are a type of those gifts prescribed in the Levitical law, but no longer of mere grains or cereals; now, instead, of flesh and blood. We are living sacrificial gifts (Romans 12:1.)

All of this is preceded by the ultimate sacrifice of Christ Himself. He has ascended and serves at the right hand of the Father offering daily each new believer who comes to faith through His sacrificial gift.

Live your life today as a believer of purpose and uniqueness. You are not a gift card offered casually before the Throne of Heaven. You have been bought with a price that no man could pay!

12/02

Content

The English language can be very difficult for those who speak other languages. It's not even easy for those of us who have spoken it since our very first words crossed our lips.

The difficulty arises mostly from the inconsistency in forming various sounds. In most languages a certain consonant or vowel will always produce the same sound when spoken. English speakers give different meaning to words that look exactly alike with as little as an accent falling on a different syllable.

One example of this is the word "content". Did you just read that "content" as in that which is contained or did you read it as "content" as in being satisfied with what one has or to lacking nothing?

As much as these two words can mean vastly different things in context, their similar spelling can tie them together in a significant way. A person being content has a lot to do with their content!

Perhaps we learn this best from the Apostle Paul as he sat chained between guards in a Roman prison. "Not that I speak in regard to need, for I have learned in whatever state I am, to be content: I know how to be abased, and I know how to abound. Everywhere and in all things I have learned both to be full and to be hungry, both to abound and to suffer need. I can do all things through Christ who strengthens me."~Philippians 4:11-13

How is it possible to be content in the most horrid of conditions? How can a person be content no matter the contents of their stomach or wallet or home? The answer is found not in the contents of our containers. It matters not what contents are in that which is passing away. It only matters what is the content of that which is eternal.

Paul's contentment was never measured on the ever-changing whims of circumstance. He used the phrase "in whatever state" to describe the limits of his contentment. Literally, he was saying that it did not matter what place or time he was in, under, around, between, up against, or going through, he would be content in the content of those circumstances.

All of this was possible because of the content of that which was eternal. Christ had filled the void of his empty soul and now the content of his relationship with Christ had provided him with the ability to be content in all things.

Take a look inside today. What is the content of the eternal in your life? If you find Jesus residing as the full content of your life, then you will also be content in whatever state you find yourself. Be content with Christ as the content of your life that!

12/03

Stop Praying!

The following story comes from Michael Green's book of illustrations which were written and compiled for use in preaching the word. As happens so many times we learn much by watching the actions of children who take God's word literally; so should we all.

Young Danny was praying at Mother's knee. "If I should die before I wake . . . If I should die. . . ."

"Go on, go on, Danny," said his mother. "You know the rest of the prayer."

"Wait a minute," interrupted the small boy. Scrambling to his feet, he hurried downstairs. In a short time, he was back. Dropping to his knees once again, he took up the petition where he had left off.

Finally his mother questioned him about the episode and issued a loving rebuke. "Son, prayer is very important. You should think about take it very seriously."

Danny explained: "Mom, I did think about what I was saying, but I had to stop and put all of Ted's wooden soldiers on their feet. I had turned them on their heads just to see how mad he'd be in the morning. If I should die before I wake, I wouldn't want him to find them like that. Lots of things seem fun if you are gonna keep on living, but you don't want them that way if you should die before you wake."

"You're right, dear," said his mother with a quiver in her voice. She thought of herself and many other grown-ups who should have stopped in the middle of their prayers to undo some wrong against another before proceeding.

Jesus taught this same truth with these words: "Therefore if you bring your gift to the altar, and there remember that your brother has something against you, leave your gift there before the altar, and go your way. First be reconciled to your brother, and then come and offer your gift." ~ Matthew 5:23-24

Now, whose toys have you been messing with lately? Stop praying! Go make things right and then the time on your knees will be sweeter than ever. AMEN!

What Kind of Friend Are You?

If you have ever been wronged even in the slightest manner you have probably felt at some point the desire to get even. I have tried to leave a lot of wiggle room in this statement on purpose for I have known some people who quickly react with an eye for an eye mentality when they are wronged. I also have known others who seem to never seek revenge even when harmed at the deepest levels.

My intent is not to set the standard for retribution based on our understanding of any given situation or altercation. My desire is to bring into focus the comparison of God's mercy which is at work in the world and how His righteous judgment can exist at the same time. It is a quandary that will not be settled in this brief devotional thought.

The answer begins, however, in establishing the fact that no one has appointed God as ruler over His own creation. He is sovereign by default. So the book of Job states, "Who gave Him charge over the earth? Or who appointed Him over the whole world? If He should set His heart on it, if He should gather to Himself His Spirit and His breath, all flesh would perish together, and man would return to dust." ~ Job 34:13-15

Truly God rules. He rules justly and could if He were to desire shut everything down immediately. God could, to use a boyhood term, simply pick up his marbles and go home. He could recall His Spirit and reclaim the breath that he first placed in the nostrils of Adam. In that moment all flesh would cease.

These verses are not written as a threat. They are intended to refresh our minds and hearts to the truth that though all of this scenario is possible, God also functions with His mercy fully intact.

Job's friends (though it is difficult to call them as such) came to Job's side with the full justice of God in view. They could only see Job's situation as the vengeful acts of a righteous God. But Job knew better and so should we.

God has not picked up His marbles and gone home. His mercies are renewed each and every day. Because He is God alone, He can be just and merciful at the same moment.

However you may have been wronged or unjustly criticized, never forget that God is on your side. Listen not to the quick revengeful statements of your "friends". Instead, remember that God's mercy is available. And as you remember this for yourself make every attempt to not be like one of Job's friends.

Destroy the Records

I would be considered a little weird by many people in one particular way. I tend to hold on to receipts and documents for an extraordinary amount of time. One example of this was several boxes full of documents that I destroyed recently. They were the financial records from my grocery business. I sold it just before beginning my ministry in the pastorate. That was over 30 years ago! I sure hope the IRS doesn't ask me for them now!

I still cannot bring myself to destroy the records of notes that I have paid off over the years. Each of them is filed away and once in a while I will stumble across one or more. I take a moment to examine the large ink stamped mark on the document that reads: PAID IN FULL!

In the days of the rule of Rome, documents of various kinds would be generated. These could be statements of unpaid debt or legal charges brought against an individual. These documents would be delivered to the home of the person so named in the parchment. After presentation, they would be nailed to the door as a public declaration.

With this picture in mind, you can better understand what Paul wrote to the Colossians. "And you, being dead in your trespasses and the uncircumcision of your flesh, He has made alive together with Him, having forgiven you all trespasses, having wiped out the handwriting of requirements that was against us, which was contrary to us. And He has taken it out of the way, having nailed it to the cross. Having disarmed principalities and powers, He made a public spectacle of them, triumphing over them in it." ~ Colossians 2:13-15

We had a death sentence nailed to the door of our lives. The charges were publicly displayed for all to see. But Christ came to the door of our hearts and ripped down the handwriting of ordinance that was against us. All debt, past, present, and future was taken by Him. He declared it His own.

Then that list of charges was nailed publicly to His cross for all to see. All who had declared us guilty were served notice that we were now and forever declared innocent of all charges. Everything has been blotted out by His shed blood. The hammer of judgment has fallen, but not upon us who believe. It has fallen squarely upon Christ Himself who took all of our sins away having made public spectacle of Satan.

We are free to go! Hallelujah!

Leave It To Beaver

How many of you remember Ward and June Cleaver? Okay, if you can't quite put your finger on these two characters, how about Theodore Cleaver? You probably know him best as Beaver. Not to leave out Wally, the older brother, but Beaver was always the one that was in some sort of predicament. You remember the general scenario of nearly every program. Beaver would get into some mischief, his friends would desert him, and he would be left to face Ward and June, his father and mother.

Somehow I feel like Beaver some days. It seems that there is always something calling my name. Something that I think needs investigating. Like the time Beaver climbed up on the billboard that had the steaming cup on it and fell inside the cup. And as usual all of his friends that had encouraged him in the adventure high-tailed it!

The Apostle Paul must have felt like Ward and June at times as he cared for churches that acted a lot like little Beavers. He had to fill the role of both parents at times, but he did so out of genuine concern and love.

He mentions this double role as he writes to the church at Thessalonica. "But we were gentle among you, just as a nursing mother cherishes her own children. So, affectionately longing for you, we were well pleased to impart to you not only the gospel of God, but also our own lives, because you had become dear to us. / You are witnesses, and God also, how devoutly and justly and blamelessly we behaved ourselves among you who believe; as you know how we exhorted, and comforted, and charged every one of you, as a father does his own children, that you would walk worthy of God who calls you into His own kingdom and glory." ~ 1 Thessalonians 2:7-8; 10-12

Paul related to the young churches under his ministry as a nursing mother who gently caresses and sings to her baby. He would in this role be like June Cleaver who would tell Beaver that he had to face his father when he came home, but at the same time would intercede for mercy.

He also was like a father in that he challenged the church to grow up and walk worthy of their role as children of God. Like Ward Cleaver, Paul was assertive, yet always dealt with those in his responsibility with exhortation and comfort.

Yes, we can remember when shows like "Leave It to Beaver" all ended well with resolution of all problems and a family intact and happy. Don't give up. Don't give in. It can still be like that in your life. God as both father and mother to us wants the whole family safely tucked in bed.

We all will have our "Beaver" moments, but God's intent is restoration before the program ends.

Giving My Best

Have you ever stopped and really considered what tempts you most? Perhaps you have and you probably concluded that it was some evil desire or habit that most often brings you into the snare of sin.

James clearly teaches this in his letter. He concludes that temptation comes when we are drawn away by our own lust which brings forth sin and ultimately death. Do you see the acronym formed by this work of temptation? *Lust....Sin...Death...LSD.* Like a poisonous drug temptation can drag you headlong into death.

You cannot stop reading James' words here though. He continued with this statement. "Do not be deceived, my beloved brethren." ~ James 1:16 Now I always thought of these words being attached to the thoughts about temptation, but here are the words that follow: "Every good gift and every perfect gift is from above, and comes down from the Father of lights, with whom there is no variation or shadow of turning. Of His own will He brought us forth by the word of truth, that we might be a kind of firstfruits of His creatures." ~ James 1:17-18

The real danger is in us focusing so much on what we should avoid that we substitute doing good or offering some good gift to the Lord thinking that this is the right thing to do and that we have achieved some spiritual advantage in doing so. James says, "Be not deceived." We have no good gift to offer, because every good gift comes from and already belongs to Him.

Oswald Chambers said in his book, *Biblical Ethics*, "Anyone will give up wrong things if he knows how to, but will I give up the best I have for Jesus Christ? If I am only willing to give up wrong things, never let me talk about being in love with Him!"

In another of his writings, *Not Knowing Whither*, he went on to say, "In seeking the best we soon find that our enemy is our good things, not our bad. The things that keep us back from God's best are not sin and imperfection, but the things that are right and good and noble from the natural standpoint. To discern that the natural virtues antagonise surrender to God is to bring our soul at once into the centre of our greatest battlefield."

Watch for the subtle temptation to offer some good thing to God, all the time thinking with pride, we have made some grand sacrifice. Avoid evil, but never substitute the sin of pride in its place.

Stretching Your Faith

How many of you remember learning how to walk? Probably none of you. At least I've never met anyone who can remember taking their first steps. The good thing about that is the fact that you don't remember those first falls either!

When children begin to walk parents must offer encouragement, but they must also allow for the elements of risks and failure to take their place in the process. Without the falls and the struggles, balance would never be possible. Ultimately maturity would be arrested by over protecting a child from the dangers of rising up and taking those first steps.

Discipleship of believers is much the same. We must allow the disciple the opportunity to fail. Is there the possibility that it can become messy? Yes, indeed! But the bumps and bruises all go into the process of growing up in Christ.

Jesus clearly demonstrated this in His dealings with the disciples. One example happened on the Sea of Galilee.

"Now in the fourth watch of the night Jesus went to them, walking on the sea. And when the disciples saw Him walking on the sea, they were troubled, saying, "It is a ghost!" And they cried out for fear. But immediately Jesus spoke to them, saying, "Be of good cheer! It is I; do not be afraid." And Peter answered Him and said, "Lord, if it is You, command me to come to You on the water." So He said, "Come." And when Peter had come down out of the boat, he walked on the water to go to Jesus. But when he saw that the wind was boisterous, he was afraid; and beginning to sink he cried out, saying, "Lord, save me!" And immediately Jesus stretched out His hand and caught him, and said to him, "O you of little faith, why did you doubt?" And when they got into the boat, the wind ceased." ~ Matthew 14:25-32

Jesus certainly knew that Peter was going to fail in his attempt to walk all the way to Him on the water. But notice that Jesus did not prevent the failure from taking place. Instead He allowed it and remained ready to save the drowning disciple.

These verses tell us that Jesus stretched out His hand and caught Peter. It was not only the hand of Jesus that was stretched. Peter's faith was also stretched.

Isn't it time to rise up and walk? Sure, you fell yesterday, but that day is gone. It's time to be stretched. Your steps may seem baby-like at first, but soon you will be running for Jesus! Just remember He's always near enough to catch you.

Servant Leadership

Sometimes out of frustration or a loss of focus in my life I become somewhat cynical. No, as a matter of fact, I become downright selfish and I cannot blame it on my circumstances or vision. It is me at work doing what I does best: Looking out for my best friend, myself.

I can imagine in times like these that I am the owner of a remote island upon which I have installed myself as the king and sole ruler. Everything goes along fine in my dream world until I take a look out over the horizon of an endless sea whereupon I see the tiny dots of boats all sailing away from my island.

And there I am. It's just me. Ruling me all by my little lonesome self. Thank God I can wake up from my dream turned nightmare. The reality of true servant leadership comes rushing back to the forefront of my mind and heart. I am once again hearing the words of Jesus loud and clear.

"But Jesus called them to Himself and said, 'You know that the rulers of the Gentiles lord it over them, and those who are great exercise authority over them. Yet it shall not be so among you; but whoever desires to become great among you, let him be your servant. And whoever desires to be first among you, let him be your slave—just as the Son of Man did not come to be served, but to serve, and to give His life a ransom for many.'" ~ Matthew 20:25-28

Jesus' words to the disciples were in response to the mother of James and John. She had come to Jesus with this request: "Grant that these two sons of mine may sit, one on Your right hand and the other on the left, in Your kingdom." ~ Matthew 20:21

Most of us would not hold it against a mother who was looking out for her kids. But her desire was driven by the same me, myself, and I mentality that I spoke of in my island dream. The only difference is that she added a fourth part to the equation: MINE.

It is interesting that the opportunity to make the request was offered by Jesus. He had framed her request with a question: "What do you wish?" Should we not pause for just a moment when this same question comes before us? The correct question is, "God, what is your will?" Only then can we find true satisfaction.

Being a disciple of Jesus produces a different leader. We are to be servant leaders who have come to serve; not to be served. And when this happens, I suggest that you take a look back out over the sea surrounding your island of existence. Those dots on the horizon will be boats full of people not sailing away, but towards you. Nothing is more attractive than a leader that serves.

Adopted

Adoption has always been part of family life. There are not many families that do not have somewhere along the family tree a son or a daughter that has been adopted. It is a good and noble process that provides protection and care for a child that through some circumstance beyond their control has been left without a family.

It is interesting that in the days which the Bible was written adoption was a very different process. Whereas, today people are interested in adopting very young children, this would be unlikely in the first century.

The person adopted was most times at a minimum a child that had reach puberty and was many times a young adult. The adopting family was primarily looking for a child that would be able to manage the inheritance that awaited him upon adoption.

The person adopted was very much cognizant of the process. They were part of the decision process though they were chosen in the beginning by the adopting parents.

The courts of that day would declare the adopted person as a rightful heir of all that the adopting parents owned. The adopted person could not be disowned. The adoption was permanent. The courts used language that referred to the adopted person as being born again.

The Apostle Paul used similar language as he wrote to the Ephesians. "Blessed be the God and Father of our Lord Jesus Christ, who has blessed us with every spiritual blessing in the heavenly places in Christ, just as He chose us in Him before the foundation of the world, that we should be holy and without blame before Him in love, having predestined us to adoption as sons by Jesus Christ to Himself, according to the good pleasure of His will, to the praise of the glory of His grace, by which He made us accepted in the Beloved." ~ Ephesians 1:3-6

What a blessed arrangement God has ordained! He has chosen to adopt us before we ever were, so that, we could forever be part of His forever family!

It's more than we can fathom in our little minds. We are the sons and daughters of God; the brothers and sisters of Jesus if indeed we are born again.

If you are not, then you can be today! He has made all of the arrangements. Call upon Jesus as Savior and God becomes your Father.

And, oh yes! Send out the birth announcements!

Just a Rebel

I am certain that I have said this before during one of my daily devotion pieces, but I must repeat myself again today: I AM A REBEL! Where we all have at least some tendency to violate the law, I have always had a real penchant to do so. Now before you think that I rob banks in my spare time, let me clarify this a little.

It is not the big laws that attract my disobedience. It's the little ones. It is those that seem ridiculous in their very creation. Somehow or another someone decided to correct a small discrepancy with a manual of procedure. The result is a burdensome set of rules that immediately sets me into motion to find a way around them. Sorry if this disappoints you in any way…

Religion is that way. It attempts to bind us under rules. In the beginning the rules seem to be there like guard rails to keep us safe.

Sooner or later, however, the rails get moved inward until all that is left is a one lane pathway that doesn't even allow two people to walk side by side much less pass in opposite directions.

Christ came to set us free so we could enjoy our freedom. Yet we have this tendency to run back to the "comfort" of the law. Somehow we convince ourselves that there is safety in the regulations.

Paul put it this way: "Therefore, if you died with Christ from the basic principles of the world, why, as though living in the world, do you subject yourselves to regulations—"Do not touch, do not taste, do not handle, " which all concern things which perish with the using—according to the commandments and doctrines of men? These things indeed have an appearance of wisdom in self-imposed religion, false humility, and neglect of the body, but are of no value against the indulgence of the flesh." ~ Colossians 2:20-23

I like Paul. He must have been a little bit like me—a rebel. He knew that no rule of religion could ever fully restrict the inner workings of the flesh. It is only when the rebel yields to the Lordship of Christ that he or she will reject the rebellious nature of the flesh.

A regenerate, restored, rejoicing rebel am I, because Christ came to be born in a rebellious, rundown, rejecting world. He died on a cross between two rebels while hundreds of religious folk ridiculed Him. He reeled under the weight of sin and the sense of His Father's repulsion.

Yet He remained until the end and rose from the retched grave to reclaim this world and reconcile a rebel like me. Amen and amen!

Turned Inside Out

If you have ever had a child leaving home you know the common refrain offered by many a parent. It goes something like this:

"Behave yourself! Remember that you are a [insert your family's last name here]."

We are reminding our children that we send them out as little representatives of the family. How they act will reflect directly upon us. In most cases our children hear us in one ear and let our words cascade out the other. Oh well, we try!

I wonder if Paul might have been thinking a little bit like a parent when he wrote the words that began what we know as the 12th chapter of Romans. "I beseech you therefore, brethren, by the mercies of God, that you present your bodies a living sacrifice, holy, acceptable to God, which is your reasonable service. And do not be conformed to this world, but be transformed by the renewing of your mind, that you may prove what is that good and acceptable and perfect will of God." ~ Romans 12:1-2

Of course, his directive was not issued so that his readers might live up to the name of Paul. These words were God's instructions to His own disciples. But, they certainly sound a lot like our words to our children as they go through the front door.

We are to actively present ourselves as living sacrifices. This is the bear minimum of the Christian experience. These words are not meant for the super Christian. This is the reasonable response of a man or woman, boy or girl that has been touched by the power of the gospel and the hand of grace.

It gets better. Where we are limited in our ability to affect the behavior of our children as soon as they are removed from our sight, God gives the answer to remaining true to a sacrificial life.

As we remain in the word of God, our minds are constantly renewed. Literally, they are metamorphosed. Our scripture verse uses the word "transformed".

This is the same process whereby a caterpillar becomes a butterfly. We are constantly being turned inside out to become what God intended us to be and furthermore to know and do His will.

Remember, you are already a butterfly even as you live a caterpillar life. Ask God today to turn you inside out so you can be all that He has intended for you. And never forget to live up to the family name!

Formula For Success

Evangelist Ron Dunn who is now safely resting at the feet of Jesus gave as an illustration in one of his messages the following formula for success.

FAILURE + FAILURE + FAILURE + FAILURE = SUCCESS

I know that this does not fit the model of this everybody-is-a-winner world that we live in today. It is, however, very much the evidence in many success stories.

It is certainly the way of the natural beast. A wolf pack has a killer instinct, but only succeeds in one of every fourteen wolf hunts. For all its cunning, speed, and strength, the polar bear will only succeed in making the kill but once in every five attempts. An adult tiger can miss nineteen out of the twenty times it hunts. You will never hear the wolf, bear, or tiger griping about bad referees, sore ribs, or incompetent teammates nor will any of these animals get a little stuffed prey just for trying hard.

Here's the truth. Life is hard and failure is part of the equation. The Apostle Peter is a prime example of this. Time and again we see Peter failing in his role as a disciple. If he was not saying the wrong thing, then he was doing the wrong thing. He was constantly reaching the wrong conclusion on matters. On the Mount of Transfiguration he was ready to build tabernacles and stay for a while. In and of itself not a bad idea, but the point was that life doesn't transpire for the most part on the mountain, but in the valley.

Walking out of the boat, he sinks beneath the waves in fear and doubt. At the trial of Jesus, he denies Him three times. After the crucifixion of Jesus, he goes back to fishing again. These are but a few of Peter's failures and this would be a sad tale if it ended here. Thank God it does not!

In the first few pages of the book of Acts we read of Peter standing before the crowd in Jerusalem. He preaches a most powerful message recounting the history of Israel and the purpose of Christ's coming.

None could deny Peter's bold words: "Now when they heard this, they were cut to the heart, and said to Peter and the rest of the apostles, 'Men and brethren, what shall we do?' Then Peter said to them, 'Repent, and let every one of you be baptized in the name of Jesus Christ for the remission of sins; and you shall receive the gift of the Holy Spirit. For the promise is to you and to your children, and to all who are afar off, as many as the Lord our God will call.'" ~ Acts 2:37-39

That day 3000 souls were swept into the Kingdom.

FAILURE + FAILURE + FAILURE + FAILURE = SUCCESS

Active Listening

I am writing this devotion as I do most days on my iPad. All day long I and another several billion people will have some electronic gadget close at hand. For the most part I think it's great; a lot of spare time is filled with productive activity. But there is a downside also.

Many of the devices people are using have an audio connection and earbuds are deeply planted in each ear. Much of what is being listened to is playing at decibel levels that are surely going to produce a society filled with hearing impaired individuals.

But there is a flip-side to the downside also.

Scientists have discovered that silence can be deafening as well. The Daily Mail published an article about Orfield Laboratory's anechoic chamber, a room that's so soundproof, it's officially listed as the "Quietest place on earth," according to Guinness World Records.

The chamber located in Minneapolis, Minnesota, is comprised of 3.3-foot-thick fiberglass acoustic wedges, double walls of insulated steel and foot-thick concrete, which enables it to be 99.99 per cent sound absorbent with a decibel rating of −9.4 dBa. Any sounds below the threshold of 0 dBa is undetectable by the human ear.

At these low decibel levels, the environment becomes so disconcerting that people have actually started to hallucinate after a period of only 45 minutes. Peace and quiet every now and then can be appreciated, but the human brain can only take so much silence.

So, how prepared are you to listen? Are you so bombarded with sounds that you cannot hear the voice of God? Or perhaps, you have been too long in a spiritual chamber of silence that you no longer have the sensitivity to pick up the still small sounds of heaven's King speaking.

Listening for the voice of God cannot be done haphazardly. Solomon said, "Walk prudently when you go to the house of God; and draw near to hear rather than to give the sacrifice of fools, for they do not know that they do evil." ~ Ecclesiastes 5:1

Make yourself ready to hear God's voice. Adjust your steps and align yourself to best hear every syllable that is sent your way. Few of us will ever have a chamber of silence that we can use and none of us must always have an earbud stuck in our ear either.

Let your ears grow accustomed to hearing God and make preparation to be an active listener.

The Saints Win!

While sitting in a restaurant in south Louisiana, I was in the company of a large group of sports fans. They were all on their way to a New Orleans Saints football game. Each one was dressed in black and gold: the team colors.

It's Sunday morning. Today thousands of loyal fans will bow before their respective gods. Now before you skip this devotion, you will have to admit that sports have become a full time idol for a lot of people. Clearly the problem here does not lie with the event itself, but the response of those paying obeisance to it.

A little fellow attended a church that had beautiful stained-glass windows along each side of the sanctuary. One day his curiosity forced him to ask who the people depicted in the stained glass were. He was told that the windows contained pictures of Saint Matthew, Saint Mark, Saint Luke, Saint John, Saint Paul, and other saints.

Sunday after Sunday he studied the men in the windows of the church. One day in Sunday School his teacher asked, "What is a saint?"

He replied, "A saint is a person whom the light shines through."

Why is it that children seem to have a better grasp of spiritual matters than we do as adults? It must be the simplicity of faith. It is through a child's eyes that the real truth of heaven's message is proclaimed.

Over and again the Apostle Paul opened his letters by addressing the individuals of the churches to whom he was writing as saints. From the Old Testament to the New Testament we are spoken of as saints. The Psalmist declared, "As for the saints who are on the earth, 'They are the excellent ones, in whom is all my delight.'" ~ Psalms 16:3

Paul prayed for the saints like this: "For this reason I bow my knees to the Father of our Lord Jesus Christ, from whom the whole family in heaven and earth is named, that He would grant you, according to the riches of His glory, to be strengthened with might through His Spirit in the inner man, that Christ may dwell in your hearts through faith; that you, being rooted and grounded in love, may be able to comprehend with all the saints what is the width and length and depth and height—to know the love of Christ which passes knowledge; that you may be filled with all the fullness of God." ~ Ephesians 3:14-19

Not a word about fans, team colors, mascots, quarterbacks, or win-loss records. It's all about saints being in the right perspective to let the light shine through so others might see Jesus. And by the way, the saints win!

Proclamations

Proclamations come in many forms and are issued for varied reasons. The idea of a proclamation is that as many people as possible will hear the intended news. We live in a world that has made it very easy to proclaim anything that a person would care to make public. That can be for the good or it can be for evil.

Digital tools like Facebook, Twitter, and You Tube allow the most insignificant happening to go viral. This has become the term that defines whether an item has really been proclaimed or not. It seems that the more weird something is, the more attention it garners.

God has been in the proclaiming business since His creative powers were released upon a planet that was dark and formless. All that He created still proclaims loudly the evidence that He alone is the God of the universe. But, invariably, throughout time men have done their best in attempting to overthrow God and seize the throne.

Nimrod tried to build a tower to heaven and failed. One king after another has proclaimed himself a god and demanded the worship of the people. In each case, God showed Himself to be God alone and each of these men passed into history's book as a failure.

When Moses came before Pharaoh to make the proclamation of Israel's freedom, this command from God came squarely against Pharaoh's own proclamation of god-ship. Needless to say, the battle was on, but the victor was never to be doubted.

One plague after another poured forth from heaven against this Pharaoh-god and all of the other gods that Egypt worshipped. Finally, as the seventh plague was about to be unleashed, God proclaimed His intent and purpose openly.

As Moses spoke to Pharaoh, he declared that this plague forward would be upon the heart of this self-made god. Furthermore, God proclaimed, "…indeed for this purpose I have raised you up, that I may show My power in you, and that My name may be declared in all the earth." ~ Exodus 9:16

Take heart today! No matter how much evil appears to be in control, God's purpose cannot be thwarted. God can put His power on display and proclaim His name even through the most wicked self-proclaimed gods.

Now, go proclaim His name!

Angels On Fire

Few of us I am afraid fully recognize the work of God going on around us daily. We pass through this life oblivious to the presence of God in our everyday affairs.

One such occurrence transpired during the time of Elisha's service as the prophet of God. Elisha had warned the king of Israel about the Syrian army's location. This greatly distressed the Syrian king who then sent a battalion to capture Elisha. The account picks up here:

"And when the servant of the man of God arose early and went out, there was an army, surrounding the city with horses and chariots. And his servant said to him, 'Alas, my master! What shall we do?' So he answered, 'Do not fear, for those who are with us are more than those who are with them.' And Elisha prayed, and said, 'Lord, I pray, open his eyes that he may see.' Then the Lord opened the eyes of the young man, and he saw. And behold, the mountain was full of horses and chariots of fire all around Elisha." ~ 2 Kings 6:15-17

Oh, that God might open our eyes today! This same God who was protecting Elisha is the One who guards us day and night. Let not your heart be troubled as you look upon the visible circumstances of life. Spend no time in consideration of what you are going to do in providing a remedy.

By faith, Elisha could see the army of God already assembled. His words of comfort to his young servant were based on fact not fantasy. They were based on hard data not a hope so of doubt. "Do not fear, for those who are with us are more than those who are with them."

When the young man's eyes were opened, he too saw what Elisha had already witnessed. A mountain full of fiery soldiers standing in defense of these two men. Here is the plentiful provision of God on display. The mountain was FILLED with God's army. It was the MOUNTAIN not the valley that was overflowing with God's army. God had the high ground! It was an army of FIRE ready to consume all that had risen against God's servants.

So, what have you arisen to discover today? What army has surrounded you during the night? Do you need your eyes opened to see the protection of God's mighty army?

Father, open our eyes and let us see not what you WILL provide, but what IS already in place at this very moment. Amen!

Happy Christmas

It's one week before Christmas! Maybe this would be a very good day to run some diagnostics on ourselves. Before you begin this set of extensive tests, perhaps you need to have some clear definitions in hand to clarify the process.

Take a look for example at the modifier we use when referring to Christmas. We use the word "happy" before all of the other major holidays, but we use the word "merry" to describe Christmas. Why?

Happy is defined as feeling or showing pleasure or contentment. Merry is defined as giving pleasure, full of high spirits, that which is marked by festivity. Now you may think that I am reaching a little here to make a point, but I believe there really is a reason that we say Merry Christmas instead of Happy Christmas.

The idea of happy focuses on the external. Someone or something makes us happy. A certain happenstance brings a moment of euphoria to us and we are happy that we were "lucky" enough to be in the right place at the right time.

Merriment on the other hand does not begin on the outside of us, but on the inside. In older times people would speak of making merry. Merry does not happen to us, we make merry happen. It has wrapped up in it an outflow of joy that cannot be contained.

That impulsive, overflowing, spontaneous disposition cannot be possible without the good news of the Christmas story flowing uncontrollably out of our inner being. We are able to be merry in spite of the crowds, traffic, or noise. We can be merry even though it may be bare under our tree. We can be merry even if there is no tree. We can be merry even if there is no one to sit next to the tree with us.

Artemus Ward, who lived believe it or not during the middle 1800's said, "Let us all be happy, and live within our means, even if we have to borrow the money to do it with." He certainly could have lived in our day. Many will try to buy happiness with the hope of having a Merry Christmas.

STOP! Hear the words of angels speaking to poor shepherds. "Do not be afraid, for behold, I bring you good tidings of great joy which will be to all people. For there is born to you this day in the city of David a Savior, who is Christ the Lord. And this will be the sign to you: You will find a Babe wrapped in swaddling clothes, lying in a manger." And suddenly there was with the angel a multitude of the heavenly host praising God and saying: "Glory to God in the highest, and on earth peace, goodwill toward men!" ~ Luke 2:10-14

It's a week early, but let me be the first to say, "MERRY CHRISTMAS!"

The First to Hear

Have you ever thought about the reason that God chose to present the news of Christ's birth to shepherds? Why not to a king or some nobleman of renown? Why not to the richest person in the area? Certainly one of these would have had the means to disseminate the news with much greater effectiveness. But He did not. He chose shepherds.

"Now there were in the same country shepherds living out in the fields, keeping watch over their flock by night. And behold, an angel of the Lord stood before them, and the glory of the Lord shone around them, and they were greatly afraid. Then the angel said to them, 'Do not be afraid, for behold, I bring you good tidings of great joy which will be to all people. For there is born to you this day in the city of David a Savior, who is Christ the Lord. And this will be the sign to you: You will find a Babe wrapped in swaddling cloths, lying in a manger.'" ~ Luke 2:8-12 / "So it was, when the angels had gone away from them into heaven, that the shepherds said to one another, 'Let us now go to Bethlehem and see this thing that has come to pass, which the Lord has made known to us.' And they came with haste and found Mary and Joseph, and the Babe lying in a manger." ~ Luke 2:15-16

Perhaps a few words about these lowly men will help you understand why God chose the keepers of sheep to proclaim the gospel first to a lost world. First, one must consider their occupation. Second, we will look at their character.

A shepherd was not held in high esteem among many. Other nations around Israel despised the occupation. The sheep herder was responsible, however, for large flocks of sheep. In most cases they were not his sheep. At times he would keep the sheep for an entire village. His job was 24/7. He would have to know the geography of his pasture like the back of his hand. He would need to know where a constant source of food and water could be found. Without him the sheep would die.

The shepherd could be trusted above measure. He was responsible for each and every sheep under his care. He would if necessary lay down his life for them as he protected them from thieves and wolves. Only a trustworthy man would be given such responsibility.

If we only take these few descriptives of a shepherd into consideration it becomes clear why God chose such men. The message of Christ's birth was of highest importance. It needed to be given to men who would protect it like a precious lamb.

God would need men who knew exactly where Bethlehem was and the quickest way there. He trusted these shepherds with the news of the Great Shepherd's birth. And like the birth of a new lamb to the fold, they would shout with joy to all they met the good news of the Lamb of God who was born in Bethlehem that night.

Would you serve as a shepherd today? "Now when they had seen Him, they made widely known the saying which was told them concerning this Child. And all those who heard it marveled at those things which were told them by the shepherds."~Luke 2:17-18

12/20

Expecting Guests

Christmas is a gathering time. We gather all sorts of things prior to this holiday. If you are like me you go to that storage spot and gather up all of the decorations. Hopefully, this puts you in the mood to gather the names of people that you will be sending greeting cards to in celebration of the upcoming event. Finally, you will begin to think about the actual gathering of people. You know the people I'm speaking of: family, extended relatives, friends, etc.

I'm not sure where our gathering tendencies came from, but it sure seems like Christmas is one time of the year that causes us to focus on that one subject. We go out of our way and travel long distances to get together. And, by the way, I think that's a good thing!

Perhaps it all began, not so much by choice, but by edict. The gathering of Joseph and Mary into a stable in Bethlehem was not by choice, but because the government had demanded it.

"And it came to pass in those days that a decree went out from Caesar Augustus that all the world should be registered. This census first took place while Quirinius was governing Syria. So all went to be registered, everyone to his own city." ~ Luke 2:1-3

Even though they were not physically in the same little space with all of their family members, the whole Joseph clan should have been in the proximity of Bethlehem. It is interesting that the first Christmas (at least as we commemorate it) was a gathering of relatives.

Have you ever noticed though, that our gatherings are seldom limited to the inner circle of family. Somehow our doors fling open and all are welcome at our tables in this season. How much was this like that first Christmas scene?

Here, in what was most likely a small cave or recess into a cliff side, was Mary and Joseph. In a short time a new Person joined their family. He came from outside of this world. He was but a guest in His own created world.

Around Him gathered His creation. The ox, the lamb, the cow, and other lesser creatures all stood in this little room with their Creator. Jesus had come to the gathering!

As you gather your families this Christmas season, will Christ sit at your table? Will He have a place in the excitement of opening gifts? Will your family be complete only when you sense His presence among the presents?

Keep the door open this Christmas. The door of your heart that is. Expect the Guest that completes your family to arrive and it will be a Merry and Holy Christmas!

	12/21

Manger In Your Heart

I was wondering who might have been the one who fashioned the feeding trough in the stable where Jesus was born. You probably are wondering why I would wonder about such things. Well, wonder no more!

The feeding trough is what we call so tenderly at Christmas time a manger. Of course, we think of our modern nativity scenes with a finely made wooden crib-like structure with nice clean hay. And don't forget the plastic baby Jesus.

Feeding troughs were used for cattle, sheep, donkeys, or horses. They were chipped out from limestone and were approximately three feet long, 18 inches wide, and two feet deep. The manger referred to in Luke 2:16 may have been in a cave or other shelter. It would have been in one of these feeding troughs that Jesus would lay to sleep after His birth.

Sometime prior to this Christmas scene in Bethlehem, a mason would have chipped away at a block of stone to form this manger. He could not have imagined that he was hewing a bed for a King.

Perhaps he thought of Israel's oppression by the Romans. He might have even contemplated the hole in his own heart that could not be filled. He may have remembered the words of Isaiah the prophet as he spoke God's words to the people: "'Listen to Me, you who follow after righteousness, you who seek the Lord: look to the rock from which you were hewn, and to the hole of the pit from which you were dug.'" ~ Isaiah 51:1

Is there a hole in your heart today? Like an empty manger or at best one stuffed with the hay of life; are you constantly trying to fill the emptiness? Have you been the mason who chipped away the stone and helped in forming an ever growing hollow in your heart?

One has come to fill the manger of the heart. His name is Jesus. Don't worry about the condition He will find your heart in today. He was not laid in a finely fashioned crib with a soft mattress, clean sheets, and a pillow for His head. He slept in a rough-hewn feeding trough and was surrounded by the hay that covered the floor of the stable.

Spend no time today cleaning the empty space of your life. Take no time trying to fashion a crib of quality into which you might invite the Savior. Declare the hole in your heart. Look to the rock from whence you are hewn and the pit from which you need deliverance.

Now sing anew the carol: Away in a manger, no crib for His bed. The little Lord Jesus lay down His sweet head.

May He fill the manger of your heart today!

12/22

Christmas In Reverse

Around 1925 some banker came up with the ingenious idea of Christmas Club accounts. You did remember that you had put that money aside didn't you?

The idea was very simple. A person would make regular deposits into an account that would mature each year prior to the Christmas shopping season. The account would then be closed and the proceeds from it would be used to purchase Christmas presents. Ah, those were the days before plastic had been invented…plastic credit cards that is!

Now I'm not saying you should not use credit cards to buy Christmas presents. I am saying that in the days of fixed budgets and Christmas Club accounts no one was fearing getting the mail in January and February. You know what I mean…BILLS!

Surely someone is calling me the Grinch, but that is not my intent at all. My illustration about Christmas Club accounts is really about how much we have prepared all year long to share the real gift of Christmas—Jesus Himself.

Have you ever noticed how Christmas was in reverse for the shepherds? They received a surprise visit by angels and had to hurry along to Bethlehem to be witnesses of the grand event of Christ's birth.

It was their response to all of this that I speak of as they lived out Christmas in reverse. "Then the shepherds returned, glorifying and praising God for all the things that they had heard and seen, as it was told them." ~ Luke 2:20

I think that we can be sure that they were not glorifying and praising God quietly. They would have been giving testimony all along the way. Tapping every person they met on the shoulder and proclaiming, "Christ is born in Bethlehem this very day!"

Christmas had just occurred for them and now they were living it out daily. You and I live our lives moving toward Christmas each year. Soon the presents will all be opened. The decorations will be stored. The bills will be due. But will we be like the shepherds?

Will be open a "Christmas Club Account" in the name of Jesus? Will we begin today making regular deposits into it?

Not money for next year's presents, but souls for heaven, a witness for His glory, and a song or two along the way throughout the coming year that tells the world that every day is Christmas for the believer!

12/23

The Equalizer Is Coming

This is a great country! There is no other place on the planet like it. Sure, others have tried to imitate it, while others are presently attempting to use it as a model, but we *are* it. By God's grace and His hand of blessing we have been letting freedom ring for over 236 years.

Our secret, although you will not find this on the front page of the newspaper, is the acceptance of this simple truth: "The king's heart is in the hand of the Lord, like the rivers of water; He turns it wherever He wishes. Every way of a man is right in his own eyes, but the Lord weighs the hearts." ~ Proverbs 21:1-2

As Christmas draws nigh once again, I cannot help but think about the King of Heaven coming to live among men. In our democratic society, we take great pride in electing presidents and representatives of the people. The best we can do, however, is to ask a person with a fallen nature to step up and do the best they can. The worst we can do is select a person who does not know Who the real Ruler of the universe is.

What amazes me is that those we elect so quickly choose to forget these fundamental truths. This has nothing to do with political persuasion. It has nothing to do with the road one takes to ascendency. It seems that those who arrive at the top of the mountain just forget whose shoulders they stood upon to get to the pinnacle and Who really is the King of the Universe.

There was a television show several years ago called The Equalizer. Robert McCall played the part of a disenchanted CIA officer who opened a detective agency. His specialty was helping those who had been squashed by the system or some other tragedy. He sought to equalize things for the little guy.

The day is coming when The Great Equalizer is going to set things right. During the time of the tribulation, mankind will shake its fist in the face of God. But know this— God's not shaking in His boots! On that day God will set about to equalize all things.

"And the kings of the earth, the great men, the rich men, the commanders, the mighty men, every slave and every free man, hid themselves in the caves and in the rocks of the mountains, and said to the mountains and rocks, 'Fall on us and hide us from the face of Him who sits on the throne and from the wrath of the Lamb! For the great day of His wrath has come, and who is able to stand?'" ~ Revelation 6:15-17

As Christmas approaches, be grateful that God sent The Equalizer in the form of a baby born in a manger. And never forget that The Equalizer is still coming again to settle the score!

12/24

Heaven's Mission Statement

If you have ever taken a mission trip before, then you know what those final hours before departure are like. There are lots of last minute decisions to be made, checklists are checked off, and all team members become fully psyched about the prospects of the endeavor.

The day before what we call Christmas is a little like taking a mission trip for us each year, but it would not have been like that in heaven. Oh, I would imagine the angels leaning over the bannister of heaven with anticipation. After all, they are created beings and they did not possess the omniscience of God.

God, on the other hand, was not anxious. He had no checklist. He was not in contact with team members.

The Father who is eternal had always planned on Christmas happening. There would be no surprises. No packing was necessary. No team would participate in the greatest mission trip ever undertaken. All would be fulfilled by One.

No suitcases were prepared because Jesus came naked to His own world. No passport was needed because He came not as a visitor, but as the Creator. No transportation was arranged, because He had been carried for nine months by His earthly mother, Mary. She would continue to do so until His first steps and then He would walk the dusty pathways of Galilee all the way to Calvary.

There would be no housing arranged. He began His mission with no room in the inn and proclaimed to His disciples during His ministry days that the Son of Man had no place to rest His head.

Finally, He would ride upon a colt, be received by royalty as a prisoner among His own people, and face rejection upon the cruel cross of Calvary. Yet not one surprise occurred as He fulfilled His mission to planet Earth.

His mission statement was revealed by angels to Joseph. "But while he thought about these things, behold, an angel of the Lord appeared to him in a dream, saying, 'Joseph, son of David, do not be afraid to take to you Mary your wife, for that which is conceived in her is of the Holy Spirit. And she will bring forth a Son, and you shall call His name Jesus, for He will save His people from their sins.' So all this was done that it might be fulfilled which was spoken by the Lord through the prophet, saying: 'Behold, the virgin shall be with child, and bear a Son, and they shall call His name Immanuel,' which is translated, 'God with us.'" ~ Matthew 1:20-23

GOD WITH US! Now that's a mission statement! The excitement is in the air!

Tomorrow…GOD WILL BE WITH US!

12/25

Whacha' Get?

Merry Christmas!

In Southern vernacular, whacha' get? Which is interpreted: What did you get? I hope it is all you desired and not all you deserved! Just kidding. I do wish you all a very Merry Christmas!

Our minds are filled with several thoughts about that first Christmas morning in Bethlehem. Some of those ideas are biblical; some are not. We have let tradition and Christmas carols dictate what we believe about the nativity scene.

One of those misnomers is the inclusion of the wise men in our pictures of the nativity. Not only do we include them, but we always number them as three. Scripture makes it plain that the wise men visited the home of Joseph and Mary nearly two years after Christ's birth and never says how many wise men there were.

"Now after Jesus was born in Bethlehem of Judea in the days of Herod the king, behold, wise men from the East came to Jerusalem, saying, 'Where is He who has been born King of the Jews? For we have seen His star in the East and have come to worship Him.' And when they had come into the house, they saw the young Child with Mary His mother, and fell down and worshiped Him. And when they had opened their treasures, they presented gifts to Him: gold, frankincense, and myrrh." ~ Matthew 2:1-2; 11

We see in these verses that the wise men came to worship Jesus as a young child in a house not in a stable. They brought Jesus three gifts, but scripture does not tell us that there was one gift per wise man.

Now don't go outside and take the wise men out of your nativity. Just remember as you put them in your yard each year that they really came a little later.

Also, don't miss the importance of the gifts they brought. Each had an important meaning in the ministry and attributes of Jesus.

They brought gold: a gift for a King. Truly Jesus is the King of Kings!

The wise men brought frankincense. This gift symbolizes the offering of prayer and the ministry of Jesus as our High Priest. He sits at the right hand of the Father on this Christmas morning making intercession for us.

Finally, they brought a very strange gift: myrrh. This is a product used to make burial ointment. These men had brought a gift that looked ahead to the great sacrifice of Jesus. It foretold the good news of the gospel: the death, burial, and resurrection of Jesus as our Savior.

Whacha' get? If you've never got Jesus, then all of the gifts in the world won't be enough. Bring Jesus a gift today: your heart. Receive from Him the greatest gift of all: eternal life!

12/26

Many Happy Returns

If you would like to buy a really ugly sweater, tomorrow will be the day. I am figuring that they will all be marked down to rock bottom prices, since everybody will be returning them to the stores today.

It's the day after Christmas and all through the house unwanted gifts are gathered with a lot more noise than a mouse. Scrunched back into boxes with very little care, everything has been placed—things no one wants to wear.

So much for Merry Christmas! Today it's many Happy Returns!

God was expecting the children of Israel to return to Him. He called for them to make it a day of happy returns as he spoke through the prophet Malachi.

"Yet from the days of your fathers you have gone away from My ordinances and have not kept them. 'Return to Me, and I will return to you,' says the Lord of hosts. But you said, 'In what way shall we return?' Will a man rob God? Yet you have robbed Me!

But you say, 'In what way have we robbed You?' In tithes and offerings. You are cursed with a curse, for you have robbed Me, even this whole nation. 'Bring all the tithes into the storehouse, that there may be food in My house, and try Me now in this,' says the Lord of hosts, if I will not open for you the windows of heaven and pour out for you such blessing that there will not be room enough to receive it." ~ Malachi 3:7-10

As you stand in lines today to make your returns think about how far you may have drifted away from the Lord. Make today a day of happy returns.

God has promised that if we return unto Him, He will return unto us. But just like making a return at the department store today, you must come with the item in your hand. What you now have must be surrendered before it can be exchanged.

The children of Israel wanted to play the game of ignorance. They wanted to have all the blessings of God while acting as if they were surrendering that which they were holding so tightly.

The truth is that God does not need your gift. He already owns all. You are the one that needs to make a return to Him and in doing so you will be more than ready to surrender all.

When you take a good long look into the face of God, everything you got for Christmas starts looking like an ugly sweater! It's time to make a return!

12/27

Roller Coaster of Time

Christmas sure seems like it happened a long time ago. Our memories are short and time has a way of both slipping away and slipping up on us.

We have only a few days left in what we recognize as a calendar year. We can most properly thank the Romans for our calendar system, though the beginning of a new year varies greatly around the world. Some cultures begin the new year in the spring, others at the end of summer, while some mark mid-autumn as a new beginning.

Actually the strike of the clock at the midnight hour will just begin a new day. Perhaps like any other, perhaps totally different from any we have experienced, but nonetheless a new day.

We get a new day each morning we arise. And in one sense we have a new opportunity every day of the year. We do, however, tend to reflect a little more as a year concludes and another begins.

It is in these final days of December that we look back with lots of emotions. These range from happiness to sadness, from the excitement of success to the disappointment of failure, and a myriad of emotional moments in between. This year has not really been any different from others. It has been the same roller coaster ride that we have been on for the entirety of our lives.

As the Apostle Paul sat in a Roman prison he wrote to his beloved friends in the church at Philippi. His words seem to hold a bit of deep reflection upon his life.

"Not that I have already attained, or am already perfected; but I press on, that I may lay hold of that for which Christ Jesus has also laid hold of me. Brethren, I do not count myself to have apprehended; but one thing I do, forgetting those things which are behind and reaching forward to those things which are ahead, I press toward the goal for the prize of the upward call of God in Christ Jesus." ~ Philippians 3:12-14

Paul seemed to have a balanced aspect when he considered the days of his life and his present position as a prisoner unjustly charged. He knew that he had not arrived yet. He knew that he was not in the driver's seat.

He knew that forgetting some things was the best while pressing on toward the goal of finally reaching the ultimate rest found only in the presence of Christ Jesus.

The roller coaster of days that mark the end of a year are upon us, but just over the hill a new and exciting ride begins. Spend these final days looking back, but keep glancing ahead.

It's going to be an incredible ride!

12/28

Thinking About Resolutions

Ah, the infomercials tell me that it is resolution time again. Most of the commercials deal with exercise equipment, diet plans, or quitting some bad habit like smoking.

Though we may not formally make a resolution, the merchants know that this is the time of the year that we are at least subconsciously thinking about them.

The word resolution means to determine an action, course of action, procedure, or method. It is at the minimum a mental state in which we resolve to accomplish some set of goals.

You know as well as I do that for the most part our resolutions tend to remain in the mental state. Sometimes we will go as far as talking a little about the steps we will take, but soon our resolutions are filed away with the recipes from our holiday feasts.

Resolutions come down to a matter of the will. You have to take that which was mere thought and put feet to it. Your resolution must rise up and become a reality.

It seems that this was the place David had come to as he wrote the longest chapter of the Bible which we know as Psalm 119. This entire psalm is about the word of God.

Early on in this chapter David said, "I will meditate on Your precepts, and contemplate Your ways. I will delight myself in Your statutes; I will not forget Your word." ~ Psalms 119:15-16

David listed four resolutions in these two verses. They are marked with the two simple words, "I will." David was speaking out of the conclusion he had already reached in his own heart.

Here is David's list:

I will meditate.
I will contemplate.
I will delight.
I will remember (not forget).

David's resolution was short and sweet. It was a four step plan with a single focus. Each step always centered upon the word of God. The steps were interchangeable. The steps were not a checklist of accomplishments and then forgotten. This was a lifelong set of actions that would be taken.

The next four days' worth of devotionals will walk you through each of these steps. I hope that it will be a blessed experience that in the end will help you to be resolved in your walk with Jesus during this upcoming year.

12/29

I Will

We begin today with a thorough look at each of the four points of David's resolution as found in Psalm 119:15-16. Do you remember them? I will meditate. I will contemplate. I will delight. I will remember (not forget). We will cover one of these on each of the following days.

Here they are in the context of these verses. "I will meditate on Your precepts, and contemplate Your ways. I will delight myself in Your statutes; I will not forget Your word." ~ Psalms 119:15-16

The first resolve that David made was to meditate on the precepts of God. When we think of the idea of meditation in our day, immediately our minds flash a picture of someone sitting with their legs folded, their thumb and forefinger pinched, and some low growling sound coming from their throats. Oh yes, and a deep concentration upon their own navel.

This is far from Biblical meditation and not even close to what David was saying he was resolved to do. He used a Hebrew word that means to ponder. That is, to weigh carefully in the mind. This is very different to the emptying of the mind used in modern meditation exercises.

David declares that he would fill his mind with the precepts of God. He would study the mandate and law of God thoroughly and with full faculties of reason in place.

This word meditate goes even further. It means to converse with one's self. To talk out the issues of God's law to the place that every point was completely understood. His self-talk could include declarations, complaints, musings, prayers, etc.

Meditation is a "get honest with God and yourself time". It is an opportunity to ask questions, levy complaints (don't worry, God will not be turned off by your complaining), lay forth supplications, and reach a deep consideration of your present standing before God.

Paul addressed this meditation process similarly in his letter to the Ephesians. "Therefore do not be unwise, but understand what the will of the Lord is. And do not be drunk with wine, in which is dissipation; but be filled with the Spirit, speaking to one another in psalms and hymns and spiritual songs, singing and making melody in your heart to the Lord, giving thanks always for all things to God the Father in the name of our Lord Jesus Christ, submitting to one another in the fear of God."~Ephesians 5:17-21

Tomorrow we will discuss David's second resolve: contemplation. Are you working on your resolution? I hope so and I hope that it will bring about a blessed new year.

12/30

Fill the Order

Welcome to day three of Steps to a Resolution. The scripture verses we are basing these devotions on are found in Psalm 119. Here they are once again:

"I will meditate on Your precepts, and contemplate Your ways. I will delight myself in Your statutes; I will not forget Your word." ~ Psalms 119:15-16

In the midst of writing what we have as the longest chapter of the Bible, David inscribed four "I wills." If we are to understand that no resolution will last without our will coming into the equation, we can then base our steps to a resolution on his "I will" clauses.

Today we will consider the second: I will contemplate.

Even though meditation and contemplation are very similar in the English language and are often listed as synonyms, these words differ significantly in the Hebrew.

Contemplation takes us much deeper than meditation. The idea is to scan or to look at intently. A visit to the doctor comes to mind here.

When we have some illness we make our way to the doctor's office. The first visit usually involves lots of questions about previous medical conditions, family history, and what is hurting at the moment. The physician will talk things over with you in an attempt to resolve your issue.

Sometimes this level of care is sufficient to determine a course of action. There are times, however, that a deeper level of testing must be done to determine the cause of your illness and to prescribe a regimen of treatment. This gives us a picture of the difference between meditation and contemplation.

Notice in our scripture selection that David meditated upon God's precepts, but also contemplated God's ways. Again, this is like our doctor visit as mentioned above. We go to doctors, because we believe and trust that they have the broad basis of medical training that qualifies them. But in our particular case, we are looking for the way all of that that will be applied to our condition.

So, as you begin to put your resolution for the new year together, begin with a time of meditation upon God's Word. You know that it contains the answer. Then begin to contemplate God's ways and make the necessary adjustments in your life to get back on the Lord's highway.

Just like a prescription written by a physician, none of this will do you any good until you fill the order and take all of the medication.

	12/31

New Year Looming

Today is the fourth installment of this mini-series on resolutions. We have been taking a deepening look into the truths that are contained in a few words written by David a very long time ago.

One of the amazing things about God's word is that it simply is not affected by time. It is fresh every day of every year. Scripture declares of itself, "Heaven and earth will pass away, but My words will by no means pass away." ~ Matthew 24:35

David's words in our selected verses contain four "I wills". These are the resolves that have become our study on resolution. Here are the two verses once again: "I will meditate on Your precepts, and contemplate Your ways. I will delight myself in Your statutes; I will not forget Your word." ~ Psalms 119:15-16

We have already looked at the first two parts of our resolution. "I will meditate on Your precepts." "I will contemplate Your ways." Today, "I will delight myself in your statutes."

The idea of delight occurs approximately 110 times in Scripture in various forms. The related concept of "please" occurs about 350 times. The particular Hebrew word used here and translated as delight is used four times by David in his writing. It is interesting that three of those times are in Psalm 119 which is dedicated to the word of God.

David looked upon the statutes (119:16), commandments (119:47), and the law (119:70) of God with delight. He looked upon these with pleasure. He handled each with an affectionate touch as one would caress a child.

His response to the fixed charge of God was complete delight. We are talking about the unchanging, unbending, everlasting precepts of a holy and righteous God and yet David was delighted to the point that he held them close like a beloved child.

I am not sure how many of us think of responding to God's law in this way. We probably spend a lot of time being somewhat Pharisaical about the commands of God. We are looking for ways to have our own way while supposedly keeping all of the ordinances.

Stop! It won't work. Be resolved today to find delight in the statutes, commandments, and law of God. As the final moments of this year come to a close and a new year looms before us, be resolved to hold close to your heart God's word. You will find yourself in a delightful situation if you do!

You actually began this devotional book with the fifth part of this study on resolutions. Turn back now to January 1 and you will find a good place to start your new year as well as refresh your memory on what you read way back when the year started.

Happy New Year to you and yours!

· ABOUT THE AUTHOR

R.E. Clark currently serves as the associational missionary for the Northwest Baptist Association in Bentonville, AR. He has ministered to these 70 churches, missions, and ministry points for the past 14 years. He earned his doctorate in ministry from the Southern Baptist Center in Jacksonville, FL.

He brings to his writing style the experiences of over 32 years of ministry as a pastor and missions leader. In addition to nearly four decades of preaching and teaching, he has either led or participated in mission trips to Mexico, Nigeria, Haiti, Bosnia, Kenya, Brazil, China, Malaysia, and the Dominican Republic.

This world-wide ministry has given him a wonderful base of insight into the application of God's word into everyday life. This was demonstrated in his first devotional book, *Glasses in the Grass: Devotions for My Friends* and continues in this devotional book as well.

R.E. is married to his wife, Trudy. Both of them have suffered the loss of their first spouses. Trudy's first husband, a police officer, was killed in the line of duty. R.E.'s first wife died from the effects of Lou Gehrig's Disease. These tragic losses add to the real life application of scripture in such a unique way. Their expanded family now consists of 8 children, 17 grandchildren, and 1 great-grandchild.

They reside in Centerton, AR.

You may contact the author through the following social media avenues:

Facebook: R.e. Clark
Twitter: GlassesnGrass
Blog: reclarkauthor.com
Email: reclark@reclarkauthor.com